Downing's Civil War Diary

BY

SERGEANT ALEXANDER G. DOWNING, COMPANY E,
ELEVENTH IOWA INFANTRY, THIRD BRIGADE,
"CROCKER'S BRIGADE," SIXTH DIVISION OF THE
SEVENTEENTH CORPS, ARMY OF THE TENNESSEE.

AUGUST 15, 1861—JULY 31, 1865

EDITED BY

OLYNTHUS B. CLARK, PH. D.
PROFESSOR OF HISTORY, DRAKE UNIVERSITY

DES MOINES
THE HISTORICAL DEPARTMENT OF IOWA
1916

COPYRIGHT APPLIED FOR

D. of D.
AUG 27 1917

PRINTED AND BOUND BY
THE HOMESTEAD PRINTING COMPANY
DES MOINES

INTRODUCTION.

Of the larger phases of the Civil War the Historical Department of Iowa has a library of published volumes quite replete. Of the official relations, civil and military, of our State to the Federal Government we have in our collections an adequate deposit. But of the proofs of the workings of the heart about the hearthstones of Iowa, where a son and support of a household is undergoing conversion into the volunteer soldier of the Republic, there is a lack.

The American Volunteer soldier of the Civil War—North and South—was in his day the most admired of all time for his soldierly qualities. For his convertability after Sumter from civil life into an effective soldier; and after Appomattox into a better citizen.

How were the best elements of the Citizen preserved throughout years in the ranks, and how was the good in the ranks carried back into life at peace? Where were the currents which blew a life out from the haven of home upon the sea of war and upon that part of such a sea which bore the standard of national as against state sovereignty? Whence came the poise in action and on march, which made of an Iowa boy the veteran soldier upon which Grant relied even in the major responsibilities of a great war?

Of Iowa soldiery in the ranks the intimate accounts are especially meager. The men who served in the 11th, 13th, 14th and 15th Infantry were as conspicuous for valor as were those of the other notable Iowa regiments, and in addition were privileged to be together from Shiloh to the Grand Review under the designation of "Crocker's Iowa Brigade." The history of that Brigade is well preserved yet there is lacking that hearthstone phase of it all which has its secret and sacred appeal to the ordinary mind.

Such a lack as to written sources did not always exist, for letters flew to and from the front which bore the individual and the collective story. There were almost as many diaries as testaments in the knapsacks of the boys. There was universal written appeal and response, of hope and of prayer, between the boy at the front and the family at home. It was such that Lincoln had in mind when he said:

"The mystic chords of memory, stretching from every battlefield and patriot grave to every living heart and hearthstone all over this broad land, will yet swell the chorus of the Union, when again touched, as surely they will be, by the better angels of our nature."

The Curator of the Historical Department of Iowa assumes the full responsibility for publishing such a record and of saying that evidences of such Iowa "chords" are both rare and necessary.

The diary of Alexander G. Downing, Co. E, Eleventh Regiment Iowa Volunteers is one of the most precious of contributions toward supplying this lack. It is published out of respect for frequent calls upon the Department for such materials, and with a degree of pride that it could have been done under the appreciative and efficient editorial oversight of Dr. O. B. Clark.

EDGAR R. HARLAN, Curator.

PREFACE.

In presenting Downing's Civil War Diary to the public, the editor wishes to set forth the exact nature and character of the work. In the first place it should be said that it is not a verbatim reproduction of the original text. This statement no doubt is enough, according to the accepted tenets of historical criticism, to condemn the work without further consideration; no attempt will be made by argument or brief to defend so gross a breach of the historical sense. However, a brief description of the original diary and an account of its publication in its present form, may both justify the course pursued and explain the true character of the published diary.

The original diary with other papers and commissions of Mr. Alexander G. Downing have been presented to the historical Department of Iowa, at Des Moines. The diary consists of two small note-books, one containing the daily entries from August 15, 1861, to the close of 1862; the other from the beginning to the end of 1863; a larger note-book for the year 1864; several large sheets of writing paper, dated and numbered consecutively, from January 1, 1865, down to the mustering out of the young veteran and his return to the harvest field in July of that year.

Another manuscript of the diarist must be mentioned as a step in the evolution of this published diary. Upon learning of the existence of the diary, the present editor suggested to Mr. Downing the desirability of preserving it in printed form. With characteristic modesty he responded that certain friends had urged the same, but that it was hardly worth it, and in any event he meant first to re-write it as it was not in shape to be printed. He thereupon set for himself the task of re-writing his diary and completed the work in the early months of 1914. This revised diary together with the original he then delivered to Curator Harlan for preservation, at the same time expressing the wish that if his diary were ever published, it should be the revision rather than the original. In fact he felt that with the revision the original was no longer of use, and it was only through Mr. Harlan's sympathetic interest and earnest solicitation that Mr. Downing consented to its preservation. Arrangements were at once entered into by Mr. Downing and Mr. Harlan for the undersigned to edit the diary for publication.

This revised manuscript is a faithful piece of work, neatly bound, which by accurate transmission, omission and amendation, is a most worthy effort at writing "the truth, the whole truth, and nothing but the truth," of a soldier's experience, after the lapse of fifty years. But it will readily be seen that there was a fundamental problem to solve before entering upon the work of preparing the diary for publication, viz.; how to make use of both the original and the revised manuscripts. It was finally determined to edit the original diary and draw upon the revision for such additional matter as would serve to enrich the simple, crude, but manifestly faithful fact-presentation of the original and so construct the material that the reader might have the advantage, without confusion, of Mr. Downing's reflections of fifty years upon his original writing. In doing this it was necessary to re-write the diary. Great care has been exercised so as not to obscure the diarist's point of view and change the spirit in which he originally wrote. The method thus adopted has had from the first the full approval of Mr. Downing.

There were entries in the original which Mr. Downing regarded of no consequence, others which he thought improper and which he consequently omitted from his revision. But all such, with his consent, have been religiously included in this volume. On the other hand, some things which he wrote in the revision have either been omitted entirely or excluded from the body of the text and placed as footnotes or included in the appendix. This is particularly the case with such reminiscent or explanatory statements which in their nature could not have been in a diary, or which would tend to discredit the work as a record of fact. The work is thus preserved as a diary. Only such material from the revision has been drawn upon as would clear up facts and make the whole more readable. It is thought that the added descriptions and experiences give a more perfect picture of the routine life of a Civil War soldier, and yet in no way change the recorded events and the currents of feeling.

The original diary was written, much of it, under the rather unfavorable conditions and trying circumstances, attending the hurry and excitement of war. Often the diarist was unable for several days, or even in a few instances for a week at a time, to set down the daily entries. Sometimes he would jot down the barest facts in a "sort of short-hand fashion," as Madison says of his "Journal," and then when he found respite from his duties, would more fully write out the entries. This he makes known to us when home on his furlough in the spring of 1864. After reaching home and being shut in upon a rainy day, he takes the opportunity, as he says, "to bring my diary down to date." Some portions of the original were much better written than others, a good example being the movements during the siege of Vicksburg, as will be seen by observing the facsimile page for June 7, 8 and 9, 1863, opposite page 120. The spelling is quite original and the writing somewhat shy in punctuation, capitalization and the use of words. Of these shortcomings in his diary, the author, Mr. Downing, was quite conscious, and on that account was unwilling to have it published in the original form.

This printed edition then, lays no claim to being what it is not, the publication of the original text without change. It is an edited edition which retains to the fullest possible degree the original in the essentials of fact and spirit. That this is so, is due to the fact that the editor had the valuable aid of the diarist himself. Every daily entry has had the approval of Mr. Downing as to matters of fact and of feeling. Every item has been cast in terms and point of view of the original writer. Thus there is preserved the spirit and thought of the youth who tho he had little opportunity for schooling beyond the merest rudiments, and handicapped in giving expression to his vision, he nevertheless wrote from the highest sense of personal honor, duty, and moral courage. These characteristics crop out all thru the diary. One reads with the feeling that this boy is a truthful and reliable witness.

In the preparation of the manuscript for publication, the editor wishes to express his great appreciation to Mr. Downing for his patient help and appreciative concern, without which the task would have been difficult indeed and the completed volume of far less value. The editor also wishes to acknowledge the valuable assistance of Mr. Edgar R. Harlan, Curator of the Historical Department of Iowa, both in his wise counsel as to the general plan and his critical reading of the proof sheets. Acknowledgment is due Miss Ida M. Huntington, Assistant Curator, for her scholarly criticism in reading the manuscript.

The editor feels that for a work of its kind, it is as worthy as it is rare and entertains the hope that it will be received as a valuable contribution to the literature of the Civil War. The author of the original diary is deserving of high praise for his foresight and conscientious work in setting down what he saw, what he experienced, and what he thought as a youthful participant in that memorable struggle.

O. B. C.

Des Moines, Iowa, March 31, 1916.

CONTENTS

Reminiscent Note 3
Chapter I. Enlisting in the United States Service........... 4
" II. In Camp McClellan.............................. 12
" III. The Mobilization at Benton Barracks............ 18
" IV. In Winter Quarters and Garrison Duty........... 22
" V. Mobilization at Pittsburg Landing and the Battle of Shiloh.................................. 36
" VI. The Battles in and Around Corinth.............. 46
" VII. On Guard at Bolivar, Tennessee................. 60
" VIII. The Battles of Inka and Corinth. Chasing Price and Fortifying Corinth................. 68
" IX. The Campaign Around Holly Springs and Retreat to Lafayette, Tennessee.............. 80
" X. The Vicksburg Campaign. Siege and Surrender of Vicksburg........................... 94
" XI. The Campaign Against Jackson, Mississippi.......127
" XII. On Guard at Vicksburg and the Fruitless Expedition to Monroe, Louisiana..............132
" XIII. A Siege of Fever and Ague. Fortifying and Patrolling Vicksburg.....................141
" XIV. Re-enlisting as Veterans.......................156
" XV. The Expedition to Meridian, Mississippi.........165
" XVI. Home on Veteran's Furlough....................173
" XVII. Mobilization at Cairo and Moving Forward to Join Sherman............................182
" XVIII. The Battles Around Atlanta. In the Field Hospital 195
" XIX. In the Hospital at Rome, Georgia. Reports from the Front.........................205
" XX. Rejoining the Eleventh Iowa at Atlanta and the Pursuit of Hood.....................217
" XXI. Marching Through Georgia. Capture of Savannah 227
" XXII. Raid Through South Carolina...................244
" XXIII. March Through North Carolina. The Last Campaign. Johnston's Surrender to Sherman 260
" XXIV. Peaceful March Through Virginia and the Grand Review at Washington.................271
" XXV. The Mustering Out. Return to the Harvest Field 279
Appendix 291
Index 310

REMINISCENT INTRODUCTORY NOTE.

During the months of July and August, 1861, the country was greatly aroused over the prospects of war. Excitement rose high when the news of the battle of Bull Run, July 21st, was flashed over the wires. I was then almost 19 and living at home on a farm near Inland, Cedar county, Iowa. Naturally I was deeply stirred over the question of war. Some of our neighbors and friends had earlier opposed the use of force in preventing secession, but I distinctly remember that my father and many neighbors and friends entertained no doubt as to the righteousness of such a course.

During these days we were at work in the harvest field. We had finished cutting our wheat and oats and during the first two weeks of August were engaged in stacking the grain. Everyone had some part in the work. Father did the stacking, while John was on the stack with him, placing the sheaves at his right hand. Albert and George drove the teams to and from the fields, while Paul and Andrew attended to watering the stock during the day.[1] Tom Toly, a strong Irishman, who had worked for us three or four summers, pitched the sheaves to father from the wagon, and Dave Cole pitched the sheaves from the shocks in the field to me on the wagon, while I arranged them on the load.

There had been some talk of raising a company of troops at Inland, but nothing had come of it. At Tipton, the county seat, a company of one hundred men was raised when the first call for volunteers was made. But as they were not then needed, they went out under the call of July 23, 1861, and became Company A of the Fifth Iowa Infantry.

I had been pondering in my mind the matter of going to join the army. On the evening of Saturday, August 10th, news came of the battle of Wilson's Creek, and that General Lyon had been killed. The First Iowa Infantry was in that battle and made glorious history for itself and for Iowa. That fact, with the excitement over the battle itself, stirred us boys in the neigh-

[1] The five boys, John, Albert, George, Paul and Andrew, are Mr. Downing's half-brothers. They are all living at this time (March, 1916) and all reside in Iowa.—Ed.

borhood, and I practically reached a decision as to what I should do.

The next day was Sunday, and everybody was talking about the battle of Wilson's Creek. Ministers spoke of it in their sermons and prayers. It was the all-important topic of the day, and for the next three days—the 12th, 13th and 14th of August, it was the topic of conversation while we were finishing our work in the harvest field. On the next day, my birthday, I began my diary and shall now let it speak.

A. G. D.

THE DIARY.

Chapter I.
Enlisting in the United States Service.

Thursday, 15th—We capped our grain stacks against rain and windstorms, and then commenced mowing wild grass for hay. This is my birthday; am nineteen years old.

Friday, 16th—I, with Tom Toly, mowed grass all day. Swinging the scythe was hard work for me and I did not cut as wide a swath as Tom did. Father went to Tipton in the afternoon and upon his return told us the war news. I am thinking some of enlisting and going to war.

Saturday, 17th—I mowed grass all forenoon and in the afternoon went to a Sunday school celebration down at Posten's Grove. I made up my mind to enlist and go and fight our Southern brethren. In the evening I went to Mr. Willey's to stay all night with Ward. Later in the evening we attended a peace meeting at Inland.

Sunday, 18th—This morning attended the Methodist church and Sunday school at Posten's Grove. Several Methodist brethren were received into the church. In the afternoon Mr. Wharton, the minister, delivered a patriotic speech and spoke of the war. He then called for volunteers and I put my name down to go for three years or during the war. About fifty-five boys enlisted and we are to go in Company E of the Eighth Iowa.

ENLISTING IN THE UNITED STATES SERVICE

(August, 1861)

Monday, 19th—I helped haul and stack hay this forenoon, and in the afternoon went to Inland with the other boys who enlisted yesterday, to see about going to Camp McClellan, at Davenport.

Tuesday, 20th—I went early this morning to Inland, where all who enlisted were to meet and go to Davenport.[1] Several of the friends came in to see us off. There were forty-five of us and at 9 o'clock we left in wagons for Davenport. After a hot, dusty ride we arrived at Davenport at 4 o'clock in the afternoon, and marched out to Camp McClellan, where they received us very kindly. We had very fine barracks to go into and the boys of the Eighth Iowa had a good supper for us. It was our first meal in the army and consisted of boiled potatoes, fried bacon and baked beans. We have lots of straw to sleep on at night. We were to meet a part of a company from Le Claire under command of Captain Foster and together form one company in the Eighth Iowa Infantry. But Captain Foster did not come, and since there are only eight Le Claire boys here we have not enough to make a company.

Wednesday, 21st—We drew our army cooking utensils this morning and one day's rations, and then cleaned up our camp. Besides a part of the Eighth Iowa Infantry, there is a part of the Second Iowa Cavalry in camp. The first day of camp life is past, and we had our first experience of a night in camp, sleeping on straw for a bed.

Thursday, 22d—Received orders this morning to get ready for review. At 1 o'clock in the afternoon we marched down into town and through the streets for a while and then back to camp. General Baker, Adjutant General of Iowa, is in charge of the camp. Our camp was named for General McClellan in the East.

Friday, 23d—There is so much delay in completing the company that the boys are beginning to think there is no hope of getting our company full. Some of the boys are joining other

---

[1] When I bade father good-by, he said: "Well, Alec, as you have made up your mind to go into the army, I want you to promise me that you will not enter into any of the vices that you will come in contact with while in the army, but try to conduct yourself just as if you were at home." Of course I was not an angel while in the army, but I always remembered father's advice, and to that I attribute what little success I have had in life—and this is my seventy-second year. Father was in his forty-sixth year, but he told me that if it were not for leaving the family alone, he would go with me. He was a strong Union man, and his father had served all through the War of the Revolution, in the command of General Wayne.—A. G. D.

companies. While waiting, those who wish may leave camp on passes. I got a pass to go home for two or three days.

Saturday, 24th—I reached home this morning at daylight, having left Davenport late yesterday afternoon, riding out with a farmer to "the forks" of the Hickory Grove and the Allen's Grove roads, and from there walked the twenty-one miles home, after night, all alone.

This is a fine day. I went over to Mr. Sparks' and accompanied him to the grove out southwest of Tipton, to a camp meeting which is being conducted by the Christian church. We got there in time for the meeting.

Sunday, 25th—I stayed over night at Sparks' and attended meeting at the grove again this morning. We had a basket dinner at noon. At the afternoon service the Lord's Supper was observed. After the meeting we started for home, a distance of eleven miles.

Monday, 26th—There was a heavy rainstorm last night. I worked all day, picking onion seed, and in the evening went down to Inland to make arrangements to go back to Davenport in the morning to join the camp.

Tuesday, 27th—I went to Davenport today and returned to Camp McClellan. A force of about five hundred men was sent down the river by boat to Keokuk, for the purpose of reinforcing the troops at that place. It is expected that they will have a fight there. I was too late in returning to camp to go with them.

Wednesday, 28th—There is nothing of importance. The camp looks as if it were deserted. There are just a few convalescents here, who were not able to go with the boys to Keokuk; there are also a few recruits coming in.

Thursday, 29th—News came that they had a fight at Keokuk; the boys that went down had a lively skirmish with the "secesh" just across the river in Missouri.[1]

Friday, 30th—No news of importance. There are still some companies arriving in camp for the Eighth Iowa, and they are still adding new recruits to the Second Iowa Cavalry, which is in camp at the Fair Grounds.

[1] This was doubtless what is known as the battle of Athens.—Ed.

ENLISTING IN THE UNITED STATES SERVICE

(August, 1861)

Saturday, 31st—Our men arrived from Keokuk this morning. They did not get into action with the "secesh" while at Keokuk as reported. The companies for the Eighth Iowa Infantry are almost completed and the regiment will be ready to leave for the South at a moment's notice. They are to receive the clothing and arms at St. Louis.

SEPTEMBER, 1861.

Sunday, 1st—We had our first preaching in camp today, both morning and evening, by the chaplain of the Eleventh Iowa Infantry. Quite a number of folks came out from town to attend the meeting. At 5 o'clock we had dress parade with the Eighth Iowa.

Monday, 2d—We are having regular drilling now: company drill at 10 o'clock in the forenoon for two hours, and in the afternoon regimental drill for two hours. Every evening at 5 o'clock we have dress parade.

Tuesday, 3d—A new company came into camp today which had only about half the necessary number, and so it was planned to have them join with us and form a full company, but the two companies could not agree on who should be captain.

Wednesday, 4th—Very fine weather. No news of importance. The Government has issued to each man a good, double, woolen blanket, which we use for covers at night in our bunks of wheat straw. There are two men to each bunk, my bunk-mate being Thomas Fossett. He is a good, conscientious fellow.

Thursday, 5th—Four men from Company A of the Eighth Iowa were drummed out of camp today. They had refused to take the oath to support the United States Government.

Friday, 6th—Nothing of importance. We have company drill twice a day now. We draw our rations every morning about 9 o'clock now. They consist of bread, beans, potatoes, bacon, rice, sugar, coffee, salt and pepper, also soap and candles. Twice a week we have salt beef and fresh beef. Each one draws enough for the day according to army regulations.[1]

Saturday, 7th—We had a big picnic dinner in camp today, given for the soldiers by the ladies of Scott county. There was

[1] Mr. Downing says that he learned later that Mr. Hiram Price (the Davenport banker) provisioned the soldiers with his own funds, which is in keeping with the well-known facts concerning the financing of the first regiments by Mr. Price and others, for the state of Iowa.—Ed.

fried chicken, bread, pie and cake by the wagon load, free to all who were hungry. The food was placed on a long table and each man could walk up and help himself. There must have been as many as five thousand who enjoyed the dinner. It was a beautiful day for the occasion.

Sunday, 8th—We had preaching in camp three times today, morning, afternoon and evening. Quite a number from the city came out to camp to attend the services. The weather was delightful.

Monday, 9th—Our company was disbanded this morning, since we could not get men enough to fill it up. Some of our boys enlisted in other companies of the Eighth Iowa. Captain Foster of Le Claire sent word to our captain, McLoney, that he would raise an entire company at Le Claire.[1]

Tuesday, 10th—I went down town this morning to see about enlisting in a battery which Mr. Little, a business man of Davenport, is trying to raise. He was planning to raise a company of two hundred men to command a battery of heavy cannon. But before night I made up my mind that he would not succeed, and I did not enlist in it. I bunked with some others in vacant store buildings, lying on gunny sacks. It rained hard all day.

Wednesday, 11th—I went up to the Fair Grounds and spent the day there. The attendance was good, there being about two thousand present.

Business is becoming quite dull. The war seems to put a stop to all improvements, and there is no demand for farm produce. Money is getting scarce, gold having been out of circulation so long that people have forgotten how it looks, and merchants say that it will not be long until silver goes the same way. For a long time now we have had wild-cat money, but everybody is afraid to go to sleep with any of it on hand for fear that it will be worthless in the morning.

Thursday, 12th—I attended the Scott County Fair again today. The attendance was about the same as yesterday. A part of the Second Iowa Cavalry is in camp here, Camp Holt.

For three days now I have been trying to find some new company in which to enlist, but not caring to go into a company of

[1] At the time some of us were greatly disappointed in not getting Captain Foster for our company, but I believe now that in the long run it was a good thing.—A. G. D.

(September, 1861)

entire strangers, I made up my mind to go home for a few days. About sundown, with two other boys, Sylvester Daniels and David Huff, I started for home, going with a Mr. Chesbro in a farm wagon.

Friday, 13th—We made the entire trip of thirty miles from Davenport last night and reached home by daylight. I went up to Tipton this afternoon and was sworn into the State service, my service dating back to August 20th. Our former captain, Mr. McLoney, and some of the other Inland boys are here, besides four of the Le Claire boys. We are trying to form a new company and everything looks good for a new company in a short time, quite a number of the boys having already enrolled. We are boarding at the hotel.

Saturday, 14th—We had company drill this morning, and some five or six new men enrolled. I went home in the afternoon.

Sunday, 15th—This morning I went to church and Sunday School once more.

Monday, 16th—I returned to Tipton this morning. Our company had no drill today on account of the rain—it rained all day. There were no enlistments. The disagreeable weather seems to make everybody feel gloomy.

Tuesday, 17th—Several new men enrolled today and things look more encouraging. I boarded at the tavern today.

Wednesday, 18th—There were more enrollments today, and there is some hope now of raising a company. The weather has become settled and everybody seems more cheerful. We have drill twice a day now, and have a good drill ground out on the town commons.

Thursday, 19th—Nothing of importance today. A few new recruits came in. There is no excitement in getting men to enlist; only plain facts are presented as to our duty to sustain the Government.

Friday, 20th—Captain Stearns of Company A of the Eighth Iowa arrived today from Davenport, coming to encourage enlistments. Several new men enrolled today. We have a fine drill-master in John F. Compton of New Liberty, Scott county. He is an Englishman, and has served five years in the Queen's Guards of England.

(September, 1861)

Saturday, 21st—We had company drill this morning. In the afternoon we had a big loyal mass-meeting in town, and we had speaking by Captain Stearns. He talked of our duty to sustain the Government. Quite a number enlisted as a result of the meeting, and it is hoped that the company may be completed so as to leave for Davenport in about eight days.

Sunday, 22d—I remained in Tipton all day, going to preaching this morning and to Sunday school in the afternoon.

Monday, 23d—The boys are beginning to enlist quite fast. A goodly number enrolled today, and we now have our company almost full. We drill twice a day. We drilled today in "double quick" through the streets of Tipton.

Tuesday, 24th—More enrolled today than any day yet. Most of the boys are from the surrounding farms, though there are a number of Tipton boys in our company. Our drillmaster keeps us on the drill ground most of the time.

Wednesday, 25th—It rained all day and we had to drill in a big barn on the edge of town. We drilled in the barn on the "double quick." On account of the rain, business of all kinds is almost at a standstill.

Thursday, 26th—We had no drill today. Instead of drilling all went to meeting. President Lincoln issued a proclamation asking that the day be observed as a day of fasting and prayer, and our company attended service twice today, in a body. The war has cast a gloom over the whole country; people are beginning to believe that it will be a long siege before it is over with.

Friday, 27th—Fine weather again. Our company was completed today and we have arranged for election of officers tomorrow.

Saturday, 28th—We had regular drill this morning and in the afternoon our election of officers. The election resulted as follows: Captain, Samuel S. McLoney; First Lieutenant, John F. Compton; Second Lieutenant, Lorenzo D. Durbin; Orderly Sergeant, Joel H. Clark. I went home this evening for the last time before leaving for Camp McClellan.[1]

Sunday, 29th—I went to meeting once more before leaving for camp. After preaching I went to Mr. Moore's, remaining there

[1] It proved to be the last time for two years and six months.—A. G. D.

THIS IS A PHOTOGRAPH OF A DAGUERREOTYPE OF MR. DOWNING TAKEN IN 1858, AT THE AGE OF SIXTEEN YEARS.

(September, 1861)

the rest of the day and stayed over night with John Moore. John presented me with a pocket Bible which he asked me to carry with me.[1]

Monday, 30th—I left home early this morning for Tipton, where at 10 o'clock about one hundred of us, with a band, left Tipton in farm wagons for Wilton, which place we reached at 4 o'clock, all covered with mud. At 5 o'clock we took the train for Davenport and arrived there at 8 o'clock. We formed in double line at the station and marched through town past the Burtis Hotel, on up to Camp McClellan, where we went into the barracks. As we passed the hotel every other man was handed a good wool blanket.

Company B of the Eleventh Iowa had supper prepared for us, consisting of boiled potatoes, fried bacon, boiled beef, baker's bread and coffee. On the way down from Wilton, Governor Kirkwood passed through the train and shook each man by the hand.

---

[1] I carried this Bible during my four years' service and read it through four times.—A. G. D.

Chapter II.
In Camp McClellan. September 30-November 15.

OCTOBER, 1861.

Tuesday, 1st—We drew our cooking utensils and rations for five days. John Batderf, Joseph Tomlinson and I were put in as cooks for the company. We have company drill four hours a day. It seems that we are in camp this time for business. My bunk-mate is James M. Fossett, a brother of Thomas Fossett. James enlisted this time instead of his brother. He's a fine fellow for a bunk-mate.

Wednesday, 2d—It rained all day. The band from Tipton left for home this morning. Our company held an election this afternoon for choosing non-commissioned officers, sergeants and corporals. It was quite a political battle, the way the boys strove for the different offices.

Thursday, 3d—It rained again all day, and although our camp is on high ground, on the bluff just east of town, yet it is a jelly of mud. It couldn't be otherwise with three or four thousand men tramping over it.

Friday, 4th—The third all-day rain. Our regiment, the Eleventh Iowa, commenced to build their new barracks, located on the east side of the camp ground. Lieutenant Durbin arrived today.

Saturday, 5th—Our company was sworn into the United States service today, by Captain Alexander Chambers of the regular army. Four men were rejected, which left ninety in the company. Fisher was rejected because he was too short—less than five feet,[1] and Lowe was rejected because he was pigeon-toed.[2] I got a pass and went to Allen's Grove to see John Moore.

Sunday, 6th—I remained all day at Mr. Moore's. Mr. Moore[3] is a Mexican War veteran.

[1] He was taken later, however, when the need of men was greater and also because of his persistence.—A. G. D.
[2] Lowe feigned to be pigeon-toed, so that he would be rejected, having got chicken-hearted. The boys jeered him.—A. G. D.
[3] Mr. Moore was an uncle of my friend and schoolmate, John Moore.—A. G. D.

(October, 1861)

Monday, 7th—I left for Davenport early this morning, riding to town with a farmer, and got back to camp at 2 o'clock. Quite a number of the boys around Allen's Grove are in camp here as members of the Second Iowa Cavalry.

Tuesday, 8th—Regular drill morning and afternoon. All men are supposed to be on the drill ground regularly every day, unless they are marked not fit for duty by the surgeon of the regiment.

Wednesday, 9th—Drill twice a day and dress parade at 5 p. m. New recruits are daily coming into camp.

Thursday, 10th—The Thirteenth Iowa are building their new barracks just north of ours. The weather is getting quite cool, especially at night.

Friday, 11th—My company, E, has ninety-seven men. They are of several different nationalities, as follows: Three from Canada, four from Ireland, two from England, two from Germany, and one from France; the rest are American-born, as follows: Twenty-three from Ohio, twenty-one from Pennsylvania, sixteen from New York, eight from Indiana, six from Iowa, two each from Michigan and Vermont, and one each from Maryland and Maine. The average age is less than twenty years, and there are eight married men.

Saturday, 12th—A number of new recruits are arriving, and the Fourteenth Iowa Infantry is being made up. Drill this afternoon. Five of the boys of my company got passes to go home for two or three days.

Sunday, 13th—We had preaching in camp this morning by the chaplain, and he gave us a good sermon. A great many people came out from town to attend the meeting, and still more came this afternoon to see us on dress parade at 5 o'clock.

Monday, 14th—We completed building our new barracks today. Each company has its own building, built of good one-inch lumber, with just enough room between the buildings for our long stationary company tables, where we eat. In front of the building, extending the entire length, is our parade ground.

Tuesday, 15th—We moved into our new barracks today, and the boys are all pleased with the new quarters. We had some

(October, 1861)

visitors. Our camp is becoming quite a place for visitors—parents and friends of the boys coming in to bid them the last goodbye.

Wednesday, 16th—Colonel A. M. Hare, who arrived today, is in command of our regiment, the Eleventh Iowa. His home is at Muscatine. More visitors in camp today, and they are usually invited to take dinner or supper with us, as the case may be.

Thursday, 17th—Our daily routine in camp is as follows: Reveille at 4 a. m., breakfast call at 5, drill at 9 and dinner call at noon; drill call at 2 p. m., dress parade at 5, supper at 5:30, tattoo at 8 and taps at 9, when every man not on duty must be in his bunk and all lights out.

Friday, 18th—Nothing of importance. At the sound of reveille every man has to get up, fall in line, and answer to his name. We then march down over the bluff to the river to wash for breakfast, going by companies, each under the command of an officer.

Saturday, 19th—The Eleventh Iowa Infantry was completed today. All the companies now have their full quotas.

Sunday, 20th—We had preaching twice today, morning and evening, by the chaplain of our regiment, John S. Whittlesey, a Congregational minister from Davenport. A number of people from town were out again to attend the services.

Monday, 21st—We received orders to keep the camp clean— have to clean up every morning. The men must all keep their clothes brushed and their shoes polished.

Tuesday, 22d—There were quite a number of visitors from Tipton today—friends of the boys from that place. The weather is cloudy and disagreeable.

Wednesday, 23d—There was a large fire in town today. New companies for the Thirteenth and Fourteenth Regiments are arriving in camp nearly every day; also new troops for the Second Iowa Cavalry in camp at the Fair Grounds.

Thursday, 24th—The flag was run up at half mast today, in honor of the death of Colonel Wentz, of the Second Iowa Infantry. Clothing and arms for our regiment have arrived at Davenport. The boys are glad to know that our regiment is to be equipped before leaving the State—ours is to be the first so equipped.

(October, 1861)

Friday, 25th—We got our equipments today. Our guns are the old-fashioned muskets made by working over the old flintlock gun, so as to use a cap in place of the flint. The musket is loaded with a cartridge containing powder, ball, and three buckshot in front of the ball. Each man is to carry forty rounds or more of ammunition all the time.

Saturday, 26th—We drilled with our new arms this morning for the first time. Some of the men are awfully awkward in shouldering arms and using the ramrod and returning it to its place. It is also quite amusing to hear some of the officers give orders when we are going through the manual of arms.

Sunday, 27th—We had regular preaching today, both morning and afternoon, by the chaplain. There was a large attendance from outside the camp at the meetings. The mornings are becoming quite frosty.

Monday, 28th—Nothing of importance today. All the boys of the company like to drill under Compton, our first lieutenant, for he can give the correct commands in the manual of arms, and he makes us toe the chalk line. He is not at all overbearing, as some of the officers are, but is kind to the men, especially to those who try to execute the commands.

Tuesday, 29th—Several new companies of the Thirteenth Iowa Infantry were sworn into the United States service today. Marcellus M. Crocker of Des Moines is to be their colonel.

Wednesday, 30th—Nothing of importance. We now have a quartermaster for our regiment, Richard Cadle of Muscatine. All think that he is a good man for the place, and will see that every man is cared for. We draw rations every five days.

Thursday, 31st—The new uniforms for the Eleventh Iowa were received today by our quartermaster. We are the first to receive uniforms before leaving the State. This is the last of October—and we are still at old Camp McClellan, Davenport, Iowa.

NOVEMBER, 1861.

Friday, 1st—Our uniforms were brought up to camp from town, and several companies drew theirs today. Every company drills four hours a day now. Some of the men have a hard time

(November, 1861)

remembering the commands of the officers and some of the officers cannot remember the correct commands to give. Some of them make as big blunders as the men.[1]

Saturday, 2d—Company E drew their uniforms today, each man receiving the following pieces: one dress coat, $6.71; one overcoat, $7.20; one pair of pants, $3.03; one pair of shoes, $1.96; two shirts, $1.76; one double woolen blanket, $2.96; one hat, $1.55; two pair of drawers, $1.00; two pair of socks, 52c; one cap, 60c; one leather collar, 14c. The total cost for each man was $27.43.

Sunday, 3d—We had company inspection for the first time, this morning at 10 o'clock, and we therefore had preaching in the afternoon only. Our entire regiment was out on dress parade in the new uniforms for the first time. Fully half of the people of Davenport were out to see us, for it was the first of the kind they had seen.

Monday, 4th—We had some visitors in camp today from Inland. Nothing of importance. The part of our uniform most talked about and criticised is the leather collar, which each man has to wear. It is a piece of stiff upper leather about two inches wide in the middle, tapering to one inch at the ends, which are fastened with a buckle. We wear it about our necks with the wide part under the chin to make us hold our heads erect. These collars the boys call "dog-collars."

Tuesday, 5th—We received strict orders today to take care of our equipment, especially our clothes and guns. Then we have to wear brass epaulets on our shoulders, which makes a great deal of extra work as they have to be kept polished.[2]

Wednesday, 6th—Drill twice a day: company drill in the forenoon and regimental drill in the afternoon. Colonel Hare for the first time commanded the regiment on the drill ground.

Thursday, 7th—Received orders to fix up for review. We packed our knapsacks, filled our haversacks and canteens, and

[1] Upon one occasion a certain captain had his company out for a drill on the town commons. The company was marching "by platoon guide right," and advancing toward a big open ditch full of water, when the captain, forgetting the correct command to give, "halt" or "right-about face," called out, "Look out for that ditch!" Now according to military tactics soldiers are not expected to move or change their course except upon specific command, and so, to the chagrin of the captain, his men went right on, plunged into the water and crossed to the other bank. A few, however, did "look out for the ditch," and the company was thrown into great confusion.—A. G. D.

[2] When we once got into active service, these epaulets were discarded, and the "dog collars" went with them.—A. G. D.

(November, 1861)

with our arms formed in line, all as if we were going on a long march. At 10 o'clock we marched down through the streets of Davenport and were reviewed by Adjutant General Baker. Then we marched back to camp. Our regiment with the new uniforms was quite a drawing card, for it seemed as if all of the townspeople were out to see us pass by.

Friday, 8th—The Thirteenth Iowa received their uniforms and equipments today. Some of our boys are absent on sick leave, having caught severe colds on account of the changeable weather.

Saturday, 9th—We received our State pay today. I got $20.60 in paper money, thus losing only about twenty-five cents on the dollar. I served forty-five days under the State.

Sunday, 10th—We had company inspection this morning at 9 o'clock and preaching at 10. At 5 o'clock in the afternoon we had dress parade and then in the evening we had preaching again.

Monday, 11th—No news of importance. Our regiment is gradually adapting itself to the military harness; the hardest thing to get used to is wearing the leather collars about our necks.

Tuesday, 12th—There is some talk of our having to stay here in camp all winter. Most of the men are getting rather restless and anxious to get to the seat of war. New companies for the Fourteenth Iowa are still arriving.

Wednesday, 13th—The weather is getting cold, which makes it rather disagreeable eating our meals at the long tables outside the barracks; besides, the coffee and victuals cool off so quickly.

Thursday, 14th—Our regular drills twice a day, company and regimental. No news.

Friday, 15th—We received orders to leave for the South and everybody is happy in the thought that we are going to leave. A great many got passes to go down town to purchase supplies, such as letter paper, stamps and the like. We had our last drill on the old camp ground yesterday and got ready today to move.

Chapter III.

The Mobilization at Benton Barracks. November 16-December 7.

Saturday, 16th—Reveille sounded at 2 a. m., and packing our knapsacks, we started at 8 o'clock for the boat down at the levee. Here we stacked our arms and waited until the quartermaster with his detail got the commissariat loaded, putting it upon our boat and the two barges, one on either side. By noon all was ready and we marched on board, some going upon the boat and some upon the barges, and at 2 p. m. left Davenport, bound for St. Louis.

We reached Muscatine about sundown and because there are so many Muscatine people in the regiment, we landed and marched uptown to Main Street. Here we had dress parade for the benefit of the citizens, who turned out in large numbers. Companies A and H are made up of Muscatine boys, while our colonel and quartermaster reside here; besides, Company I is from Louisa county just west of this place. After the parade we marched back to the boats and left at once for Keokuk. Our boat is the "Jennie Whipple," and Company E is stationed on the hurricane deck.

Sunday, 17th—We had a pretty stiff introduction to our first night on a river boat, for it snowed in the night. My bunk-mate, James Fossett, and I lay down on the deck with our heads to the smoke-stack instead of our feet, in order to avoid lying with our heads down hill. By morning we were covered with snow, about two inches deep. At 8 a. m. we landed at Montrose, where two of our companies were transferred from our boat to another boat in order to lighten our boat for the purpose of passing through the rapids just above Keokuk. We reached Keokuk in safety about noon and went on shore to cook some provisions. At dusk we returned to the boats, our company being transferred to another boat which lay at Keokuk all night while the "Jennie Whipple" proceeded down the river.

Monday, 18th—We left Keokuk at daylight and ran all day without accident or incident. We again tied up for the night, for fear of encountering a "secesh" battery on the banks. The weather is delightful and riding on the "Father of Waters" is very enjoyable.

Tuesday, 19th—We started down the river again at daylight and reached St. Louis at 3 p. m. We landed and marched to Benton Barracks, where we were to be at home. Just as we left the boat it commenced to rain and we marched the whole way in a downpour of rain which soaked our clothes through and through. Reaching the barracks we built fires to dry our clothes before retiring for the night.

Wednesday, 20th—The first thing this morning was to finish drying our clothing, after which we cleaned up and burnished our guns. There are several thousand troops, infantry, cavalry, and artillery here in camp. The barracks are ordinary frame structures and built around the drill ground. The Eleventh Iowa is located on the west side of the ground. We have large quantities of firewood on hand.

Thursday, 21st—We took up our regular company and regimental drills again, and have a very fine drill ground.

Friday, 22d—New troops are arriving all the time, and there are something like forty thousand men in the barracks at present. This camp has the appearance of being nearer the seat of war. It is a novel experience for us country boys to see so many men all armed for war, some on guard duty, others leaving for the front, while still others are arriving. The commissary work of the camp is thoroughly organized. Each company has a detail of cooks which serves a week at a time and then is relieved by another shift. The cooks go to the quartermaster and get the rations for five days at a time. The food is cooked in kettles hung in a row in the rear of the barracks, and is served on long stationary tables, each accommodating a full company. Our rations are about the same as at Camp McClellan, except that we have our first taste of "hard-tack" instead of bread.

Saturday, 23d—We cleaned up today, preparing for our first inspection and review at Benton Barracks. I sent $10.00 home today, the surplus of my State pay.

Sunday, 24th—We had our first regular company inspection this morning at 10 o'clock, and at 2 p. m. we had general review, then at 5 o'clock we were on dress parade, but as it is Sunday there was no regular drilling.

Monday, 25th—Nothing of importance. Camp life is a big change from life at home. In the army, every man simply obeys orders; he knows his place and keeps it. Our officers generally are kind to the men, especially if a man tries to do his duty.

Tuesday, 26th—Our drills now are, company drill at 10 a. m., battalion drill at 2 p. m. and dress parade at 5 p. m. We commenced battalion drill today.

Wednesday, 27th—No news of importance. We enjoy our drilling under First Lieutenant Compton. He has the company under perfect control. The boys always make an effort to execute his commands and we are never ashamed of our drilling when other soldiers are standing by observing our movements.

Thursday, 28th—The weather is very warm and pleasant. The regiment is becoming quite proficient in battalion drill, Colonel Hare seeming to understand the movements quite well. When the Colonel gives the orders to the different company officers, he usually simply says to Compton, "You know how to move your company."

Friday, 29th—We had inspection for pay today, which includes inspection of knapsacks and equipments. After inspection and pay, I went down town on a pass and purchased a portfolio,[1] a paper weight and a pocket knife for army service.

Saturday, 30th—We had our first general review today, including the infantry, cavalry and artillery. The parade ground was full of soldiers, most of them full-armed for active service. And thus ends the month of November at Benton Barracks, St. Louis, Missouri.

DECEMBER, 1861.

Sunday, 1st—We had a big snowstorm last night. It came my turn to go on camp guard for the first time. It takes some five hundred men to go around the camp.

Monday, 2d—It turned warm today and the snow is all gone. I was on guard for the first time here at the barracks. We have to walk the beats with our overcoats on. A man on this, the

---

[1]This portfolio, together with my Bible, I carried through my four years' service.—A. G. D.

(December, 1861)

west side, of the camp was engaged in cleaning his rifle today, when by some movement it was accidentally discharged and hit and killed a soldier on the other side of the grounds.

Tuesday, 3d—Nothing of importance. It is quite noticeable that the men are now holding their heads erect without wearing the "dog collars" around their necks.

Wednesday, 4th—Company drill in the forenoon and battalion drill in the afternoon. We get the St. Louis papers in camp every morning and keep posted on the movements of all parts of the army in the field.

Thursday, 5th—No news of importance. There are troops from all of the western states here in camp and working together in harmony.

Friday, 6th—Very warm and pleasant. There are soldiers drilling almost all the time. Our drill ground is level but well drained, so that even after a heavy rain it is soon dry again.

Saturday, 7th—The Eleventh Iowa received marching orders today, and we are to carry forty rounds of extra ammunition, besides our cartridge box of forty rounds. There was no drill or dress parade today on account of an all-day rain.

Chapter IV.
In Winter Quarters and Garrison Duty. December 8-March 8.

Sunday, 8th—Reveille sounded this morning at 2 o'clock. We jumped out of our bunks, packed our knapsacks, and got started for the railroad station by daylight. As we left the barracks and entered the main street leading down to the city, the sun away to the southeast, just above the hills, showed its face—a regular ball of fire. How glorious it was! I think I shall never forget it. Arriving at the railroad yards, we stacked arms and went to loading our commissariat onto the cars—coal cars. At noon we boarded the train for Jefferson City, riding in box-cars and open cars, and reached our destination at 6 p. m.

While loading our train at St. Louis, we heard the church bells calling the people to worship. It made many of us think of home and I wonder if the folks at home were thinking of us boys here at the seat of war. For here there is no church for us, and when we get orders to go, there is no stopping for Sunday.

Monday, 9th—We left the cars and marched up through town, where we were met by the Forty-seventh Illinois Infantry, who turned out to receive us, presenting arms. They took us into camp about a mile southwest of town. Here we pitched our tents and for the first time went into camp.[1] I went on guard.

Tuesday, 10th—I was on camp-guard all last night, and until 9 o'clock this morning, when I was relieved. The order of the day was cleaning up camp and our clothes. Our camp is on high ground and we have plenty of wood for fires and for cooking. We also have good water, but have to go a half mile for it.

Wednesday, 11th—I am having my first experience of living in a tent. We are under the strictest military rules, and we are just beginning to realize that a soldier's life is not all glory.

---

[1] We had left our train standing on a siding east of the city alongside a fine piece of timber, the ground covered with a heavy sward of blue grass. Some of the boys thought the grass would be just the place upon which to lay the ponchos and sleep on them for the night, and they did so. But it was a mistake, for the ground was cold and damp and a number of the boys caught hard colds from which several of them never recovered. My bunkmate, James Fossett, was one of those, and with the cold taken that night and later, he was sent to the hospital suffering from inflammatory rheumatism. He never again returned to the company, being finally discharged for disability, on October 17, 1862.—A. G. D.

IN WINTER QUARTERS AND GARRISON DUTY 23
(December, 1861)

Thursday, 12th—We received our first month's pay today. Each man in Company E received pay for twenty-six days of service in the month of October, amounting to $11.25, a little less than a full month's pay. I received my first Government pay as a soldier in the United States service, getting a ten-dollar gold piece[1] and one dollar and twenty-five cents in silver. I expressed $10.00 home.

Friday, 13th—The Eleventh Iowa is at home now in wedge tents, with four men to a tent, and we are experiencing more changes in living. Irish potatoes have been dropped from our rations and we have no tables now at which to eat our meals. When the orderly sergeant draws the rations, the company cook calls out for every man to come and get his portion—of hardtack, bacon, sugar, salt, pepper, soap and candles. The cook makes the coffee, boils the beans and salt beef (fresh beef twice a week), and at noon calls each man to get his day's rations of bean soup and meat. The coffee he makes three times a day, each man having his own tin cup for his coffee. Each one prepares his own bacon to suit his taste, many eating it raw between two pieces of hard-tack. Every one has his own plate, knife and fork.

Our regiment received marching orders with ten days' rations, and so we have to leave just as we were getting settled in our tent camp.

Saturday, 14th—We struck our tents early this morning and at sunup marched down to the landing on the Missouri river, where under the quartermaster a large detail of men worked nearly all day loading our commissariat on board the boats. At sundown our regiment, with a part of the Second Illinois Cavalry, started up the river.

Sunday, 15th—We landed at the little town of Providence, Missouri, about sunup and experienced our first day's march after the "secesh." It was a delightful day. The few belated grasshoppers and crickets which escaped the cold spells were singing their farewell songs. We were all awake and keyed to the highest pitch, felt prepared to meet ten thousand "secesh" at any moment. A detail of cavalry was leading the way, and when at

[1] This was the first gold I had seen for months and, as it proved, the last I saw during the war.—A. G. D.

times our marching was delayed, each man anxiously wanting to know the cause, would peer forward over the shoulder of his file leader; but there was nothing to see.

At noon we stacked arms and ate our first lunch upon a march, and in the "secesh's" country at that. Here we rested about two hours, until the cavalry returned. They reported that there was not a "secesh" to be seen in that part of the country, and I guess all heaved a sigh of relief in the thought that there would be no fighting today. We were ten miles out from our landing. Hastening our return march, we reached our boat at sundown, and boarding it, proceeded up the river.

Monday, 16th—We reached Boonville at sunup, and landing, remained there about two hours, when we again boarded the boat and crossed to the other side of the river. We lay on the boat here till dark, when Company E and three other companies started for Boonesboro, seven or eight miles distant. Reaching the town we surrounded it and waited for daylight. On our way out we marched through some very heavy timber, where the sound of our tramping and the rattle of our bayonets aroused the many wood owls, and of all the hideous noises I ever listened to—it made my hair stand on end!

Tuesday, 17th—This morning we entered the town and made a search of all the houses for "secesh." We took seven prisoners, besides some arms and ammunition. This being a great apple country, we found stores of apples in the houses, and helping ourselves, we filled our haversacks. By one o'clock we had finished sacking the town and started back to our boats, arriving there at dark.

Wednesday, 18th—The four companies of cavalry that accompanied us up the river (also by boat) went on a scouting expedition yesterday toward the town of Glasgow. They captured and brought in this morning one hundred and fifty-five kegs of powder which they found hid in haystacks. We stored the powder in the hull of our boat, and at 2 p. m. left this place for an all-night run on our return to Jefferson City. But we are quite uneasy for fear of an explosion from our cargo of powder.

Thursday, 19th—We reached Jefferson City this morning at sunup after an uncomfortable night's ride. The water in the river is very low and it seems that we were fastened on sandbars

(December, 1861)

half the time. Then when the boat was under way, the boat hands, one on each side of the vessel, were constantly calling the soundings, "six feet," "ten feet," "no bottom," etc., in that dreadful, drawling sound, keeping it up all night, and with the thought of that powder on board—it was not a good night for sleeping. But we landed, and marching out to the camp, pitched our tents where we were before. We got back all safe and sound, with one exception, for one of our company took the smallpox and was left at the pesthouse at Boonville, with only his bunk-mate to care for him. The weather is quite cool.

Friday, 20th—We finished cleaning our clothing and accouterments and spent the rest of the day in cleaning up our camp and parade ground, besides bringing in firewood from the timber near by. When we got back we found the Thirteenth Iowa here in camp, having arrived on the 11th day of the month, during our absence.

Saturday, 21st—Nothing of importance today. I went on guard. There is some talk of making Jefferson City headquarters for the various detachments of the army within fifty miles of this place.

Sunday, 22d—It snowed all day, the snow falling in large flakes, and the weather is fast turning colder. I was detailed on camp guard and with my overcoat on walked my beat for two hours at a time. At about 4 o'clock in the afternoon five companies of our regiment received marching orders to go at once, and striking our tents we hastened down to the railroad station on the bank of the river, where we had to stack arms and wait four hours for the train. The weather by this time had turned intensely cold and we were compelled to build fires to keep warm, but no firewood was at hand. The boys spied a lot of canoes stored away for the winter under a warehouse; these we appropriated and had used up forty or fifty of them before our train finally came. When the train did come, we discovered to our dismay that it was made up of stock cars, bedded with straw. We boarded the cars at 8 p. m. and settling ourselves as comfortably as possible, with our rifles in hand started at midnight for California, Missouri.

Monday, 23d—We arrived at California about sunup, almost frozen; it cleared off during the night and a cold northwest wind was blowing. Leaving the train we entered the several churches in town and built fires to warm by, Company E going into a Catholic church, where the sexton and his wife brought us some hot coffee. We then put into winter quarters, occupying vacant houses and storerooms and made all the "secesh" skedaddle. The companies in quarters here are B, E, G, K and H, under command of Lieut. Col. William Hall. We just learned why it was that we were rushed up here last night. It had been reported at Jefferson City that a train with "secesh" prisoners was to pass through this place today, bound for St. Louis, and that their sympathizers in this locality were planning a raid on the train to liberate the prisoners.

Tuesday, 24th—We raised a flag pole today and ran up the Stars and Stripes high in the air, amidst cheering and singing the old song, "Columbia."

"Long may it wave,
O'er the land of the free and the home of the brave!"
This afternoon we went over town and compelled all the secessionists to take the oath. Quite a number of the boys are sick with bad colds, the result of the hard exposure coming up on the stock cars the other night.

Wednesday, 25th—This is a beautiful day, the snow having nearly all disappeared. The boys had a fine time today, this being our first Christmas experience in the army. There was no roast turkey with cranberry sauce and we all missed mother's mince pies, cake and doughnuts. But we bought some pies and cakes of the citizens here, which with our regular army rations made a good dinner and something like a square meal. In the evening some of us boys went to the tavern to get our suppers, costing twenty-five cents apiece, and we had hot biscuit and honey in the bargain.

Thursday, 26th—By orders Company E boarded the cars this morning for Lookout Station farther on, about twelve miles from California. I bade my bunk-mate, James Fossett, goodby at the hospital, where he is confined with inflammatory rheumatism. His suffering is something intense, and he is unable to turn himself in bed, but I left him in the hands of a good nurse.

Friday, 27th—We went into winter quarters here, and that with the intention of cleaning the "secesh" out of this part

IN WINTER QUARTERS AND GARRISON DUTY 27
(December, 1861)

of the country. Our company is the only one here, and our captain is in command of the post. There are but few houses in this place, and we are quartered in a vacant storeroom, one-half the company upstairs, the other below. We who are below built our bunks on the counters, one on each side of the room. We keep two picket posts at night, ten men at each post, on the sides where the railroad enters. We also have a day patrol on the railroad.

Saturday, 28th—We had to send two patrols of five men each down the railroad track each way from the station. There is always some danger of the track's being torn up by organized bands of the "secesh" in this locality.[1]

Sunday, 29th—I am staying at the tavern on account of having taken a severe cold. As we are here without the regimental surgeon, the captain marked me "not fit for duty." The landlady is very kind to me and is helping break up my cold. The company had to clean up this morning for inspection.

Monday, 30th—We made all the citizens at this place take the oath; they have to take the oath not to aid or shelter those who are fighting against the Union. There are but few men left in this locality, they having enlisted, some of them in the Union army, but most of them with the South.

Tuesday, 31st—The boys are all preparing for New Year's Day celebration. Thus ends 1861.[2]

JANUARY, 1862.

Wednesday, 1st—I am back with the company again. The boys are having a big chicken dinner today, Lieutenant Compton having bought four dozen chickens and presented them to the company for a New Year's dinner.

Thursday, 2d—Nothing of importance. The weather is quite cold, but since we are in a building with stoves and plenty of wood, we do not suffer from the cold. Lookout Station is a

[1] William Dwiggans died of typhoid fever on this day, in the hospital at Jefferson City. His was the first death in Company E. He was a good boy and a dutiful soldier.—A. G. D.
[2] The last day of 1861 found our regiment stationed as follows: Company E at Lookout Station, Companies B, G, K and H at California, Companies A, C, D, F and I at Fulton, all in the State of Missouri, and not far apart. They were all in winter quarters, occupying vacant store buildings. We saw some pretty hard service during the month of December, but only in the suffering by exposure to the cold weather.—A. G. D.

small town on the railroad between California and Jefferson City; there is a store, tavern, and twelve residences, some of which are vacant, and the country around is heavily timbered.

Friday, 3d—Mrs. Hemmenway gave some of the boys permission to have a dance at her home last night. Quite a number of the boys went and they declare that they had a good time. The girls of the locality were there and most of them either smoked or chewed tobacco. They would dance a while, then rest and smoke, but those that chewed did not care to stop.[1]

Saturday, 4th—Some of the boys went out today on a 'possum hunt. They were very successful, as this is a good 'possum country, especially over on the banks of the Missouri river.

Sunday, 5th—Nothing of importance. Everything is very quiet and it appears lonesome today. Our company had no preaching today, as our chaplain is with another part of the regiment. The weather has become quite warm. Regular picket and patrol duty at night.

Monday, 6th—This is a very fine day. The boys went out on another 'possum hunt and brought in six.

Tuesday, 7th—Nothing of importance. It rained all day. Our company is divided into messes, seven in all, and each has a cook. Each mess draws its rations every five days, according to number, and the rations are placed in the care of the cooks. Some of the cooks are not well posted on cooking. Cook number 7 wanted to cook some rice for dinner and put his kettle on filled with rice. Presently he began dipping out rice, as it was running over, and he soon had his third kettle filled with rice. In finishing it up he let it scorch and to overcome that he put in some molasses, which the boys foraged out in the country, and so mess number 7 will have sweet scorched rice for some days to come.[2]

Wednesday, 8th—The boys have been gathering persimmons and walnuts today—got lots of them.

Thursday, 9th—Some of the boys go out into the country almost every day on foraging expeditions and bring in an abun-

---

[1] Craven Lane, a member of Company E, died of lung fever on this day at Jefferson City. He had been with us but a short time and was a very quiet boy.—A. G. D.

[2] Cook number 7 did not hear the last of it for some time. We all recommended him as being a good hand to cook rice.—A. G. D.

dance of things to eat, so that with our regular rations we are pretty well supplied.

Friday, 10th—It is cool and cloudy, with some rain. We get our mail every day, as the railroad is open between here and St. Louis.

Saturday, 11th—Our company were all vaccinated today as a protection against smallpox. The regimental surgeon came down from California to do the work. Our captain called the company up in line, and every man had to take his medicine.

Sunday, 12th—Dr. Smith, a resident here, had his horse stolen last night. This morning Lieutenant Durbin with ten men went out to find the thief, but they returned this evening without finding him.

Monday, 13th—Some of the boys have been getting whiskey in this locality and today Lieutenant Compton with Carl Frink and John White went to find where they were getting it, but they returned late in the evening without finding the distilling plant.

Tuesday, 14th—Lieutenant Compton with five men went out to capture the man who fired into a passenger train last summer and killed the conductor. When the man saw them approaching to surround his house, he started to run for the timber. He refused to surrender and the men fired on him, shooting him through the thigh, but upon seeing that the man was severely wounded, Lieutenant Compton gave the order to let the man remain at his home.

Wednesday, 15th—Nothing of importance. Got some more pies and doughnuts from a man and his wife who come in three times a week with them, to sell to the boys. We usually lay in a good supply.

Thursday, 16th—A squad of the boys went out scouting[1] and took one man a prisoner, besides bringing in nine mules and six hogs. They took the man to headquarters, turned the mules over to the regimental quartermaster, and the hogs we made use of as so much extra pork for the company.

Friday, 17th—Warm and pleasant. Nothing of importance. Some of the boys are quite sick from the effects of vaccination, though on some of them it did not work. Mine worked fine, and

---

[1] This was really a foraging expedition which at that time they spoke of as "scouting."—Ed.

some of the boys took virus from my arm and vaccinated themselves. The surgeon vaccinated a few of the boys as many as four or five times before it took.

Saturday, 18th—Some of the boys went out on a scouting expedition, but did not meet with any success.

Sunday, 19th—Lieutenant Durbin and some of the boys went out scouting. They brought in a lot of corn to feed the horses; also some walnuts, hickory nuts, corn meal and molasses. The lieutenant took a "secesh" flag from a schoolma'am.

Monday, 20th—It snowed some today and turned colder; the weather is very changeable. I wrote a letter to father and enclosed $20.00 of the $26.00 I received from the Government on the 8th inst.

Tuesday, 21st—Nothing of importance. Everything is very quiet in this locality. We have nothing but the regular camp duty to perform. Mess number 7 have now used up all their cooked rice.

Wednesday, 22d—Orderly Clark, Sergeants Spencer, Sweet and White went out on a scouting expedition and brought in a pair of ponies and some things to eat.

Thursday, 23d—It is warm today. Nothing of importance. The land around Lookout Station is heavily timbered and there are no large farms. Negroes are very scarce here. The war has put a blight on this part of the State.

Friday, 24th—It snowed a very little today. Soldiers are marching past here for St. Louis. The roads are in a fearful condition. Our company would like to leave this place for more active service. Our picket and patrol duty is very light, though it is all-night duty. None of the men on the scouting expeditions have been hurt or wounded.

Saturday, 25th—The report came that we were to be brigaded today—the Eleventh, Thirteenth, Fifteenth and Sixteenth Iowa Regiments are in one brigade. Hurrah for Iowa! The four regiments are to form an Iowa brigade and the organization will date from today.

Sunday, 26th—We had preaching in our quarters this forenoon and in the evening a few gathered for prayer meeting. Our quarters were not very inviting for a minister. There was no

(January, 1862)

tuning fork for the music and we had no chairs, most of the boys standing during the preaching.

Monday, 27th—The regimental surgeon came down from California to look over the convalescents in our company; he revaccinated all on whom the vaccine had not worked.

Tuesday, 28th—One of the Missouri boys who enlisted in our company while at Jefferson City asked me to go with him to spend the evening with a family about two miles out, where there were three or four young ladies. One of the young women was his best girl and he wished to bid her goodby before we left for the South. He assured me that we would have plenty of good things to eat and that there would be no danger, and so I finally decided that it would be safe to go. We had a very enjoyable time and about midnight started for our quarters, running all the way.[1]

Wednesday, 29th—Our company has had a fine time while at Lookout Station and the men are all in good health with the exception of two or three who are suffering from varioloid as a result of vaccination.

Thursday, 30th—A part of our company went out into the timber to gather persimmons. They are very plentiful in this locality; the trees are quite large and some of them are loaded with the finest fruit.

Friday, 31st—This is the end of January. Company E has been at Lookout Station thirty-seven days, and while our army service has not been hard, yet we are anxious to leave for more active service.

FEBRUARY, 1862.

Saturday, 1st—I commenced cooking for twenty men of our company. None of the boys likes cooking, so the seven messes have been consolidated into three with a cook for each. Mess numbers 1 and 2 have been united, becoming mess number 1, and I am to be the cook.

Sunday, 2d—Nothing of importance. We had preaching in the forenoon and prayer meeting in the afternoon.

---

[1] We arrived safely at our quarters, but I made up my mind never again to take such a trip while in the enemy's country.—A. G. D.

(February, 1862)

Monday, 3d—The captain with eight men went out on a scouting trip to rout some "secesh" from an island in the Missouri river, where they were trying to recruit a company.

Tuesday, 4th—A squad of the boys went out on a scouting expedition, but did not accomplish much in the way of getting supplies for the company.

Wednesday, 5th—Nothing of importance; the regular routine of camp life. Our company has this locality pretty well disciplined as to the people's duty toward the Government.

Thursday, 6th—Very fine weather. There is one woman in this locality of whom the boys are afraid, for she has a large kettle of water hanging on the crane over the fireplace. This she keeps at the boiling point, and whenever any of the boys come around her premises, she is out with the hot water. They have to take lively steps to keep out of her way.

Friday, 7th—No news of importance. The boys had a dancing party at the depot, and some of the girls in the neighborhood who are somewhat lively were there—they seem to enjoy smoking when out in company.

Saturday, 8th—It is the same old thing over. We cleaned up our accouterments for inspection tomorrow.

Sunday, 9th—Company inspection this morning. We had preaching by the chaplain in the forenoon, and the boys had prayer meeting in the evening.

Monday, 10th—Nothing of importance. A squad of men went out into the country for supplies and brought in some corn meal, molasses and honey.

Tuesday, 11th—It snowed today and turned quite cool. Some troops marched past here on their way to St. Louis.

Wednesday, 12th—Our mail goes east every day at 11 a. m. and comes in from the east at night. This is a cold night.

Thursday, 13th—It snowed some today, and we all stayed close in our quarters, as the weather was so disagreeable. It is a very cold night.

Friday, 14th—This is Valentine's Day and some of the boys are having a great time sending out valentines to the girls in this locality; others are sending valentines to their old home sweethearts.

IN WINTER QUARTERS AND GARRISON DUTY

(February, 1862)

Saturday, 15th—We received a very large mail from home today. The papers say that General Grant has taken Fort Henry, on the Tennessee river.

Sunday, 16th—The weather is warm and pleasant. It is reported that Fort Donelson with several thousand prisoners has been taken by General Grant.

Monday, 17th—This is a very beautiful morning. The good news came that Grant has really taken Fort Donelson. Lieutenant Compton called out the company with arms, and we fired a *feu de joie* to celebrate the victory.

Tuesday, 18th—It is cloudy and quite cool. News came that Fort Henry has been taken and we fired a *feu de joie*. Some of the boys are afraid that the war will be over before we have a chance to have the honor of being in a battle.

Wednesday, 19th—News came that Roanoke Island has been taken by our men. It is reported that our company will leave for California, Missouri, in three or four days and all are rejoicing that our stay here is about over.

Thursday, 20th—No news of importance. Grant's recent victories have made the Union sentiment stronger in this locality, which will be a big help to the few Union men left here.

Friday, 21st—We are to bid goodby to Lookout Station tomorrow. Some of the good people living here are sorry to see us go. May they have success for their loyalty to the Union cause.

Saturday, 22d—This is Washington's birthday. We packed our knapsacks early this morning and left Lookout for California, arriving at 2 p. m. The roads were quite muddy. In camp again at California, Missouri. We pitched our tents on the commons south of town.

Sunday, 23d—We attended church today at the different churches in town, some of the boys going to the Catholic church. We had prayer meeting in camp in the evening.

Monday, 24th—Nothing of importance. Our company now has a company cook. He cooks the beans and salt beef for all, but each man draws his rations every five days, makes his own coffee and cooks his salt bacon to suit himself.

Tuesday, 25th—No news of any importance. There is some

talk of our having to stay at this place all summer. We have company drill twice a day and with the other four companies of our regiment here now, have dress parade at 5 p. m.

Wednesday, 26th—Nothing of importance. We are in a regular tented camp here, and it seems more like being in the army than it did at Lookout Station.

Thursday, 27th—There are no hopes of leaving this place. We cleaned up for inspection and muster tomorrow. The five companies of the Eleventh which went to Fulton, Missouri, last December, are still at that place.

Friday, 28th—We had company inspection with all accouterments on ready for a march, and the regiment was then mustered for pay. Thus this month ends, finding us at California, Missouri.

MARCH, 1862.

Saturday, 1st—It is very cold with a strong northwest wind blowing. We drilled with our overcoats on for the first time, and even then we could not keep warm.

Sunday, 2d—It is still getting colder. The ground is frozen and we have no fires in the tents—the men are suffering day and night from the cold. Had company inspection this morning.

Monday, 3d—It is turning a little warmer. There are just a few of the boys in the hospital here and they are well cared for; their bedding is kept nice and clean and their food is well cooked.

Tuesday, 4th—Nothing of importance.

Wednesday, 5th—Company E had prayer meeting this evening in a vacant room close by their quarters. It is reported that we are to leave for the South in two or three days. The war has certainly struck this place a hard blow. There are many vacant houses and most of the storerooms are standing empty. There are but few men left in town, most of them having gone to war. Families are divided, each member having gone to the army of his choice; there are fathers against sons and brothers against brothers. They are so determined for the side they take that many are killed in the neighborhood by their neighbors, and some even by members of their own families.

(March, 1862)

Thursday, 6th—No news of importance.

Friday, 7th—Orders came for us to get ready to leave for St. Louis, and everybody is happy. Drill was discontinued for the day.

Saturday, 8th—The boys are in fine spirits because we have orders to leave. All are at work getting ready—some are mending their shirts, pants or coats, others their socks or shoes, or anything which needs fixing up before leaving for the South.

Chapter V.
Mobilization at Pittsburg Landing and the Battle of Shiloh.
March 9-April 20.

Sunday, 9th—Had a cold rain all day. There was no church for us today. The quartermaster with a detail of men loaded some of the supplies on open cars, the wagons being taken apart and loaded. The mules and horses were put in the stock cars. The cars came for us about 9 p. m. and we finished loading about midnight and left for Jefferson City, some of the men in box cars and others in open cars with the baggage.

Monday, 10th—We arrived at Jefferson City about daylight. Our regiment came together here this morning after being separated since the 22d of last December. We left for St. Louis about 8 a. m., our train being made up of almost every kind of car known, and arrived about 3 p. m. We went aboard the "Great Western."

Tuesday, 11th—We lay at the wharf all night, loading the quartermaster's supplies. At 8 a. m. we left St. Louis for Cairo, Illinois. Our entire regiment is on the one boat, a side-wheeler. Company E is quartered on the hurricane deck, and a cold wind blowing makes it rather disagreeable for us. We lay up for the night one hundred miles below St. Louis. We have big times getting our rations cooked, for there is but one place to get boiling water to make coffee, and only one place at the fire where we can broil our bacon. Each man slices his bacon, puts it on the ramrod, and holds it close to the fire under the boilers. We all have to take our turn, and since there are eight hundred men, there is some one at the fire all day and part of the night. The captain of the boat declared that we were "the d———st set of men to eat" that he had ever seen in his life.

Wednesday, 12th—We started again on our voyage at daylight. A high cold wind was blowing all day. We landed at Cape Girardeau, Missouri, remaining there for a short time, and then proceeded on our journey, arriving at Cairo, Illinois, at 2 p. m., where we waited for further orders. Late in the afternoon

PITTSBURG LANDING—BATTLE OF SHILOH

(March, 1862)

we received orders to go up the Tennessee river and left Cairo about sundown. At Cairo there are gunboats and a large number of transports loaded with troops, and provisions for the army up along the Tennessee river.

Thursday, 13th—We stopped at Paducah, Kentucky, a short time and then early this morning came up the river to Fort Henry, arriving in the afternoon. There are about twenty transports at this place, loaded with troops. Fort Henry is a dilapidated place. The Tennessee river is very high, the water being out over the banks, and the lowlands are flooded for miles on both sides of the river.

Friday, 14th—We left Fort Henry at dark last night, going on up the river, and arrived at Savannah, Tennessee, this afternoon. The river seems to be lined with transports loaded with troops going up-stream. There are two gunboats in our fleet, also two tugboats and several barges.

Saturday, 15th—It rained all day. It seems so dark and gloomy. We lay on the boats all day, but we are expecting to receive orders to go on up the river. Boats loaded with troops are passing us and going on up to Pittsburg Landing, Tennessee.

Sunday, 16th—We are still lying on the boats waiting for orders. Two gunboats came down from Pittsburg Landing. The weather is very disagreeable, with rain every day and rather cold besides.

Monday, 17th—We received orders to disembark in the morning and everybody is rejoicing, for it is getting very tiresome on the boats—we have been on the boats seven days now. Details of men worked nearly all day at unloading our commissariat. The landing place is nothing but a jelly of mud—there are so many mules, horses and men passing back and forth.

Tuesday, 18th—We left the boats and marched out about two miles from Savannah. We pitched our tents near a big orchard. Details of men went to the timber with teams to get firewood for our camp.

Wednesday, 19th—There are about ten thousand men of all arms in camp at this place. We are expecting marching orders every day. Our camp is on high ground, but there has been so much rain that the water stands on the surface. We cut brush and place it on the ground in our tents to lie on at night.

(March, 1862)

Thursday, 20th—It is cloudy, chilly and very disagreeable weather. A great many of the boys are getting sick with the chills and fever, and the doctors are no account. We have no drill nor dress parade; we seem to be just stopping here in the mud. Troops are passing here every day going up the river. The boys are getting anxious for a fight.

Friday, 21st—It is cloudy and cold. Captain Chambers' battery of six guns arrived today. Orders came for us to embark at once, and we struck our tents and got ready to start. After waiting six hours for the order to fall in, the order was countermanded and we had to pitch our tents again.

Saturday, 22d—It is disagreeable weather—a cold rain from the north. The Thirteenth Iowa started to Pittsburg Landing, about ten miles up the river. The Eleventh Iowa is expecting marching orders any time.

Sunday, 23d—The Eleventh Iowa received marching orders, and we struck our tents and got on board the "Westmoreland." The quartermaster had all of the commissariat on the boat by noon and we left for Pittsburg Landing. We reached the landing at dark and remained on the boat for the night.

Monday, 24th—We disembarked and marched out about a mile and a half from the landing, where we pitched our tents. Our camp is located in what is called Jones' Field.

Tuesday, 25th—We had company drill twice today. We have a fine drill ground. Our water here is good, there being several springs a short distance to the east and to the west of our camp. The camp of the Thirteenth Iowa is on our left, while to our right are the Eighth and Eighteenth Illinois. These three regiments with ours, the Eleventh Iowa, form the First Brigade of the First Division of the Army of the Tennessee, under the command of Maj. Gen. John A. McClernand. Col. Abraham M. Hare of our regiment is in command of the brigade. Dresser's battery of six guns is encamped just in front of the Eleventh Iowa.

Wednesday, 26th—The weather is getting very warm. We have plenty of firewood near by for the cooking, and running water a short distance away where we do our washing once a week.

Thursday, 27th—It is warm and dry today. The trees are

(March, 1862)

beginning to leaf out. Troops are arriving every day and going into camp all along the roads about two and a half miles from the Landing.

Friday, 28th—It is warm and dry—it is delightful. There is nothing of importance going on. Our camp is well protected on the left by the Tennessee river and by Owl creek on our right flank. Most of the camp ground lies high and just rolling enough to keep the ground dry. Our camp—the First Brigade of the First Division—lies almost due north and south, so arranged for the purpose of giving the brigade a good drill and parade ground. The camps of the different brigades, all through the woods, face in any desired direction, except the regiments out in front, which are so arranged as to be facing the enemy should they have to form a line of battle.

Saturday, 29th—A large detail from the brigade was sent to cut and clear away some timber between Jones' Field and a small field just to the south, so as to throw the two fields together, making it possible for the First Division to form a continuous line to be reviewed by the commanding general of the army, General Grant. Companies A, B and C received Belgian rifles today for their old muskets.

Sunday, 30th—This is our first Sunday in camp in the "Sunny South." We had company inspection with all accouterments on, by the colonel of our regiment, Colonel Hare.

Monday, 31st—Our regular drills are: Company drill from 10 to 11 a. m., battalion drill from 3 to 5 p. m., and dress parade at 5 p. m. We have a splendid drill ground in a large field. Received orders to get ready for review by General Grant tomorrow morning at 10 o'clock.

The country around here is quite rough and the soil is very poor. There is a great deal of gravel and there are some rocks, but the soil works very easily. The timber here is mostly white oak.

APRIL, 1862.

Tuesday, 1st—Our Division, the First, was reviewed this forenoon by General Grant and Maj. Gen. J. A. McClernand. While the review was in progress three men were seen on the roofs of two small log houses at the southern end of Jones' Field, taking notes on our maneuvers, the number of men in line, etc. They were dressed in butternut suits although, it is said, they had claimed to be Union men; yet when the review was ended no trace of them could be found.

Wednesday, 2d—It rained all day and we had no drill. The men remained in the tents, reading the Bible, magazines and papers, or writing letters home.

Thursday, 3d—We had drill as usual today and also general review, by General McClernand. We have no guard duty at this camp, but the troops of the front camps have to keep out a strong picket line.

Friday, 4th—It rained and hailed this afternoon, and by night it got very warm. We were ordered under arms at 6 p. m., and we formed a hollow square on the parade ground. We remained in line until 10 o'clock, when we were ordered back to our tents. It was reported out in front that the rebels were advancing in force from Corinth, but at 10 o'clock the word came that they had bivouacked for the night.

Saturday, 5th—We had company drill this morning as usual. Lieutenant Compton took the company out on the drill ground this afternoon for company drill, and he said: "Now, boys, we drill in earnest for an hour, then return to our quarters, put away our rifles, and then to the branch for bathing." It was warm, but the men all went into it and after a hard drill we had a good wash-off in the branch.[1]

Sunday, 6th—The long roll sounded about half-past seven in the morning, and at once we formed a line of battle on the regimental parade ground. At about 8 o'clock we were ordered to the front, and marching out in battle line, about one-half mile, we met the rebels at Water Oaks Pond. Dresser's battery was just in front of our regiment, we acting as a support to it. The rebels came up on our right, compelling us to fall back about eighty rods to our second position, where we remained until we were again flanked, when we fell back to within about one hundred yards of our parade ground, where we lay down on the brow

---

[1] This was the last time that Lieutenant Compton ever drilled our company, for the poor fellow was killed in the battle on the next day, Sunday, a little after noon. He was a fine drillmaster, and kind to his men, especially to those who tried to do their duty.—A. G. D.

PITTSBURG LANDING—BATTLE OF SHILOH
(April, 1862)

of a hill awaiting the approach of the rebels in front. While in this position, Thomas Hains of Company E took off his hat, placed it upon his ramrod, and holding it up, shouted to the boys along the line to see what a close call he had had while out in front, for a minie-ball had passed through the creased crown of his hat, making four holes. Before he could get his hat back on his head, a small shell burst over us and mortally wounded him.

By this time the rebels were marching right oblique, just in front of us, in double line of battle with their two stands of colors flying. By order we waited until we could look them in the eye and then rose up and fired a volley at close range into their ranks, throwing them into great confusion. We then made a bayonet charge, capturing one of their standards, and together with the Eleventh and the Twentieth Illinois Infantry we captured Cobb's battery and retook General McClernand's headquarters. In this charge Company E met its greatest loss of the day.

My musket became so dirty with the cartridge powder, that in loading it the ramrod stuck fast and I could neither get it up nor down, so I put a cap on, elevated the gun and fired it off. But now I had no ramrod, and throwing down my musket, I picked up a Belgian rifle lying at the side of a dead rebel, unstrapped the cartridge box from his body, and advanced to our company, taking my place with the boys. While in this position I witnessed a wonderful sight—thickly-flying musket balls. I have never seen hail falling thicker than the minie balls were flying in the air above us, though too high to do any harm. Our ammunition soon ran out and the entire regiment was ordered to the rear to replenish our cartridge boxes.

When leaving with my company for the rear to restock our ammunition supply, I passed a severely-wounded boy (a stranger to me) who begged me to help him to the rear and out of danger. I stooped down and let him put his arms around my neck, but finding that I could not rise up with him hanging on my neck, I assured him that he would be safe there among the logs, and explained that if I should stay with him, I would surely be taken a prisoner, so left the poor fellow to his fate.

After filling our cartridge boxes, we again formed in line of battle close by the cavalry field and right in the midst of heavy brush timber. Here we remained for about two hours, when we were ordered by General Grant (in person) to a position on the extreme left of the Army of the Tennessee, in support of Dresser's battery, being placed in line by Webster of General Grant's staff, just to the left of the siege guns. Here we were engaged for more than two hours. The Fifty-fifth Illinois and the Fifty-fourth Ohio were placed to our left in support of two batteries hard by the river. Here about 5 o'clock in the evening, three regiments of Buell's army, just arriving, helped to repulse the fearful charge of the rebels.

The Eleventh Iowa was taken from its brigade early in the morning and remained separated all day. Now with the end of the day's fight, and after dark, we retired a few rods distant from our last line of action and without food or shelter bivouacked for the night, lying down on the wet ground in the rain.

This was our first battle and our company was hard hit, our losses being as follows: Killed, Lieut. John F. Compton, Serg. Ezra McLoney, John R. Buckman, George Croak, Thomas M. Hains and Carlton Frink; mortally wounded, George W. Simmons and John W. Dwiggans; severely wounded, Elmore Chrisman and John T. Rice.[1] About ten other boys were slightly wounded.

Monday, 7th—It rained all night. The battle was renewed this morning at 6 o'clock, by our forces under General Buell. The Eleventh Iowa formed and marched forward with parts of broken regiments, in support of the left center of Buell's army, whenever needed. It was very trying for us thus to stand in line of battle, shells exploding over our heads and cutting off limbs of trees, spent minie balls flying all about us, yet not being able to get into action, because of the line of battle just in front of us. The rebels were fighting desperately, but falling back all the while with great slaughter of men. About 3 p. m. the rebels in front of us began to retreat, with Buell's army after them, but we remained in line. About an hour later the report came that the rebels had left the field, and we were ordered back to our camp in Jones' Field, arriving there about dark. We had not been in our tents since Sunday morning and they were still standing, but a great many had been hit and badly torn by shells and minie balls. We found the body of a rebel soldier

[1] Rice finally died on April 19th, from the effects of the wound and typhoid fever.—A. G. D.

(April, 1862)

lying in my tent; he had been wounded and apparently had gone in, crawled between our bunks and bled to death. We carried the body out to the parade ground and then got a shovel to clean away the blood from the place where the body had lain in the tent.

Tuesday, 8th—We formed a line of battle early this morning and remained in line about two hours.[1] So many men throughout the camp were firing off their loaded rifles, preparing to clean them, that the officers thought a battle was in progress out in front. About 9 o'clock word came in from the front that there was no rebel in sight, and we were ordered back to our quarters. We spent the day in burying the dead, both our own and those of the rebels.

Our battle line had been at the south end of Jones' Field, where a few days before we had cleared the timber for a review ground. This place was fought over so often by both armies and the dead lay so close that one could walk on dead bodies for some distance without touching the ground. There were over three thousand five hundred dead on the battlefield, and something like five hundred dead horses. Seven hundred bodies of the rebels were put into one grave. It is an awful sight to see the dead lying all about. It rained this forenoon, but cleared off this afternoon. The heavy rains have soaked the ground, making it very muddy. About five thousand of our forces arrived today.

Wednesday, 9th—Fifteen hundred more of our troops arrived. We are still burying the dead. It rained again today. The ground is so thoroughly soaked that it is difficult to dig the graves deep enough and keep out the water. We bury our dead by companies, all of one company in one grave, and if only one of a company is killed, the body is placed in a grave by itself. The bodies of the rebels' dead are placed side by side in long graves. The carcasses of horses are removed by burning them.

Thursday, 10th—We are still burying the dead. The lieutenant of Company F was buried today. Nearly all of the dead

[1] It has been said by some that from General Grant down to the commonest private in the ranks of the entire Army of the Tennessee, all the men cared for on Monday afternoon, the second day of the battle of Shiloh, was to get back to their camps. I cannot believe the statement, for on Tuesday, the 8th, when we were ordered into line of battle, on that gloomy, rainy morning, and a cold wind blowing from the northwest, I know by the sentiment of the boys in my own company, that they would have gone to the front then if ordered to do so. We felt that the loss in our company was too great not to follow up the victory.—A. G. D.

have been buried now, but there are some of the wounded still dying. I was detailed with two others to bury three of the rebels' dead. We went out about a half mile north of the camp to a stony knoll where one body lay, and worked all forenoon, the ground being so hard and stony, to dig even a shallow grave into which we rolled the body and covered it the best we could. In the afternoon we dug a double grave for two who had died of mortal wounds.

Friday, 11th—It rained all day. Troops have been arriving by the thousands every day since Sunday.

Saturday, 12th—It is still raining every hour and the floors of our tents are very wet.[1] Our camp has become very muddy, which, with constant rain and the braying of mules day and night, makes it a very gloomy time.

Sunday, 13th—It is clear and warm today. We had battalion drill again, twice today. Not more than two hundred of the regiment are fit for duty. Major Abercrombie, who drilled us, gave us a lecture about getting out to drill. He assured us that the battle we just had would be classed as a skirmish in comparison with what we would have to go through with before this war is over. The boys declared that if he called this battle a skirmish, they would like to know what he called a real battle.[2]

Monday, 14th—We had inspection of arms this forenoon. Most of the boys in our company picked up rifles from the battlefield and got better rifles than they had. But it makes it quite difficult for the quartermaster to supply the extra ammunition required for the different kinds of rifles. The weather is quite warm.

Tuesday, 15th—There's nothing of importance.

Wednesday, 16th—No news of importance.[3]

---

[1] We had not yet learned how to take care of our health, for in place of raising our tents from the ground and building our bunks about eighteen inches high, as we did in later camps, we just laid down our rubber ponchos on the bare ground, covered this with a blanket, then lay down with another blanket for a cover. Our bedding thus was often damp, and it is no wonder that so many of the boys became subject to fevers and rheumatism.—A. G. D.

[2] Major Abercrombie's words were quite true, as we found out later by experience.—A. G. D.

[3] There was much discussion among the men over the great battle we had just been through, the battle of Shiloh. The question why the Confederates lost the battle, I should answer as follows: First, they were four hours late in making the general attack on that Sunday morning. The Confederate generals, instead of sending some of their staff officers before daylight to spy out and report to the commanding general what they had seen (according to a report of H. C. Lockett of

PITTSBURG LANDING—BATTLE OF SHILOH 45
(April, 1862)

Thursday, 17th—The day is fair. Had battalion drill again.

Friday, 18th—No news of importance.[1]

Saturday, 19th—Nothing of importance. Everything appears to be so lonesome.

Sunday, 20th—John T. Rice, a member of Company E, Eleventh Iowa, was buried this afternoon with military honors.[2] He died of his wound accompanied with fever. Three other men who died of disease were also buried today. We learned that Wilson Simmons of Company E died of lung fever on the 15th at Mound City, Illinois.

General Bragg's staff), should have had their first line of battle at the Union picket line by that time, and then charging our pickets and coming in upon the first camps, they could have captured them before they could have dressed; then pushing on to the other commands, they could have put them to rout before they could have formed a line of battle. But their being so late in making the first attack gave our commanders time to form into line. As it was, whenever the Confederates advanced our forces were in shape to fire volleys into them and easily throw them into confusion, thus making their advance slower and more irregular during the day.

In the second place, the Confederates starting four hours late in the morning made them more than six hours late in the afternoon, so in place of being ready to make their last charge of the day at 1 o'clock they did not make it until almost 7 o'clock in the evening. By that time it was too late, since the Union generals had formed a strong line of artillery, supported by all the infantry, who stood loyally by their colors. Then, just before the final charge, one brigade of Buell's army had already arrived and formed in line, and the day was forever lost to the Confederates.—A. G. D.

[1]While the battle of Shiloh was a Union victory, nevertheless it was dearly won, and could easily have been a defeat. Even at that time the men in discussing it, pointed out some of the mistakes made by the Union forces. I wish to point out how the day at Shiloh was almost lost to the Union Army. In the first place, when the different commanders called out the troops under arms at 6 o'clock on Friday evening, April 4th, they kept them in line until midnight, when, since the immediate danger was past, they ordered them to return to their quarters. Then it was that a great mistake was made, for instead of sending the men back to camp, they should have been put to work, every man with shovel, pick or axe, digging trenches, throwing up breastworks and fortifying their camps. Thus by the morning of the 6th they would have had two or three lines of works. That this was not done must of course be charged to General Sherman. Each man behind the works would have been equal to five men in the open. General Prentiss' men, protected in the old, sunken roadway, in making their attack upon us, proved the worth of a man protected, to one out in the open. The mistake cost the Union army more than a thousand men, besides those captured.

In the second place, when the Union army was attacked on that Sunday morning, there were but four regiments in line of battle and ready for the assault of the Confederates. The officers did not succeed in forming a continuous line of battle until late in the day. Regiments and brigades would march to the front and form in line, but they were usually unsupported by troops on the right and left at the same time. This enabled the Confederates to come in on the flanks and the rear, thus compelling our forces to fall back or be captured. This continued till late in the afternoon, when Webster succeeded in forming a continuous line of artillery, supported by all arms. This, together with the arrival of Buell's brigade, which formed a line on the left, saved the day to the Union cause for all time to come.—A. G. D.

[2]Rice was buried in the Shiloh National Cemetery, Pittsburg Landing, Tennessee, his grave being 175, Section 9.—A. G. D.

Chapter VI.
The Battles in and Around Corinth. April 21-July 27.

Monday, 21st—Our camp is becoming more unhealthy all the time, and the odor from the battlefield at times is very disagreeable. This is the result of the heavy rains followed by warm weather.

Troops are arriving here every day and going on to the front. The army is advancing on Corinth, Mississippi, and we hear that there is almost continuous skirmishing between the outposts of the two armies.

Tuesday, 22d—It is quite pleasant again after some rain—thunder showers. The wheat fields are looking fine.

Wednesday, 23d—We have company drill twice a day and more of the boys are getting out again for drill. The artillery men are receiving fresh horses to replace those killed in the battle. The weather is beginning to get very warm.

Thursday, 24th—No news of importance.

Friday, 25th—We struck our tents early this morning and marched about three miles to the southwest, and went into camp again, camp No. 2. We were brigaded over again. It rained all day.

Saturday, 26th—Our regiment is now brigaded with Iowa soldiers, the brigade being completed today. Our brigade is composed of the Eleventh, Thirteenth, Fifteenth and Sixteenth Iowa Infantries, with Colonel Crocker in command.[1] We were inspected today by the general inspector of the army, and had all our accouterments on.

Sunday, 27th—Today we had company inspection. We had to go to work and clean up our camp and parade ground. The camp is in the timber. The water is very scarce and poor at that.

Monday, 28th—We had company drill at 9 a. m. The weather is getting very warm; the sun shines hot, and we are sweeping

---

[1] The brigade dating from April 27, 1862, became known as "Crocker's Iowa Brigade." It remained together throughout the war and maintains an organization to this day.—A. G. D.

(April, 1862)

our camp with brush brooms. We are being kept quite active, the doctors, we hear, having told the officers that the men would have better health if kept at work.

Tuesday, 29th—We received orders this afternoon to march out towards Purdy, about twelve miles, to be in readiness as a supporting column to General Wallace in command of the right. He was expecting to be attacked by the rebels and sent for reinforcements. We went in light marching order without knapsacks, and we have to lie on our arms at night.

Wednesday, 30th—We were routed from our beds of leaves at 4 o'clock and moved on two miles farther in the direction of Purdy, when we received word from General Wallace that we were not needed. We marched back to camp, arriving here about noon, in a heavy rainstorm, soaked to the skin and covered with mud. We had lain all night with rifle in hand, in a heavy timber, on beds of leaves, without blankets, and some of the boys caught cold. The Eleventh Iowa was inspected today for pay. Thus ends this month in old Tennessee.

MAY, 1862.

Thursday, 1st—We received marching orders, and striking our tents moved four miles further toward Corinth. All of the Sixth Division moved forward today. We went to work and cleaned up our camp in a heavy piece of timber. This is camp number 3.

Friday, 2d—It is warm and pleasant. The water is very scarce at this camp and poor in quality. We hear the sound of cannon in the front every day. The Sixth Division is in the second line of battle, but we are building no fortifications, as we are moved from right to left, as the case may be, in support of either wing of the army whenever reinforcements are called for.

Saturday, 3d—We struck our tents and at 7 a. m. started in the direction of Corinth. After marching eight miles we pitched our tents for camp number 4. All of the sick boys have been sent to the hospital set up at camp number 2, which we left a few days ago. General Pope has taken Farmington, out to the left of our army. There was some very heavy cannonading this afternoon.

(May, 1862)

Sunday, 4th—It rained nearly all day. We received orders to cook four days' rations and be ready to march at a moment's notice. Henry L. Sweet of our company died of fever this morning at the Division hospital.

Monday, 5th—Nothing of importance. We did not get orders to move, so we had our regular drills today.

Tuesday, 6th—We had battalion drill this afternoon. News came that Yorktown has been taken. New troops are still arriving and our lines are being extended to the right and left. A second line is supporting the artillery in the front line and the second line's flanks are supported by the cavalry.

Wednesday, 7th[1]—We struck tents this morning, and moving three miles around to the right, cleared away the heavy timber and brush for our camp number 5. Our camp is just at the edge of the vacated breastworks of the rebels, they having lost them by being outflanked by our forces. Lieutenant Anderson of Company A returned from home today, having been on furlough.

Thursday, 8th—It is very warm today. Our major drilled us—the regiment—in the manual of arms. Company E went out in the evening to reinforce the pickets.

Friday, 9th—We heard some very heavy firing off to the left towards Farmington. General Pope was compelled to fall back from Farmington, but has again taken the town.

Saturday, 10th—The Eleventh Iowa went out today to reinforce pickets again. Our cavalry had quite a skirmish with the rebel pickets out on the flanks while driving them in.

Sunday, 11th—The Iowa Brigade moved two miles to the right, nearer to Corinth, and some of our boys came in upon the rebel pickets. We established another camp—camp number 6. The Eleventh Iowa was relieved from picket duty this evening.

Monday, 12th[2]—Batallion drill today. Sixteen of the boys of our regiment failed to appear for the drill and later they were put into a squad by themselves under an officer and put through the drill until dark—that was their punishment for disobeying orders.

[1] John W. Dwiggans of Company E, who was severely wounded at the battle of Shiloh, died on this day at Paducah, Kentucky.—A. G. D.
[2] On this day George T. Willcott of Company E died of fever in Scott County, Iowa, and George W. Simmons died of his wounds at Tipton, Iowa. This makes Company E's loss in the battle of Shiloh, nine—six killed and three dying of their wounds.—A. G. D.

THE BATTLES IN AND AROUND CORINTH

(May, 1862)

Tuesday, 13th—We received marching orders this forenoon, and striking our tents at noon, started off towards the right. We marched four miles and went into camp—camp number 7. There was some skirmishing with the pickets today.

Wednesday, 14th—We cleaned up our camp today and had company drill twice. There was some heavy musketry firing on the front lines, and the artillery was in action on both sides, but not much damage was done.

Thursday, 15th—We were expecting to be attacked today by the rebels' making a charge on our front line and were ordered to fall in with two days' rations in our haversacks. We marched out about a mile, and forming a line of battle, remained there till dark—about six hours—when we moved toward the right wing and up to camp. The entire right wing of the army has moved around farther to the right.

Friday, 16th—Nothing of importance has taken place today, but I think we will have a fight soon. We have plenty of rations, but the drinking water is very poor. The health of the men is better, however, since we have become more active, and the men are getting back their old-time vigor. Some of the boys who have been sick are now returning to the regiment. Major Abercrombie is in command of the regiment while Colonel Hare and Lieutenant-Colonel Hall are at home recovering from wounds received at Shiloh.

Saturday, 17th—We were ordered to strike tent and march out to the picket line and form in line of battle. Here we remained in line until after dark. There was heavy cannonading and musketry firing all along the line and it continued all day. We pitched our tents in a heavy piece of timber and established camp number 8, in our siege of Corinth.

Sunday, 18th—Our brigade threw up four miles of fortifications, earthworks, and also forts for the artillery. We were expecting to be attacked by the rebels' making an effort to turn our right flank, so we were in line of battle all day. The pickets have been fighting all day, for the only action taken by the rebels was trying to drive in our pickets.

Monday, 19th—We were ordered to strike our tents and move to the right, but just as we were ready to fall into line, the order was countermanded and we were ordered to go to throwing up breastworks. It was reported that the rebels were going to come out of their breastworks and attack us. The pickets were fighting all day, and there was brisk skirmishing and cannonading all along the front. Our entire picket line has been reinforced by extra men.

Tuesday, 20th—Things are a little more quiet today, the cannonading not being so brisk, although the skirmishers are keeping up a lively firing all along the line.

Wednesday, 21st—The right wing moved up closer upon the fortifications of the rebels and although they tried to drive our men back, they failed in the attempt. There is very heavy cannonading and skirmishing. The left wing of our army is under command of General Pope. The earthworks between the two armies are getting very close to each other.

Thursday, 22d—Things were a little more quiet this forenoon, but there was some very heavy cannonading off on the left flank this afternoon. Skirmishing is still going on between the pickets. There are not many men being killed on either side, since they are well protected by their respective fortifications; it is when they have to advance on skirmish in the open that they suffer losses.

Friday, 23d—We formed a line of battle at 4 o'clock this morning, but the rebels did not make their expected attack. The army generally now forms a line of battle every morning at 4 and remains in line until about 6 o'clock. It rained some today, and on account of the wet weather it was only at times that there was activity along the lines.

Saturday, 24th—The Eleventh Iowa went out on picket at 5 o'clock this evening. It was reported in camp that General Beauregard is moving all of his heavy ordnance and his entire army to the south with a view of evacuating Corinth. The report says that teams loaded with munitions of war are leaving Corinth every day.

Sunday, 25th—We stood in line of battle out on picket all night, and were relieved at 9 o'clock this morning. There's a report in camp to the effect that General Pope is desirous of mov-

(May, 1862)

ing his command around by the left flank to get into the rear of Corinth and cut off the retreat of the rebels. General Halleck, however, would not give him permission, as he did not want to take any chances in allowing his army to be divided, thereby giving the rebels the opportunity of attacking and defeating each part separately. It is estimated that Halleck has about one hundred thousand men in his command here about Corinth, and we hear that Beauregard has about the same number.[1]

Monday, 26th—It is very warm. Had company drill twice again today. There was very heavy cannonading off on the left flank.

Tuesday, 27th—Things are quiet all along the lines today. Our supplies and ammunition are hauled by team from Pittsburg Landing. We still draw our full army rations every five days.

Wednesday, 28th—Some very hard fighting out on the right flank. Our men were driven back from their line, but rallied and regained the ground lost. In the mix-up we took some prisoners and there were some killed and wounded on both sides.

Thursday, 29th—There was heavy cannonading today off on the left flank and the pickets are still fighting. General Pope cut the railroad and with the aid of the Second Iowa Cavalry burned a train of cars and took one thousand stand of arms.

Friday, 30th—Corinth was evacuated during the night. Upon leaving, the rebels burned the depot and several houses, besides a large amount of other property, and also blew up their powder magazine. They burned some cars loaded with their own supplies which they could not get away because they had no engineers. At daylight General Pope with his force entered Corinth and then went in hot pursuit of the rebels.

Saturday, 31st—There was still some fighting today with the fleeing rebels, and we took some prisoners, but the main part of the army had too much of a start on us.

The Eleventh Iowa received four months' pay today. I drew $53.00. We had to make settlement at this time for all clothing purchased.

---

[1] Beauregard had been reinforced and now had a force of 50,000. See Rhodes Vol. III. page 628.—Ed.

JUNE, 1862.

Sunday, 1st—It rained all day. I took "French leave" this morning and went into Corinth. The town appears to be deserted and it is a dilapidated looking place, as so much of it has been destroyed. I found it to be a fine place, however, on high ground, and when rebuilt it will be beautiful. There are two railroads running through the town and there are good schools and a college. The country around is rich and the farms are well fenced.

Monday, 2d—I was one of a hundred men detailed to clean up our camp ground. Pope's men who went in pursuit of the rebels are returning and going into camp in and around Corinth. I spent $1.00 for peaches and bread at the sutler's tent.

Tuesday, 3d—The weather is very hot. We have no picket duty now, but get plenty of exercise by regular drills, having company drill twice a day. We also get exercise in keeping the camp clean; have to sweep it every morning.

Wednesday, 4th—Nothing of importance. Some of the troops are returning to Pittsburg Landing, a part of them to go down the Tennessee river and then up the Cumberland to reinforce the army in eastern Tennessee, and the others are to join the forces going down the Mississippi.

Thursday, 5th—We received marching orders with one day's rations. It is reported that General Buell will move with the Army of the Ohio into central Tennessee. It is clear and hot today.

Friday, 6th—We struck our tents and at 7 a. m. started on our march. We marched through Corinth and went into camp again about a mile northwest of town, making camp number 9. The Eleventh Iowa went out on picket.

Saturday, 7th—I stood out on picket all day. We were relieved from picket this evening about dark. We were posted in a heavy timber about two miles out, on one of the main roads leading to town. Water is very scarce and poor at that. We have to go a mile from camp for our drinking water, and to a branch the same distance to do our washing.

Sunday, 8th—We received orders to clean up for inspection and a detail of men was put to work cleaning up the parade

(June, 1862)

ground. We have a fine drill ground out in a large field. But the camp being out in the open, the sun beats down pretty hot upon the tents.

Monday, 9th—It is dry and hot. We are at work building fortifications here on a large scale, Corinth being an important point for either army to hold, as it is the key to Mississippi and Alabama. The bulk of the Army of the Tennessee is left here, while detachments of the original hundred thousand under Halleck are being sent to other commands to act as reinforcements.

Tuesday, 10th—It is dry and hot. I wrote a letter to father enclosing $50.00 of the $53.00 which I received from the Government on May 31st, and in greenbacks at that. I had $1.86 coming to me over and above the allowance the Government makes for clothing, which is $40.00 a year.

Wednesday, 11th—I was on guard today at General Todd's headquarters. The weather is very hot. The teams all went to the river for provisions. We are establishing a good camp at this place. We raised our wedge tents up from the ground and built bunks for our beds instead of lying down on the ground.[1]

Thursday, 12th—The farmers living about here are cutting their wheat; some have already begun stacking. Wheat here is good, with some especially fine fields, but some fields were entirely destroyed during the siege of Corinth. The corn is not as good on account of the cold, wet spring.

Friday, 13th—It came the Eleventh Iowa's turn to go on picket today. The teams still have to go to Pittsburg Landing, twenty-two miles from Corinth, for provisions and ammunition for the army.

Saturday, 14th—We came in from picket this morning, having been relieved by the Thirteenth Iowa. We do not have much idle time here, for besides keeping our camp and clothing clean, we have picket duty and fatigue duty on the fortifications.

Sunday, 15th—There were five hundred men from the Sixth Division detailed to go out and cut down the timber in front of the fortifications around the camp. The trees are cut so as to make them fall outward toward the approach of an enemy; the branches are then sharpened, making what is called an abatis.

---

[1] This was the first time that we built bunks for our beds, raised up from the ground.—A. G. D.

(June, 1862)

The trees in a space six hundred feet wide and twenty miles long are being felled. We had company inspection at 5 o'clock in the evening.

Monday, 16th—It came my turn for the first time to go on fatigue. Our men are throwing up a line of breastworks and building some very strong forts. I worked all day at one of the big forts built for the siege guns. The fort is fifteen feet high, with a ditch in front fifteen feet wide and ten feet deep. At the top within each fort the guns will be mounted on a dirt platform about ten feet high so as to afford a good view in front. When the works are completed on this grand scale it will require one million men to defend them.[1]

Tuesday, 17th—It is very hot. Nothing of importance.

Wednesday, 18th—It is very hot, but the troops are in fine spirits. Some of the boys who were wounded at Shiloh, together with those who went home on furloughs on account of sickness, are now returning to their commands.

Thursday, 19th—Drill is now all dispensed with on account of the hot weather. But the men are kept busy at fatigue and picket duty.

Friday, 20th—Our regiment went out on picket this evening. Water is very scarce out on the picket line and so we have our canteens filled in the evening before we go out.

Saturday, 21st—We were relieved this morning by the Thirteenth Iowa. Some of the fruit in this locality is beginning to ripen and we will have some variety in our rations.

Sunday, 22d—We had company inspection at 5 o'clock this evening. Our chaplain, John S. Whittlesey, died of diphtheria on May 11th at Durant, Iowa, and our regiment has no chaplain at present. We have no services on Sunday now, except that some of the companies occasionally have prayer meetings.

Monday, 23d—Nothing of importance. I went out to the branch a mile from camp to do my washing. Burtis Rumsey of our company has been sick for about two weeks and he begged me to take two of his shirts along and wash them for him, so I

---

[1] These works were never completed, the commanding general having called off the work. It was a good thing that it was discontinued, for the heavy work during the hot weather would have greatly injured the men.—A. G. D.

(June, 1862)

did. I used a small camp kettle which the company cook has set aside for boiling clothes. Some of the boys in the company hire colored women to wash their clothes. I prefer to do my own washing.

Tuesday, 24th—Our camp was inspected today by the brigade commander. Colonel Hare arrived in camp today. The boys were very glad to see him come back to the regiment.

Wednesday, 25th—The weather is very hot today and our camp is becoming very dry and dusty. Twenty-seven men were detailed this morning to clean up our camp for general inspection.

Thursday, 26th—The Eleventh Iowa went out on picket. The Third Brigade of the Sixth Division was inspected by the general inspector of the army. Men and camp both passed inspection quite satisfactorily.

Friday, 27th—We were relieved from picket this morning by the Thirteenth Iowa. Blackberries are beginning to ripen and seem to be plentiful. Fresh fruit with our rations will lighten our work.

Saturday, 28th—It rained this morning and the air is nice and cool. We worked most of the day cleaning up for another inspection—polishing our shoes, belts, cartridge boxes and muskets, besides sweeping the camp ground.

Sunday, 29th—We had inspection this morning at 8 o'clock by the general inspector. Colonel Hall and Captain McLoney arrived from home this morning. The Colonel had been wounded at Shiloh and went home to let the wound heal. Mrs. Hall is with the Colonel in camp and the men of the regiment have great respect for her; she is so kind to the sick in the regimental hospital.

Monday, 30th—The Eleventh Iowa was mustered for pay this morning. The men all looked fine—well and clean. None had on ragged clothing and few were absent from the regiment on account of sickness.

This ends June, with us in a good camp near Corinth, Mississippi.

JULY, 1862.

Tuesday, 1st—Received orders to cook four days' rations and be ready to move at a moment's notice. We had everything in readiness when late in the evening the order was countermanded.

Wednesday, 2d—I went out about a half mile from camp to pick blackberries, and I picked a gallon of them and sold them to the hospital steward for $1.25.

Thursday, 3d—The Eleventh Iowa went out on picket duty. I was on guard at division headquarters, my post being in a large orchard, and my orders were to keep all soldiers out of it.[1]

Friday, 4th—The Eleventh Iowa came in from picket. The weather is very hot. This is my first Fourth of July in the army. Things appear so lonesome. The battery boys of our brigade took their battery of six guns out a short distance from camp and fired a salute to celebrate the day.

Saturday, 5th—There is nothing of importance. Everything seems quite dull. There are but few whites left in Corinth and we seldom see white natives anywhere. There are some colored people in town, women and children, but the able-bodied men have all been taken off with the rebels. Some colored men are coming into camp from the plantations.

Sunday, 6th—It is very hot today. We had company inspection this morning. No news of importance.

Monday, 7th—No news of importance. We have to haul our water for the camp. The springs where we get our drinking water have become very low on account of the dry weather. Our quartermaster has to send the teams three miles distant for water. I went out about four miles to the south with a squad of men to slaughter some cattle and to bring in some fodder for the mules.

Tuesday, 8th—The rebels in this locality are not making much of an effort to retake Corinth. The report in camp is that they have sent the greater part of their forces east to reinforce their army in and around Richmond. News came this evening that General McClellan has been whipped and is now retreating from Richmond.

Wednesday, 9th—Nothing of importance today. Our regiment went out on picket again. Our picket line and reserve post are both in heavy timber and so we do not have to be in the hot sun while on duty.

[1] Such orders soon got to be a joke with the men, they in a quiet way giving the commanding officers to understand that they did not go down South to protect Confederate property. In a short time all guards were taken from orchards or anything which the men wanted for food.—A. G. D.

(July, 1862)

Thursday, 10th—The regiment returned from picket this morning at 8 o'clock, the Thirteenth coming out to relieve us. The roads are becoming very dusty and a regiment of men with a few mules can kick up a big dust. The soil is a sandy loam, and so fine and of such a color as to look like smoke from even a short distance.

Friday, 11th—Nothing of importance today. The weather is very warm. The entire army is engaged on the fortifications and in felling trees, and besides picket duty we have to keep the camp clean and our accouterments polished. Every man has his rifle in readiness.

Saturday, 12th—We had company inspection again as usual. A good many negroes are coming into camp. Some of the men who are strong enough to work and who want to be free are given work on the fortifications. A number of the officers are adopting negro boys as servants, and some of the most intelligent boys are being sent North to be educated.

Sunday, 13th—No news of importance. Some of the men occasionally get into religious discussions. There are two of them rather strong in the Universalist doctrine. One of them who reads the Bible a good bit got into a discussion today with some of the men. While some of the boys are church members in their homes, there are a good many who are not.

Monday, 14th—The weather is very warm; it is sweltering. I was detailed with a squad of men from our regiment under command of the quartermaster to go out with the trains to get some corn and fodder for the mules and horses. The Government has adopted the policy of paying for all material taken on a foraging expedition. But this is upon one condition only, viz.; the quartermaster issues a requisition on the Secretary of War for all material taken, and then if the owner of the property can prove his loyalty to the Government, he will get his pay for the same; if he cannot prove it, he will be classed as a rebel and will get nothing.

Tuesday, 15th—No news from Richmond.

Wednesday, 16th—Our regiment went out on picket. I went on camp guard.

Thursday, 17th—It rained all last night and everybody is thankful, as it has become so dry and dusty. There are a few cases of sickness in our regiment, due to the extremely hot weather—a few cases of typhoid fever and some are suffering from chronic diarrhea.

Friday, 18th—The weather is very hot. Colonel Hare took the regiment out on the drill ground for battalion drill, but we remained out only a half hour, since four or five men were overcome with the heat and had to be taken back to their tents.

Saturday, 19th—Everything is very quiet. With the exception of a few cases, the health of the men in camp is generally good. But the men are becoming restless. All would rather be in active service, for this camp service will never bring the war to a close.

Sunday, 20th—No news of importance. The weather is very hot. We had company inspection this morning, after which, because of the intense heat, the men remained in their tents. None were out during the day except those detailed on duty.

Monday, 21st—It is very warm and dusty today. There are some fine orchards around Corinth and the apples and peaches are beginning to ripen now. Fresh fruit will help out our rations and add freshness and variety.

Tuesday, 22d—We removed our tents and had a general clean-up of the camp. We made brush brooms, took down all tents, swept the ground, then pitched our tents again.

Wednesday, 23d—Our regiment is out on picket today. It rained all day. We seldom see any of the rebel cavalry in this locality, yet we always maintain a strong picket line so as not to be taken by surprise. We are expecting them to make a raid upon Corinth any time.

Thursday, 24th—We were relieved from picket this morning by the Thirteenth. Wild fruit is becoming plentiful and while on picket we added quite a variety to our rations.

Friday, 25th—The quartermaster drew some clothing today for our regiment. The regiment was out for drill today, with better success than the other day when it was so hot.

Saturday, 26th—Nothing of importance. Much of our time in camp is taken up with the question of rations. During this hot weather the regular army rations are drawn, but the men use very little of the salt bacon. But the bacon being issued, the company cook takes care of it and now has a wagon load of it stacked up beside his tent, anyone being permitted to go and help himself to it. At noon the company cook prepares the bean soup and cooks the pickled beef, after which he calls out for every man to come and get his portion. All the other rations are issued every five days, each man carrying his portion in his haversack. We have had no Irish potatoes issued for eight months now, but fresh beef we draw, sometimes twice a week, and it is cooked for us by the company cook. The rations are all of good quality with the exception of crackers, which at times are a little worm-eaten.

Sunday, 27th—We had regimental inspection this morning by Colonel Hare. We received orders to march in the morning. The Eleventh Iowa lost two men by disease while here in this camp—such is the penalty of camp life.

Chapter VII.

On Guard at Bolivar, Tennessee. July 28-September 11.

Monday, 28th—We struck our tents and at sunup started on our march for Bolivar, Tennessee. Our guide took us on the wrong road and we countermarched about ten miles, thus not being far from our starting point. The guide was tied and taken back to Corinth.[1] It is very warm and the roads are dusty. Our road being on high ground, we found water very scarce, and what little we got was of poor quality. General Tuttle is in command of our division, the Sixth.

Tuesday, 29th—We got on the right road and started at 8 o'clock this morning. We marched twelve miles and bivouacked for the night. The weather is extremely hot and the roads are very dusty. Orlando Stout of Company E fell out of the ranks today, and getting too far behind, was taken prisoner.

Wednesday, 30th—We camped on a large "secesh" plantation last night. The owner of it being a general in the rebel army, we made ourselves at home, killing all the cattle that we wanted and taking all the honey that we could carry away with us. We started at 8 o'clock this morning and marched fourteen miles, when we bivouacked for the night.

Thursday, 31st—We started at 8 o'clock this morning and arrived at Bolivar at 12 o'clock noon. We went into camp two miles east of town on the banks of the Hatchie river. Our camp is in a fine piece of timber, well shaded. I was almost played out when we arrived in camp; the weather being so hot, it was hard work to carry knapsack and accouterments and keep up with the company. Our officers are expecting to be attacked at this place and have put three or four hundred negroes to work throwing up breastworks. There is some very pretty land in this part of old Tennessee and there are some very nice farms. The timber here is chiefly of white oak, but there is some poplar and beech. Bolivar is a fine town and has one railroad.

[1] I never learned what became of him.—A. G. D.

AUGUST, 1862.

Friday, 1st—All hands are at work cleaning up our camp. We have a very pretty camping ground right on the bank of the river. The entire Crocker Brigade is in this camp and is in command of General Crocker.

Saturday, 2d—I was detailed on brigade guard this morning, but was taken sick while at my post and was relieved at 11 a. m.

Sunday, 3d—When the sick call was made this morning, I went to see the doctor for the first time. I was threatened with fever and the doctor gave me three "Blue Mass" pills and marked me off duty for three days.

Monday, 4th—I slipped out today between two guards and going up the river about a mile to a bakery near a mill, I bought a dozen apple pies. I returned safely to camp and sold the pies to some of the boys for double what I paid for them. Orders are very strict against absence from camp, for it is reported that a large force of the rebels is in this locality, and they may charge upon our camp any time.

Tuesday, 5th—The Eleventh Iowa drew two months' pay today. I received $26. We are able to purchase most any kind of goods needed, right here at Bolivar only two miles from camp.

Wednesday, 6th—I went on guard again. The boys are having high times today; all having plenty of money, they are making it lively in camp. But those on guard duty are having hard work because of the hot weather; for with dress coat buttoned up, all accouterments strapped on, and carrying musket at right shoulder shift, one can easily see what warm work it is walking the beat.

Thursday, 7th—Nothing of importance. Everything is quiet in camp. The rebels are not giving us much anxiety yet, but our officers are not napping; a strong picket is constantly kept in line.

Friday, 8th—No news of importance. The officers are having considerable trouble in keeping the boys from getting through the lines. We have regular brigade guard to keep the men in camp, yet every day a few slip through when the guards are walking in opposite directions. But now, every morning at guard mount, the officer of the day gives strict orders that guard number 1 shall walk his beat so that he will be looking at guard number 2, and continuing thus around the entire camp, so that all getting to the end of their beats at the same time face about and proceed as before, each looking toward the guard ahead of him.

Saturday, 9th—The weather is very hot and during the day the men not on duty keep close to camp. There are some fine orchards in this locality and we get plenty of fruit now, as all orchard guards have been removed. The men are given passes and every day four or five from each company go out to get fruit.

Sunday, 10th—We had company inspection this morning. We received orders to sweep the camp twice a day from now on. Our new chaplain, Chauncey H. Remington, conducted preaching services in the evening on the regimental parade ground.

Monday, 11th—I wrote a letter home today and sent a ten-dollar bill in it. I am sending home nearly all my pay from the Government, with the understanding that father is to keep it for me.

Tuesday, 12th—We just learned that Ebenezer McCullough of Company E died of chronic diarrhea at Corinth, on the third of this month. His home was at Davenport, Iowa.

Wednesday, 13th—The weather is very hot. I was on camp guard today when one of the guards suddenly became sick. I was number 24 in the first relief, and the man next to me, number 25, got sick. He called out to me, "Corporal the guard number 25." It then became my duty to repeat the same call, "Corporal the guard number 25," to the guard next to me, number 23, who made the same call to the guard next to him, and in this way the call went down the line to guard No. 1. Guard number 1 then sent the same call to the corporal of the guardhouse, who went out to guard number 25 to see what he wanted. When he was found to be sick another guard was brought out to relieve guard number 25.

Thursday, 14th—The Eleventh Iowa was ordered to move across the river, which we did this afternoon and went into camp on a low piece of ground. Our regiment is to guard the railroad track for four miles. We have to go on duty every other day and have to see that the rebels do not come and tear up the track.

(August, 1862)

Friday, 15th—There was a very heavy rainstorm last night. We pitched our tents and built the bunks in them today, and are again quite well settled in camp. This is my birthday—twenty years old, and I have done a hard day's work, setting up our tent and building bunks, after having been all night on picket. I have now served almost a year in the army and it has been an active year's work, too.

Saturday, 16th—Ten men from each company are detailed every morning to stand on picket, while the others patrol the railroad tracks. The first thing we do is to form a line of battle every morning at 4 o'clock.

Sunday, 17th—Nothing of importance. We had company inspection early this morning. Because of the hot weather, all men not on duty stay close to their tents in the shade.

Monday, 18th—We are having some very hot weather. Since coming to Bolivar, each man is permitted to cook his rations in his own way, and so every man has a frying pan of some sort, and a tin peach can in which to boil his coffee. One man in our company, "Long John," as the boys have nicknamed him, is a great coffee drinker. He carries a two-quart peach can strapped to his haversack, and every day buys up one or two rations of coffee from the boys who do not use much.

Tuesday, 19th—We received orders that two companies are to go out every three days about four miles east of the camp, to guard the railroad at the deep cut. On the third day they are to be relieved by two other companies from the regiment. It is a dangerous place to be on picket.

Wednesday, 20th—Nothing of importance.

Thursday, 21st—There is one train a day over the railroad. It is a combination train, and comes in at 6 p. m. and departs at 8 o'clock in the morning. The train does not run at night for fear the track might be torn up, as the rebels are so near.

Some very hot weather now. We get all the fruit that we want here, and have plenty of other rations at this camp. We have fresh pork and sweet potatoes. The potatoes we either boil in kettles or bake in ashes.

Friday, 22d—No news of importance. The rebels are not making any attacks on us, but they keep us busy watching them.

Saturday, 23d—Some very hot weather today. It is my turn off duty today, but I dread the picket tomorrow on the main road going into Bolivar.

Sunday, 24th—I went out on picket this morning to remain at the one post for twenty-four hours. I was on vedette for eight hours, two hours at a time. The vedette has to stand out in advance of the reserve post, one hundred yards or more. This post is about three miles east from Bolivar on the main road, having a high rail fence on either side. If the rebels should make a raid on the town, they would have to come in on this road.

Monday, 25th—Companies E and K went out on railroad guard, to the deep cut about four miles east of our camp. We went to relieve Companies C and H and are to stay out two days. We have to patrol about five miles of the track to the east of our reserve post, making nine miles of track to guard. Our reserve stays in a schoolhouse located on a high piece of ground close by the railroad. We have to keep a strong picket line all night. Our drinking water here is excellent, and we have all the peaches and apples that we can eat. Some rain this evening.

Tuesday, 26th—We remained on railroad guard all day again. Nothing of importance happened, but we had quite an exciting time for a while last night. When George Cush of Company E was on vedette, he thought he heard someone ahead of him in the brush, and gave the usual command to halt, but without response. Then as the noise continued he let fire, and although he hit nothing, yet that shot was enough to arouse the whole reserve post, and we remained in line the rest of the night, thinking that the rebels would make a charge on us before daylight. In the morning, upon investigation, we concluded that the noise must have been made by a hog or a calf, for there was not the least sign of the rebels. But the boys of the company began teasing George about his scare, and it is not likely that they will let him know the last of it for some time.

Wednesday, 27th—Companies G and B came out this morning to relieve us from picket duty at the big cut. We have had very little rest while on picket and patrol during the last forty-eight hours. Our regiment has begun building fortifications here at Bolivar; some negroes drifting into camp have been put to this

(August, 1862)

work. The rebels to the south of us are getting bolder, and have driven in some of our outer pickets.

Thursday, 28th—Nothing of importance. We are enjoying a well-earned rest in camp today, after having been without sleep for forty-eight hours. Our camp ground is getting dryer and more settled, and the weather is more pleasant.

Friday, 29th—No news of importance. We are all on fatigue duty today, building rifle-pits and a fort. Our fortifications are not on high ground, but in case of an attack upon our camp, they would give us ample protection.

Saturday, 30th—We are on guard every other day now. I am on picket post again on the main road out east from our camp. There are thirty of us with a captain in command. I stood on vedette for eight hours. Our reserve post is close by a farm house owned by a man named Patrick. He has a great many slaves who are out in the fields picking cotton, and they have a colored foreman, a slave at that, over them. But Patrick himself is the "driver," though he seems to be kind to his slaves, who are mostly women and children. Patrick had been forced into the army of the Confederacy, but he escaped, and returning to his plantation, he hopes now to remain within the Union lines.

Sunday, 31st—Our pickets at the south edge of town were driven in by the rebels, and expecting to be attacked, the right wing of our detachment was in line of battle all day. We have now been in camp at this place all month and the work which we have been called upon to do has been very strenuous. I was on picket half the time, patrolling the railroad, and I spent the other half on special picket and on fortifications. I have been in good health.

SEPTEMBER, 1862.

Monday, 1st—We were expecting to be attacked today and so were in line of battle most of the time. Our pickets to the south of town are still skirmishing.[1] The weather is very hot.

[1] It was the belief in camp that there was only a small force of the enemy in the locality of Bolivar, but that they were quite active to make our commanders think that they were here in large force to take the place, and so make us keep a large force there while their real objective was Corinth. We had then but a small force at Corinth while the Confederates had their main army in the vicinity of Iuka, Mississippi, with the view of capturing Corinth.—A. G. D.

Tuesday, 2d—There was some fighting south of town this morning and there is still some skirmishing. Old Patrick and several other citizens left, for they were afraid that the rebels would catch them and hang them. They had violated their oaths to support the Confederacy and then when the Union army took this section they had sworn to support the United States, and now thinking that this place would be retaken, they got out so as not to fall into the hands of the rebels.

Wednesday, 3d—Our regiment had to fall in line of battle this morning at 2 o'clock so that if the rebels should attack us they would not find us in our beds. The rebels did not appear and a big detail was put to work on the fortifications. When these works are completed a small force can hold them against a force five times the size.

Thursday, 4th—Companies E and K went out on railroad guard at the deep cut, to relieve Companies C and H. We are guarding the road for a distance of seven miles. We have some very strict orders on guard; every man has to be on guard all the time, as the rebels may come out of the brush at any moment, and if we should be caught napping, some of us would surely be killed.

Friday, 5th—We are still on guard at the big cut, with cartridge boxes on and muskets by our sides. It was reported that the rebels were coming to attack us last night and there was no sleep for us. They did not come, but I hope that they will not deceive us any more.

Saturday, 6th—We were relieved this morning by Companies B and G and arrived in camp at 11 o'clock. All are glad to get back to tent for a good rest, after having been on duty for forty-eight hours.

Sunday, 7th—There have been no rebels to see us yet. Things are very quiet today; the weather being so hot, no one cares to stir.

Monday, 8th—It rained all last night. Bolivar has a town clock which can be heard as far out as our camp. The town watchman keeps calling out the hours till 2 or even 4 o'clock in the morning, ending with his monotonous "all's well." The feeling of the boys is that all is not well when hundreds of men have to be out on vedette with drawn muskets ready for a fight, and that the watchman had better dispense with the announcement until this war is over.

Tuesday, 9th—Nothing of importance. We are still working on the fortifications; those at work are relieved from picket duty at night. The rebels are not as bold as they were a few days ago. The talk in camp is that our brigade will leave in two or three days for Corinth.

Wednesday, 10th—We finished building Fort Hall, on the north side of town, and when the artillery boys get the cannon mounted, we will be ready for the rebels.

Thursday, 11th—The brigade received marching orders to leave in the morning at daylight and we packed our knapsacks today. The talk is that we are to go to Corinth. A small force is to be left here to hold the fort, and it will require a large number to take it. Bolivar has some loyal citizens who will be protected in this way, but we are sorry to bid these people good-bye, perhaps for all time to come. We have been in camp here forty-two days and all the time engaged in hard service—on picket, fatigue and patrol duty, besides often in line of battle.

Chapter VIII.
The Battles of Iuka and Corinth. Chasing Price and Fortifying Corinth. September 12-October 31.

Friday, 12th—We struck our tents at daylight and at 8 o'clock left Bolivar for Corinth, Mississippi, about forty-five or fifty miles distant. We marched fifteen miles and bivouacked for the night on the banks of the Hatchie river. The weather is very hot and the water is scarce, which, together with the dusty roads, makes traveling hard work. The men, however, are in good health and spirits; only a few found it necessary to call on the doctor for aid in having their accouterments carried.

Saturday, 13th—We started at 7 o'clock and marched fifteen miles. Bivouacked for the night on the banks of the Tuscumbie river. It was very warm and dusty marching, but all held their places in the ranks. It is said that the rebels' cavalry which kept up close to our rear guard, had something to do with keeping the men in line, for anyone falling out behind would surely have been taken prisoner.

Sunday, 14th—We started early this morning with General Crocker in command and marched fifteen miles without stopping to get a drink. But several of the men became overheated, for it was a dreadfully hot day and the roads were dusty. We reached Corinth at 1 p. m., and going out a mile south of town, stacked arms and remained there the rest of the day. We were nearly famished when we reached Corinth. Our road was on a pine ridge, hot and dusty, with a mile to water on either side, and it was utterly impossible for one to fall out of rank, get water, catch up and get back to his place in line. It was one of the hardest marches I have ever been on.[1] On passing through the town, by the college grounds, the young lady students worked hard at drawing water from the well and giving it to the men to quench their thirst. We bivouacked in a large cotton field, as our teams had not yet arrived with our tents. It commenced to rain about sundown and we lay on the ground without any protection.

[1] The fast march and doing without water so long was all uncalled for, as after we got to Corinth we did nothing but lie around.—A. G. D.

THE BATTLES OF IUKA AND CORINTH

(September, 1862)

Monday, 15th—We pitched our tents and built our bunks today. It had rained all night and rained some more this afternoon. The men are not pleased with this camp ground, as it is low and level. There will be a great many on the sick list if we remain here. On account of the dry weather all summer, the springs no longer furnish the branch with running water, and we are compelled to get our drinking water from a stagnant pool. Our former camp here in Corinth, which we left in July, was on high ground and all had hoped that we would be permitted to occupy that spot, but we were disappointed in that—such is the life of a soldier.

Tuesday, 16th—We drew some clothing today; I got a rubber poncho, which cost $2.50. It is about three by six feet, with eyelets every six inches all around the edges, so by four men going together in bivouac and putting their ponchos over a pole resting on two forks, they will have a roof that will turn rain better than any canvas roof. They are good, heavy rubber cloth.

Wednesday, 17th—Our division started at 6 o'clock this morning, leaving all our baggage in the tents. Each man is carrying sixty rounds of ammunition, and only such teams as are needed to haul extra ammunition are taken along. The whole Union army, excepting a small garrison left at Corinth, is on the move. We are marching out to the northwest, but the men do not know where they are headed for. We marched twenty-five miles today, and went into bivouac for the night. We got our gum blankets just in time, as it rained nearly all day, and the roads became very muddy, especially where the artillery went. The men built fires tonight to dry their clothes.

Thursday, 18th—It rained all night and till about 10 o'clock in the morning. We were on the march again for fifteen miles and then bivouacked for the night. We have traveled forty miles in the two days and learn that we are about ten miles from Corinth.

Friday, 19th—Each man was ordered to have sixty rounds of cartridges, and leaving our bivouac, we marched a short distance and formed a line of battle waiting for the sound of cannon from Rosecrans' men in and around Iuka, on the opposite side of the rebels. Not hearing anything we slowly moved forward about four miles through the woods, remaining all the while in line of battle. We drove the rebel pickets in. At noon the Eleventh Iowa was on a high piece of ground in open field awaiting orders. Some of the boys started fires to boil their coffee, and the rebels, seeing the smoke, opened with a few shots from a battery of four-pounders. Then our battery of heavy guns, lying in front of us, suddenly opened up on them and soon put them out of business. But the boys put out their campfires in short order. When the rebels first opened fire upon us, I was lying on the ground resting my head upon my knapsack and a ball passed just over me, striking the ground at my left. That was a closer call than I cared to have and I did not think of taking a nap again.

Saturday, 20th—We remained in line of battle all night and early this morning advanced in a line about two miles, when we received orders to march on into Iuka. The rebels retreated during the night, and General Rosecrans' forces are after them. We learned this morning that a battle had been fought yesterday here by Rosecrans' forces alone. When we were waiting for the sound of Rosecrans' cannon, we could not hear them on account of an unfavorable wind. The rebels attacked him and made the fight come off a day before the time set for our capture of them. The Sixteenth Iowa of Crocker's Brigade had been detached from us and sent forward, being the only regiment of our brigade engaged in the fight. Their loss was fourteen killed. The Fifth Iowa in Rosecrans' army was trapped in an ambush which was made with a battery masked in green leaves, and lost forty-one killed. The rebels were driven out and left their dead and wounded on the field. Quite a number of our wounded are now being brought into town from the battlefield. Iuka is a nice place with some good buildings. It is well supplied with good water from splendid springs. There is poor farming land around here, it being quite rolling in this part of Tennessee. The timber, mostly pine, is rather scrubby.

Sunday, 21st—We lay around all day in the camp which the rebels vacated. Their tents are badly torn, but the wooden bunks are in good condition. The wounded have all been cared for and the dead were buried today. A detachment of our army is still in pursuit of the rebels. Our brigade has been detailed to garrison this place and we expect our tents to arrive soon. I was detailed on camp guard this morning.

THE BATTLES OF IUKA AND CORINTH

(September, 1862)

Monday, 22d—No news of importance. Rain last night. Foraging parties are bringing in all the fresh pork that we can use, besides plenty of sweet potatoes. Our crackers, having been kept in storage so long, are musty and full of the weevil web, and there are no trains from Corinth to bring a fresh supply. We often clean them the best we can and bake them again in ashes or in skillets.

Tuesday, 23d—We moved out of the old camp in the woods and went into bivouac in a large field. We are obliged to form a line of battle every morning at 2 o'clock and remain in line until after sunrise. A few of the rebel cavalry are still watching us in this vicinity. Our entire division is at this place, but it is thought that we shall soon leave for Corinth, as Iuka is not a very important point to hold, but Corinth, because of its two railroad lines, is very important.

Wednesday, 24th—The first train of cars came in today from Corinth and we expect now to receive a fresh supply of hardtack. We have been on one-third rations by foraging; now, however, it seems we have to do without, for we have cleaned up everything for a distance of ten miles in all directions.

Thursday, 25th—Our knapsacks and tents arrived today by train from Corinth, and it will be more like living now. We have excellent water here, and there are large hotels for invalids, this having been a health resort for Southern people. There are quite a number of mineral springs here, some of sulphur and others of iron.

Friday, 26th—I was on fatigue duty down in town today, helping to dismount the guns and load them with the ammunition upon the cars to be shipped to Corinth. We are preparing to leave Iuka as soon as possible, but it is slow work, as the railroad is in bad shape, and there is only one train a day.

Saturday, 27th—Company E went out today with the teams to forage for corn and fodder. We were out northeast about seven miles and found plenty of corn, but not much fodder. The boys also took some chickens and two fine hogs. The farmers in this section are not rich, their farms being on the bluffs of the Tennessee river, but they seem to have plenty and some to spare. When the quartermaster sends teams out to forage, he calls for a company or perhaps a whole regiment, and they go and take what they want without asking for it, but the officer in charge always gives the owner of the property the quartermaster's receipt.

Sunday, 28th—It rained all day. I went out on picket. David Huff, Leroy Douglas, Wm. Esher and I were together at one post. We had strict orders to keep a sharp lookout for the rebel cavalry. We are expecting to be attacked.

Monday, 29th—We were relieved from picket this morning, and for the first time in several days we rested in camp all day. The weather is hot and sultry, with quite cool nights. The rebel cavalry seem to be all around us, but for fear of getting hurt they keep their distance.

Tuesday, 30th—Nothing of importance. We received orders to drill.

OCTOBER, 1862.

Wednesday, 1st—The Eleventh Iowa was ordered down into town last night, for it was expected that the rebels would make a charge into town to burn our rations. We think, however, that they want our rations for their own haversacks. We formed a line of battle and lay in the streets all night, but the rebels did not show themselves. We received orders to march at daylight this morning. The cars came in from Corinth at 4 o'clock this morning, and the sick men, our baggage, and the remainder of our stores were loaded up and sent to our headquarters at Corinth. By noon Iuka was expected to be entirely evacuated by our men. Our regiment marched twenty-three miles and bivouacked for the night within six miles of Corinth.

Thursday, 2d—We started this morning at 7 o'clock, and reaching Corinth at 10, we marched out two miles west of town where we pitched our tents in the timber for camp. Water is very scarce. I took six canteens and started to find water, but to get it I must have traveled in all four miles. The balance of the day I served on camp guard.

Friday, 3d—I was on camp guard all last night, on the second relief. Troops were coming in all night. This morning about daylight the Sixth Division was ordered out, and marching out about two miles to the northwest, we met the rebels in force and formed a line of battle. Our pickets having been attacked about

(October, 1862)

sunrise, the battle now commenced in earnest and lasted all day. There was some hard fighting in the afternoon, particularly off on the right, and our men soon fell back to the first line of breastworks. About 3 p. m. the Iowa Brigade was flanked and had to fall back to the second line of breastworks, but the brigade, with the exception of the Fifteenth Regiment, did not get into the thick of the fight.[1] The fighting continued till dark, and after that there was some very heavy cannonading.

Saturday, 4th—During the night all was quiet and our brigade fell back to the last line of fortifications which, extending almost around the town, had been built in the last few days. Here we lay in line of battle all night. The rebels commenced to throw shells into town this morning at daylight. I was still on guard with the teams and we had to get out of that place in double quick. The rebels threw some ten or twelve shells before our battery in Fort Robinet could get the range of them, but when they did, they opened on them some sixty-four-pounders and soon put the rebel's battery out of commission. I was relieved and went to join the regiment, which had been advanced to support a battery. About 10 o'clock the rebels made a charge upon Fort Robinet, to our right, and tried to break our lines at that point but failed. This charge was made by a Texas cavalry, dismounted; they came clear over into the fort, driving some of our artillerymen from their guns, but they were soon overpowered, some being killed and some taken prisoner. The colonel of the regiment planted their flag on our fort, but he was almost immediately killed. The rebels' dead just outside of the fort lay three or four deep and the blood ran in streams down the trenches. The rebels finally withdrew about 4 p. m., leaving their dead and wounded. The Iowa Brigade was placed to the left of Fort Robinet, in support of a battery, but did not become engaged during the day. Some of our forces started after the fleeing rebels. We received orders to be ready to march in the morning, and have to lie in line of battle all night.

Sunday, 5th—The entire Sixth Division, taking up the line of march[2] this morning at 6 o'clock, marched five miles and then

---

[1]The record of the losses of our brigade is as follows: The Fifteenth, eleven killed, sixteen wounded; the Thirteenth, one killed, fourteen wounded; the Sixteenth, one killed, twenty-one wounded; the Eleventh, three killed, eight wounded.—A. G. D.

[2]As we passed the field hospital of the Confederates on the Corinth

formed a line of battle. We heard some very heavy cannonading out on the Hatchie river, in our front. General Hurlbut had cut off the retreat of the rebels at the bridge crossing the river, but after a hard fight they got away and continued their retreat to the south, on the east side of the river. We resumed our march at 1 p. m. and after covering ten miles stopped for the night. The Second Iowa Cavalry was ordered back to Corinth.

Monday, 6th—We started this morning at daylight and crowded the rebels very hard all day, capturing their trains and some of their artillery—ammunition, arms and caissons. I never saw such a stampede in all my life. They drove their wagons and artillery through the timber, over fallen trees, two and three abreast, wiggling through the standing timber as best they could with every teamster for himself. Some of the artillery men took the cannon off the running gears, and throwing them into gullies, covered them with leaves. Everything imaginable was strewn along the road—tents, bake ovens, corn meal, fresh beef and a great many other things; some of their supplies they burned up, to keep from falling into our hands. We captured some of General Price's headquarters' supplies, among such a buffalo robe which the men tore up for souvenirs.[1]

Tuesday, 7th—We kept on the march last night till 1 a. m., when we stopped in bivouac. The men were all very tired, yet were willing and anxious to go on if only they could capture Price, or even a part of his army. Leaving our bivouac at 8 o'clock this morning, we again started after Price. We soon came upon the rebels and shelled their rear guard almost all day. We took a great many prisoners. It is reported that they are breaking up

battlefield, we saw eighteen of their dead, evidently having died from wounds, lying side by side, and almost black in the face, which at the time was said to have been caused by their drinking a mixture of water, vinegar and gunpowder. Our army had barrels of vinegar, one for each regiment, so stationed as to permit the men to come and help themselves. Now, our quartermaster, in hastily removing the commissary's supplies back of the inner lines during the battle, had, for lack of facilities, left standing these barrels of vinegar. It is supposed that the Confederates took the vinegar and made a drink of it, for after the battle there was no vinegar to be found.—A. G. D.

[1]During that day's march I saw, I think, the meanest man in the Union army. We had just started up a long, steep hill when I noticed one of our men coming out of a one-room log hut by the roadside. As he passed us, with an oath, he growled that he had gone into the hut to get something to eat, but all he could find was a half-bushel bag of corn meal. This the woman, who by the way had the courage to stay with her home, begged him not to take, as it was all the food she had, but he took it. Then when about halfway up the hill, the bag of meal, in addition to his accouterments, becoming too heavy, he with another oath, dumped half the meal out on the ground and ran on to catch up with his command. For such a man I cannot find words to express my contempt.—A. G. D.

into small bands and getting away through the timber and are scattering in every direction.

Wednesday, 8th—We did not get into bivouac until late last night, and again started on our march early this morning. We marched until 3 p. m., when we halted to rest, going into bivouac for the night in a large field of cow-peas, near the town of Ripley, Mississippi. We ran out of rations and foraging parties were sent out. They brought in sweet potatoes and fresh pork, which is all we have to eat. I picked some cow-peas and cooked them; they are rather strong, yet better than nothing to eat. The report is that the rebels have scattered out and escaped, and that we shall not follow them any longer. We are so far from our base of supplies that we are in danger of being captured.

Thursday, 9th—We have received no rations today and the boys have been pitching pretty freely into the cattle and hogs in this locality. The rebels are reported to be at Holly Springs, Mississippi. We moved on nearer Ripley and are three miles east of town. It is very warm and dusty; water is scarce along the way.

Friday, 10th—We have received no rations yet and have nothing but fresh meat and sweet potatoes to eat. Our brigade went out about four miles on a scout, to escort a battery to another part of the army. The weather is very hot and about 3 o'clock in the afternoon it commenced to rain, the roads soon becoming very muddy, for the dust was so deep. At dark we reached our old bivouac, where we had been the night before last, and stopped for the night. A cool wind followed the rain and some of us went into negro huts, built fires and dried our clothes.

Saturday, 11th—We were routed out this morning at 1 o'clock and started for Corinth, seventy miles distant. It soon began raining, and after marching six miles in the rain we met our provision train. We stacked our arms by the roadside, drew some rations and had a good square meal again. The hard-tack and coffee, with the bacon broiled on our ramrods in the fire, tasted mighty good—better than any pound cake eaten at home. While resting here and feasting, a number of the boys who had gone into the negro huts, caught up with us. They were in the cabins, nice and dry, and thought when we were routed out in the night, that it was to form in line, but in the morning found out their mistake and hastened to catch up with the command. A few of them were taken prisoners by the rebel cavalry following us. After our meal we continued our march till we reached the Tallahatchie river, and bivouacked in heavy timber on the banks of the river. We traveled thirty-five miles today, the weather being quite cool.

Sunday, 12th—We started early this morning and marching thirty miles arrived at Corinth just at dark. The soldiers are all very tired and worn, having marched about sixty-five miles over a heavy road in two days. We came into Corinth over the ground we had fought over in the battle of October 3d and 4th. This battlefield is a terrible sight and gives one a horrible picture of war. Our men having hurriedly gone in pursuit of the fleeing rebels, the burial of the dead was left to the convalescents, together with such negroes as could be found to do the job. Many of the dead bodies had become so decomposed that they could not be moved and were simply covered over with a little earth just where they lay.

Monday, 13th—Quite a large mail awaited us here. We cleaned up our camp grounds and pitched our tents in order. All are glad to be in camp again, as sleeping on the damp ground in bivouac, without any protection whatever, as we did the last week, is hard on the health.

Tuesday, 14th—No news of importance. We washed our clothes today. We have to haul our water about two miles, and it is poor at that. The horses and mules are taken by the men to water.

Wednesday, 15th—We are once more getting settled in camp. Our duties are not as laborious as they were at Bolivar and Iuka. We have begun the building of forts and rifle-pits, close in, all around Corinth, so that a small force can hold the place. We are pulling down some of the vacant houses to make room for fortifications. But the fortifications will not be on as grand a scale as those built here during the summer. They will be smaller, too, than the fortifications which protected us during the battle here.

Thursday, 16th—We have a beautiful camping ground; it is well situated on high ground which affords good drainage and in case of rain will dry off quickly. The weather is very warm and pleasant, with signs of autumn on every hand, and a northern autumn at that. We have warm days and cool nights, and the foliage of the forest is turning many different colors.

Friday, 17th—Everybody is now busy in the routine duties of camp life. The Government is having some deep wells drilled here in our camp; one of them is now completed and we are enjoying plenty of good water, although it is quite a job to draw it. We draw the water by means of a bucket attached to the end of a rope which runs upon a pulley fastened upon a tall pine tree standing near the well. The bucket is about four feet long and has a valve in the bottom. There are always some of the men at the well waiting for their turn to draw water.

Saturday, 18th—It is reported that General Bragg is marching on this place.[1] Colonel Hare has not been with us for some time and will not be with us again. We have just learned that he resigned his commission on August 31st, on account of the wound which he received at the battle of Shiloh. He was respected by all the men of the regiment, and we are sorry to lose him.

Sunday, 19th—Nothing of importance. This is our first Sunday in a quiet camp for more than two months. We had company inspection this morning and dress parade at 5 o'clock in the evening.

Monday, 20th—No news of importance. We are again drawing regular army rations, having a railroad to our base of supplies. There is little to be secured by foraging around Corinth, as the rebels' attempt to retake the place has resulted in keeping a large force of our men here and food and feed has been almost cleaned up, with the men for a part of the time on short rations.

Tuesday, 21st—Some very fine weather. We have received orders to have company drill twice a day now, and dress parade every day at 5 p. m. We are getting over the effects of our hard service of the past two months.

Wednesday, 22d—We had brigade inspection today with all accouterments on. There is a report in camp that the army is soon to make an important move south into Mississippi. It is

[1]This was one of those mere rumors, for we know by history that General Bragg was not around there at the time.—A. G. D.

(October, 1862)

rumored that there are soon to be some changes of brigade and division commanders.[1]

Thursday, 23d—No news of importance. The roads are quite dusty.

Friday, 24th—I went to wash clothes today. Company washing squads are sent out daily, except Sundays. A squad consists of eight men with a captain, a lieutenant and two sergeants. This method is necessary because we have to go so far, two miles, and a smaller group could easily be taken by the rebels' cavalry.

Saturday, 25th—It is very cold today. It snowed about two inches this afternoon. We are well fixed for a mild winter in camp, with plenty of wood for fires in our Sibley tents.

Sunday, 26th—The Eleventh Iowa was detailed to work on the fortifications under construction down in town. It was quite cold all day, and disagreeable, as the snow is still on the ground.

Monday, 27th—Our entire regiment was at work on the fortifications. Nathan Chase and William Cross of my company had a fight today, all over some trivial matter. It seems that it is enough to have to fight the rebels without the men fighting among themselves. They were put into the guardhouse.

Tuesday, 28th—The regiment worked on the fortifications today for the third day in succession. I was not with my company though, being on other fatigue duty. The forts under construction are arranged so that if one fort should be captured, the guns of two other forts could be turned upon the enemy in that one. The floors of the forts and the rifle-pits are raised from four to ten feet by filling in earth, and then laid with the lumber from the houses which were pulled down to make room for the fortifications. The ramparts are faced on the outside with long woven baskets of hickory withes and filled with earth to keep them in shape. The forts are built with a view of standing some time, and should last for four or five years. We commenced drawing bread instead of crackers.

Wednesday, 29th—The Eleventh Iowa was detailed to clean up and smooth a tract of ground for inspection. We are to have

[1] There was a sentiment even then among the rank and file of the men, that General Grant was the man to lead them. Some expressed the opinion that in the course of time he would be placed in command of all the armies of the United States. The men had the utmost confidence in his leading the army to complete victory.—A. G. D.

(October, 1862)

general inspection of the army here at Corinth, and it is to be made by General Grant.

Thursday, 30th—The weather is quite warm again. We were at work getting ready for general inspection, cleaning camping ground, clothing and accouterments. Our camp is now in fine shape and the men are well rested. Some of the sick and wounded who have been absent for some weeks are returning to camp.

Friday, 31st—This was general muster day, and we were reviewed this afternoon by the commanding officer, General McArthur. The general says our division is hard to beat, declaring that it would be difficult to find a better-looking number of men armed for active service than the Sixth Division. After the review we were mustered for pay. The weather is very warm and the roads are dusty.

Chapter IX.

The Campaign Around Holly Springs and Retreat to Lafayette, Tennessee. November 1-January 11, 1863.

NOVEMBER, 1862.

Saturday, 1st—I was on guard today. The Sixth Division received orders to march in the morning.[1] We are to go in light equipment, leaving here our knapsacks and tents, which are to be put in storage.

Sunday, 2d—We struck our tents, packed our knapsacks and sent them into Corinth for storage. The sick were all left in the hospital at Corinth. We started at 2 p. m. and marched fourteen miles, when we bivouacked for the night. The roads are very dusty and the weather is quite cool, but we are breaking the chill by building campfires.

Monday, 3d—We started at 8 this morning, and marched eighteen miles. We cannot get much sleep at night because the army is so large; it is about 10 o'clock every night before we get into camp. But the weather is quite cool and the roads are good for marching. We went into bivouac for the night in a large vacant field. We passed through some rich farming country today, which the foraging parties had not found. The farms have good buildings and fences, and the crops are bountiful.

Tuesday, 4th—We started rather early this morning and arrived at Grand Junction at 9 o'clock in the evening. The army has burned the fences along the road and set fire to many deserted houses.[2]

[1] The Eleventh Iowa regiment was within fifty miles of Corinth for two hundred and thirty-four days, and in that time took active part in the two days' battle at Pittsburg Landing, the siege of Corinth, two months of garrisoning and fortifying Corinth, forty-two days in fortifying and garrisoning Bolivar, the battle of Iuka and garrison duty there, the two days' battle of Corinth and then the pursuit of the enemy and return to Corinth. During all this time Company E was with the regiment performing its full duty. The losses of our company were nine killed in battle and five dying of disease, making fourteen of the company whose bodies were laid away under the green sod.—A. G. D.

[2] Our march these two days was marred by the disgraceful spectacle of the waste and destruction of property. Some men set fire to the autumn leaves in the fence corners along the road. A high wind blowing soon spread the fire, which laid waste the timber and burned some farm buildings, together with their contents. Such destruction of property was the disgrace of our army—but it was at the seat of war.—A. G. D.

(November, 1862)

Wednesday, 5th—It was cold last night to lie in open bivouac. A cold northwest wind was blowing, and although we built fires to sleep by, yet the night was very uncomfortable, for while one was warm on the side next to the fire he was freezing on the other. We lay still all day to rest, but many of the boys slipped out in small squads for forage; they ran all over the country and fetched in fresh pork by the wholesale. I was in a squad of six with our corporal and we came in with our haversacks filled with sweet potatoes. On returning to camp, we passed too close to the colonel's tent, and he happened to be standing outside taking a sun bath. He called the corporal to his side, asked him where he had been, where he belonged, and taking out his penknife, cut from the corporal's blouse his chevrons and gave him an order to his captain, reducing him to the ranks.[1] The rest of us passed on to our tents. While we were out foraging, the colonel issued an order directing each orderly sergeant in the regiment to have his company fall in line every thirty minutes for roll call, and every man not answering to his name was either to be put in the guardhouse or on extra duty. I was caught, but being a pretty good friend of the orderly, I got off easy. He ordered me to carry a kettle of water to the company cook, telling me that since this was my first offense, he would let me off with that. None of the boys was punished very hard.

Thursday, 6th—The Sixth Division remained in bivouac here at Grand Junction, while a part of the army moved on to Holly Springs. We have roll call now every hour during the day.

Friday, 7th—The weather is fine with quite cold nights. We are on half rations now, because there are no trains through from Corinth.

Saturday, 8th—Nothing of importance. A large detail from the Sixth Division was sent to clear a place for a drill ground down on the second bottom of the creek south of our bivouac.

Sunday, 9th—We moved our camp to higher ground today, and are now in camp on the banks of Scott creek.

Monday, 10th—We have plenty of water at this camp, but are on short rations, having nothing but "gruel" and sweet potatoes to eat. What the boys call gruel is made from flour and corn

---

[1] This, it has always seemed to me, was a mean, contemptible thing for the colonel to do.—A. G. D.

meal. The quartermaster issued some flour and meal today, each man drawing his portion and cooking it to suit his taste. The usual method of preparing it is to make a dough and then bake it in the hot ashes or in the frying pan. Some of the new regiments from the North are equipped with shelter tents, each man carrying his part of the tent on his knapsack. The boys have nicknamed the new tents "dog tents." [1]

Tuesday, 11th—The same old thing over. We are still in camp and on short rations. The quartermaster tells us to be patient three or four days more, when he expects to have full rations for us. I hunted about an hour through a ten-acre cornfield, thinking I might find an ear of corn and parch it to help relieve my hunger, but the field had been picked over so thoroughly that I did not even find a nubbin.

Wednesday, 12th—Nothing new. The weather is quite cool. This makes our eighth day on short rations, but the quartermaster assured us today that he would have some provisions for us tomorrow. New troops are arriving every day and passing on out to the front.

Thursday, 13th—The railroad is repaired now and the cars came through today to Grand Junction from Corinth, loaded with provisions. Our tents and knapsacks also arrived. We pitched our tents, drew rations this evening, and commenced to live again. It looks like home once more. Three new recruits for our company arrived today from Iowa.

Friday, 14th—Nothing of importance. The Eleventh Iowa is in the Third Brigade commanded by General Crocker; the brigade is in the Sixth Division commanded by General McArthur; the division is in the Seventeenth Army Corps commanded by General McPherson.

Saturday, 15th—It rained all day and we had no drill. No news. We have the Sibley tents now and are in good shape for cold weather. The tents are large, one accommodating eighteen or twenty men, and it is supported by a center pole which rests on a tripod. Fires are built on the ground floor in the center

---

[1] Our boys were inclined to ridicule the idea of a man having to carry his tent on his back, and gave them the nickname "dog tent." But at that very time some of the boys would have been glad for a chance to carry as good tents, for when we were out on the march our tents had to be left in camp or else put in storage, and we would have to bivouac without any protection.—A. G. D.

(November, 1862)

and there is a round hole at the top of the tent for the smoke to escape. The men sleep in Indian fashion with their feet to the fire.

Sunday, 16th—We had another heavy rain today which caused Scott creek to overflow and our camp was almost flooded over. It seems that we shall have to move the camp.

Monday, 17th—We moved our camp today onto the hills back from the creek. We raised the tents from the ground about three feet, by digging trenches and setting staves which we made from the red oak trees growing so plentifully here. Then we elevated our bunks about eighteen inches from the ground with the staves and lumber torn from vacant houses in the vicinity.

Tuesday, 18th—We cleaned up our camp ground and finished setting in order our new camp. We have a very fine camp now and it looks quite homelike. It is located in rather open, wooded ground and the different colors of leaves on the trees make it look quite grand. The nights are getting frosty.

Wednesday, 19th—I was detailed to help the general quartermaster draw supplies for the division. There were about one hundred men and we went with teams to La Grange, Tennessee. The supplies consisted of sugar, flour, pickled beef, pork, salt and vinegar, these all in barrels, with coffee and rice put up in sacks, and crackers or "hard-tack," salt bacon, pepper, soap and candles in boxes. The feed for the animals consisted of oats and shelled corn in sacks, and hay in bales of four or five hundred pounds each. Loading these on the wagon was heavy work, especially the big bales of hay, which required the strength of all who could get hold to lift them. We got a taste of another phase of war.

Thursday, 20th—We had division drill by General McArthur this forenoon, and in the afternoon we had battalion drill under Lieutenant Abercrombie. Our drill ground proved to be poorly suited for division drill, on account of the ravines and washed-out gullies.

Friday, 21st—No news of importance. We are now in the regular routine of camp life, with drill twice a day. The quartermaster received a consignment of clothing and blankets for some of the men of our regiment.

Saturday, 22d—It is dry and the weather is quite pleasant.

After the regular drills we cleaned up camp for inspection. There is no news, but the report in camp is that the division will start for the front in four or five days.

Sunday, 23d—Nothing of importance. We had general inspection this forenoon and in the afternoon the boys were permitted to remain in their tents—some were reading, some writing letters home, while others were mending their clothes.

Monday, 24th—We draw rations now of equal parts of meal, flour and crackers, and in amount equal to a one-pound loaf of bread. We have no means for baking bread, so each man turns over his flour and corn meal to the company cook, who boils it into a mush. Then at the noon hour he calls out and the men go and get their portions. Some of us fry the mush with a little bacon, which makes a very palatable dish. But I cannot understand why it is, that with a railroad open to our base of supplies, the quartermaster cannot draw full rations of crackers for the men.

Tuesday, 25th—Division drill in the forenoon and battalion drill in the afternoon, as usual. We had a practical demonstration during our division drill of the difficulty of drilling on uneven ground. While our column was advancing in line of battle by right flank, up hill and down hill, and across ravines and gullies, the line at times became badly broken; men occasionally fell into the gullies and had to be helped out; it became pretty exciting and even quite laughable, for there was always some one struggling to stay in his place in the line.

Wednesday, 26th—Nothing of importance. The boys had the laugh on our commanding general this afternoon when we were returning from drill; he was riding at the head of the division and when crossing the creek at a rocky ford he was thrown from his horse. The boys declared that the horse was O. K., but that perhaps the real cause of his ducking was Southern rum.

Thursday, 27th—I signed the allotment roll for my father to draw $10.00 of my pay at home. The division received orders to be ready to march tomorrow morning. We are to pack our extra clothing in our knapsacks, which are to be stored at La Grange. Our tents are to be taken with us, the quartermaster delivering them to us every night so that we will not have to lie out in all kinds of weather.

(November, 1862)

Friday, 28th—We packed our knapsacks ready to be sent to La Grange, and striking our tents started at 6 o'clock. We marched eighteen miles and went into camp for the night. Our cavalry drove some five hundred rebels out of Holly Springs this morning. The entire army is on the move and is in command of General Grant. It is reported that we are to effect a junction with General Sherman's army in the rear of Vicksburg.

Saturday, 29th—We started this morning at 6 o'clock and arrived at Holly Springs at 10 o'clock. We remained there about two hours and then moved on to Waterford, eight miles distant, where we went into camp. We drove the rebels before us nearly all day and there was some skirmishing. The fighting in the streets of Waterford was sharp and the buildings were burned. There was heavy cannonading in the front late in the day. There are thousands of negroes, women and children, of all shades of color gathered at Holly Springs. The roads by which we marched were lined with them. The best of the negro men have been taken South by the rebels to work on their fortifications.

Sunday, 30th—We lay in camp here at Waterford all day and I wrote a letter to John Moore. I was on picket last night, but was relieved this morning. There was some skirmishing and cannonading out on the Tallahatchie river today. Several troops passed here going out to the front. The land in this part of the country is very rough and very poor. The soil is sandy and is easily worked.

DECEMBER, 1862.

Monday, 1st—We lay at this place, Waterford, until about 6 o'clock in the evening, when we struck our tents and started on a night march.

Tuesday, 2d—We marched ten miles last night and then went into bivouac for the rest of the night. The rebels are falling back without much resistance. We left our bivouac at 10 o'clock this morning, crossed the Tallahatchie river over the railroad bridge and after marching four miles, went into camp. We are near the town of Abbeville, where the rebels were strongly fortified. They deserted the place early yesterday morning after burning the station, but left large quantities of their supplies which they could not move before they had to flee. After they had crossed the bridge, which is a mile long, they set fire to it, but it failed to burn. Our cavalry is after them today and have taken several prisoners. It rained all day today.

Wednesday, 3d—It rained all night, but the weather is rather cold. We moved our camp today and set it up again in a deserted camp, one mile from Abbeville, which the rebels had built for winter quarters.

Thursday, 4th—Our entire company went out on picket duty this morning with the orders to keep a sharp lookout for rebels. The sentinels out on the front are ordered to stand in secluded places, as they are in danger of being picked off by the rebel sharpshooters. It rained all day again.

Friday, 5th—The rain continued all night. We were relieved from picket this morning about 9 o'clock. Troops are passing to the front and there is some heavy cannonading in that direction.

Saturday, 6th—I was on duty today with a foraging party of our division, to help load the wagons with corn and cotton. We brought in seventy-five loads of cotton worth about $40,000. At one plantation some negroes were out at work picking cotton, while others were baling it in the gin houses, but we drove into the houses and loaded up without asking for the privilege. The Sixth Division almost every day brings in from seventy-five to one hundred loads of corn or cotton. This part of the state is thickly settled and the settlements are rich, there being a great deal of corn and cotton.

Sunday, 7th—No news of importance. The weather is getting quite cool. The chaplain of our regiment is not with us at present and we have no preaching on Sundays, though we have prayer meeting in the evening. We had regular company inspection this evening. Our guard and picket duties are light at this place.

Monday, 8th—The Sixth Division is running a mill now, the quartermaster having taken possession of a grist mill which he is running day and night. We are now drawing full rations of meal instead of crackers and we have plenty of fresh pork and sweet potatoes. The boys have confiscated every bake oven in the country; each company has from three to five, and by keeping them hot all day we bake all the corn bread needed. We all appreciate full rations after our fast at Grand Junction.

(December, 1862)

Tuesday, 9th—No news of importance. Our foraging parties destroy a great deal of property unnecessarily, especially when the owner of a plantation is away with the rebel army—then there isn't much left when the boys get through.

Wednesday, 10th—Our troops are still moving out to the front. It is fine weather for marching. There is very little sickness among the men now.

Thursday, 11th—I was on the picket line again today. Picket duty is less dangerous now than it was, as the rebels have fallen back. We maintain a brigade guard at this camp.

Friday, 12th—Nothing of importance. I was relieved from picket this morning. New regiments from the North are arriving and passing out to the front to hear their first roar of cannon.

Saturday, 13th—I was on duty again today, going out with about two hundred men from our division to bring corn. We got one hundred loads, and although it was not a good day for snapping corn, yet the corn being quite good it did not take long to fill a wagon.

Sunday, 14th—No news of importance. We had company inspection as usual on Sunday morning. There are no foraging parties sent out on Sundays, but brigade and picket duty are performed every day and night.

Monday, 15th—The railroad bridge across the Tallahatchie river is repaired now, and the first train came through today. The cars can run as far as Oxford now. The quartermaster of our division has brought together at this place about $1,000,000.00 worth of cotton, which is to be shipped to the North.

Tuesday, 16th—The Sixth Division received orders to be ready to march in the morning. We have been in the rear of the army and we are now to move forward. The railroad being in operation now, it is said that our base of supplies will be moved forward and established at Holly Springs, Mississippi.

Wednesday, 17th—We struck our tents this morning and at 10 o'clock started toward Oxford. We went into bivouac for the night within four miles of the town. The weather is fine for marching and we have good roads.

Thursday, 18th—We started at 6 o'clock this morning and arrived in Oxford at about 10. We were inspected by General

(December, 1862)

Grant, passing through the town by platoon. We marched on eight miles out from town and went into camp along the railroad. Grant has his headquarters in Oxford. It is a fine town, on high ground and well built up with fine homes of the rich planters. A college is located here, with good buildings.[1] The surrounding plantations are well fenced and have good buildings.

Friday, 19th—The boys worked all day setting up their tents. The boys of our company cut down a red oak tree from which we made staves, set them in trenches dug in the ground, and had just finished putting up the tents, when at 5 p. m. the long roll sounded to form in line. We were ordered to march to the station to board the cars for Holly Springs, as the rebels had taken the place and burned our rations. But we did not go, as another regiment nearer the station got there ahead of us and we were marched back to our camp, with orders, though, to be ready to start for Holly Springs in the morning. We had expected to stay here several days and are sorry to have to leave the place, for it would have made us an excellent camp ground, being on a south hillside with timber just thick enough for shelter.

Saturday, 20th—We struck our tents early this morning and marched twenty-one miles back toward Holly Springs. It is a disappointment to have to retrace our steps and the boys are not as jolly as they were when going south. Holly Springs is said to have been taken and our supplies cut off. We have been put on half rations.

Sunday, 21st—We left Abbeville this morning and marched through to Holly Springs, twenty-two miles. It was warm and dusty traveling. We arrived at dark, going into bivouac in the north edge of town, and I tell you the boys made the boards fly, for as the teams had not yet arrived with our tents, we pulled down vacant houses to build bunks and windbreaks to protect us from the cold wind.

Monday, 22d—The rebels before leaving town burned several houses, altogether some two or three squares, besides burning about one million of our rations, and we are again short of food. On that account the boys are not in the best of humor, and every

[1] Our diarist must have seen either the University of Mississippi, opened in 1848, or Union Female College, a Cumberland Presbyterian college, founded in 1854.—Ed.

(December, 1862)

man has practically a free hand to take anything that he can use or that he may want; and there are no officers out looking for corporals to reduce to the ranks as was done on our way south. Any citizen who in any way had aided the Union army found his property set on fire by the rebels under the pretext that it had caught fire from our burning supplies. We received word that we are to stay here until further orders.

Tuesday, 23d—No news of importance. We pitched our tents this morning. I was out on a foraging train for some corn, but we got very little, as this section of the country is pretty well cleaned up. We are now on half rations.

Wednesday, 24th—Nothing of importance. It is quite cold and our extra clothing, underwear, is in storage at La Grange, Tennessee. There is no chance to draw new clothing now.

Thursday, 25th—General Rosecrans's division passed here today on their way to Memphis. This is rather a gloomy, dry Christmas. We are still on half rations. But in spite of it, the boys are all enjoying themselves. They are taking everything that they can lay their hands on, carrying to their tents couches, rockers, chairs, tables, books, bric-a-brac—in fact, all kinds of household articles. Some of the boys, who are lovers of fancy books, sent home by express some of the most costly bound volumes. Holly Springs has certainly paid dear for burning our supplies.

Friday, 26th—The Fourth Division commanded by General Logan passed here today on their way to Memphis. Nearly all of the troops which started on the expedition south have now returned.

Saturday, 27th—Nothing of importance.[1]

---

[1]The days of the latter half of the month of December were the darkest we had seen up to that time and, as it proved, they were the darkest days of the entire Union army during the whole four years of war. Our armies, all along the line, East and West, had not been successful. The second 600,000 men had been called for during the summer, and the loyal men of the North responded nobly, most of them being on the field by December, ready for action. But there was an element in the North holding nightly meetings and declaring that the war was a failure; there was also talk of England's recognizing the Confederacy; then there were discouraging letters from the home folks to the men in the field, for the times were hard and the situation looked very bad to them. They would, in writing to us, ask what we thought of the outlook, and almost to a man, the reply would be that we would push ahead until we were successful, for our loss already had been too great to give up the struggle short of going to the bitter end.—A. G. D.

(December, 1862)

Sunday, 28th—The weather is quite cool. We are pretty hard on clothes in the army. My bill for clothes up to this time is as follows: One overcoat, $7.20; two dress coats, $13.42; four pair pants, $12.12; two pair double woolen blankets, $5.12; three pair drawers, $1.50; two pair shoes, $3.12; three woolen shirts, $2.64; one rubber poncho, $2.73; four pair socks, $1.04; one hat, $1.55; one cap, 60c; one knapsack, $1.56; one haversack, 56c; one canteen, 44c.[1]

Monday, 29th—We had company drill this morning and received orders to be ready to march in the morning. We have been at Holly Springs nine days now, and the town is almost deserted.[2]

Tuesday, 30th—We struck our tents and started at 10 a. m. We reached Coldwater by noon and stopped for our mess. Our colonel must have been cold and in a hurry, for he gave the order, "Front right dress! Stack arms! Break ranks! Get rails and build fires! G— D—!" It amused the boys and they were not long in building fires and preparing hot coffee. At 1 o'clock we left for Moscow, Tennessee, along the railroad, and after a day's march of twenty miles went into bivouac for the night within one mile of town.

Wednesday, 31st—We left our bivouac at 6 a. m. and entered the town of Moscow at 7 and were then ordered to move to Lafayette, Tennessee, on the Memphis & Charleston Railroad thirty-five miles east of Memphis, where we are to guard the railroad. The town is located on the Wolf river and is surrounded by heavy timber.

JANUARY, 1863.

Thursday, 1st—We have become somewhat indifferent about keeping our camp in the best possible order, for we have been disappointed so often in soon having to leave a camp which we took pains to build. We have, however, fairly good bunks in our tents, made of brush and leaves. Our duties are very la-

---

[1] Then there was that leather collar ("dog collar") to make us hold up our heads; it cost fourteen cents, but it was enough and the only one needed during the four years of war.—A. G. D.

[2] When we passed through Holly Springs going south, the town looked very pretty, and no property was destroyed. But when the place was surrendered to Van Dorn by our traitorous colonel in command of the small garrison, and that without the firing of a gun, then it was that destruction followed. When we had to come back to find our stores burned and live on half rations, our men were not in the best of humor; they did not care then if the whole town was destroyed.—A. G. D.

(January, 1863)

borious here, for besides the regular picket duty, we are almost constantly at work repairing the railroad. Today four companies were on picket patrol and at work repairing a railroad bridge. I was on picket duty with the countersign "helmet." The army is on half rations, but we expect more soon, as a provision train came through today from Memphis. The Third Division went to Memphis. The weather is clear and cool.

Friday, 2d—We are now on less than half rations and the outlook for anything better in the next few days is not good, although a train was expected to come through from Memphis today.[1] The railroad east and west from us has been torn up; the rebel cavalry seem to be able to destroy it as fast as we can repair it.

Saturday, 3d—A work train came in from Corinth today, and troops are coming in from the front. It is said they are bound for Memphis where they will take transports down the river, to go into camp just above Vicksburg. The Fifteenth Iowa left camp here and took up quarters down in Lafayette.

Sunday, 4th—I was on picket again today. A work train came in from Memphis, and four trains passed through going to Memphis; but none of them brought provisions, and as our provisions are so low, the division quartermaster sent all the teams to Memphis to bring provisions.

Monday, 5th—A report came to camp that the forces under Sherman made an unsuccessful attack upon Vicksburg.[2] We are shut out of communications now as well as of provisions; we have had no mail for a month.

Tuesday, 6th—We received a large mail today, coming through from Memphis, and it is quite jolly in camp. Besides this, our teams returned from Memphis with loads of provisions, and we hope soon to have something more to eat. A report was circulated in camp today that peace had been declared, but no one takes the report very seriously.

Wednesday, 7th—The quartermaster placed a strong guard around the corral where the provision wagons were parked last night. But some of the boys of my company and of Company

[1] The train the day before did not have provisions.—A. G. D.

[2] They failed because of the strong fortifications and the fact that Grant failed to make his attack in the rear of Vicksburg at the same time, as planned.—A. G. D.

K were determined to have something to eat without waiting on the slowly-moving formalities. They slipped through the guard line in the night to the wagons and succeeded in getting away well loaded, having secured a small chest of tea and two boxes of crackers, which they divided among the boys of the two companies before daylight. Expecting Van Dorn's cavalry to make a dash into town today, we formed a line of battle at 2 o'clock and awaited the attack. But no cavalry appeared, and in the evening all our teams with a strong guard were sent out to forage corn and fodder.

Thursday, 8th—Although it is now quite warm, we are still waiting for our knapsacks containing our underwear which were stored at La Grange, but we were again disappointed in not getting them today as expected. Our boys have never been so bent on foraging as they have since going into camp here. Last night a squad of boys from Company K were out looking for whatever they could find, but apparently with little success, until returning to camp they passed by the camp of the Sixteenth Iowa, where they noticed two dressed hogs hanging up to cool during the night. What did they do but deliberately walk up and carry off one of the carcasses to their own camp! They immediately cut up the meat, put it into kettles over fires, cooked it, and divided it among the boys of their company, all before daylight. This morning when a squad of the boys of the Sixteenth Iowa walked along our regimental camp in quest of that missing hog, they did not see even a sign of meat, bone or campfire embers.

Friday, 9th—It is reported in camp that we are soon to go to Memphis for duty. Several cases of smallpox have broken out in the camp of the Sixteenth Iowa Regiment. All who had not been vaccinated before had to take their medicine. The country along the Charleston & Memphis Railroad from Memphis to Iuka, a distance of about one hundred miles, and for some miles on either side of the line where our armies are in camp and on the march, has been laid waste and is almost desolate. The men are desperate enough for anything. Vacant houses on plantations or in towns and villages have been burned. Many of these were substantial buildings with stone chimneys, which generally remained standing after the burnings. These the boys hilariously spoke of as headstones and on passing them would call

(January, 1863)

out: "Here stands another Tennessee headstone," or a "Mississippi headstone," as the case might be.

Saturday, 10th—Two trains loaded with provisions came through on the railroad from Memphis, and we drew five days' full rations. This was the first time that we drew full rations in forty days, but we have no way of drawing extra clothing, and our knapsacks in storage again failed to come today. The First Brigade passed by on its way to Memphis.

Sunday, 11th—We received orders to be ready to march early in the morning for Memphis. The report in camp is that we are to go on down the Mississippi river. The Fourth Brigade of the Third Division came in at 5 o'clock in the evening and relieved our brigade. A detail from the Eighty-first Illinois Infantry furnished the picket guards to relieve our post where I was on guard with Corporal McBirney and Privates John Esher and George Eicher, all of my company. We are all glad to leave this place, as it is low, damp and unhealthy, which with the smallpox makes it a bad camp.

Chapter X.
The Vicksburg Campaign. Siege and Surrender of Vicksburg.
January 12-July 4.

Monday, 12th—We struck tent early this morning and at 8 o'clock took up the line of march, the entire Sixth Division being on the road bound for Memphis. Companies E and K are on rear guard. The day being fairly warm and quite pleasant, we covered twenty miles without incident, and bivouacked for the night within nine miles of Memphis.

Tuesday, 13th—We left bivouac this morning at 6 o'clock and moved on to within a mile of Memphis, where we went into camp. The day was cloudy, threatening rain, and by evening had turned quite cool, with a high wind blowing. The ground being very rough here, the setting up of our tents was pretty slow work.

Wednesday, 14th—It rained all night and much of the day. Our tents failed to turn the water, as the strong wind blowing literally drove the rain through the canvas, making it as wet where we lay as on the outside. There is no hay or straw to lie on at night and no lumber to be had for floors, but the quartermaster is providing us with plenty of cordwood, and having the Sibley tents we build fires in the center of them to warm ourselves and dry our clothes. A great many of the boys got permission to go down town to spend the night. We signed the payrolls for two months' pay and were expecting to receive our pay today, but for some reason it failed to come.

Thursday, 15th—It turned cold during the night and the rain of yesterday turned into snow which continued all day. Our camp is in a frightful condition, there being six inches of snow on mud a foot deep. Half the men of the Sixth Division go into town over night. The Eleventh Iowa received two months' pay this afternoon, and now only a few of us remain in camp, the most of the boys putting up in the city instead. We are expecting any moment to receive orders to break camp here.

Friday, 16th—The snow continued today with a high wind. I loaned Lieutenant Spencer $15.00.[1] I went to the city today

---
[1] Mr. Downing informs me that, as was the common practice, this loan was evidenced only by a verbal contract.—Ed.

(January, 1863)

to purchase some supplies, spending in all $1.00. This evening we received our long-looked-for knapsacks with our extra underwear, which was quite welcome. Those of us who were not fortunate enough to secure extra underclothes when at Holly Springs, as some did, were obliged to wear one undersuit for forty-nine days without changing. When we now cast them aside, some of the boys declared that there was almost enough life in their clothes to walk.

Saturday, 17th—It was cold and stormy all day. I spent the day down in the city, and bought a few more necessary articles—spent $1.25. Five hundred rebel prisoners passed up the river today, being taken to a Northern prison. This evening we got orders to be ready to leave.

Sunday, 18th—Bright sunshine, with cold northwest wind blowing. We struck our tents early this morning, loaded the wagons, and started for the river. Upon reaching the city commons, on a high bluff overlooking the landing, we stacked arms and remained there in the mud all day. About dark we were ordered to go aboard the transports. Our regiment with two others, the Eighteenth Wisconsin and the Ninety-fifth Illinois, together with a part of the Second Iowa Battery, embarked on the Marie Deming, where we bunk tonight.

Monday, 19th—We worked all day loading our supplies on the transports. The Ninety-fifth Illinois finished their loading today and are now lying in waiting. The river is quite wide here, one and one-half miles, and is fast rising. There are four mortar boats and one gunboat here, besides a large fleet of transports, some of which are loaded with troops to go down the river, while others are coming from the North with fresh troops. The rebel gunboat, "General Bragg," has just been captured here.

Tuesday, 20th—Another cold, wet day. We completed loading our regimental supplies about noon, and at 4 o'clock started for Vicksburg. We tied up for the night about forty miles below Memphis. The boats are overcrowded, and because of the cold weather there is much suffering.[1]

[1] Starting on this trip ended seventy-nine days of campaigning in northern Mississippi and western Tennessee. For suffering from exposure, part of the time no tents at night, nearly all the time on half rations or less, for forty-nine days no change of clothing, and more than sixty cloudy days with rain or snow, this campaign proved to be one of the most laborious campaigns during our four years' service.—A. G. D.

(January, 1863)

Wednesday, 21st—The weather continues cold. At daylight our fleet started on down the river, reaching Helena, Arkansas, at 10 o'clock. We left Helena at noon with thirteen transports loaded with troops and tied up for the night sixty miles below. The transports dare not run at night on account of being fired upon by the rebels from the banks of the river. They fire on us even on the day run, but before we can get our boats to the banks to give them chase, they are gone and out of sight.

Thursday, 22d—Today we enjoyed the first warm, clear day for more than two weeks, the snow having entirely disappeared. Our fleet continued all day without a stop. We met the White river expedition returning to Memphis from Napoleon, Arkansas. We tied up for the night about one hundred miles above Vicksburg.

Friday, 23d—We continued our journey again at daylight and by evening reached a point about ten miles above Vicksburg, where we drove our fleet ashore and remained on the boats all night. Fully seventy-five boats loaded with troops are assembled here, while the fleet of gunboats is lying in the river two miles below us. The country is very low here, the land on either side of the river being about twenty feet below the water in the river, which is kept within its banks by levees. The river is rising, and about three miles below us the levee on the Louisiana side has broken, and the land is being flooded.

Saturday, 24th—We had some rain early this morning, followed by a heavy fog which lasted all day. Boats loaded with troops are constantly arriving and landing at different points along the river where the men are going into camp. Some of our boys are quite sick, the result of using the river water on the way down. Accidents are not common here considering the large number of men crowding as they do, but today a private of the First Kansas Infantry fell from the boat and was drowned before help could reach him.

Sunday, 25th—We moved up the river today about a mile and disembarked on the Louisiana side, going into camp right on the bank. We are from ten to fifteen feet below the water in the river, while the levee is twenty-five or thirty feet higher than our camp. Company E was to go on picket, but the order was countermanded, and then at dark a detail of one thousand men, I being

(January, 1863)

one, from our division, was chosen to go down the river to work on the canal which is being cut across the point of land opposite Vicksburg. It is a fearful mudhole to work in. A large number of negroes are put on the job. The rebels try to shell the place, but their shells all fall short.

Monday, 26th—Today I was one of a detail of two thousand men sent down the river a few miles to repair the break in the levee on the west bank of the river. The break is two hundred feet wide and the water rushes through with terrible force. I was glad when the order came to return to camp, for I would rather risk my life in a battle than to work another day on that break. An increasing number of men still lying in the boats are getting sick from drinking the poor river water; the new recruits just arriving from the North are especially affected.

Tuesday, 27th—Wood for fuel is becoming very scarce in camp, and also on the transports. The Thirteenth Iowa, with thirty of us from my regiment, were detailed to go with the transports up the river for wood. We reached the woodyard about thirty miles up the river at dark and Company C of the Thirteenth Iowa was detailed for picket. There are six thousand cords of wood piled up here.

Wednesday, 28th—We had ten or twelve teams at work all day hauling wood to the boats. I worked till noon with the detail of men hauling wood and loading the transports, while the other detail was on picket. In the afternoon our detail was on picket and the others completed the loading. We were called in from picket at sundown and with all on board the transports started on the return trip, reaching our camp a little before midnight.

Thursday, 29th—We have plenty of wood now. At about 2 o'clock this afternoon a brisk fire opened between our men and the rebels. We have not yet heard what was the cause of it.[1] A scouting party seventeen miles out from the city had a skirmish with the rebel cavalry, but there were no losses outside of several horses. A report came into camp that Port Hudson has been taken by our forces.

Friday, 30th—Everything is quiet today. It came my turn to

[1]This was down at Vicksburg, where there was some heavy cannonading between our gunboats and the Confederate batteries.—A. G. D.

go on duty. Another gunboat came down the river today. General McArthur moved his headquarters from the boat, lying here in the river, out into a plantation house nearby. Things are very expensive here; butter is fifty cents a pound and cheese is forty cents.

Saturday, 31st—A scouting party of about two hundred men mounted on horses and mules, and carrying one piece of light artillery, came upon a rebel camp some eighteen miles out and engaged in a fierce fight. After standing their ground for two hours the rebels left for the tall timber. They left their supplies to our men, who burned all that they could not bring with them, and returned to camp with only five or six men wounded, bringing one lone prisoner.

FEBRUARY, 1863.

Sunday, 1st—We had an all day rain and the river is rising; the bottom land on the east side of the river is already under water. It came my turn to go on fatigue today. A detail of four hundred men was again sent down to work on the break in the levee. Our chaplain preached to the regiment this afternoon.

Monday, 2d—An exciting time down at Vicksburg last night was reported in camp this morning. One of our gunboats ran the blockade and while passing their batteries, the rebels fired exactly one hundred and thirty shots at her, but did not hurt her. Our gunboats blew up one of the rebels' steamers which was tied at the wharf just below the city, and then ran another battery below without being hurt.

Tuesday, 3d—Cloudy and cold. The levee is the only thing of interest and importance. We are still at work on the levee, but the water is almost to the top now, and it is breaking at so many points that the land on both sides of the river is being flooded. Our camps will have to be moved to higher ground farther from the river. Some of the camps are already being moved. I bought a supply of bread today for a dollar.

Wednesday, 4th—Rain all day, and the whole country is being flooded over. General Grant has sent five or six expeditions along the river to find some way to move the army on to higher ground in the rear of Vicksburg, and also to solve the problem of getting our fleet and gunboats past the rebels' batteries with-

(February, 1863)

out running the risk of having them destroyed. I wrote a letter to John D. Moore, Inland, Iowa.

Thursday, 5th—Weather pleasant. I was detailed to go out on picket, but the order was countermanded. There is some talk of our leaving the place. It is reported in camp that on account of the flood the work on the canal had to be given up, and that an effort would be made to turn the current of the river through the canal, thus letting the river cut it.

Friday, 6th—We hear that we are to move up the river to an island where General McPherson's command is. About one hundred transports with troops aboard are tied up along the levee on the Louisiana side, awaiting orders to go up the river, while still others are being loaded. The plan is to go into camp at different points to do garrison duty, making it safer for fleets to pass at certain points.

Saturday, 7th—While waiting for orders, I went down to a daguerreotype gallery[1] and had my likeness taken. The water is still rising and the report in camp is that our division is to proceed up the river to Lake Providence, Louisiana, and cut the levee to let the water of the Mississippi through to the lake from which it would be carried into the Red river.

Sunday, 8th—Orders came for the detail of men to quit the work of repairing the levee and for our entire division immediately to embark on the transports. The Eleventh and Thirteenth Regiments went on board the "Empress" and loaded all their supplies after night; at the last moment the Tenth Ohio was ordered to take passage with us.

Monday, 9th—We left for Lake Providence, seventy-five miles above Vicksburg, at 10 o'clock this morning, and reached our destination at dark. There were six transports and one gunboat in our fleet. We found the First Brigade of our division already here and at work cutting the levee.

Tuesday, 10th—This is a clear, warm day. We disembarked early this morning and marching out about one mile from the river to Sparrow's plantation, we pitched our tents on the large lawn of the plantation house, bordering the lake. Mr. Sparrow, the owner, is a congressman in the rebel congress, and he and his family having gone away, left their negroes in charge of the

[1] Among the numerous "camp-followers" was also to be found the picture man.—Ed.

plantation. Our colonel has established his headquarters in the plantation house. The First Kansas out on scout duty today got into a skirmish with the rebels and lost two men killed and eight wounded.

Wednesday, 11th—A large detail from our brigade began work on the canal from the Mississippi river to Lake Providence. About three hundred negroes are working on it. The canal is being cut twenty rods wide and when completed will be three-quarters of a mile long with a fall of twenty feet. I paid out thirty cents for some necessary articles, and also loaned thirty cents to Clark.

Thursday, 12th—A dreadful rain during the night flooded our beautiful camp on Sparrow's lawn. The ground being so nearly level, it will take some time for the water to run off. It cleared off in the afternoon and it is nice and warm. The grass and trees are beginning to look green; peach trees are in full bloom. I wrote a letter to brother John.

Friday, 13th—The mail today brought me a letter from Jason Sparks and the monotony of camp duties was broken with good news from home. The weather is quite warm and we no longer need fires in our tents. Things are growing very fast and the farmers in this locality are planting their corn.

Saturday, 14th—A heavy rain all night stopped our digging for a time, and the fatigue party did not begin work on the canal until 1 o'clock in the afternoon. It is terribly muddy and the water hinders our digging; we wheeled out more water than mud. The following strange epitaph I noticed on a tombstone in a cemetery located in a grove near the town of Lake Providence:

> "Remember man, as you pass by,
> As you are now, so once was I,
> As I now am, so you must be,
> Prepare for death and follow me."

Sunday, 15th—We had another all night rain, which again stopped work on the canal. We moved our tents a little distance, to get out of the mud, going onto higher ground, closer to the lake. We are still in the plantation lawn, however, which comprises about twenty acres and has a great variety of shrubbery and tropical trees.

(February, 1863)

Monday, 16th—It rained all night and some today. Our canvas tents are no good in shedding water. I was on guard today, but on account of the heavy rain and high wind all the guards were taken off duty.

Tuesday, 17th—Another all night rain, which continued all day today. Our camp is again becoming very muddy. Company E went on picket duty today. Our camp guard has been taken off.

Wednesday, 18th—We came in from picket this morning. The day is warm but cloudy. News came that another one of our gunboats accompanying a barge loaded with hay ran the blockade at Vicksburg.

Thursday, 19th—I was off duty today and went to town to have my likeness taken.[1]

We now have five hundred negroes at work cutting the levee at Lake Providence, and Captain Elrod of the Thirteenth Iowa has about one hundred negroes at work picking cotton—last year's crop left in the field.

Friday, 20th—There is some talk of our having to move our camp again. News came that our gunboats were throwing shells into Vicksburg, one every fifteen minutes, driving the rebels back, and that our mortar boats were damaging some of their water batteries.

Saturday, 21st—Yesterday was clear and warm, but today it rained all day. We have had full rations ever since leaving Memphis. Today we received eight days' rations with an extra ration of desiccated potatoes. Orders came to clean up for inspection.

Sunday, 22d—Dress parade was dispensed with today on account of the smallpox scare. One case of smallpox was discovered in Company K. Instead of the regular inspection, the doctor vaccinated all who could not show a scar less than a year old.

Monday, 23d—General Logan's division arrived today, accompanied by the Seventeenth Engineers' Corps with pontoon bridges.

---

[1] Upon inquiring of Mr. Downing how he came to have his "likeness" taken twice so close together (see Feb. 7), he laughingly confessed that it was not because the first was not a good picture, but because it was not a proper picture. Said he, "To tell the truth, I had it taken dressed in a major's uniform, and it wouldn't have been safe to let it be seen." He destroyed it and had another taken.—Ed.

(February, 1863)

They bring the news that our men are still throwing shells into Vicksburg, and that the rebels are vacating the place. Our quartermaster went out into the country with the teams and brought in nineteen loads of cotton.

Tuesday, 24th—There was quite a fire today in the town of Lake Providence, burning several vacant houses. In the excitement our men found two rebel flags. The Eleventh and Thirteenth Iowa received orders to embark with three days' rations, and taking passage on the "Marie Deming" left for Greenville, about sixty-five miles up the river, to reinforce the brigade there.

Wednesday, 25th—We arrived at Greenville at 9 o'clock in the morning and reported to the commander of the post, who informed us that he did not need reinforcements. He had just defeated a force of three hundred with a battery of six light guns and lost but three men. We remained, however, during the day, leaving for our camp down the river at 10 o'clock at night.

Thursday, 26th—We reached our camp this forenoon in a rain which continued all day. General Quimby's division just went into camp here, from up the river. The regimental quartermasters are bringing in large quantities of cotton every day.

Friday, 27th—We received orders to clean up for general inspection. Captain Beach of Company H of the Eleventh Iowa having been appointed to go after and bring back any deserters from our brigade, left for Iowa to get all such found in the State.

Saturday, 28th—Our regiment was mustered for pay at 9 o'clock this morning, and at 10 o'clock we had general inspection with all accouterments on, by the inspector general of the Seventeenth Army Corps, General William E. Strong.[1] I got an order today from the captain on the sutler for $1.50.

[1] Iowa may well be proud of the Third Brigade of the Sixth Division, Col. M. M. Crocker commanding. It is composed of the following troops, viz.: The Eleventh, Thirteenth, Fifteenth and Sixteenth Iowa Infantry. It turned out for inspection 1,935 rank and file. * * * Since I have been a soldier, it has so happened that I have seen many brigades of many different army corps, both in the Eastern and Western armies, but never have I seen a brigade that could compete with this Iowa brigade. I am not prejudiced in the slightest degree. I never saw any of the officers or soldiers of the command until the day when I saw them in line of battle prepared for inspection. * * * I cannot say that any one regiment of the brigade appeared better than another—they all appeared so well. The Eleventh was the strongest. It had 528 enlisted men and 20 officers present for duty, the Thirteenth 470 enlisted men and 22 officers, the Fifteenth 428 men and 29 officers, the Sixteenth 405 men and 33 officers. In the entire brigade there was not to exceed a dozen men unable to be present for inspection.—Roster of Iowa Soldiers, Infantry, Vol. II, p. 279.

MARCH, 1863.

Sunday, 1st—We had regimental inspection by the colonel at 2 o'clock, and our regiment showed itself in good trim. Boats are passing daily, loaded with troops for Vicksburg. I was on camp guard and the evening seemed to be very long and lonesome. It put me in mind of the long evenings just before the battle of Shiloh, and I thought how soon there might be another such a battle.

Monday, 2d—Being off duty I got a pass this afternoon and went to town. The quartermaster drew wedge tents for the regiment and clothing for some of the men. I drew a new haversack costing fifty-six cents. Our army is in good condition in equipment, provisions, clothing and munitions of war, and the health of the men is good with the exception of the new regiments, in which there are many sick. The work on the canal continues, with about a week's work to complete it; we still have the large force of negroes on the job.

Tuesday, 3d—Everything is quiet. I went down town again this afternoon. Our men have pulled a steam tug up on the bank and the engineers have a force of a thousand men re-calking it.

Wednesday, 4th—The engineers finished calking the steam tug and with ropes attached to it some five or six thousand men succeeded in pulling it overland to the lake where it is to be launched. I crossed the lake in a skiff to the south side to buy some notions of a sutler with the Fourth Division. Among other articles, I purchased a diary for seventy-five cents, for the purpose of keeping a record of my army life. We were ordered to prepare for inspection.

Thursday, 5th—We had regimental and camp inspection this morning at 10 o'clock, conducted by a major of General McPherson's staff. We came out in splendid order. The officers of the Eleventh Iowa met at 6 o'clock this evening to draw up resolutions demanding the hunting down of all Copperheads in the North. The steam tug was started on the lake today to inspect and make sure of the outlets from Providence Lake through the Tensas river to the Red river. These outlets must all be open before we let the water into the lake.

Friday, 6th—I was detailed to go on picket with Company D. Had quite a thunderstorm this evening.

(March, 1863)

Saturday, 7th—It is quite showery and things are growing fine. Farmers throughout here are putting into corn most all the land that is not flooded. There are few white men here and most of the able-bodied negro men are forming companies and regiments for the army of the North, to be under white officers.

Sunday, 8th—Company E went on picket this morning. Had a fearful hailstorm late this evening.

Monday, 9th—We were relieved from picket at 9 o'clock this morning. The Thirteenth Iowa had battalion drill this afternoon. Hear some heavy cannonading in the direction of Vicksburg.

Tuesday, 10th—We heard again that Port Hudson was taken, and also that Rosecrans had a battle, but can learn nothing definite. A squad from our regiment mounted on mules and horses had an exciting experience while out scouting, about twelve miles from camp. Seeing some chickens in the yard of a farm house, they thought they might as well get a few to take along with them. When some of the boys, dismounting, entered the yard to catch the chickens, they were met by the woman of the house with a bucket of scalding hot water and they had a hard time trying to keep out of her way. Some of the boys got a touch of the hot water, but they caught their chickens.

Wednesday, 11th—All is quiet. The commissioned officers of our brigade had a meeting at brigade headquarters for the purpose of considering ways and means for arming the colored men, since they have been declared free. The plan is to put them under good officers for garrison service, thus relieving that number of men for the more important places in the front. They also passed resolutions calling upon the loyal people of the North to put down those at home who are opposing the prosecution of the war; if need be they would use force by calling for soldiers from the front. The men at the front feel that this opposition to war at home is helping to prolong the war, by encouraging the rebels.

Thursday, 12th—The Eleventh Iowa received two months' pay, I receiving $26.00. We commenced to cut the levee today, but shortly after we got started the order was countermanded.

Friday, 13th—The weather is quite pleasant and all is quiet. There is nothing of importance.

(March, 1863)

Saturday, 14th—I was on guard at Colonel Crocker's headquarters in the old Sparrow house and had a fine room to stay in over night. The Sixteenth Iowa got two months' pay today. Major Wilson of the Thirteenth Iowa left today for his home in Iowa on a thirty-day furlough, and I sent $35.00 home by him. The weather is quite warm.

Sunday, 15th—We had an all day rain. I was relieved from guard at 9 o'clock a. m. We see very little of our chaplain at this camp, for he is seldom here and we have no one to occupy the regimental pulpit. Two brigades of General Quimby's Division boarded the transports and left today for Vicksburg.

Monday, 16th—The Eleventh Iowa turned their old Sibley tents over to the quartermaster and drew wedge tents in their stead. They finished cutting the levee today and let the water through from the river to the lake. The roar of the water rushing through the canal can be heard a mile.

Tuesday, 17th—The Third Brigade got orders to drill four hours today. Three transports went up the river today. The water in the lake is rapidly rising since the canal is cut through and our regimental camp along the edge of the lake will, in a few days, have to be moved to higher ground.

Wednesday, 18th—We now have company drill four hours a day. The fatigue duty at this camp has not been very laborious, as the officers put negroes to work, very few of our men working any toward the last. The lake is still rising and already overflowing the bottom land at places. We are expecting to receive orders to leave soon. The weather is warm, the trees are all leafed out, and everything is growing fine.

Thursday, 19th—I was again on duty today. Company drill at 9 o'clock and battalion drill at 2 o'clock. The troops which were in camp at the south side of the lake are on the move, going aboard transports to go down the river to find higher camping ground.

Friday, 20th—Nothing of importance today. We have drill twice a day. I received a pass and went to Lake Providence. The water is already in the streets and the army sutlers occupying vacant buildings will have to move out tomorrow. I purchased a tin plate and spoon for thirty cents.

(March, 1863)

Saturday, 21st—The Eleventh Iowa received new guns, the Enfield rifle, and everyone is pleased with the exchange. Receiving orders to move camp, we struck our tents at 3 o'clock p. m. and moved two miles and went into camp in a cottonfield close by the levee just above the town of Lake Providence. On account of the flooding waters we had to travel a distance of four miles to reach the point. General Logan's Division moved up the river about four miles.

Sunday, 22d—I worked all day setting up our tent, my two tent mates being on duty. General Logan's Division started for Vicksburg today. It commenced to rain this evening.

Monday, 23d—It rained nearly all day and our new camp has become very muddy. Today I read the two books of Chronicles in the Bible, sixty-five chapters in all. Our picket duty here is very light at present.

Tuesday, 24th—It rained all night and day, and our camp is almost covered with water. The report in camp is that we will go down the river in a day or two.

Wednesday, 25th—A division of troops passed our camp going down the river, while General Logan's Division came back again going on up the river.

Thursday, 26th—It is very warm and pleasant, and the mud is drying up fast. We have no need for camp guards at this camp. We drew six days' rations. The Eleventh and Fifteenth Iowa Regiments received orders to move at once down the river. We immediately struck our tents and by 10 o'clock p. m. were on board the "Superior" with all the quartermaster's supplies, but the boat is to lie here all night. Everything seems to point to a movement upon Vicksburg, and the report is that the fleet, protected by the gunboats, will have to run the blockade, while the troops will have to move by land through Louisiana and cross the river below Vicksburg.

Friday, 27th—We started down the river at daylight this morning and landed about three miles below Lake Providence. We pitched our tents on the lawn of a fine plantation, some distance from the house. We found plenty of boards with which to build our bunks. We are situated about ten feet lower than the water in the river, but the levee is strong here, being well sodded over. Our camp is in the open, unprotected by shade trees. On

(March, 1863)

coming down the river we saw our camp ground on the Sparrow plantation all flooded over, and the country as far as we could see was under water. The town of Lake Providence looked desolate with the houses standing in the water.

Saturday, 28th—No new developments today. We had orders to clean up for inspection. I went to the commissary headquarters and drew a hat and a blouse, costing $4.78.

Sunday, 29th—We had a heavy rainstorm last night, blowing down several tents. Today it is quite rainy with a cool wind blowing. Being off duty today I remained in camp and read through the Book of Psalms.

Monday, 30th—A cool wind again today. Several boats loaded with troops went down the river today bound for the vicinity of Vicksburg. I am in hopes that they will do something.

Tuesday, 31st—Warm and pleasant today. More troops passed down the river. I commenced cooking for the captain and officers of our company.[1] I was considered a pretty good cook at home, but having so few utensils here, I fear there will be quite a contrast.

APRIL, 1863.

Wednesday, 1st—It continues warm and pleasant. All is quiet. I went up town to the division quartermaster to buy provisions for the officers, the captain giving me the money with the order to purchase ten days' provisions. When I returned the captain noticed among the items of the bill "20 lbs. codfish," and exclaimed, "Why, Alexander, what in thunder are you going to do with salty codfish? You have enough to do the whole company, and there are but three of us!"[2]

Thursday, 2d—Weather warm and pleasant. No news.

Friday, 3d—The Eleventh Iowa signed the pay rolls for four months' pay. Boats loaded with troops are passing down the river every hour of the day. Our entire division is again drilling four hours a day. We have a fine drill ground.

---

[1] It seems that Private Downing was to get $5.00 per month as cook. See the entry for May 2d.—Ed.

[2] There was some suspicion that the codfish deal was some April Fool business, but I declare that it was all done in dead earnest. But I began to figure that it was a pretty large ration of codfish for ten days and the matter having been noised about, I was not very careful to lock the codfish in the mess chest. The boys soon found out where they could find codfish after night, and at the end of a week it had all disappeared. I was thankful.—A. G. D.

(April, 1863)

Saturday, 4th—Nothing of importance. The weather is getting very warm, but it is pleasant. I wrote another letter to Jason Sparks.

Sunday, 5th—We had company inspection at 10 o'clock this morning and regimental inspection at 5 p. m. I did not go out on inspection, having to prepare an elaborate dinner (some of that codfish), and after dinner I had a good many dishes to wash —tin plates, cups and knives and forks. I read the following chapters today: Isaiah, ninth chapter, second to the eighth verse; Psalms, twenty-second chapter.

Monday, 6th—Four loads of sanitary goods from Iowa were landed today for the Eleventh Iowa. Colonel Hall arrived this morning from home and the boys were glad to see him. One year ago today he commanded the Eleventh Iowa at the battle of Shiloh. The boys are all in fine spirits. The Sixteenth Iowa received their pay today. It is reported that our cutting of the levee at Lake Providence will prove of no avail, as the channel of the Tensas river is so narrow, and it is impossible to cut out the big overhanging trees, so as to make it wide enough for a fleet to pass through. The project will have to be given up as impracticable.

Tuesday, 7th—The sanitary goods were issued to the different companies of the regiment today; the boys are pleased with the many good things that came from Iowa. Received orders to clean up for inspection.

Wednesday, 8th—General Townsend, of General Halleck's staff, from Washington, D. C., made a speech to the Sixth Division of the Seventeenth Army Corps today, on the question of arming the colored men. He urged loyal men to accept commissions as officers in colored regiments. General McArthur, commander of our division, spoke also, and the boys cheered them a great deal. Steps were taken to raise two regiments of colored troops at this place and give them arms. The Fifteenth Iowa received their pay today.

Thursday, 9th—The Eleventh Iowa received four months' pay today, I receiving $3.00 a month here and father drawing $10.00 a month at home. The boys of our regiment send a large amount of their money home every pay day.

(April, 1863)

Friday, 10th—William Mills, secretary to the president of the Sanitary Commission of Iowa, visited our regiment today. He is down here among the different Iowa regiments distributing the sanitary goods donated by the loyal people of the State. The health of the Eleventh Iowa is very good, and the boys are feeling fine. Our regiment reports five hundred and twenty men for duty.

Saturday, 11th—The Eighth Iowa passed down the river today. We had no drill this afternoon, but were ordered to clean up for inspection. April has been warm and pleasant every day, but today we had a high wind.

Sunday, 12th—Eight gunboats went down the river today. The boys feel quite lively and are anxious to get into action again. We had company inspection in the morning and regimental inspection in the afternoon, with dress parade at 5 o'clock. Some of the men of our regiment were caught in a trap today. They went up into a pigeon house a short distance from camp and were having a game of "chuck luck" when someone informed the officer of the day, who took some guards, surrounded the house, entered and made a quick dive for the rubber poncho, taking all the money lying on the figures, almost $200, and arresting all the participants. He put the fellows in the guardhouse and turned over the money to the hospital steward.

Monday, 13th—Our nice weather was broken today by an all day rain. A large number of transports loaded with troops went down the river; the Twenty-fourth Iowa was on board. I went down to the sutler in the Fifteenth Iowa camp and bought a bushel of potatoes, paying $2.50.

Tuesday, 14th—Another rainy day. I went to town two miles up the river this morning in a canoe, with the cook of Company K (I am taking cooking lessons from him) to buy provisions. I bought ten pounds of ham and other things for $3.95. I wrote a letter home to Albert Downing and enclosed $10.00 in it. General Quimby's Division landed at Lake Providence this afternoon. It is reported that the expedition that was trying to find a way to get the army past Haines's Bluff on the Yazoo river has been forced to give it up on account of the floods. The river is flooded for a hundred miles up from the mouth, and four miles on either side. It is thought that they will have to run the fleet past the batteries at Vicksburg and march the army down the Louisiana side and then across the river on high ground below Vicksburg.

Wednesday, 15th—General Quimby's Division passed on down the river today, and another large fleet of boats loaded with troops passed us for Vicksburg. It is thought that Vicksburg will soon be attacked. Things seem quite lively at present.

Thursday, 16th—The weather is very pleasant. Mrs. Hall, the wife of our colonel, returned to camp today from the North. Another large fleet went down the river today.

Friday, 17th—The Sixth Division was reviewed today by General McArthur. We heard some very heavy cannonading last night down toward Vicksburg. The report is that four gunboats and six transports with five hundred thousand rations on board ran the blockade. Another large fleet loaded with troops went down the river today.

Saturday, 18th—Weather pleasant. Had some rain this evening. Another large fleet loaded with troops passed down the river just after dark.

Sunday, 19th—Warm and pleasant today, but we had quite a storm last night. We had company inspection at 3 o'clock and dress parade at 5 o'clock. The boys all feel quite lively; no one is reporting to the doctor.

Monday, 20th—The Sixth Division received marching orders, and the First and Second Brigades started down the river. Our brigade, the Third, has orders to be ready to move at a moment's notice. We heard some cannonading this morning down toward Vicksburg. Companies E and K went out on picket. I remained in camp to guard the company's property. We have a fine camp at this place, but are glad to leave for the front, as staying in camp will not bring the war to a close.

Tuesday, 21st—We struck our tents and at 3 o'clock in a heavy rain embarked on board the "Platte Valley." We had all the supplies loaded by dark and during the night left for Milliken's Bend to join the other brigades. The boys all feel very fine.

Wednesday, 22d—We landed at Milliken's Bend early this morning and went into camp on a large plantation about a mile from the levee of the river.

SIEGE AND SURRENDER OF VICKSBURG

(April, 1863)

Thursday, 23d—Brig. Gen. M. M. Crocker took command of our brigade today. I got a pass to go down to the landing to buy bread for the officers' mess in my charge. Our troops are encamped by the thousands all along the Mississippi river, for thirty miles up from Vicksburg. There is much sickness among the new troops in camp here, caused by using the river water and by camping on the low ground. Many of them have already died and their bodies have been buried upon the levee instead of in the low ground. It is reported that five of our transports loaded with supplies for the army below ran the blockade last night. One of the transports when almost past was hit by a solid shot and sunk.

Friday, 24th—We are now in camp twenty miles above Vicksburg. Received orders to clean up our camp ground and to have company drill forenoon and afternoon. A large detail was put to work and when the camp was put in order we had our regular drills, one hour each time. A large fleet of troops came down the river this morning.

Saturday, 25th—Our division received orders to get ready to March. All the sick are being taken to the hospital and we are storing our supplies[1] upon the boat. We have to go in light marching order, one tent to each company and with five days' rations.

Sunday, 26th—We struck our tents this morning at 5 o'clock and loaded them on the boat and at 2 p. m. with knapsack on took up our march. By night we were within one mile of Richmond, Louisiana, on the railroad running from Vicksburg to Monroe, Louisiana, where we bivouacked for the night.

Monday, 27th—It rained all day and we marched into Richmond early this morning, taking shelter in cotton sheds, vacant houses, and any shed that would turn water. The Third Brigade is quartered in gin houses and negro shacks. White and I had a fine bed to sleep in last night. The land here is so nearly on the dead level, that it is almost impossible to keep out of mud and water, but we have plenty of cotton for bedding.

Tuesday, 28th—It cleared off this morning and we left Richmond at 10 o'clock, marched nine miles and went into camp on Holmes's plantation, about eight miles from the Mississippi and

[1] Tents and extra baggage.—A. G. D.

due west from Vicksburg. We took possession of all the vacant houses and sheds on the plantation. The roads are very muddy and many of the trains got stalled. Some of the wagons loaded with ammunition sank down to the axles and much time and labor were consumed in getting them out. There was some fighting at Grand Gulf today.

Wednesday, 29th—The teams all went back to the landing this morning for provisions and the boys cleaned up our camping ground. We have first-rate grub now, hard crackers, sowbelly, green tea, besides fresh beef every fifth day. We draw full rations every five days when in camp, and every three days when on the march. The boys live fine. I wrote a couple of letters today.

Thursday, 30th—Our provision train returned from the landing today. There was some very heavy cannonading at Grand Gulf today, where it is reported that the rebels are strongly fortified. Some of our transports ran the blockade at Vicksburg last night. The Eleventh Iowa was mustered for pay today. The sergeant-major reports the regiment as having five hundred and fifty men fit for duty.

MAY, 1863.

Friday, 1st—News came that General Sherman has again made an attack on Haines's Bluff, the same as last fall when the plan failed because General Grant failed to co-operate with him. The plan is to be tried again this spring. A large ammunition train passed through here for Carthage, Louisiana. General Crocker left the command of our brigade, to take command of the Seventh Division of the Seventeenth Army Corps. The boys are all sorry to see him leave.

Saturday, 2d—The weather has been warm and quite pleasant for several days and the roads are drying fast. Things are very quiet here. Colonel Hall is now in command of our brigade. We have drill twice a day, though this afternoon there was none, in order to give the boys time to wash their clothes and clean up for inspection. I received $5.00 from Captain McLoney, for the month of April, as cook for the officers' mess.

Sunday, 3d—News came that our army took five hundred prisoners at Grand Gulf. General Steele's Division passed here today. There is an Iowa brigade in it, consisting of the Fourth, Twenty-sixth, Thirtieth and Thirty-first Infantry. The men all look fine and there are none from the brigade in the hospital.

Monday, 4th—The Eighth, Twelfth and Thirty-fifth Iowa Regiments passed here today on their way to the front. They are all fine-looking men. I feel in hopes that Vicksburg will soon be in our hands. Our division is in the rear, most of the other troops having gone on ahead of us. Our army is in strong force at this place, and there is no danger of the rebels' cavalry making a raid on the base of our commissary supplies here.

Tuesday, 5th—The Fourth Iowa Cavalry passed here this morning. It is a fine regiment of horse. Four hundred and forty-four rebel prisoners captured at Grand Gulf were taken by here this morning to be sent to our prisons in the North; they are a hard-looking set of men. News came today that our men have taken Grand Gulf with two thousand prisoners. If this is true it gives us a road to Vicksburg over high ground, which means the fall of Vicksburg.

Wednesday, 6th—The Sixth Division trains all went to the landing this morning for ammunition. Wagon trains are passing back and forth all the time, hauling provisions and ammunition for the army at Grand Gulf. We had battalion drill this afternoon.

Thursday, 7th—One hundred and fifty prisoners captured at Grand Gulf were taken past here this morning; they all looked quite downhearted. A large train of provisions passed here for the army below. The roads are drying fast, which is making the hauling and marching better. The boys are all anxious to leave this place and move to the front. This is a low, unhealthy locality. An old negro here has picked up more than a thousand overcoats and blankets and is storing them away in his hut. These are thrown aside by the men marching out from the landing. On becoming warm and getting tired of their loads, they begin to unload about the first day's march.

Friday, 8th—General Blair's Division, composed of Ohio and Illinois troops, went by today on their way to Grand Gulf. All day teams were returning to the river landing for provisions for the army at Grand Gulf. We received orders to send all the sick back to the hospital at Memphis, and prepare to march. Our regiment has battalion drill twice a day now.

Saturday, 9th—It is quite pleasant. Had battalion drill this forenoon. The boys are all in fine spirits, expecting at any moment to receive marching orders. Our division teams returned from the landing with provisions and went on down to Carthage, where they will load them on boats for Grand Gulf.

Sunday, 10th—Our brigade received orders to march at 5 o'clock tomorrow morning. Regimental inspection at 8 o'clock this evening showed the regiment to be in fine order. Companies D and E went out on picket this evening.

Monday, 11th—We started this morning at 5 o'clock and marched about eight miles, when we stacked our arms until 3 p. m. We continued our march to Perkins's Landing about forty-five miles below Vicksburg as the river runs, or twenty miles as the crow flies. Here we bivouacked for the night. The country here is very low and often overflows. The large plantations, such as Perkins's, Holmes's and Jeff Davis's, are usually planted to cotton. The work is all done by slaves driven by overseers who live on the plantations, while the owners, planters, reside in more healthy localities.

Tuesday, 12th—We took up our march at 5 o'clock this morning and marched sixteen miles over very fine roads. This is a very rich country, and before the war, was prosperous, but now looks quite desolate, the buildings and fences having been burned by our troops. At the approach of our army the people fled, leaving all behind them. At noon we halted for lunch, and since it was so fearfully hot, remained here during the heat of the day in the shade of evergreens. The Eleventh Iowa was situated just opposite the residence of General Bowie, said to be a descendant of the inventor of the bowie knife. The main Bowie residence was burned and household articles, among which is a grand piano, are strewn about the large lawn. The outbuildings, on a grand scale, were not molested. The lawn contains about forty acres and is planted in all kinds of tropical trees and shrubbery, with cisterns and fountains at different points. The plantation borders the west bank of Lake St. Joseph, the public highway being just between it and the lake. This plantation, containing

(May, 1863)

several thousand acres, is all planted to corn, which is now in tassel and silk. Our march today was along the west bank of the lake with a continuous cornfield on our right. When night came we were still by the lake, where we went into bivouac.

Wednesday, 13th—After an early breakfast we left bivouac at 6 o'clock and took up our march. By noon we reached the Mississippi river, where we took boat, and going down about two miles landed on the east bank at Grand Gulf or Hard Times Landing—where the town once was. The town was destroyed just a year ago by the Union fleet, and there is nothing left but the streets and sidewalks. We went into camp here to stay until relieved.

Thursday, 14th—News came today that Richmond was taken. I took a walk and reviewed the rebels' works about here. They were strongly fortified with heavy ordnance on the high bluff, about two hundred feet above water, with the river for a distance of two miles running straight to the bluff. This made it a very dangerous place for our gunboats to approach. But after two days' shelling, our gunboats with two or three transports succeeded in running the blockade and landing below the fort.[1] The river coming with such force is fast washing away the bank and we hope that we may soon move from this place. The Third Brigade of Blair's Division arrived late last night.

Friday, 15th—News came again that Richmond has been taken, and that all of General Lee's supplies are cut off. The Third Brigade of General Blair's Division landed at this place today and went into bivouac. A gunboat came up the river from Port Hudson. Reports are coming in that General Grant is routing the rebels wherever he comes upon them in force. There are some prisoners and wounded being brought in from the front. The wounded are taken to the hospital and the prisoners to the North.

Saturday, 16th—The weather has been quite warm for several days. Troops are arriving every day and some of them are going to the front. It is reported that our men are shelling the rebels at Vicksburg and are getting no reply. We received a

---

[1] At the time of the capture the first troops marched down and crossed the river onto high ground some two miles below, while our main army came into the rear of the enemy, who were compelled to surrender, leaving all their heavy guns.—A. G. D.

(May, 1863)

dispatch from General Grant this afternoon, saying that his headquarters is in the State House at Jackson, Mississippi. The troops are in fine spirits.

Sunday, 17th—There was some very heavy cannonading out at the front today, and word came that a battle was fought at a place called Champion Hills, with heavy loss on both sides. The rebels are falling back towards Vicksburg. The river is falling and troops are still arriving. General Lauman's Division arrived last night.

Monday, 18th—A despatch from the front informs us that General Grant has taken the railroad bridge across the Big Black river in the rear of Vicksburg. The troops also took some prisoners. The Eleventh Iowa, accompanied by a gunboat, went on a scout up the Big Black river to destroy a bridge which the rebels had built in the last few days. This river empties into the Mississippi a short distance above our camp.

Tuesday, 19th—All is quiet here at Grand Gulf. We heard some heavy cannonading up at Vicksburg. The Third Brigade of General Lauman's Division arrived this afternoon, and about 10 o'clock our brigade (the Third of the Sixth Division) and the Third Brigade of Lauman's received orders to embark at once for Vicksburg. The Eleventh and the Thirteenth got on board the "Queen Forest."

Wednesday, 20th—This morning found us going up the river, when about 10 o'clock we landed three miles below Vicksburg. The rebels commenced throwing shells our way and we dropped down the river to a point six miles below the city. But at 4 o'clock we returned to the place we had reached in the morning, and landing on the west bank marched across the point of land just opposite Vicksburg. Here we boarded the boats again and awaited orders. The mortar boats are throwing shells into the town. Our armies about Vicksburg have taken a great many prisoners. It is reported that our men have taken Haines's Bluff, and that General Grant has commenced action all the way around his line of battle.

Thursday, 21st—Early this morning, at 6 o'clock, we moved up the river and entering the Yazoo river we reached Haines's Bluff, where we landed and stacked arms. Here we remained several hours awaiting orders. General Sherman has just taken

(May, 1863)

Haines's Bluff and now is uniting with General Grant's forces in surrounding Vicksburg. At 4 o'clock we again took boat, returning down the river to Young's Point, where we landed, and marching across the point again took the boats. We passed on down the river below Vicksburg to Warrington, Mississippi, where we landed, and marching out about five miles, went into camp for the night.

Friday, 22d—This morning we moved out a short distance from our bivouac and formed a line of battle. The rebels commenced throwing shells at us, and continued it all day; but as their guns were aimed too high, our greatest danger was from the falling limbs of trees hit by their shells. Four companies, including Company E, were sent out on the skirmish line. Company B had one man killed[1] and one wounded. We withdrew after dark and moved five miles farther on toward the right wing of the army and bivouacked in a cottonfield for the night. We were in heavy timber all day, which with the rough land, all hills and gullies, afforded us some protection. We are on the extreme left of Grant's army, which almost encircles Vicksburg.

Saturday, 23d—We started this morning at daylight and marched five miles to General McPherson's headquarters at the center of the army. Here we lay until 4 o'clock in the afternoon, when we marched back to our old place on the extreme left. The rebels again commenced to shell us, but the shells went over our heads. The Eleventh Iowa went on picket. Our men are shelling the rebels from all sides, and they are falling back behind their fortifications. When passing the headquarters of the Seventeenth Army Corps today, I saw a most dreadful sight at the field hospital; there was a pile, all that a six-mule team could haul, of legs and arms thrown from the amputating tables in a shed nearby, where the wounded were being cared for.

Sunday, 24th—The rebels tried to shell us again this morning, but could not get range of us. There was not much fighting today, our men having orders not to advance. Our siege guns, mortar boats and gunboats are throwing shells into the rebels day and night. We were relieved from picket this afternoon by another regiment.

---

[1] Jacob S. Deeter.—Roster Iowa Soldiers, II, p. 309.

(May, 1863)

Monday, 25th—Fighting commenced this morning all along the line, but it proved to be mostly picket fighting. There was also some heavy cannonading and the mortar boats and the gunboats were in action. Our command, the Sixth Division, lay in bivouac all day. In the evening the rebels came out and captured some of our pickets, and we then formed a line of battle. The First Missouri Battery threw some shells into the rebels' camp after night. General Lauman's division arrived this morning, but did not get into action.

Tuesday, 26th—It was quiet all along the line last night. The rebels came out with a flag of truce, asking permission to bury their dead, killed during the day. Our brigade started towards the right this morning, and arriving at McPherson's headquarters at the center, we went into bivouac for the night. Our march was over hot and dusty roads. Our guns commenced to shell the rebels again this afternoon.

Wednesday, 27th—Our brigade, with four others, all under the command of General Blair, left this morning for Benton's Crossroads. The expedition is to keep General Johnston from coming in to reinforce the rebels at Vicksburg. Cannonading and picket firing opened up early this morning. Our army, by sapping and mining after night, is gradually working its way closer to the fortifications. Our men are well protected during the day by earthworks.

Thursday, 28th—Last night we bivouacked twenty miles east of Vicksburg and remained there till noon, waiting for rations. We then moved on ten miles and went into bivouac for the night. The country is very rough in this part of the state and there are only a few small farms to be seen. Water is scarce, our main reliance being cistern water.

Friday, 29th—We started on the move early this morning and after marching about ten miles came upon the rebel pickets. We drove them in and forming a line of battle advanced towards them about two miles, our batteries throwing a few shells. But the rebels refused to take a stand and finally withdrew altogether. It was a small detachment of Johnston's army. We lost one killed and two wounded. Our regiment went out on picket.

Saturday, 30th—Our expedition started back this morning for Vicksburg. We received orders to burn the buildings along the

(May, 1863)

way and drive in all the cattle we could find. Our road ran along the south side of the Yazoo river, through rich bottom land planted to corn and cotton. The plantations are well improved with fine buildings. This bottom land is from one and one-half to two miles wide and springs in the bluffs pour out excellent water which runs in streams to the river. We got our fill of good water. When we halted at noon for lunch Company E, on rear guard, stopped in the sheds of a cotton gin in order to escape the hot sun. We had been there but a few minutes when some straggler set fire to the cotton, which being very dry and scattered about soon made a big fire, driving us out. The fire burned some sheep, a yoke of oxen and a wagon, besides other articles which we had taken en route.

Sunday, 31st—We camped by the river last night, and early this morning started for Haines's Bluff. We marched along some fine cornfields. We reached Haines's Bluff in the afternoon, and went into bivouac to the south of that place. We were as far east as Mechanicsville, forty-two miles from Vicksburg. On this raid we burned some fine plantation houses and other improvements. I saw only one residence left standing, and that was where the family had the courage to remain at home. The weather has been hot and the roads dusty.

JUNE, 1863.

Monday, 1st—We lay over here below Haines's Bluff all day, the boys being very tired after their long march. We ran out of provisions last night and could not draw any today. Some of the boys went out into the country to see what they could forage. We heard the roar of cannon at Vicksburg all day.

Tuesday, 2d—We lay here in bivouac again all day. Our quartermaster drew some clothing for the regiment. I drew a pair of shoes, a shirt and a canteen. We are still without provisions. We spent the day in cleaning our clothing and equipments. There was some very heavy cannonading at Vicksburg today and we are expecting to receive orders to leave soon for the lines in the rear of Vicksburg.

Wednesday, 3d—We lay still again today, but all improved their time cleaning up their accouterments. We drew two days' rations, which relieved our hunger. We received orders to march early in the morning. Colonel Chambers returned from the North today. He is to take command of our brigade, a thing a great many of the boys were sorry to learn.

Thursday, 4th—We left early this morning to join the army in the rear of Vicksburg, and arrived at General McPherson's headquarters about 5 o'clock in the evening. Here we stacked arms and formed a line of battle. Our men are still shelling Vicksburg day and night. We are here on high ground, but cannot see the town of Vicksburg.

Friday, 5th—We remained in line of battle all night. Our brigade lay in bivouac all day. The Governor of the State of Iowa made a speech to the Iowa Brigade. Adjutant General Baker and Congressman Wilson of Iowa spoke also. The Sixteenth Iowa went out on picket. Skirmishing has been going on all day, and our men are digging rifle-pits.

Saturday, 6th—Several companies from our brigade were detailed to go out last night and work as sappers and miners on the rifle pits. Our forces are working their way closer to the rebels' works every day, and Vicksburg is now almost completely surrounded. The rebels are running short of provisions, it is said, and are anxious for reinforcements to break the siege. They made attacks today on our outside lines at four or five different points, driving in our pickets.

Sunday, 7th—The rebels made an attack on our forces at Duck's Point, Louisiana, where, it is reported, two negro regiments met the attack and captured two hundred prisoners and five pieces of artillery. Who says that the negro will not fight? I say he will fight! Arm the negroes and let them fight for their liberty! There are some Northern troops with them at Duck's Point, and together they make a strong garrison.

Monday, 8th—The Third Brigade received their knapsacks this morning. The boys are at work building sheds of the canebrake which is so plentiful in this part of the State. Fighting is still kept up and reinforcements are arriving every day. Vicksburg must and shall fall this time!

Tuesday, 9th—The weather away down south in Dixie is getting quite warm. The soldiers are all in good health and fine

JUNE.

Sunday 7.

The rebels attacked our men at dud[?] from Sd. there was some negros troops at that place they whiped the rebels out nicely taking 200 prisoners and 5 pieces of artillery. who sais that the negrow wont fight I say they will right arm them and let them fight for their liberty.

Monday 8.

The 3rd Brig received their knapsacks this morning. the boyes is hard at work to day at pulling up houses out of line. the corn is very plentey in this part of the state. fighting is still keep up and not reinforcements is rising every day. Vicksburg must and shall fall this time.

Tuesday 9.

The wether is geting quite warm a way down south in diky. the soldiers is all in good helth and fine spirits. times is quite lively good news from all directions. the moter boates thres shell all day and night in to town.

FACSIMILE PAGE OF THE ORIGINAL DIARY. ENTRIES FOR JUNE 7, 8, AND 9, 1863.

(June, 1863)

spirits. Times are quite lively, with good news from all directions around Vicksburg. Our mortar boats are throwing shells into town day and night.[1]

Wednesday, 10th—The cool morning was followed by a rain all day ending at dark in a heavy windstorm. Companies E and D of the Eleventh Iowa worked all last night in cutting a road through the canebrakes to the rebels' breastworks. Skirmishing has been going on all day.

Thursday, 11th—The Thirty-fifth Iowa received marching orders. A report is that General Burnside with eight thousand troops went on an expedition up the Yazoo river today. Cannonading has been heard on all sides all day. News came that General Banks has Port Hudson surrounded and is now besieging the place.

Friday, 12th—Our brigade receiving orders, moved out about a mile and again went into camp in a large hollow; we fixed up bunks and made a nice camp. I was out last night again with a large detail from our brigade digging rifle pits, working all night with rifle in one hand and pick in the other, digging trenches to protect ourselves in the daytime. There was skirmishing and heavy cannonading all day, and after night by their lighted fuses we sometimes could see the shells from our mortar boats coming over the city and down to the ground before they exploded.

Saturday, 13th—The Eleventh Iowa moved out towards the rear about four miles, to relieve the Ninety-third Illinois on picket. The land around here is very rough and heavily timbered. There is an occasional small farm. The people around here are all rank secessionists.

Sunday, 14th—Company E moved back as a reserve and to do police duty. Six of our companies are out on picket. There was heavy cannonading today by our men, the rebels in return throwing a few shells now and then. It is reported that one of our shells exploding in the streets of the town killed six women. Women and children as well as the men are shut in and are of course helping to consume the small store of provisions, but there is no way of escape.

---

[1] We were all confident that Pemberton would soon be compelled to surrender Vicksburg, for we had him completely surrounded.—A. G. D.

(June, 1863)

Monday, 15th—Our brigade is all broken up, most of it being on picket duty facing Johnston's army and acting as a reserve, and doing police duty between the two lines of battle. Johnston is reported to be out on the Big Black river with about ten thousand men, in an attempt to get into Vicksburg, but he's afraid to come for fear of getting whipped. The boys are having fine times picking blackberries and plums. I quit cooking for the captain, and was recommended as a first-class cook. John Lett took my place as cook for the officers.

Tuesday, 16th—We have had several days of very warm weather which became very hot yesterday, but today there is a high wind accompanied by thunder. The Eleventh Iowa signed the payroll today for two months' pay. Cannon have been roaring all day and the place still holds out. General Grant still feels confident that he can take the place, and the army is in fine spirits. Only a few tents are used now, and they are only for the sick and wounded.

Wednesday, 17th—Our mortar boats are shelling the rebels day and night, and the constant roar of cannon is something dreadful to listen to. Our regiment drew some clothing from the quartermaster today. We just learned that we are to remain out here on picket. The boys are having easy times picking blackberries and plums. They are quite plentiful, and come as a Godsend to us. Water is becoming very scarce, for the branches which we have to depend upon have now stopped running, and all we can get is the water left in the sink holes in the creek bottom.

Thursday, 18th—We have had strong wind and thunder for three days now, but no rain. I was on duty today for the first time in two and a half months, for while I was cook I had no other duty. Skirmishing and cannonading are still going on. News came that our army is in the rear of Port Hudson and that fighting is going on there. I wrote a letter today for John Ford, of my company. Ford had shot off his right thumb by an accidental discharge of his rifle, and when it came time for him to write to his sweetheart, he called upon me to do it for him.[1]

---

[1] I undertook the job for Ford, but did some perspiring before I finished the letter, and I would never undertake it again. The letter went through and he received a nice one in reply.—A. G. D.

(June, 1863)

Friday, 19th—It is again quite warm. Every morning at about 2 o'clock we have to form a line of battle, so that if the rebels should come in upon us we would be ready for them; but I do not think they will come. On account of the very poor water here, several of the boys are down with the fever and ague.

Saturday, 20th—By order of General Grant all the artillery opened upon Vicksburg this morning, and the bombardment continued throughout the day. It is reported that the rebels have lost six hundred, killed and wounded, many of these being killed during the first two hours of the firing. Our left is holding quite tight. The sky was hazy today and the heat at times was very oppressive.

Sunday, 21st—Things are quite still all along the lines today, but the mortar boats continue to throw shells day and night. Our chaplain preached a sermon to us this afternoon; his text was from John, fourteenth chapter and second verse. It was the first sermon our regiment has heard for nearly six months.

Monday, 22d—It is quite still along the lines today and there is no news of importance. Some troops were sent out in the rear today, and our regiment received orders to be ready to march at any time. It is thought that Johnston is trying to break the siege by attempting to make a move from the Big Black river, and by Pemberton's striking our lines at the same time and place, they hope to effect a union and escape. But General Grant is leaving nothing open. He has ordered the felling of large trees across the highways to prevent the moving of their artillery.

Tuesday, 23d—Fighting is still going on. A force of thirty thousand under command of General Sherman was sent to rout Johnston. The Eleventh Iowa, with the exception of Company E, went on an expedition[1] in the direction of the Big Black river. Company E was left here for picket duty.

Wednesday, 24th—I was on picket today, each man going out every other day, and the orders are very strict, no one being allowed to go through the lines unless he can show a pass signed by General Grant. Our men are digging tunnels under the rebel forts and laying powder to blow them up. When a fort is blown up our forces are to make a charge at that point and capture the

[1] To join Sherman's forces.—Ed.

rebels. The report is that the rebels are planning to cut their way out through our lines. News came that Port Hudson has been taken, together with a great many prisoners.

Thursday, 25th—Everything on the outside is quiet as usual. Our engineers blew up one of the main rebel forts, and the infantry rushing in tried to hold the place, but on account of the fierce cross firing had to fall back to their rifle pits. A number of our forces were killed, including one colonel, and a number were wounded. Only a few of the rebels were killed by the explosion, not many being in the fort at the time. Our cannon opened up all along the line. A negro in the fort blown up, was thrown high up in the air and came down on his head within our lines unhurt.[1]

Friday, 26th—I went on picket again this morning with very strict orders as to passes and keeping cartridge boxes on day and night. The rebels are becoming active and desperate in their determination to get out, for their provisions are very low. No news from the rear.

Saturday, 27th—Our company is still on picket here about five miles southeast of Vicksburg, while the other companies of the regiment are with our brigade out on the Big Black river. There is no telling when we shall be relieved from picket; yet our boys are pretty well satisfied, for we have plenty of blackberries and we drew three days' rations today.

Sunday, 28th—I was sent out on picket duty today and everything is quite still along the line. It is also quiet at the front, except along General Logan's Division, where the rebel sharpshooters are trying to silence our batteries. News came that Port Hudson had not been taken, and that instead General Hooker was falling back. The little news we get from the Potomac is discouraging, but since we are so sure of a victory here at Vicksburg, we can stand discouraging reports from the Potomac.

Monday, 29th—Fighting is still going on and our guns around Vicksburg seem to be making a new onslaught today. Our men blew up another rebel fort, but did not attempt to rush in, since the guns from the other forts are so arranged as to defend any other point along the fortifications. Everything on the outer

[1] A photograph was taken of the negro and the boys had him on exhibition for a few days at five cents admission.—A. G. D.

(June, 1863)

lines has been quiet. I came in from picket this morning. The boys of my company are all in fine spirits, and although the blackberries are getting scarce, peaches and apples, which are plentiful around here, will soon be ripe.

Tuesday, 30th—Our company was mustered at 9 o'clock this morning by Captain McLoney. Major Foster came in today and made a demand upon the general picket officers that our company be relieved from picket duty at this place. We had a fine time at this place. Our work here has not been laborious, but we had to be on constant duty and ready with all accouterments on, for any emergency. The abundance of canebrakes here fortunately made it unnecessary for us to sleep on the ground.

JULY, 1863.

Wednesday, 1st—A detail of the Seventeenth Iowa came out this morning to relieve us, and a team came this afternoon to haul our baggage, but we have not yet received orders to leave. Captain McLoney went down to the headquarters of the picket officers to get an order to move. The report is that our men blew up another rebel fort. It is said that a man on one of our mortar boats made a wager that he could pull the lanyard longer and fire a larger number of shells than any of his comrades, but he was overcome by the concussion and dropped dead just as he stepped from the boat. He gave up his life for a vain wish.

Thursday, 2d—We loaded up our baggage and started at 8 o'clock to join our regiment and brigade in camp on the Big Black river, about ten miles distant. We found our command cutting away the trees which were cut down to keep General Johnston from coming in our rear after Vicksburg should surrender.[1]

Friday, 3d—We received orders to be ready to march at a moment's warning. Getting the orders we started about 10 o'clock at night for Messenger's ford on the lower Big Black river, about four miles from our bivouac, and reached the ford at midnight. We are to stop Johnston from crossing the river, as it is thought he is making an effort to cross at the ford to strike Sherman's right flank.

[1] It was reported that Pemberton had raised the white flag, asking for terms of surrender. This being the case, our forces were set to work clearing the road for our artillery; for we understood that upon the surrender of Vicksburg, we were to pursue Johnston's army.—A. G. D.

Saturday, 4th—A despatch came that Vicksburg has been taken and that Pemberton has made an unconditional surrender to General Grant. The terms include the surrender of his army of twenty-seven thousand men, one hundred siege guns, one hundred and twenty-eight field guns, and eighty thousand small arms.[1] Early in the day the rebels drove some of our skirmishers in, but in the afternoon we commenced to shell them and they withdrew. They surrendered soon after. Our company went out on picket this evening. This has been a hard Fourth of July; I don't want to see another such a Fourth.

---

[1] There were no provisions to give up and General Grant issued Government rations to all the prisoners taken.—A. G. D.

Chapter XI.
The Campaign Against Jackson, Mississippi. July 5-July 26.

Sunday, 5th—We came in this morning at 10 o'clock from an all night picket along the Big Black river. We were relieved by General Tuttle's Brigade. Our brigade then fell back a mile and went into bivouac in heavy timber. The rebels all left last night, it is thought, for Jackson, Mississippi, with the forces of Sherman and Ord in pursuit of them. Sherman passed us, crossing the Big Black at Messenger's ford, while Ord's army crossed the river over the railroad bridge. There is great rejoicing in camp over the fall of Vicksburg and the boys are singing songs and celebrating.

Monday, 6th—We have had very changeable weather for a week now—hot and sultry, then cool and pleasant, then warm and hazy. The Eleventh Iowa received two months' pay today. I got $37.25; of this, $11.25 was allowed for clothing not drawn. The Thirteenth Iowa and the Tenth Ohio Battery went out on picket duty.

Tuesday, 7th—A high wind today ended in rain tonight. Colonel Chambers of the Sixteenth Iowa, who has been commanding our brigade, left for Vicksburg this morning to obtain release from this command in order to return to the regular army. The boys of the brigade are glad to see him leave. Colonel Hall takes charge again of our brigade. I went on brigade guard tonight. Our countersign is "Vicksburg."

Wednesday, 8th—I came off guard duty this morning at 9 o'clock. There was a hailstorm last night and everything looks nice and green, notwithstanding the fact that there has been no rain for two months. But it is hot and the corn has suffered a great deal. All the fields are planted to corn, as that was the surest way to get food for the rebel army.

Thursday, 9th—There is no news of importance and we have had no chance yet for newspapers. We have scant news while out here in the woods, sometimes getting no mail for eight or ten days at a time. All our teams went to Vicksburg today for provisions. The forces of Sherman and Ord are still pursuing Johnston.

Friday, 10th—News came that there was fighting at Jackson, Mississippi, General Sherman having pushed Johnston back to that point. Troops are passing on to the front to reinforce Sherman. News came also that General Lee was making a raid into Pennsylvania.[1] Colonel Chambers returned from Vicksburg today, and has again taken charge of our brigade. The men of our brigade are all in good health at present. The weather is hot and oppressive. No more at present.

Saturday, 11th—The Eleventh Iowa started at sunup this morning for Jackson, Mississippi, as an escort for two hundred and forty-five wagons loaded with provisions and ammunition for General Sherman's army. By night we were within one mile of Clinton, where we went into bivouac, closely corralling the wagons. We rode on the wagons a part of the time during the journey. Whenever they came to a stretch of good roads, the teamsters would put the horses on the run, and in order to keep up we had to climb onto the loaded wagons. We suffered for lack of water today, for the rebels in their retreat polluted the branches they crossed by killing and throwing into the streams their worn-out horses and mules, hoping thus to strike a blow at us. Their march was marked by the buzzards flying above or feeding upon the carcasses of the slain animals.

Sunday, 12th—We started this morning at sunup and arrived at General Sherman's headquarters at 10 o'clock. Two regiments of Sherman's army came out to reinforce our train guard. They feared that the rebels' cavalry would make a raid on the train before we could reach the main army. We arrived safely without losing a single wagon. Cannonading is going on quite lively from both sides. Good water is very scarce here, and the few wells and cisterns which we can draw upon are crowded all the time; I stood with two canteens for more than an hour waiting for my turn.

Monday, 13th—We left this morning at 3 o'clock on our return trip *via* Black river bridge, with a train of two hundred and fifty empty wagons. We took with us sixty-one prisoners, giving

[1] This seems to have been the first news from the battle of Gettysburg—a week after the battle.—Ed.

them the first free ride they have had for some time. We all rode on the wagons, standing, and in order to keep from falling out when the teams made a lurch, we removed the canvas covers so as to hold to the bows. The road was lined the whole way with troops going to reinforce General Sherman. The day was cloudy, and we were thankful, as it kept the deep dust from rising somewhat. We reached the bridge at dark and went into bivouac. I was on a detail to guard the prisoners during the night. The paroled prisoners are all being sent out of Vicksburg to their homes. They are a hard-looking set of men.

Tuesday, 14th—We lay here in bivouac at Black river bridge all day, and we are glad for the chance to rest and clean our clothes. The cars from Vicksburg can run only to the river, since the bridge is burned and the railroad track is torn up for five miles east of the river. A train load of provisions came out from Vicksburg today, and a part of the provisions and ammunition have been loaded upon wagons and started with an escort for Jackson.[1]

Wednesday, 15th—A train of provisions and ammunition arrived from Vicksburg this morning. Late in the afternoon they finished loading the wagons with the provisions and ammunition for Jackson, and our regiment was ordered to accompany them. We started late and after marching six miles stopped for the night. We received orders to keep a sharp lookout for the rebels' cavalry, as they had crossed the Pearl river and had captured and burned a part of the train just ahead of ours.

Thursday, 16th—We left our bivouac with the wagon train at an early hour and moved on quite rapidly, expecting to be attacked at any moment. We passed the place on the road where the train just ahead of us was attacked by the rebel cavalry, which captured and burned fifteen of the wagons, taking with them the mules and carrying off the drivers and guards as prisoners. This was a terribly hard day for us. We were not allowed to climb the wagons, but were ordered to keep up with them, and with muskets loaded and bayonets fixed, be ready to fight at the drop of a hat. Then, too, the weather was awfully hot, and the dust kicked up by the mules was stifling; besides this, we were

---

[1]The men generally dreaded this kind of service, for it was exceedingly dangerous. Then, too, much of the journey had to be made on the run—but it is a soldier's business to obey orders and do the best he can.—A. G. D.

almost famished, the little water we could find being unfit for use because of its sickly odor. But late in the afternoon we arrived at Clinton, where we were relieved by another regiment and went into camp with our brigade which was stationed here.

Friday, 17th—We heard that our wagon train went through to Jackson without attack, and that the rebels evacuated the place this morning, with Sherman's forces in hot pursuit. We hear that Johnston, after crossing the Pearl river, burned the bridges behind him and is now in rapid retreat on the other side. News came that Meade had taken Richmond, Virginia, together with thirty thousand prisoners. Things are very lively here today—there is singing and rejoicing.

Saturday, 18th—Our wagon trains now move unmolested back and forth from Vicksburg to Jackson, since there are few of the rebels' cavalry left in this section. Our brigade is to remain here at Clinton as a reserve to escort wagon trains when needed. We hear that Sherman is still after Johnston. Our camp here is quite low and damp, and a great many of the boys are coming down with the ague.

Sunday, 19th—Company E with three other companies, one from each regiment, went out on picket this morning. Our company is stationed on the south side of a vacant field. Off to the north on the other side of the field and just in the edge of the timber on high ground, we can see the rebel cavalry, but they are careful to keep their distance. We have fine times on picket now, with little danger of being attacked and plenty of fruit to eat. We have green corn, too, and the fields nearby are being pretty well picked over. One of the boys came in with a hundred ears of corn. He roasted fifteen of them in the campfire ashes, ate all of them, and declared that he could eat two or three more.

Monday, 20th—We came in from picket this morning and this afternoon moved our regimental camp onto higher ground. Some of our boys are having a time with the ague and fever. The Fifteenth and Sixteenth Regiments were ordered out to Miller's Creek to guard a wagon train. The Thirty-fifth Iowa passed us on their way to Vicksburg with five hundred prisoners from Johnston's army. Orders came to prepare to march.

Tuesday, 21st—Our brigade started for Vicksburg this afternoon. We covered five miles and went into bivouac. It is extremely hot, and having had no rain for so long, the roads are very dusty. Our entire army is falling back to Vicksburg.

Wednesday, 22d—We started this morning at daylight and marched all day. We stopped for the night along Baker's Creek, just beyond Edward's Station. The roads are alive with troops returning to Vicksburg. It is reported that Johnston's army is falling back to Columbus, Mississippi.

Thursday, 23d—We were off by 4 o'clock this morning and reached Big Black river bridge by noon. It had rained very hard here yesterday and last night, overflowing the river and causing the deep dust to become deep mud. This made our traveling very heavy, and since the rain set in again this afternoon, we moved on only about three miles and went into bivouac.

Friday, 24th—We remained here in bivouac all day. Orders came for our brigade to return to Black river bridge and remain there until relieved by General Sherman. The cars are coming through now from Vicksburg twice a day. We are very anxious for mail, having had none for many days, and are disappointed in not receiving any today. We put in our time today cleaning clothes.

Saturday, 25th—Our brigade returned to the bridge and went into camp, with Colonel Chambers in command of the entire post. Our army field hospital is located here and the convalescents are being cared for in it. Refugees by the thousands are at this place and are still pouring in by the hundreds from every direction, ahead of Sherman's returning army. It is a wonderful sight to see; they are of all colors and ages, though mostly women and children. I bought a gold pen today from the sutler for $2.00, and had the misfortune to lose it before night.

Sunday, 26th—We were relieved by an Iowa brigade from Sherman's army, which just arrived, but we remained in bivouac all day, awaiting orders. One of General Sherman's foraging trains came in; they are going to forage for oats. News came that there was fighting going on at Charleston, South Carolina. It was quite hot this morning, and in the afternoon we had a hard rainstorm. A great many of the boys in camp here are sick with the chills, while others are almost worn out by the hard service.

Chapter XII.
On Guard at Vicksburg and the Fruitless Expedition to Monroe, Louisiana. July 27-September 3.

Monday, 27th—Our brigade started for Vicksburg at 4 o'clock this afternoon. We moved only four miles, when we stopped for the night. The country is very rough and the heavy rains have made the roads very muddy.

Tuesday, 28th—We started early this morning and though it was hot and sultry, we reached Vicksburg at 10 a. m. So we finally entered Vicksburg after more than eight months in trying to take the place. In the afternoon we moved out a few miles to the north of town and went into bivouac. While in Vicksburg we saw some of the paroled prisoners leaving for their homes. They were indeed sorrowful-looking beings—all in rags and without food; yet they were ready to fight for their cause to the bitter end.

Wednesday, 29th—We passed a miserable night, for we had no tents and the ground was wet from yesterday's rain; besides, the ground is so rough and hilly that we can hardly find a place big enough to camp on. Things dragged on slowly this morning, so I had a chance to run around some to view the fortifications. The rebels were strongly fortified, and had dug large caves under ground at the foot of the hills just off from the roadway to protect themselves from our shells. Troops are going aboard the transports, some down the river to reinforce General Banks at Port Hudson, and others north to aid General Dodge in Tennessee and northern Mississippi.

Thursday, 30th—It is quite hot and sultry. There is no news of importance. Colonel Hall has again taken command of our brigade. I bought a two-pound can of butter, paying $1.25, and five loaves of bread for fifty cents.

Friday, 31st—The weather continues hot. Our men are at work raising the gunboat "Cincinnati," which was sunk during the siege of Vicksburg. She was a fine boat. A detail of men was sent to bring our tents today, but they failed to get them.

AUGUST, 1863.

Saturday, 1st—The quartermaster received some clothing for our regiment. I drew a pair of pants for $3.05 and a shirt for $1.46. A certain number of men from each company will be permitted to go home on a thirty-day furlough, and the boys of our company are looking forward to the time, wondering who will be the lucky ones.

Sunday, 2d—The teams went to the wharf down in Vicksburg for our tents. The three boys from our company drawing furloughs were Sylvester Daniels, Daniel E. Sweet and Major Christmas, and they left for home today on a thirty-day furlough.[1] I sent $1.00 with Sweet to buy postage stamps for me and $2.00 to buy me a gold pen.[2] I also sent $5.00 to father by Daniels.

Monday, 3d—I was on camp guard today. We got our tents and pitched them today, and also, because of the intense heat, built shades in front of them by setting up forks and poles covered with brush. It is the report that we are to remain here on garrison duty. Our work is very light, however, as we have no picket duty.

Tuesday, 4th—The heat is intense today. We finished putting up the brush shades and also completed our bunks. It seems like home once more. Our regimental payrolls were made out today, while the Thirteenth Iowa received their pay. Major Foster is now in command of our regiment.

Wednesday, 5th—The heat continues as yesterday. The Eleventh Iowa signed their payrolls today, and the Fifteenth Iowa received their pay. I was on fatigue duty all day. We had dress parade this evening for the first time since May 19th. The boys came out in fine style. Troops are leaving every day to reinforce different commands of the army of the West.

Thursday, 6th—The Eleventh received pay today; I got $26.00, my full payment for the two months, for the Government has discontinued the "allotment rolls," as sending a portion of a soldier's pay to his parents is called. Our colonel ordered a bake oven for the regiment, so in a few days we will draw fresh bread instead of hardtack.

[1] In drawing lots for furlough, our diarist tells me, the officers favored the married men. Mr. Downing himself did not care about a furlough.—Ed.

[2] I am using this pen in re-writing the manuscript of my war diary fifty years later, and in my seventy-second year.—A. G. D.

Friday, 7th—It is quite sultry today. There is no news of any importance. The Sixteenth Iowa received their pay today.

Saturday, 8th—Quite pleasant today. We cleaned up our clothing and accouterments for inspection. We are getting fixed up very nicely in our camp and all are feeling fine. Only a few of our boys are sick and in the hospital at present. I loaned George Toyne (Company E) $25.00 today, until next pay day.[1]

Sunday, 9th—I was detailed on a foraging party today. There were two hundred men and one hundred wagons, accompanied by a squad of cavalry as a picket guard. We went up the Yazoo river bottoms about five miles and loaded our wagons with green corn, which we found in abundance. It was very hot, and the work was strenuous, besides its being on the Lord's Day—but such is the life of a soldier.

Monday, 10th—We are living on fresh bread now; we got our first today, baked in the new oven. Each man is allowed to draw a one-pound loaf per day. We again have company drill twice a day, with dress parade at 5 o'clock. The weather is fearfully hot, day and night.

Tuesday, 11th—No news from the Army of the Potomac nor from Charleston, South Carolina.

Wednesday, 12th—We had a fearful windstorm today, though no rain. Everything in camp is moving along fine and the boys are quite cheerful. We have plenty of wood, canebrake and Spanish moss for our use and our camp is in good shape.

Thursday, 13th—It is rumored that our brigade is to go to Natchez, Mississippi, in a few days, but we cannot tell whether it is true or not. I was on police duty today, for the first time, down in Vicksburg. There are more than a hundred men detailed each day to keep order in the city, and nobody is allowed on the streets without a pass from the provost marshal. We work on eight-hour shifts, and each man has a certain part of a street to patrol for two hours at a time, after which he is off duty for a period of four hours. I was on duty in a residence district, and while I was walking my beat, a lady came out of her home for an afternoon's walk. I of course had to ask her to show her pass. I must have looked pretty fierce to her, with

[1] Mr. Downing explained that Toyne's family at home was in need and that it was a very common thing for a single man to loan a married comrade money to send home to his family.—Ed.

(August, 1863)

loaded gun, fixed bayonet and all accouterments on. I asked her kindly for her pass and she answered that she had none, whereupon I told her what my orders were; that she would have to return to her home and not come out on the streets again without a pass, or I would have to take her to the provost marshal's office. She thanked me very politely as I closed her gate, saying that she wanted to obey orders and that she would send out and procure a pass before going on the street again. This lady is certainly experiencing war at her own dooryard, yet she showed the good breeding of the Southern lady.

Friday, 14th—All is quiet. Orders came today to send all of the sick home on thirty-day furloughs.

Saturday, 15th—This is my birthday—twenty-one years old today. I was detailed to help dig a grave for the body of Rufus C. Walter, of Company G, who died last night. He had been wounded and lived here in camp in a hammock which was tied to trees, or to posts set in the ground when there were no trees.

Sunday, 16th—We had regimental inspection this morning at 8 o'clock. The regiment showed itself in splendid order. A man from the Fifteenth Iowa was buried this morning, having died of fever.[1] Some of the sick boys of our regiment started home today on their furloughs. Mark Titus was the only one from our company, though some of the boys still have the fever.

Monday, 17th—Our company went out on picket this morning. There is always danger of cavalry raids, particularly evenings. Some more of the sick boys were examined this morning by the doctor. The boys were hoping to get a sick furlough. There is some homesickness in the regiment, but a number will be made well by a thirty-day furlough. I am in good health and it is more than a year since I have had to report to the doctor, and then he marked me "not fit for duty" for only three days.

Tuesday, 18th—We were relieved from picket this morning. It looks pretty bad in walking the streets of Vicksburg to see the destruction caused by our shells. Many buildings are completely demolished, while others have great holes made in their walls —I counted as high as ten holes in a wall. I noticed a shell lying in the bottom of a cistern, whose fuse must have been put out

[1] John Chrismore, Knoxville, Iowa. He died August 15th and was buried in National Cemetery at Vicksburg, Section G, grave 172.—Roster Iowa Soldiers, Vol. II, p. 926.

when it struck the water and so it only knocked a hole in the wall, but it drained the water out of the cistern.

Wednesday, 19th—A thunderstorm last night cooled the air some, though it is still extremely hot. There was a boat blown up this morning down at the wharf and thirty or forty lives were lost, mostly negroes. The boat was being loaded with ammunition and the explosion was caused by a negro's dropping a box of loaded shells. A number of persons thrown into the water were rescued from drowning.

Thursday, 20th—It has rained most of the day. On dress parade this evening orders were read for the brigade to prepare to march in the morning with ten days' rations and one hundred rounds of ammunition. The sick are to be left in camp.

Friday, 21st—We packed our knapsacks and started at 10 o'clock for the landing two miles above Vicksburg and a mile below our camp. Our regiment with the Thirteenth went on board the "Fanny Bell," and at dark started up the river.

Saturday, 22d—After an all night run, we landed this morning at daylight at Goodrich's Landing, on the Louisiana side, from which place we marched two miles up the river and went into bivouac, where we remained all day. There were four brigades in the expedition, comprising about five thousand men, and commanded by Brigadier General Stephenson. There is a camp of several thousand negro refugees here, old men, women and children, they having fled from the plantations. They are fed on Government rations doled out to them, which cannot take the place of their accustomed corn bread and pork. They are poorly cared for, the place being a miserable camp of filthy hovels, and are dying by the hundreds of disease and neglect.

Sunday, 23d—Our expedition broke camp this morning and started for Monroe, Louisiana, on the Washita river, seventy-five miles northwest of Vicksburg. By 1 o'clock we had covered ten miles, in a burning hot sun,[1] without water to drink, and through neglected fields of hemp standing from ten to fifteen feet high. The cavalry went in front to break down the hemp, and were followed by a six-gun battery and our army wagons, after

[1] Oh, that hot sun on our heads! It was frightful! There was no air to stir even a leaf; it was like going through a fiery furnace! But stopping in that God-forsaken country to hunt for water would have been a greater punishment than going on without water—so we kept straight on.—A. G. D.

(August, 1863)

which the hemp was pretty well flattened for the infantry to pass over. The men and animals suffered awfully. Many artillery horses gave out and some of the men were sunstruck. Many of the boys fell out of the ranks during the trip and had to be cared for by the doctor. Finally at the end of the ten-mile journey we reached the banks of the Tensas river, and though the water was stagnant, in mere pools, we threw ourselves down, brushed aside the green scum and drank that hot, sickly water to quench our thirst.

Monday, 24th—Spending the night here we started early this morning and moved on to Bayou Mason only seven miles further on. Here we remained during the balance of the day and for the night. There being no bridge, we had to wade the bayou to enter the town. Our cavalry routed about one hundred and fifty of the rebels in a camp on the west bank of the bayou. Most of our way today was shaded by forest trees. The country here is low and heavily timbered with cypress and the ground is covered with masses of palm leaf. We noticed driftwood high up in the trees, some forty or fifty feet, and were told by the natives that it was carried there last winter when the "Yanks" cut the levee up at Lake Providence, flooding the whole country. So we were permitted to see some of the results of our attempt at directing the waters of the Mississippi.

Tuesday, 25th—We took up our march at 4 o'clock this morning and journeyed seventeen miles, when we stopped for the night. Our brigade took the rear, the Eleventh Regiment acting as rear guard. The day's march was through swamps and bayous and land heavily timbered. Now and then we noticed a field with a little log hut in it, occupied by a poor white family, whose head was away with the rebel army, or with a cavalry squad in this section.

Wednesday, 26th—Getting an early start again this morning, we covered sixteen miles and camped for the night on Oak Ridge. This ridge is on a dead level and only about twenty feet higher than the bottoms where the cypress grow so luxuriantly. It is covered with oak and fine large walnut, also magnolia and a few other semi-tropical trees. To reach the ridge we had to wade across Bayou Lee. Our cavalry had preceded us and routed a small detachment of rebel cavalry. They were nicely fixed up at this place. Our boys went in on their nerve at foraging.

(August, 1863)

Thursday, 27th—Leaving our Oak Ridge bivouac early this morning we journeyed fifteen miles more and stopped for the night on the banks of Bayou Said, only seven miles from Monroe, our destination. During the day we crossed another ridge known as Pine Ridge, which is eight miles across and about twenty feet above the surrounding land. It is beautifully covered with yellow pine, growing so straight and tall, seventy-five to one hundred feet. We noticed a few small clearings with log huts. This is the worst bivouac we have yet occupied. It is full of poisonous reptiles and insects, centipedes, jiggers, woodticks, lizards, scorpions and snakes of all kinds—I have never seen the like. Some of the boys killed two big, spotted, yellow snakes and put them across the road—they measured about fifteen feet each. The ground is covered with leaves ten inches deep, and the water of the bayou has a layer of leaves and moss fully two inches thick.[1]

Friday, 28th—We had company inspection this morning and then started out for Monroe, expecting to have a little fight in taking the town. But upon reaching the place we found that the rebels had withdrawn, leaving at 6 o'clock in the morning. General Logan's Division entered the town at 10 o'clock, while our brigade had come within a mile of town, where we again went into bivouac. In the afternoon there was a heavy rain. The rebels have a hospital here, with about fourteen hundred sick and wounded. Monroe is a nice town, well situated, and has some fine buildings. Strict orders had been given us not to kill any livestock on this expedition; all persons caught in the act were to be arrested. But some of the boys of our regiment had killed a hog and were in the act of cutting it up when the general of our division came riding along with his staff. The boys were caught in the very act. General Stephenson halted, and wanting to know by what authority they had killed the hog, he was going to have them arrested on the spot. But they had one fellow equal to the occasion, who explained that they had killed a wild hog. They were out in the timber getting wood with which to build fires,

---

[1] This proved to be our most dangerous journey in all our four years' service. The natives told us the next morning that no Southern soldiers could have been hired to do what we did. I have often wondered and would like to know, just as we did then, why we were sent into this forsaken section of the country, and during the most sickly time of the year, at that! The natives we saw were a white-livered set; they were all ardent sympathizers of the secession cause.—A. G. D.

(August, 1863)

when some wild hogs there made a charge upon them, and in self-defense they had killed the boldest one; they then thought that as they had killed it they might as well bring it in and have some fresh pork. The general rode on.

Saturday, 29th—We had a heavy rain during the night and the day opened cloudy and dismal. Our entire expedition started on the return journey for Vicksburg. We covered twenty-six miles and camped for the night on Oak Ridge. Some of the men had found too much of the "Southern bay rum," and imbibing quite freely, became so topheavy on the way that they had to be hauled all day.

Sunday, 30th—We left Oak Ridge and covering but ten miles went into bivouac on the banks of Heff river. Some of the men on account of the bad water and climate are suffering with the chills and fever. The boys were raiding all the sweet potato patches they found along the way, today.

Monday, 31st—We left Heff river and marched through to Bayou Mason, eighteen miles, and stopped for the night. While marching today some of us heard the report of a rifle, and we learned that a member of the Seventh Missouri had committed suicide by shooting himself. He stepped out of rank into the brush and putting the muzzle of his gun under his chin, touched off the trigger with his toe and blew his head off. We were mustered for pay upon reaching Bayou Mason.

SEPTEMBER, 1863.

Tuesday, 1st—We lay here at Bayou Mason all day to rest. The boys are very tired after marching for twelve days, with the weather much of the time so fearfully hot. Then on account of the bad water, exposure and fatigue, a large number are sick, many of them not able to carry their accouterments, while others are too sick to walk and have to be hauled. The boys made the sweet potatoes suffer today. Received orders to start tonight at midnight and march to the Mississippi river.

Wednesday, 2d—We left Bayou Mason at midnight and marched through to the river, eighteen miles, without stopping, reaching Goodrich's Landing at 7 o'clock this morning. General Stephenson planned our march so that we should pass through

(September, 1863)

that terrible ten miles of hemp at night, thus avoiding the heat.[1] Our brigade led in the march all the way. The day is very hot and sultry. General Logan's Division has taken the boats down the river for Vicksburg.

Thursday, 3d—The boats arrived this morning and we embarked immediately, pushing out at 10 o'clock for Vicksburg. The Eleventh and the Sixteenth Iowa were on board the "Samuel Gotz." We were crowded on the boat, and the heat of the sun was frightful. We reached Vicksburg at 3 o'clock in the afternoon, and disembarking, marched to our old camp.

---

[1] All were thankful to him for it; for, if there is such a place as hell, this piece of road is a sample of the road leading to Satan's residence. —A. G. D.

Chapter XIII.
A Siege of Fever and Ague. Fortifying and Patrolling Vicksburg. September 4-December 2.

Friday, 4th—The weather today is intensely hot. Those who are not sick spent the day in washing their clothing. Over half of the boys in our regiment are sick with the fever and ague, all because of the very poor water we had to drink while on the march, the weather being very hot and sultry.[1]

Saturday, 5th—No news of importance. The weather continues hot and sultry. Many more of the sick are being sent home on furloughs or taken to hospitals. Although half of our number are sick with the chills and fever, yet a kind Providence has certainly favored the soldiers of the Union armies in this region; for though in past years it was a common thing for the people here to have a siege of cholera or yellow fever, we have thus far been spared such a scourge.

Sunday, 6th—The sick in our regiment were sent away this morning, thirty-one in all. Those who could stand the trip North were given a thirty-day furlough, and the very sick were taken to the general hospital here in Vicksburg. The men whose thirty-day furloughs have expired are returning to their regiments.

Monday, 7th—Things are quiet and there is no news of importance. Our chief concern is taking care of the sick, as the weather is yet quite hot. This is a lonesome day with so many of our company sick in the hospital, while six are home on furloughs and three more are soon to go. This leaves but a few of us for duty. I tell you, it looks pretty discouraging.

Tuesday, 8th—Captain McLoney is going home for thirty days and there are still others from our regiment going on furloughs. We have no drilling, dress parade, camp guard or picket duty to perform, nor yet fatigue duty—our whole duty at present is to help care for the sick boys.

---

[1] The results accomplished by this expedition were meager indeed, while the suffering endured by the men engaged in it was very great. Many died from the effects of the hardships to which they were subjected, and many never fully recovered from the diseases contracted while passing through that malarious region, and that during the hottest days of the summer.—A. G. D.

(September, 1863)

Wednesday, 9th—Still more of the boys are coming down with the ague. I had a shake of it myself today, for the first time in my life. I passed through all the degrees of fever and chill. Am thankful tonight to find that I am still among the living.

Thursday, 10th—I reported to the doctor this morning for the second time in the space of two years. The doctor thought that I was in no immediate danger, for which opinion I thought he was not very well posted, but he gave me the "Blue Mass" pills, telling me to be sure to take them and not throw them away as so many of the boys do. I told him that I did not come for the purpose of getting medicine to throw away, for I had been too near dying. He assured me that I was a long way from dying.[1]

Friday, 11th—We moved our camp to the south of Vicksburg, two miles, just within the fortifications. The ground is low and level here, and the water is scarce. It is not a good place for the sick to get back their health. But there is danger of a raid by the rebels' cavalry from this point.

Saturday, 12th—Company E went out on picket this morning. I did not accompany them, as I had another chill yesterday and was not strong enough to go. The teams brought in our poles, lumber and planks and those of us left in camp worked all day building bunks and putting up the brush shades in front of the tents.

Sunday, 13th—There was regimental inspection this morning with accouterments on and in full dress. Some of the companies have the appearance of a "corporal's guard." Company E, being on picket, was not on inspection, but later they were relieved. The Thirteenth Iowa went down town to act as a provost guard. Our chaplain having resigned, we have no religious services at present.

Monday, 14th—Companies A and B started out with teams on a foraging expedition of three days. A detail of forty men was sent down to the wharf to unload a boat of ammunition.

Tuesday, 15th—The weather continues sultry and hot. We have our camp fixed up quite comfortably again. There are not

---

[1] The doctor's exact words were: "Oh, you're a long ways from dying!" Perhaps I was more frightened than sick. But when a sick man is near a regular hospital and sees from three to six dead men carried out every day to the "bone-yard," as the boys used to say, it does not look very encouraging to him.—A. G. D.

(September, 1863)

many of the sick in the regiment now, most of them having been sent away, and others of us who were sick are getting stronger. I am on duty again, having been to see the doctor only the one time.

Wednesday, 16th—I was on division guard today. There are several negro regiments in camp in the vicinity of Vicksburg; they made a good appearance today for their first time on review. They were reviewed by the commander of the post. As a rule there are inferior officers in charge, and it would be a good thing if they would drill in the manual of arms themselves.

Thursday, 17th—We had a cool rainstorm this afternoon which was quite refreshing. The sick in the general hospital here in Vicksburg are improving and are being sent home on thirty-day furloughs.

Friday, 18th—It is reported in our camps that General Rosecrans has taken Chattanooga, Tennessee, and that General Burnside took two thousand prisoners and twelve pieces of artillery without firing a gun. We hope that the report is true, for Chattanooga will afford our army there a strongly-fortified place.

Saturday, 19th—Company E went out on the picket line today. The nights are getting cooler and the middle of the day, though warm, is not so oppressive. Since our rainstorm it begins to look like autumn; the trees are beginning to turn various colors and the sun shining over the timbered hills in the late afternoon makes a landscape grand to look upon.

Sunday, 20th—We had dress parade this evening at 5 o'clock and important orders were read to the command. The first is, that our division is now to be known as the First Division of the Seventeenth Army Corps; second, that on a march we are to carry only nineteen pounds, and third, that we are to be ready to form a line of battle at a moment's notice. The reason for the last is that the rebels have driven in our pickets on the right and may make a raid. News came that a battle is being fought on the Chickamauga river, to the south of Chattanooga, with heavy loss on both sides.

Monday, 21st—Three companies were sent out on picket today. I was on camp guard today. It is reported that the battle south of Chattanooga is still in progress, and also that our gunboats are throwing shells into Charleston, South Carolina. We

(September, 1863)

hear that there was a riot in Mobile, when six hundred women and children demanded bread of the city.

Tuesday, 22d—Everything is very quiet. We learned that Alexander Ragan of Company E died at Benton Barracks, St. Louis, on the 9th of this month. His is the first death in our company since August 3, 1862, when Ebenezer McCullough died at Corinth, Mississippi, on that date.

Wednesday, 23d—The weather is quite cool and the boys are beginning to fix up for winter by siding up the tents and building chimneys. There is some prospect of our brigade having to remain here for the winter. The Second Brigade of our division is still at Natchez. We are raising our tents and bunks about twenty-four inches from the ground. The openings around the tents we close up with boards torn from buildings, and having the wedge tent which accommodates four, we build our bunks for two men, one on either side, with the fireplace and chimney in the rear between the bunks. This makes a pretty good house for winter quarters.

Thursday, 24th—There is no news of importance. I have entirely recovered and am in good health again. Our regiment, as also the entire brigade, is slowly regaining its strength and increasing in number. The boys from the hospitals are taking their places and those on furlough are returning and bringing new recruits with them.

Friday, 25th—It is quite warm today. I was on fatigue duty, accompanying the quartermaster's wagons into Vicksburg to draw supplies for the regiment. The bales of hay and sacks of corn taxed our strength in loading them. Some of the boys on furlough returned today.

Saturday, 26th—There is still some shaking with the ague among the boys, but the health of our regiment is gaining slowly. We have no drill in camp at present, but we are on duty almost every day, our routine running as follows: Picket duty every other day, and the alternating days on fatigue duty either in Vicksburg or in camp, and then, once a week for twenty-four hours at a time, we are on provost duty in Vicksburg.

Sunday, 27th—It continues quite warm and all is quiet. We had company inspection early this morning, after which those

(September, 1863)

not on duty were free to go about, and I attended services at the Baptist church in the city. It seemed like home to attend a regular church service on a Sunday morning. This church building is of brick and during the siege four or five cannon balls passed through the walls at different places.

Monday, 28th—I went out on picket today, on the public highway from Vicksburg to Warrington. We have to maintain a heavy picket with strong reserve at all the public highways leading from this place.

Tuesday, 29th—I came in from picket this morning in a rain which continued all day. We learned that a boat twenty miles up the river from Vicksburg, burned and sank last night in midstream, with a large number of lives lost. The boat was loaded with provisions for the army here at Vicksburg.

Wednesday, 30th—It rained all day. I was on fatigue, helping to clean up the review ground. We are to have general inspection in the next few days by General McArthur, our division commander, and General McPherson, corps commander. Our company is returning to its old-time form and numbers.

OCTOBER, 1863.

Thursday, 1st—We had brigade inspection this morning at 7 o'clock, by General McArthur. Colonel Hall of our regiment is in command. There were three regiments of infantry, one of cavalry and three batteries. In the afternoon I was on fatigue duty, and part of the time in a heavy rain; this is our third successive day of rain.

Friday, 2d—The weather is quite cool for this time of year in the "Sunny South." There is no news of any importance. Things are very quiet.

Saturday, 3d—Orders have been issued to fortify Vicksburg so that a small force can hold the place against one five times the number; the fortifications are to be on the highest ground in the city. I was on duty at a picket post three miles below Vicksburg, on the east bank of the Mississippi. There were four privates and two corporals at the post, the corporals taking their turns in standing out in front as vedettes.

Sunday, 4th—Our brigade was reviewed this morning at 7 o'clock by General McPherson, major-general commanding the

(October, 1863)

Seventeenth Army Corps. The pickets were not relieved until about noon, and so we missed the inspection. The boys are in camp today reading or writing letters.

Monday, 5th—Everything is very quiet here, although as the health of the men is improving our duties become more laborious. Every regiment that can be taken from Vicksburg is being sent to reinforce the armies at other posts. General Sherman has been ordered to proceed to Chattanooga and thus all of the Fifteenth Army Corps will be taken from the vicinity of Vicksburg.

Tuesday, 6th—Our brigade went into Vicksburg this afternoon at 2 o'clock to be in the review, together with the entire army at this place. We were reviewed by Major General U. S. Grant. The report in camp is that General Grant has been ordered by the War Department to report at Louisville, Kentucky. All are sorry to see him leave. Just after dark, the Eleventh Iowa was ordered out on picket, it being expected that the rebel cavalry would make a dash into Vicksburg in the morning.

Wednesday, 7th—Six regiments were stationed at the different roads last night to reinforce the regular pickets. But the rebels did not make their appearance as it was reported they would. Our regiment was relieved at 10 o'clock this morning by the Thirteenth Iowa. We were struck by a fearful rain and windstorm last night.

Thursday, 8th—The Eleventh Iowa went out again on picket this morning, relieving the Thirteenth. I did not accompany the regiment, because I was on camp guard. The weather is quite cool and there is no news of any importance.

Friday, 9th—The rebels have made no attempt at a raid into Vicksburg, but seem to be at their old trick of making our officers believe that they are in this vicinity in large force. Our officers, however, are on their guard, and are not to be caught napping. They continue a strong support of the pickets. The Eleventh and the Thirteenth again exchanged places, our boys coming from picket. A report came that Rosecrans had been whipped at Chattanooga, by Bragg's army.[1]

---

[1] In fact, Rosecrans with his army in Chattanooga had been surrounded by Bragg, who had possession of the railroad, and Rosecrans' army had to depend upon long hauls by wagon for their supplies.—A. G. D.

FEVER AND AGUE—FORTIFYING VICKSBURG

(October, 1863)

Saturday, 10th—The Thirteenth came in and the Eleventh again went out on picket this morning. I was relieved from camp guard after two days' steady duty, and accompanied my regiment on picket. About dark our brigade received orders to be prepared to march at 6 in the morning, with one day's rations in haversacks and four days' rations in the wagons.

Sunday, 11th—We left this morning according to orders and marched fifteen miles, when we stopped to eat dinner. We then continued our march about five miles farther, and at 4 o'clock we reached the Black river bridge, just ten miles out from Vicksburg, thus making a circuit of twenty miles to reach this important point.

Monday, 12th—We remained here in bivouac all day, and shall probably continue at this place several days. Our brigade was sent here to relieve the Third Brigade of General Tuttle's expedition toward Jackson, Mississippi. It turned very warm today. It is raining this evening, and we have no tents in which to stay.

Tuesday, 13th—This is election day for the soldiers of Iowa, they having been given the right to vote while in the army. No one is permitted to electioneer for his favorite candidate and those who persisted in doing so were arrested and put in the guardhouse. General Tuttle, the commander of a division, is from Iowa and is the candidate for governor of the State on the Democratic ticket, against Colonel Stone, formerly of the Twenty-second Iowa Regiment, who is the Republican candidate for governor.[1]

Wednesday, 14th—General Tuttle's division left early this morning on their expedition, carrying eight days' rations. General Logan's Division is also in the command, and there is a total of about ten thousand men—infantry, artillery and cavalry. Our brigade moved into the tents of the Third Brigade of Tuttle's Division, the Eleventh Iowa occupying those of the Fifth Minnesota.

Thursday, 15th—The weather is quite cool and pleasant and we are enjoying the rest afforded us, for the duties here are not laborious: all we have to do is to keep the camp clean and serve on picket. We had regimental inspection this afternoon.

[1] Stone was elected, even without the soldier vote, by a large majority. Mr. Downing has the distinction of having cast his first vote while in the service.—Ed.

(October, 1863)

Friday, 16th—I went on picket this morning. We have to keep a strong picket line for fear of the rebels' cavalry making a dash into this place and burning the provisions stored here. The large camp of refugees is still maintained here by the Government. The cars are running back and forth through here from Vicksburg, coming out at 11 a. m. and returning to Vicksburg at 3 p. m.

Saturday, 17th—We had regimental dress parade this evening, after which an order was read to us giving us our drilling program while stationed here. Beginning tomorrow the Eleventh and the Thirteenth are to have skirmish drill in the afternoon of every other day, and the Fifteenth and Sixteenth are to practice battalion drill on the alternating days.

Sunday, 18th—The Thirteenth went up to Messenger's ford on picket. We had our regular company inspection this morning. In the afternoon I went to the refugees' camp to hear a colored man preach. There was a large number of negroes and they had a joyful time; their singing and shouting beat all that I have ever listened to. They were so happy that they did not cease shouting until after sundown.

Monday, 19th—We were out this morning for our skirmish drill. The scouting expedition returned from Jackson this afternoon and occupied their old camp, while we had to go into open bivouac for the night. The expedition had little difficulty in routing the rebels at Jackson, but lost five or six men killed and quite a number wounded.

Tuesday, 20th—General Logan's Division returned to Vicksburg today. Our brigade pickets were called in and we were expecting also to return to Vicksburg, but had to remain here in bivouac all day. The health of our regiment is quite good now, and most of those away on sick furlough have returned to the regiment.

Wednesday, 21st—Our orders came and we left this morning at 6 o'clock for Vicksburg. We arrived in camp at noon, twelve miles from where we started. All is quiet here and no news of any importance.

Thursday, 22d—We are glad to be at home again in camp after eleven days' absence. Most of that time we were in bivouac

(October, 1863)

without any protection—two nights in soaking rainstorms. Our heavy duties begin again—fatigue duty and camp guard, fourteen of our number being on guard today. Our regimental payrolls for two months' pay were made out and we signed them today. There is no news from the army in the East, and all is quiet here in the West.

Friday, 23d—It rained all day, but that did not affect our camp routine. I was on camp guard, and large details were out at work, as every day, on the fortifications.

Saturday, 24th—The weather is quite cool. I worked all day building a fireplace in my tent, while my bunk-mate was out on duty. The boys are all fixing up for winter just as if we were going to stay here all winter.

Sunday, 25th—I went out on picket today. We keep a strong picket guard along the entire line. The rebels' cavalry are not as bold as they were two or three weeks ago, for they know that we are becoming more thoroughly entrenched every day; besides this, they have been pretty well driven out of this section.

Monday, 26th—Everything is quiet. A thousand men are at work every day on the fortifications. The fortifications are being built on a small scale, but are built all around the edge of town so that a small force can hold the place. The cannon are arranged so that they can be turned in any direction.

Tuesday, 27th—The Eleventh received their pay today, and then went out on picket. Picket exchanges are directed by the aid-de-camp of our brigade, who rides out every morning with the picket relief, and after posting them, brings the retiring picket into camp and disbands them.

Wednesday, 28th—The weather is getting quite cool, particularly the nights, and a little fire in our tents in the evening makes it quite comfortable and homelike. It is different on picket, where no fires are allowed, except on the reserves' posts. Troops are leaving Vicksburg nearly every day, going to northern Mississippi and western Tennessee to occupy garrisons made vacant by General Sherman's men going to the relief of the army cooped up in Chattanooga.

Thursday, 29th—It is quite pleasant today. The Mississippi river is slowly rising. Produce is very high here at Vicksburg and fruit and vegetables are scarce this fall because of the large armies in and around this section for more than a year. What little stuff has been grown by the farmers was confiscated by the soldiers before it was matured, so what we get is shipped down from the North, and we have to pay about four prices for it. Potatoes and onions are $4.00 a bushel, cheese (with worms) is fifty cents per pound, and butter—true, it's only forty cents a pound, but you can tell the article in camp twenty rods away. Vicksburg being under military rule makes it difficult for the few citizens to get supplies, which they can obtain only from the small traders who continued in business after the surrender, or from the army sutlers. No farmers are allowed to come in through the lines without passes, and even then no farmer, unless he lives a long distance from Vicksburg, has anything to bring in.

Friday, 30th—We had a downpour of rain last night which continued most of the day. Our camp is flooded, the dry run beside it having become a raging torrent, and our camp ground is under water from one to four feet. Some of the boys put all their belongings on their bunks and others left for higher grounds.

Saturday, 31st—The water has left our camp in a frightful condition, and we got orders to move the camp to higher ground tomorrow. This was general muster day.[1] I went on fatigue today. William Green of our company, not having recovered from his sickness, left for home this morning on a thirty-day furlough. I sent $50.00 to father by him.

NOVEMBER, 1863.

Sunday, 1st—We moved our camp about a half mile onto higher ground this morning. The quartermaster had our lumber and wood hauled from the old camp and we worked all day pitching our tents and rebuilding the bunks, fireplaces and chimneys. It has been a busy day with us, although it is the Lord's Day, but a true soldier cannot halt when duty calls. I was very thankful that I did not have to be on the picket line, so that I could have a hand in fixing up our tent.

Monday, 2d—It was my turn on the picket line today. Our picket post is three miles below Vicksburg on the main road to

---

[1] A general "muster day" was a day observed throughout the army by general order mustering the soldiers for pay.—Ed.

FEVER AND AGUE—FORTIFYING VICKSBURG 151
(November, 1863)

Warrington, and I was stationed right on the bank of the Mississippi. Our reserve post has one lieutenant, one sergeant, two corporals and thirty privates. Six men under a sergeant go out on the public highway from four to six miles, twice a day, to see that there are no rebels advancing.

Tuesday, 3d—Though the weather has been warm for two days, we are fixing up our tent for any cold snap that may come later on, for the report now is that we will remain here at Vicksburg all winter. I finished building the fireplace in my tent. The quartermaster has a detail of men with teams cutting and hauling wood from the timber for the winter.

Wednesday, 4th—It is still quite warm. I was on fatigue at the fortifications. The men are pulling down some fine residences and using the material in building the forts. It is pretty harsh and severe business to order a family, brave enough to stay all through the siege, out of their home and tear down their house before their eyes, to build into fortifications, but this is war. We are fortifying the place so that ten thousand men can hold it against any force that has a mind to come.

Thursday, 5th—It rained all day and on account of it the fatigue party did not work on the fortifications. Our camp number 3 is located on the town commons, and because of no timber near by the northwest wind has a full sweep over the camp. No news of importance.

Friday, 6th—I was on fatigue again, but on account of rain last night the detail did not go to work until 1 o'clock this afternoon. Some of the heaviest siege guns obtainable are being mounted on raised platforms in the forts.

Saturday, 7th—I was on fatigue duty again today. Two brigades of General Logan's Division went out to the Black river post to relieve General Tuttle's Division, which came in and is to take boat for points up the Mississippi river.

Sunday, 8th—No work today, only picket duty, and all is very quiet here. General Tuttle's division left Vicksburg this morning for Memphis.

Monday, 9th—An order was read at dress parade today announcing that ten men from each regiment would be detailed to go home to their respective states to solicit recruits for their regiments. Lieutenant Alfred Carey has been selected to represent Company E of the Eleventh Iowa.

Tuesday, 10th—I was on a detail of two hundred men with one hundred teams to haul the commissary supplies and ammunition from the transports to the storehouses and magazines constructed near the new forts. It is heavy work, and as to handling the ammunition, quite dangerous. General Grant has given orders that Vicksburg must be well fortified and supplied with munitions and provisions, and that it must be held against all possible attack, for it cost too much to obtain it, besides its being a point of the greatest strategic importance.

Wednesday, 11th—It is very pleasant after four or five days of quite warm weather. I was on picket again, the first time for a week. Two brigades of General Crocker's Division arrived from Natchez to reinforce the troops here at Vicksburg. Two negroes entering an old vacant Confederate magazine today were blown to pieces. They were smoking and it is supposed that the loose powder on the floor in some way became ignited. The explosion was heard for miles around. So much again for the filthy habit of smoking.

Thursday, 12th—The two brigades of General Crocker's Division were at his request ordered back to Natchez today, because of a threatened attack of the rebels at that place.

Friday, 13th—My same old duty again—picket. There was no fatigue detail today, as the fortifications are almost completed. Two or three forts, however, are yet to be built just outside of the rifle pits.

Saturday, 14th—The weather is quite warm, but windy and smoky. Wild grapes are still growing. There is no change; all is quiet and no news. We still maintain our regular picket of two thousand men.

Sunday, 15th—We had the regular Sunday inspections, company at 10 o'clock and regimental at 4. It is pretty strict discipline to call us out on the Lord's Day for two inspections, when our daily duty is so laborious.

Monday, 16th—On picket today. The weather is warm and pleasant, though the cool nights give warning of approaching

FEVER AND AGUE—FORTIFYING VICKSBURG

(November, 1863)

winter. With our high picket post and the beautiful landscape, finer than an artist could paint, picket duty in the daytime is a delight.

Tuesday, 17th—The report in camp this morning was that General Sherman had been killed and his force captured on a railroad train east from Memphis. Another report this afternoon says that the train was attacked by the rebel cavalry, but that the troops formed a skirmish line and routed the rebels, and that Sherman is safe; but men were killed and wounded on both sides.[1]

Wednesday, 18th—The weather is still warm. Our fatigue duty is not so laborious now, but the picket duty is becoming more strenuous if anything on account of the activity of the rebels' cavalry. The Eleventh Iowa signed the payrolls today.

Thursday, 19th—All is quiet and there is nothing of importance. The report in camp is that the Sixth Division will remain at Vicksburg all winter; we are thankful if that is the case, as we are comfortably fixed for winter.

Friday, 20th—It is rainy and blustery today, but otherwise all is quiet. We received two months' pay, being paid in crisp new greenbacks. The paymaster always has a guard with him to guard the strong iron box containing the bills.

Saturday, 21st—The weather is quite cool today. The Fifteenth Iowa got their pay today. Pay time for the soldiers is the time for the gamblers.[2] It is then that they start up their "chuck luck" games. These banks or games are set up south of town, about the springs where the boys from our brigade go for their water.

Sunday, 22d—This morning when our detail was relieved from picket, we were marched to brigade headquarters and put to target shooting. This is to be done regularly from now on, in order to give the boys practice. To encourage good marksmanship a reward is given; those who hit the bull's-eye are excused from picket duty, once for every time they hit the mark.

Monday, 23d—It was warm and pleasant again with rain in the afternoon. The "chuck luck" banks at the spring are in full operation this morning. At each bank there are from twelve to twenty of our boys down on their knees laying their money on

[1] See Sherman's Memoirs, Vol. I., pp. 371-72.
[2] That is, gambling among the soldiers themselves.—Ed.

certain figures, as the "banker" throws the dice. After each throw the operator picks up the largest number of dollars. Some of the men in less than five days lose every dollar received from the paymaster.

Tuesday, 24th—The weather is clear and cool, and the regiment is in good health. No news of importance.

Wednesday, 25th—Out on picket. The guard continues strong and the officers are very strict.

Thursday, 26th—I returned from picket and all is quiet. I loaned $5.00 to Corporal Daniel E. Sweet, until next payday. All of the furloughed men are back now.

Friday, 27th—A detail of men, two of them from Company E, was sent as a guard to go up North with some deserters from our army. Upon being caught, the deserters were brought back, court martialed, and will now be confined in one of the United States military prisons.

Saturday, 28th—A detail of forty men from our regiment was sent into town on provost guard. Our orders were to arrest all citizens and soldiers found upon the streets without passes from the commander of the post here or from the provost marshal, and take them before the latter for investigation and punishment.

Sunday, 29th—We learned that there had been several spies in the city getting plans of our fortifications; they also got medical supplies and other articles of value to the rebels, and smuggled them through our lines at night. Special precaution is taken and the guard is to be continued. We were relieved this morning by a detail from the Thirteenth Iowa.

Monday, 30th—The weather continues with pleasant days and very cool nights. I loaned $5.00 to Thomas R. McConnoll. No news of importance.

DECEMBER, 1863.

Tuesday, 1st—All is quiet. We had dress parade this afternoon at 5 o'clock. I wrote a letter home today.

Wednesday, 2d—We now have a good market house established here which has cut the cost of provisions; formerly the army sutlers had a corner on everything. I bought a barrel of potatoes for $4.00, which, without the market house, would have

FEVER AND AGUE—FORTIFYING VICKSBURG

(December, 1863)

taken $12.00 out of my month's pay. The provisions come from the North and are sold by retailers occupying stalls in the market house. They are usually at it as early as 3 o'clock in the morning.

Two brigades came up from Natchez this morning and went out to Black river bridge to reinforce the post there. A report reached camp to the effect that General Grant has raised the siege of Chattanooga and put Bragg's army to rout, gaining a glorious victory. We threw up our hats and cheered for Grant. Sherman routed Longstreet from the siege of Knoxville, Tennessee. Everything seems to be coming our way again.

Chapter XIV.
Re-enlisting as Veterans. December 3-January 27, 1864.

Thursday, 3d— I went out on picket this morning. An order was read on parade this evening, announcing that all soldiers who will re-enlist for three years or during the war will be enrolled in the Veterans' Corps, and receive a bounty of $400.00 and a thirty-day furlough. Some of the boys signed their names at once.[1]

Friday, 4th—The rebels seldom show themselves near our front. The loss of Chattanooga and Knoxville is a staggering blow to them. News came today that General Grant had another engagement with Bragg, near Dalton, Georgia, and again whipped him.

Saturday, 5th—The re-enlisting of the men for three years is proceeding rapidly. Most of the boys are in favor of seeing the war brought to a close before they quit the job, while others say that they have seen enough of war, declaring that they have done their duty.

Sunday, 6th—I went on patrol guard in the city today, and shall be on guard off and on all night, looking for spies. I attended the evening services of the Baptist church while off duty after a two-hour shift. The weather is nice and warm, as it has been for many days.

Monday, 7th—I was relieved from patrol this morning. Thus far we have not succeeded in locating any of the reported spies. This patrol duty is quite hard, since when we have a few moments for rest the only place is a vacant room over a store, without fire; furthermore, lying down on the floor is not very inviting because of the graybacks running over the floor.

Tuesday, 8th—Everything is marching along fine. The finishing touches are being put upon the outside forts and the heavy guns are mounted and ready for action. The floors of the forts and rifle pits are all laid with the lumber torn from the houses which were removed to make room for the forts, so when it rains

---
[1] I was not yet in from picket and so knew nothing of what was going on.—A. G. D.

RE-ENLISTING—VETERAN REGIMENTS

(December, 1863)

while the men are occupying the forts, they will not need to tramp through the mud. News came that General Bragg was retreating with Grant after him. General Grant is the man for us yet. All are loud in their praise of Grant, and declare that he is the coming man of the time, that we will have him at the head of all of the United States armies before the war is ended.

Wednesday, 9th—Another twenty-four hours duty on picket, which with the time occupied in going out and returning makes about twenty-six hours each time.

Thursday, 10th—It is pretty cold weather now, somewhat cloudy and windy. Our regiment furnished the patrol for the city today, composed of a captain, a lieutenant, two sergeants, eight corporals and forty privates.

Friday, 11th—The Eleventh had regimental inspection with accouterments and full dress. The boys are continuing to re-enlist for three years or during the war. Officers from the corps headquarters are out among the different regiments urging re-enlistments. They argue that the war will be over anyway by the time the first three-year service shall have expired, and they might as well avail themselves of the extra bounty. Then, too, they say, "What a fine thing it would be to be called a veteran of the war!"

Saturday, 12th—It came the Eleventh Iowa's turn to go on reserve picket, down in the river bottom. It is a fine place for a reserve post, plenty of wood to burn these rather cold nights.

Sunday, 13th—We were relieved from picket and arrived in camp about noon. For a wonder we did not have inspection of any kind on this, the Lord's Day. It rained some this morning, but turned off quite clear in the afternoon.

Monday, 14th—A pleasant day and all is quiet. This is wash-day in camp. But since there are so many negro women here, thankful for the job, and who do it so cheaply, most of the boys hire their clothes washed. I got my week's washing done for twenty-five cents. In the early morning we see dozens of negro women going to the springs, each with a tub of soiled clothes on her head and a pail in each hand, singing "the day ob jubilee hab come." In the evening they return with the clean clothes in the same fashion, many of them singing some quaint negro melody.

(December, 1863)

Tuesday, 15th—Quite cool this morning, with a high wind all day. Quite a number of the Eleventh Iowa have re-enlisted, though only eighteen of our company.

Wednesday, 16th—It rained nearly all day, commencing about 1 o'clock in the night. I being on picket had a hard night of it, for the water at our post in the bottom stood about a foot deep. It was a fearful night to be out on picket; one could not even find protection standing, let alone lying down.

Thursday, 17th—It cleared off and has turned quite cold, consequently the boys not on duty keep pretty close to the fires in their tents. There are no "chuck luck" banks in operation now—it is too cold, and then the boys' money is all gone.

Friday, 18th—No news. Our camps are good and there will be no suffering since we have plenty of wood for fuel. The boys feel quite lively staying in camp so long at one time, but I think a march would do us all some good.

Saturday, 19th—All is quiet around Vicksburg, and the weather is quite mild and pleasant, though quite cold at night. Our camp was cleaned up for inspection. I was out on picket again, though on higher ground than the previous time out.

Sunday, 20th—Quite pleasant weather. We had our regular company inspection at 9 o'clock today with dress parade at 5 o'clock.

Monday, 21st—The Eleventh Iowa furnished the provost guard for the city, though I had to go with a picket squad.

Tuesday, 22d—Relieved from picket this morning. It was quite cold last night. I was on an outpost and our detail consisted of a sergeant, a corporal and twelve privates. We took turns standing on vedette, one hour at a time.

Wednesday, 23d—The weather continues quite pleasant. There is no news. All is quiet here. There has been no foraging for two months now, for the reason that there is nothing left to forage. I often wonder what the farmers in this section live on; whatever they have certainly cannot be in abundance. The citizens of Vicksburg are a little more fortunate; that is, if they have the greenbacks, for since July 4th, last, Confederate scrip is no longer legal tender. Some people still have a little gold and silver, which comes from its hiding place when their larders run low.

(December, 1863)

Thursday, 24th—I went on picket again this morning. Late in the evening the Eleventh and the Fifteenth Regiments were ordered out to a little town called Redstone, as it was reported that a strong force of the rebels was there. At 10 o'clock at night a detail of sixty men from the Thirteenth and Sixteenth Regiments was sent out to reinforce our pickets, as it was feared the rebels' cavalry would make an attack upon Vicksburg in the early morning.

Friday, 25th—It was a false alarm. The rebel attack did not materialize and we came in from picket at the usual time. The extra force from the other two regiments returned late in the aftrnoon. The camp is a lonely place with so many out at Redstone, and it is Christmas Day, too. I went to the regimental hospital and purchased from the steward a nice mince pie for my Christmas dinner, costing me fifty cents.

Saturday, 26th—The Eleventh and the Fifteenth Iowa returned from Redstone, and they report that there was no sign of the rebels out there. The rebels being out there was all a humbug. The regiments were sent out there so that the officers in town could have a spree on Christmas.[1]

Sunday, 27th—I was again on provost patrol in the city, and with two others was assigned to the mule corral, the meanest place one could possibly be stationed at; for all we had to do was to see that the four mules penned up there did not kick down the fence.

Monday, 28th—The commanding officers of our post here are "conscripting" every able-bodied citizen for military duty. The order applies to blacks as well as to whites, and aims to provide artisans for labor in connection with the army and army posts.

Tuesday, 29th—I was on camp guard today. The weather is quite pleasant. News came that General Schofield is to be removed from the Department of the Missouri and that Rosecrans is to be placed in command. People are rejoicing over the change. Schofield is in command of a corps with Grant.

Wednesday, 30th—The veterans of the Eleventh Iowa were sworn into the United States service today. There were ten from Company E, as follows: Nathan Chase, George Cush, Leroy

---

[1] Many thought at the time that it was a put-up job to give the boys a march—and I still believe it.—A. G. D.

Douglas, Frank Johnson, James Martin, James Newcom, Henry Newans, James Rankin, Burtis Rumsey, and Orlando Stout.

Thursday, 31st—The weather has been generally mild this month, though changeable, but today it capped the climax. There was a strong gale from the northwest, accompanied by rain and snow. This is regular muster day. The Eleventh Iowa was mustered at 10 o'clock, and we all had to fall in line by companies, and march to the colonel's tent, where we answered to our names as they were called. This is a poor day for "Veterans;" the re-enlisting is not progressing very fast.

JANUARY, 1864.

Friday, 1st—This is a cold New Year's Day, but things are quite lively in camp, the boys being in fine spirits. I got a pass to go down town this afternoon and found the stores all closed for the day. This is the beginning of the year 1864, and this cruel war still continues to rage in the land. I pray to God that it may come to a close before this year does; but, if not, may all things be done to the glory and praise of God, for He is a God of battles. May this war come to a close and our nation be at peace once more, and may slavery be wiped out so that there shall be no more slaves in America.

Saturday, 2d—I was detailed for picket again this morning, and the post I drew stationed me on the bottom land. It began to rain late in the afternoon and continued into the night and I was soon standing in water. I tell you, it is poor comfort on picket. The commanding officer banished three women from our lines today. The case against them grew out of a meeting on last Thanksgiving Day. They attended the meeting held in the Presbyterian church and when the minister prayed for the President of the United States, for the success of our arms, and for the Stars and Stripes, saying, "May they continue to float over the land of the free and the home of the brave," the three women got up and indignantly walked out. They were banished for disloyal conduct.

Sunday, 3d—It cleared off this morning and it got quite cool. I was at my post this morning, standing in water a foot deep. When our relief came they had to go back almost to town before

RE-ENLISTING—VETERAN REGIMENTS

(January, 1864)

they could cross the swollen creek to reach our post. The "Veteran" excitement was raging when we got back to camp. This afternoon we had a meeting of our regiment, when Major Foster made a speech on the subject of re-enlisting, and I re-enlisted. A large number in our brigade and throughout the Seventeenth Army Corps have re-enlisted. Abraham Brown of our company died yesterday, here in the Vicksburg hospital. He was a good man.

Monday, 4th—An order was issued by the War Department cancelling the previous order giving the large bounties to soldiers for re-enlisting, but it is not to go into effect until midnight of the 5th inst. Re-enlisting is going on at a lively rate. Company E today secured the necessary number entitling it to be a veteran company—the first one in the regiment, Company K being the second. General McPherson delivered a speech before the Iowa Brigade, expressing his desire that the entire Seventeenth Army Corps might become a corps of veterans, and I think there is no doubt but that it will.

Tuesday, 5th—The Eleventh Iowa went in today as a veteran regiment, for three years more if needed. Our brigade will also go in as a veteran brigade. It is quite stormy, with a wind from the northwest. I went on picket again, down on the river bottom, two miles below.

Wednesday, 6th—The time for re-enlisting with the bounty expired last night at midnight. The boys who re-enlisted are now looking forward to going home on a thirty-day furlough in the spring.

Thursday, 7th—Pleasant weather again after several days of cold. Our brigade now provides the provost guard for the city, which takes each regiment down town every fourth day. The work is thus becoming heavier for our brigade. All is quiet in camp.

Friday, 8th—I was on fatigue duty, hauling wood for the picket post out in an open field. General Hunter reviewed our brigade today and inspected Company E. It is reported that he is to take command of the Seventeenth Army Corps. All of us hope that it is a false report, for we do not wish to lose General McPherson.

(January, 1864)

Saturday, 9th—I was on picket guard down town and all is quiet. The ice floe is running quite strong in the Mississippi and has been for some days, which is rather a new thing to the people of Vicksburg. They say the like has never been known, at least in such large quantities, and that this is the coldest winter they have had for fifty years, although there is no snow as yet.

Sunday, 10th—We had company inspection this morning. A brigade from here was sent up the river on transports to Greenville, to rout the rebels who have set up a battery there, blockading the river and stopping navigation.

Monday, 11th—The weather has been very warm for several days and there was a heavy thunderstorm last night. All is quiet in camp, but the men in the old regiments, having re-enlisted, are becoming restless and want to move, for remaining in camp will never bring the war to a close.

Tuesday, 12th—It is cloudy but warm, and the ice is still coming down the river. Our duties here in camp are lightening up some. All is quiet and there is nothing of importance.

Wednesday, 13th—I was on patrol down town. Things are quiet there, but the streets are quite muddy. The patrols have strict orders to arrest all soldiers found down town without passes, as well as citizens who are caught on the streets without passes. It is not a very pleasant duty, this thing of stopping everyone on the street and requiring him to give an account of himself.[1]

Thursday, 14th—There is a rumor that our army has taken Charleston, South Carolina. Some of our guard early this morning stole a big fish from a fisherman who was taking a load to market. It weighed forty pounds and was divided among the boys. I took a piece to my tent and cooked it, but I might as well have eaten a piece of crow, for it was tasteless and tough. It proved to be a channel cat.

Friday, 15th—Camp and picket duty are becoming very light as compared to one month ago. Some of the regiments sent to Minnesota and western Iowa to drive back the Indians, are returning to camp. It is reported that the Sixteenth Army Corps will soon return from Chattanooga. We hear also that General Sherman will command an expedition from Vicksburg across the state to Meridian, Mississippi.

[1] Mr. Downing explained that spies in Vicksburg had gotten some Union uniforms, and that special precautions were again taken.—Ed.

RE-ENLISTING—VETERAN REGIMENTS
(January, 1864)

Saturday, 16th—The weather has been warm and pleasant for a week. We have our regular daily drills and dress parade. It came my turn to go on the picket line again. The Thirteenth Iowa received their muster rolls, and when they are filled out, the regiment will be sworn into the United States service as a veteran regiment.

Sunday, 17th—We had an all day rain. Company inspection early this morning. The Eleventh Iowa received their muster rolls and the boys are anxious to be sworn into the service and start for home on their thirty-day furloughs.

Monday, 18th—It cleared off and turned quite cool. Nothing—nothing new; still lying in camp. The men are becoming restless and anxious to move on to another place, and to accomplish something.

Tuesday, 19th—The weather is quite pleasant. No news. On picket again and all is quiet. We see nothing of the rebels about here.

Wednesday, 20th—The Thirteenth Iowa was today sworn into the service for three years as a veteran regiment.

Thursday, 21st—All things quiet in camp and no news. The weather is pleasant, though a little frosty every night. The army could stand a long siege, for we have plenty of wood and the quartermaster has in storage a large supply of provisions. This is fine soldiering.

Friday, 22d—The weather is quite warm and it looks almost like spring—grape vines are beginning to start.

Saturday, 23d—Warm weather. Still lying in camp and all is quiet—no news.

Sunday, 24th—After company inspection this morning, I went to church down in the city; went again in the evening. They have regular church services and Sunday school every Sunday.

Monday, 25th—The Eleventh Iowa Regiment was today sworn into the United States service for three years or during the war, and now we are a veteran regiment. Our company had an election of officers, but it did not amount to anything, as it was vetoed by the colonel, and men of his own choice were put into the offices. The role of officers as elected is as follows:[1]

[1] The men had been promised the right to elect their own officers if they re-enlisted.—A. G. D.

(January, 1864)

Captain..........................S. S. McLoney
First Lieutenant................William Spencer
Second Lieutenant.............Joseph Tomlinson
First Sergeant ....Lewis Elseffer
Second Sergeant....................David Huff
Third Sergeant....................Hiram Frank
Fourth Sergeant.................John A. White
Fifth Sergeant............Alexander G. Downing

Tuesday, 26th—I went on picket today. The weather is quite warm. Vicksburg, on the east bank of the Mississippi, is built on very high ground. It is quite rough and rolling here. There are some nice buildings here—a very fine court house, six good church buildings and a number of very nice dwellings, besides some large warehouses and stores. During the siege the houses were all more or less damaged, there being scarcely a single building that was not in some way injured. There are very few of the old citizens living here at present, as the military rule of the Union army is not good for their peace of mind.

Wednesday, 27th—We have battalion drill now every afternoon, and today our regiment was reviewed by General Chambers. A division of the Sixteenth Army Corps from Chattanooga landed here last night.

Chapter XV.

The Expedition to Meridian, Mississippi. January 28-March 6.

Thursday, 28th—Some of the troops that are going out on an expedition to Meridian, started on their way this morning. It is rumored that the Seventeenth and Sixteenth Army Corps are to make a raid across the State of Mississippi for the purpose of destroying the railroad running from Vicksburg to Meridian, and that General Sherman is to be in command of the expedition.

Friday, 29th—Everything is working fine here at present. We can hear nothing about the army in the East. Some of the brigades have moved out to Black river bridge, since there is a better camping ground at that place; they also have good water there and plenty of wood and provisions. But we are still lying in camp with plenty to live on and our duty is very light.

Saturday, 30th—We cleaned up our camp for inspection. Troops are still landing here for the purpose of going out on the raid.

Sunday, 31st—Regimental inspection today and the usual dress parade. All things are quiet in camp and no news. I attended church services in the afternoon. Since the arrival here of the large number of reinforcements, the rebels have all left this vicinity, retiring beyond the Black river. In all probability they are informed as to our contemplated expedition and are concentrating their forces to dispute every mile of the way to Meridian.

FEBRUARY, 1864.

Monday, 1st—The weather is nice and warm today, as it has been for several weeks. A part of General Tuttle's Division arrived in camp from some point up the river. The Crocker Brigade (Third Brigade of the Fourth Division of the Seventeenth Corps) received orders to prepare to go with the expedition, taking twenty days' rations of hard-tack, salt, coffee and sugar. We are to start in the morning at daylight. Meridian is one hundred and sixty miles east of Vicksburg.

(February, 1864)

Tuesday, 2d—Our pickets were relieved last night about 10 o'clock preparatory to going on the expedition, but we did not get off this morning because the quartermaster failed to get the rations loaded yesterday, so we have to remain in camp for another day. I went on camp guard this morning. Our orders are to leave all equipage in camp, taking only our blankets and one hundred rounds of ammunition. The convalescents are to remain here to guard the camp.

Wednesday, 3d—We started this morning at 8 o'clock and marched to the Black river, where we bivouacked for the night. Our brigade was train guard for the provision train. Our entire expedition is supposed to have about twenty-five thousand men, composed of infantry, artillery and cavalry, with one engineers' corps in charge of a pontoon bridge. The weather is fine for marching. General Crocker's Division has started ahead.

Thursday, 4th—We started to move at 8 o'clock and by night reached Bolton Station, where we went into camp. Our brigade being in the rear did not get into camp until 11 p. m. There was some skirmishing by Crocker's Division, which lost three men killed and several wounded. Two men were killed by a ball from the rebels' battery striking the top rail of a rail fence, which broke and struck the two men, knocking off their heads and spilling their brains about. It was a gruesome sight. Their bodies were buried where they fell.

Friday, 5th—We left our bivouac this morning at 8 o'clock and moved forward about fifteen miles. General Liggett's Division was assigned the advance today, while our brigade was taken from the supply train and placed immediately in Liggett's rear. General Hurlbut's Division is on a road just off to our left. There was some skirmishing, though with little loss to either side. We drove the rebels out of Clinton this morning and at dark routed them from Jackson, capturing one piece of artillery and some prisoners. We did not get into bivouac until 10 o'clock.

Saturday, 6th—Our army did not move until in the afternoon, because of having to lay the pontoons across the Pearl river. The rebels had burned the bridges, twenty-eight in all, after crossing. I was detailed this morning as special guard at the Seventeenth Corps headquarters while out on this expedition. Things are quiet in the rear.

THE EXPEDITION TO MERIDIAN, MISSISSIPPI
(February, 1864)

Sunday, 7th—We started early this morning and after reaching Brandon, about thirteen miles east of Jackson, went into bivouac about a mile from the town. There was no skirmishing in the front today, the rebels rapidly falling back. Our men set fire to the town this evening and burned almost the whole town. Most of the citizens had fled from the place before our forces entered. We captured a great quantity of tobacco here.

Monday, 8th—We left bivouac at 8 o'clock and covered seventeen miles today. There was some skirmishing in front. The roads were good and but few bridges to cross. All is quiet in the rear. This section of the country is heavily timbered, mostly pine, and the soil is quite sandy. It is thinly settled through here.

Tuesday, 9th—Starting early this morning we reached Morton about noon, where we went into bivouac and remained the balance of the day. The rebels took their first stand here, forming a line of battle, but our two corps being brought together to engage them, they feared to risk a battle and hastily fell back. The Sixteenth Army Corps then passed ahead of the Seventeenth, taking the advance in pursuit. It is estimated that the rebels have a force of fifteen thousand men. Our army is burning all railroad and public property on the way. This town even is literally wiped out, for when the citizens flee before our army and leave their homes vacant, there is always someone ready to set the vacant houses on fire.

Wednesday, 10th—We left Morton early this morning, and covering fifteen miles, reached the town of Hillsborough at about 3 o'clock. There was some skirmishing in front with a loss of three to the rebels. By the time the rear reached town it was all on fire, the citizens having fled. Our army moves rather slowly, on account of the bridges being burned, and the engineers must rebuild or throw out the pontoons. But things are marching along fine.

Thursday, 11th—We moved but ten miles today, when we went into bivouac. Our men are foraging on the way, especially for meat, of which there is a plenty of fresh pork. Some of the foraging parties sent out today were captured and roughly used by the rebels. General McPherson had his headquarters in a large mansion on a rich plantation today. There had been hun-

(February, 1864)

dreds of slaves on this plantation, but all the able-bodied negro men were taken along by the rebels for their army.

Friday, 12th—We reached Decatur at 10 o'clock this morning and went into camp. The rebels attacked the provision train of the Sixteenth Corps and killed twenty of the mules before our men could rally and put them to rout. The town was burned before we left it. Things are marching fine.

Saturday, 13th—We left Decatur early this morning and marched fifteen miles before going into bivouac. The Sixteenth Corps corralled their train and leaving a brigade to guard it pushed forward after the rebels. Skirmishing in the front continued and was brisk at times. The weather is pleasant and the roads are fine for marching. There is still plenty of forage along the way. This morning I saw a woman with her children forcibly moved out of her residence, all the household goods and the house set on fire. The deed was ordered by our officers, for they had been informed that her husband was out in the brush with his rifle, killing Union soldiers at every opportunity. The plantation home had the appearance of wealth.

Sunday, 14th—We marched fifteen miles again today and went into camp for the night. The Seventeenth Corps also corralled their wagon train, leaving two brigades as a guard. There was some skirmishing in the front today, but we learn that the rebels have left Meridian without making any resistance, retiring to the south. Some of our men occupied the town late this evening. Things are marching along fine.

Monday, 15th—After two hours' marching our army entered Meridian at about 10 o'clock this morning and went into camp. The rebels are still retreating, and detachments of our army are pursuing them. The infantry is sent out in all directions tearing up the railroads, burning the ties and twisting the rails. Large numbers of cars, some engines and the depot have been burned, as also the store buildings and many residences. It is a terrible sight to look upon. Forage is plentiful in this vicinity.

Tuesday, 16th—After a rain yesterday, it is quite cool today. General Crocker's Division went on to the town of Enterprise, to destroy the railroad there, while the Sixteenth Corps went to the north destroying the railroad. General McPherson has his headquarters in a fine residence in the west part of town and his headquarters' guards, twenty-eight of us, occupy the negro huts close by. We are at present short of rations and all I had for dinner was some tough fresh beef, which the more I fried, the tougher it got.

Wednesday, 17th—The different troops are returning to camp here after destroying about one hundred and twenty-five miles of railroad, stations and all public property. All is quiet around here.

Thursday, 18th—Our provision trains came in from the rear today and we are thankful for the hardtack which we have been without for three days.

Friday, 19th—The quartermaster is sending out large foraging parties today, while the army is preparing to start back toward Vicksburg tomorrow, after destroying everything within our lines. There are no more rebels to be found in this vicinity.

Saturday, 20th—The weather is quite cool and has been for several days. We left Meridian early this morning for Vicksburg, followed by large numbers of contrabands and refugees. Some of the negro women have their bedding tied up in quilts, carrying them on their heads, each with a bundle of clothing in one hand and in the other a corn pone and pieces of bacon tied up in a red handkerchief.

Sunday, 21st—The weather is fine for marching. After a night's rest, we started early this morning and reaching Decatur, went into bivouac. The provision trains aim now to keep one day's march in advance of the army.

Monday, 22d—We had a long hard day's march, with our brigade leading the corps. There were some wide swamps to cross and we had to build corduroy roads of rails and pine trees, over which to move the artillery. It was late before we went into bivouac.

Tuesday, 23d—We left at 8 o'clock and by noon had reached Hillsborough, where we were ordered to go into bivouac for the night. We caught up with the supply trains here and getting a fresh supply of provisions we are to lie over to give them a start again. All is quiet on the return.

Wednesday, 24th—The army left the Hillsborough bivouac

over different roads. Our brigade went in advance of the Sixteenth Corps to assist the engineers in laying the pontoons across the Pearl river. This is a good section of the country for forage. We selected twelve men from our entire headquarters' guard of twenty-eight to go out on forage, and they brought in six hundred pounds of bacon, twenty-five live chickens, one hundred pounds of honey and other articles. Several of us are up tonight cooking the chickens, which with the other things will fill our haversacks. We shall live well now. We are camping on a large plantation.

Thursday, 25th—The main army moved only eight miles today, when it went into camp for the remainder of the day and night. This is to give the Sixteenth Corps time to cross the river. Our brigade was the first to cross the river, and we went on as far as Canton, about fifteen miles north of Jackson. Here we went into camp and are waiting for the army to catch up. All is quiet. The weather is quite warm. Peach trees are in bloom and the wild grapes are getting green.

Friday, 26th—General McPherson with the main part of the army left camp at 8 o'clock in the morning and after an all day march arrived at Canton after dark. They crossed the Pearl river at 10 a. m. and then reloaded the pontoons and destroyed what remained of the bridge. Just before going into camp two men were shot dead by the accidental discharge of a gun which they were pulling out from the back end of the wagon.

Saturday, 27th—We remained here in camp all day. A number of foraging parties were sent out and some of them were captured by the rebels, and so did not have the privilege of enjoying their booty with their comrades. Canton is a very nice little place, and our army did not destroy the town because so many of the citizens remained in their homes.

Sunday, 28th—The supply trains started on ahead for Vicksburg, taking with them about six thousand contrabands and refugees—men, women and children, both white and black, of all sorts and sizes. The rebels drove in our pickets today, but did not come any closer. The report is that it is Wheeler and his cavalry.

Monday, 29th—The rebels drove in our pickets again last night and there was some skirmishing, but when we commenced cannonading they fell back. General McPherson has his headquarters here in a fine residence, and I am one of three men who have to walk the beat in front of his headquarters; we had the same duty the entire expedition, when his headquarters was in a residence or in his tent in bivouac.

MARCH, 1864.

Tuesday, 1st—We left Canton at 8 o'clock this morning, our brigade taking up the rear. There was some skirmishing with the rebels' cavalry, which began early in the morning before we got started. Bullets commenced to fly and the guards formed a line to protect the headquarters' baggage. Finally, however, the rear guard opened a light battery on the rebels, who soon dropped back out of danger. The army, on account of an all day rain which made the roads very muddy, covered only eight miles, and went into bivouac, our rear not getting in, however, till 4 o'clock in the morning.

Wednesday, 2d—Orders were issued this morning for the army not to destroy any more property while on the march. We just learned that while we were in Canton, General Hurlbut levied a tax on the citizens, compelling them to furnish corn meal and other articles of food for the army. Today we marched fifteen miles, reaching Clinton Crossroads by night, where we went into bivouac. The rebels are still following us and there was some skirmishing in the rear, which at times made it necessary to bring the light artillery into action.

Thursday, 3d—We got into motion early this morning and marched twenty miles. We bivouacked for the night within twenty-six miles of Vicksburg and not far from our forces at Big Black river bridge. The rebels ceased following us today. The weather and roads were fine for marching.

Friday, 4th—The army left bivouac at daylight this morning and the vanguard reached Vicksburg at 2 o'clock, while our rear did not get in till dark. We found our camps, clothing and all in good shape. The Sixteenth Army Corps went into camp out east of Vicksburg. We were relieved from the duty of headquarters' guard this morning. The expedition was out thirty-two days, and marched three hundred and twenty-five miles; it destroyed an immense amount of property, thus inflicting a tremendous blow to the Confederacy, and foraged on the country the whole way.

Saturday, 5th—We are all glad to get back in camp again and to sleep in the bunks instead of lying on the ground in open bivouac. The boys spent the day in washing clothes and cleaning guns and accouterments.

Sunday, 6th—The weather is quite pleasant today, and has been for several days. We had company inspection early this morning, and in the afternoon we had preaching in camp, followed by dress parade at 5 o'clock.

(March, 1864)

Chapter XVI.
Home on Veteran's Furlough. March 7-April 22.

Monday, 7th—The Thirteenth Regiment started for Iowa today on their thirty-day furlough. Our regiment received three months' pay, and all who re-enlisted were given a part of their bounty money, $160.00 each. The bounty, with my regular pay, after settling for six months' clothing, $8.00, gave me $207.00.

Tuesday, 8th—I was detailed with six men from the Eleventh under me, as special guard at the roundhouse. We were detailed about midnight to relieve the Ninety-fifth Illinois, which will accompany a part of the Sixteenth Army Corps down the river, and then on an expedition up the Red river. The Seventeenth Army Corps is going home on veterans' furlough.

Wednesday, 9th—It rained all day. We are still on guard at the roundhouse. Troops are on the move, both up and down the river as fast as the transports can carry them. New troops are to garrison Vicksburg from now on. We are glad to leave the place, for we have been in and around Vicksburg for more than fifteen months, and have seen some very hard service in that time. But there is something about Vicksburg, the Gibraltar of the West, that is really fascinating.

Thursday, 10th—It rained all day yesterday, and today it is quite cool. The expedition that is going up the Red river left this afternoon. Regiments are leaving every day for the North, going home on their veterans' furloughs. We are still on guard at the roundhouse.

Friday, 11th—The Iowa Brigade turned over their tents and camp equippage to the general quartermaster, preparatory to going up the river. General Grant is now at the head of all the armies of the United States, just where we have wanted him ever since the surrender of Vicksburg.[1]

---

[1] After Vicksburg, General Grant was sent to Chattanooga, Tennessee, and succeeded in raising the siege there, and then at Knoxville, defeating two Confederate armies all in the space of a few days. That covered Grant with glory in the estimation of us Western men, and we then declared that he was the man to send to Washington, D. C., and to take command of the Eastern as well as the Western army.—A. G. D.

(March, 1864)

Saturday, 12th—All the men of the Iowa Brigade who did not re-enlist have been formed into a battalion until the veterans return. Major Pomutz of the Fifteenth Iowa is in command. All the non-veterans of the old regiments are to remain at Cairo, Illinois, until the veterans return from their furloughs.

Sunday, 13th—The Eleventh and the Fifteenth Iowa, together with the Twelfth Wisconsin, all veterans, went aboard the "Continental" this afternoon and about dark left for the North. I could not go with my regiment, as I have not yet been relieved from guard duty at the roundhouse.

Monday, 14th—It is quite cool today, after three days of warm weather. We are still on guard at the roundhouse. The contrabands are all being put to some kind of work, or enrolled in the army. As the Government has to feed them, they will partially pay their way by working.

Tuesday, 15th—We were relieved from guard at the roundhouse, and I received my transportation papers from the provost marshal. I was promoted today from "high private in the rear rank" to sixth corporal in the front rank, my commission to date from March 1, 1864.[1]

Wednesday, 16th—This is a beautiful day. I left for home on my thirty-day furlough. I embarked with the Fifteenth Iowa and the Thirty-second Illinois, on board the "Olive Branch." We left for Cairo, Illinois, at 3 p. m. We say adieu to thee, Vicksburg, the Gibraltar of the West! We leave thee with some pleasant memories, notwithstanding the many hardships we had to endure while with thee! Before we left Vicksburg the railroad station caught fire and was completely consumed with two thousand bushels of oats stored there.

Thursday, 17th—Our boat has been running steadily since starting, it having stopped but once, and that was to take on wood for the boilers of the engine. The time has passed without incident.

Friday, 18th—It is quite cool today with a rather sharp wind blowing, which with our crowded condition makes it very uncomfortable. The Thirty-second Illinois received their pay on

[1] This was indeed a surprise to me, as I had never asked for any office. The expression in quotations was a war-time saying, a joke of the privates.—A. G. D.

(March, 1864)

board today, and no doubt the gamblers will get their hands in before we land.

Saturday, 19th—It is quite cool. We reached Memphis at 4 o'clock this morning and remained all day, not starting on our trip till late this evening. The supply train of the Sixteenth Army Corps was unloaded here from our boat, and we took on the Thirty-fifth New York Infantry.

Sunday, 20th—It is quite cool today. We ran all day, but we have a big load, crowding every nook and corner of the boat; we are more crowded than before reaching Memphis. The sergeant in charge of us six guards had our haversacks replenished at Memphis.

Monday, 21st—We reached Cairo at 4 o'clock this morning and I went ashore with my comrades to the Soldiers' Home for breakfast. We then went to the provost marshal's office for our railroad transportation from Cairo to Davenport. We boarded the train at noon and arrived at Centralia at 5 o'clock. We had to lie here until after midnight when we took the Illinois Central for La Salle, Illinois. The train was so crowded that in order to get a comfortable place, we bought sleeping berths. The weather is cold here, and we saw snowbanks for the first time in two years.

Tuesday, 22d—We reached La Salle at 2 o'clock this afternoon and changed cars for Davenport, arriving at our destination at dark. I took lodging at the Davis House. The taverns are all crowded, because of so many soldiers coming home on their furloughs.

Wednesday, 23d—I left all my accouterments and clothing at the hotel. Before starting for home, I purchased some clothing and other articles, all amounting to $46.50. Among other things, I bought a blouse and vest, a hat, shirts, boots, pen, and my first watch, for which I paid $17.00. I started for home at 10 o'clock, and as it is seeding time and the roads are muddy, there were no teams in town from my neighborhood, so I had to walk the entire distance, all alone. I reached home at 8 o'clock and found all well, and getting along fine.

Thursday, 24th—I went to Mr. Elseffer's and spent most of the day there, taking dinner with them. Lewis Elseffer is a mem-

(March, 1864)

ber of my company and was detailed as clerk in corps headquarters, thus could not return with us.

Friday, 25th—I remained at home all day visiting and talking over some of my experiences. One change I find in myself, and that is the discomfort in sleeping in a warm room, as the custom in the homes is, for it is more than two and a half years since I have slept that way.

Saturday, 26th—The friends of the boys in our company gave a dinner for us today at Mr. Ray's, and father took me over. It was a cold, cloudy day and the roads were muddy, but all the friends came out and gave the boys a warm greeting—and a fine dinner we had. We all enjoyed ourselves and are thankful to those who got up this dinner for the returned soldiers. It would be fine soldiering if one could have such dinners in the army. May this war soon come to a close that all may enjoy home, and help where we are needed.

Sunday, 27th—I went with father to meeting today, in our old church at Inland, and attended the Communion of the Lord's Supper with the Disciples. They have no minister at present, but meet every Lord's Day to break bread. It rained nearly all day.

Monday, 28th—I went to Tipton on horseback today, accompanied by John D. Moore, who enlisted in Company E of the Eleventh Iowa Infantry. All of the Inland boys who went before have re-enlisted as veterans, and four or five others besides John Moore are going to enlist in our company and go to the front when we return. I saw several of the boys of my company today, who live at Tipton.

Tuesday, 29th—I attended a supper this evening given for the veterans of my company, at the home of Mr. J. W. Stanton on York Prairie. On account of the bad weather, dark night and muddy roads, there were not many there, but we had a fine supper and a pleasant evening with friends.

Wednesday, 30th—I remained at home all day. Times appear to be very dull and lonesome. My brothers are having a siege of the measles. I am thankful that I have had them, for measles in the army causes more soldiers to be discharged for disability than anything else. I long to see this cruel war come to a close.

(March, 1864)

Thursday, 31st—I went to a party this evening, given in honor of the veterans, over at Mr. Hatch's, on Yankee Street.[1] There were not many present, but all enjoyed themselves. I found a new road to travel, a mile from this place—if all goes well. Things are very quiet in this settlement, but almost every young man here is thinking of returning with us to help bring the war to a close. It does us good to see the loyal sentiment among the people at home. The general belief at home is that the war cannot last more than a year longer.

APRIL, 1864.

Friday, 1st—The same old thing over and over. I almost wish myself back in the army; everything seems to be so lonesome here. There is nothing going on that is new, and there is no work of any kind.

Saturday, 2d—They had a very cold winter here in Iowa and the ground has been frozen so deep that it is slow in thawing out. Farmers, as yet, have sown but little wheat, but they have everything ready to push the seeding as soon as the ground will permit. It is quite pleasant today, but the roads are very muddy yet, and there is no news of any importance.

Sunday, 3d—I went to our church again this morning, it being the day for preaching. In the evening I went to see a young lady friend.

Monday, 4th—It rained all last night and nearly all day. I attended a party this evening at Mr. Fossett's and we all had a fine time which passed off very rapidly. There were fourteen couples present. I remained over night with my old bunk-mate, James. I enjoyed my visit with him, talking over the times when we started into the service together.

Tuesday, 5th—I took dinner at Mr. Curtis's today, and had a fine dinner. Two other soldier boys were there, Mr. Curtis's son, Homer and Thomas Fossett, both of the Twenty-fourth Iowa Infantry. The citizens in and around Inland are very loyal, and the vicinity is well represented in the Eleventh and Twenty-fourth Regiments.

[1]Yankee Street was the name given to an adjoining neighborhood.—A. G. D.

Wednesday, 6th—I went to Tipton to attend the celebration of the 6th of April, the day on which two years ago we fought the battle of Shiloh. I went with a team, taking a load of the young people of the community with me. The roads were awfully muddy and once we stuck in the mud. The citizens gave a dinner in honor of the veterans of Company E, and though I cannot brag on the dinner, there were a great many present. Although we had a muddy time of it, yet all seemed to enjoy themselves. At a meeting in the court house in the afternoon, Major Foster of the Eleventh Iowa delivered a speech before a large audience.

Thursday, 7th—It rained all day, and I remained at home. As the boys are all down with the measles, I am helping father with the farm work between showers.

Friday, 8th—Another wet day and I stayed at home all day. It is so lonesome that I almost wish I was back in the army; although if I did not have to go back, I could enjoy myself a great deal better. May God hasten the day when this cruel war will be fought to a close, so that the soldiers may return to their homes and friends. What a cruel thing this war is! Think of the thousands of our brave men suffering in the hospitals and in the camps, and many being killed on the battlefield. And yet, think of the everlasting Copperheads in the North, how they sympathize with the South! Such men as they are not fit to be compared with the negroes of the South! I would like to see such men as they are be made to go down there and fight for the South, and be compelled to live on mule beef at that!

Saturday, 9th—It is cool and quite pleasant. I stayed at home all day and did some writing (brought my army diary up to date). The farmers are still lying by waiting for the weather and the ground to get fit for seeding. There is no news of any importance from the army.

Sunday, 10th—It is still raining; there appears to be nothing but rain, rain! I went to meeting again this morning, and accompanied Mr. Sparks home for dinner. Jason Sparks is going to enlist and return with us to the front. In the afternoon we all went to attend meeting at the Inland schoolhouse, but the preacher didn't come, and so I spent the balance of the day with the family of Mr. Willey, and remained there till late in the evening.

Monday, 11th—It was rainy all day, but I went to farming this morning for the first time for nearly three years. As the boys are all sick and as it is impossible for father to hire help even for a few days, I made up my mind that it was my duty to help father to get his seeding done. I started in drilling wheat, but after a while I had to stop on account of the rain.

Tuesday, 12th—It rained almost the whole day; it does look as if it would never quit raining. I gave father $110.00 today, to keep for me until I return from the war. That makes $360.00 altogether that I have placed in his hands to put out on interest till I return. There is nothing of any importance here.

Wednesday, 13th—It is cloudy and very cool. I helped father put in his wheat today, harrowing all forenoon and drilling in wheat in the afternoon. James Kelley, a soldier of the neighborhood, home on a furlough, came over to help me out for a few days.

Thursday, 14th—Another cloudy, disagreeable day! I drilled in wheat all day and Kelley did the harrowing. The boys with the measles are getting along fine and will be well in a few days if they don't take cold.

Friday, 15th—It is cloudy and quite cool. I harrowed all day, and I think that it is the last day's work that I shall do on the farm for some time, unless this cruel war soon comes to a close.

There are two families in this locality who are Copperheads and opposed to the war. They are members of the "Knights of the Golden Circle," but are very quiet at present. They do not, however, give dinners to the returned veterans. About eighteen months ago, they, with some others, north and west from here, were giving the loyal people of the county a great deal of trouble, going so far as to recruit a company of cavalry for the rebel army and drill them at the county seat. Finally, some of our brave soldiers, Tipton boys, home on furlough, made it so hot for the would-be rebel soldiers, that they disbanded, and have not been seen drilling since.

Saturday, 16th—It is clear and quite cool today. My brother John and I went up to Tipton this morning. Things are pretty lively in town; but there are not many of the veterans in today. I went to the harness shop and bought a saddle as a present to father. I called on Mrs. Willey, she and her husband having been good friends of mine. Mr. Willey was a member of the Twenty-fourth Iowa, but died in the spring of '63 at Milliken's Bend, above Vicksburg. On our way back home I stopped at the home of Mr. Robedie and took supper with the family.

Sunday, 17th—It is cloudy and quite cool. There was some rain today, but toward evening it cleared off and became quite pleasant. I attended church at the Sparks schoolhouse, where the few members of the Christian church in this settlement have organized a church. They have prayer meeting and communion every Sunday at 10 o'clock, with preaching every fourth Sunday. May God help those who are trying to keep His holy laws, and may He help the churches all over the world, that they may do much good in bringing sinners to repentance and into the service of the Lord their Savior. After services I went home with John Moore, perhaps for the last time this spring. John and I spent the early evening at the home of Mr. William Listenwalter.

Monday 18th—I stayed at home all day. Father finished sowing his wheat today. John D. Moore with Henry Clark left this morning for Davenport to go into Camp McClellan—Clark is a veteran of my company, while John is a recruit for the company. Jason Sparks could not go with them on account of having the measles. Dr. Clark went to see him and certified that he was not fit for duty.

Tuesday, 19th—I attended a party last night at Mr. Ray's and did not get home till daylight this morning. William Green and Jeremiah Argo came home with me for breakfast and left for Camp McClellan. Green is one of the veterans of Company E and Argo is a recruit for the same. The weather is getting warm, the ground is in fine condition for putting in the crops and the farmers are all quite busy seeding. I sowed some barley today for the first time. This evening I went over to Mr. Sparks's to see Jason, who is getting along well with the measles, and in a few days will be able to leave for the army.

Wednesday, 20th—I remained at Mr. Sparks's over night and coming home this morning stopped at the postoffice. I got a letter from Thomas R. McConnoll, my bunk-mate and one of the

(April, 1864)

non-veterans whom I left at Vicksburg. The non-veterans are all at Cairo now awaiting our return.

Thursday, 21st—This is a warm, pleasant day and I bade farewell to my home folks and friends and started back to the army, my thirty-day furlough being almost up. I went on horseback, brother John going along as far as Allen's Grove, to Uncle John Moore's to remain over night, while John returned home, taking back the horse which I rode. Though the spring has been very late, the farmers here have all their small grain in and it is starting fine. The country around Allen's Grove is very nice farming land; it is rolling, with plenty of timber and close to a good market; it is becoming very thickly settled. Scott county, Iowa.

Friday, 22d—I started with Uncle John this morning for Davenport, but one of his neighbors, Mr. Lathrop, soon overtook us and as he had to go to town anyway, I rode with him and Uncle John returned home. I reached Davenport by noon and went to the Davis House for my dinner, after which I called for my knapsack and accouterments and made a bee-line for Camp McClellan. Eight companies of the Eleventh Iowa have already reported and it is expected that we shall leave for the South in a few days. I went down town and got my new watch repaired—costing $2.00—and purchased a few necessary articles, such as a diary, pocket dictionary, stationery, etc., costing in all $3.15.

Chapter XVII.

Mobilization at Cairo and Moving Forward to Join Sherman Before Atlanta. April 23-June 8.

Saturday, 23d—Company E reported for duty this morning, and in addition ten recruits. Our regiment has more than one hundred recruits. We signed the pay rolls this forenoon, and were expecting to receive our pay, one month's, but as Company B has not yet arrived in camp, the paymaster withheld the pay. I swapped watches with Henry Clark, trading my cylinder escapement watch for his American lever watch, and gave $10.00 to boot. The boys still keep straggling into camp, and all who have reported are in high spirits and glad to return after their thirty-day furlough.

Sunday, 24th—It is raining again—there is nothing but rain and mud. Company B is now in camp and we received our pay today, including $50.00 of the new bounty. I got $63.00 in all. We received orders to be ready to move in the morning at 6 o'clock, and go to Cairo, Illinois. It rained all day and so we had to stay in camp. We had preaching here this afternoon. I had a couple of likenesses taken yesterday and today I am sending them away.

"Disappointment is the common lot of man."

Monday, 25th—And still it is raining! Reveille sounded at 5 o'clock this morning and we strapped on our knapsacks and all accouterments, and at 7 o'clock marched to the station, where we boarded the cars and started for Cairo.

We bade old Iowa farewell, perhaps never to return, for in the course of the coming events it is improbable that all will get back, but if the Lord is willing, I hope that we may be spared to return again. Crossing the Mississippi at 8 o'clock, we arrived at La Salle about noon and changed cars—exchanged fine coaches on the Rock Island for rather poor ones over the Illinois Central. Leaving La Salle at 3 o'clock we passed through Bloomington at dark, soon after which many of us took berths for the night. This morning just before leaving Davenport, I sent $50.00,

(April, 1864)

my bounty money, to father by Solomon Lichtenwalter, who had come to Davenport to see us off. I then borrowed $5.00 of Thomas Armstrong, to run me till next pay day.

Tuesday, 26th—We stopped at Centralia this morning for breakfast, and arrived at Cairo about 5 o'clock in the evening. Our regiment received new tents, and marching up the Ohio, we went with our non-veteran comrades into camp just above Cairo. There are about twenty thousand troops in camp at this place, and a large expedition is being fitted out here, to start in a few days, but there is no certainty as to where it is going.[1] Most of the Seventeenth Army Corps is camped here awaiting orders. It is being reorganized and fitted out with Springfield rifles and cartridge boxes.

Wednesday, 27th—It rained all day and there is no end of mud in our camp, which is on very low ground. Cairo is improving very fast, a great many buildings having been erected since this war broke out. The veterans still keep coming in on every train; the Eighth Iowa arrived today. About two thousand troops went aboard the transports for Huntsville, Alabama.[2] We will be glad when we get orders to leave this mudhole.

Thursday, 28th—It is cloudy and misty, and suffocating smoke is settling over our camp at times—and there is no end of mud. There is no news of any importance and we lay in camp all day, with no drill or dress parade. We are expecting orders to board the transports for Huntsville, Alabama. I went down town this afternoon to purchase a few articles. Things are awfully dear here. The soldiers are all supplying themselves with stationery and little articles needed on a long campaign.

A Regiment: A body of men, either horse, foot or artillery, commanded by a colonel and consisting of a number of companies, usually from eight to twelve.

A Reserve: A select body of troops in the rear of an army, reserved to sustain the other lines as occasion may require.

—A. G. Downing.

Friday, 29th—It is quite cool and cloudy, with some rain this afternoon. The Ohio river is rising fast. The veterans keep

[1] The expedition was fitted out for the campaign against Atlanta, under the command of General Sherman.—A. G. D.
[2] Clifton, Tennessee.—A. G. D.

(April, 1864)

arriving daily at Cairo. The Seventeenth Army Corps is being reorganized as fast as possible and sent up the Tennessee river and landed at Clifton, and is then to march across to Huntsville, Alabama. Our mustering rolls are being made out and we are to be mustered in tomorrow. I received my discharge from the old service, dated December 31, 1863, and sent the certificate home for father to keep till I return.

Saturday, 30th—The Eleventh Iowa was mustered today for pay. The regiment numbers about six hundred men present for duty, and but few are absent on account of sickness. General McPherson is having his entire corps (the Seventeenth) armed with new Springfield rifles, and our regiment today turned over to the quartermaster the Enfield rifles and old accouterments to draw the new rifles and accouterments. Most of the men feel that the Enfield rifle is better suited to our use than the new one, for it has a bronze barrel, hence easier to keep clean, as the outside does not require extra polishing.

I took a walk this afternoon over Cairo to view the town. There is a great deal of building going on, even if it is one of the biggest mudholes in the State of Illinois. The town may be said to be on stilts, for the buildings rest on posts, ten or twelve feet from the ground, and of course the sidewalks are the same. There are only two or three really nice buildings in the town. But it is a very important place for our armies, as it is the mobilizing point for our army on the Mississippi and the Tennessee rivers.

MAY, 1864.

Sunday, 1st—The Eleventh Iowa signed the pay rolls this morning for two months' pay. Six of the boys were robbed of $30.00 last night. Our regiment drew the new rifles and accouterments this afternoon. The Government is fitting out all of the veteran regiments with new equipments.

We received orders this afternoon to go on board the transports at 5 o'clock, and we struck our tents and turned them over to the post quartermaster. The Eleventh, the Fifteenth and part of the Thirteenth Iowa are on board the "John H. Dickey." We were ordered to carry five days' rations. Our destination is supposed to be Huntsville, Alabama.

(May, 1864)

Monday, 2d—We left Cairo at 1 o'clock in the night and arrived at Paducah, Kentucky, at 10 o'clock today. We were sent here to reinforce the troops at this place, as it was reported that the rebels, thought to be Forrest's command, would make a raid into Paducah for the purpose of destroying our supplies. We went ashore while the transports with large details of men were sent back to Cairo for ammunition and provisions. I was detailed this morning for the first time as corporal of the guard. We have a force of about five thousand men at this place, with but one fort.

Tuesday, 3d—We remained in bivouac all day. The transports did not return today as expected. The recruits of the Eleventh Iowa were formed into a battalion and drilled twice a day, by Captain Kelly of Company D. We had our first dress parade this evening, since returning from furlough, and the regiment looked well in their new uniforms, but it was very awkward in the manual of arms because of the new recruits. An order was read on dress parade making some promotions of non-commissioned officers in Companies A and H, since they went in as veterans. Paducah is a nice town and contained about seven thousand inhabitants just before the rebellion broke out.

Wednesday, 4th—We lay here all day awaiting the boats. Nathan Chase, a veteran of our company, got into trouble with some men of the Fifty-third Indiana Regiment and one of them shot him twice, one ball going through his right arm and the other taking effect in his mouth, but neither wound is dangerous. The trouble was caused by drink. The health of the regiment is good, yet there are several sick, some with light attacks of the ague, and they are sent to the hospital here at Paducah. The transports arrived late this evening and we received orders to go aboard early in the morning.

Thursday, 5th—Reveille sounded at 4 o'clock and by daylight we were on the boats. At 8 o'clock we started up the Tennessee river, our destination, we suppose, being Clifton, Tennessee. Our fleet consists of eleven transports and two gunboats, one of them in advance and the other taking the rear, so that if we should be attacked by light batteries from the bank, the gunboats would be ready for action and silence them. Then each transport has a squad of men with rifles in hand ready for action in case we should be fired upon by the guerrillas. The weather is pleasant and everything is working fine.

Friday, 6th—Our boats tied up for the night, but early this morning, at 4 o'clock, we continued our journey. The river is deep and narrow here, which with the high bluffs, makes it a dangerous place for bushwhackers, but we were not molested on the trip. We reached Clifton at 3 o'clock in the afternoon and disembarked, marched out about two miles and went into bivouac.

Saturday, 7th—Our new wedge tents were issued to us this morning by the quartermaster, and we worked all day pitching the tents and building bunks. I was on fatigue duty as corporal, in charge of a squad of men cleaning the grounds. We have a fine camp at this place with very good water. The health of the men is excellent and they are all in fine spirits. There was a flying report that the rebel general, Forrest, has been captured, but we don't know as to the truth of it.

Sunday, 8th—All is quiet. We had dress parade this evening and an order was read to the effect that the troops should drill two hours a day in company or skirmish drill, and besides that, the recruits should drill four hours a day; also that there are to be four roll calls a day, and company inspection every morning at 8 o'clock. There are about five thousand men in camp under command of Brig. Gen. F. M. Force, and all are in fine spirits and well fitted for a fight. The general quartermaster has large quantities of rations and ammunition here, and there are some three or four thousand beef cattle for our meat supply. This camp puts us in mind of our camp at Pittsburg Landing, two years ago, but I do not think that we will have such a battle as we had then, although the rebels' cavalry is quite active.

Monday, 9th—The weather is warm and pleasant and things are growing fine. The order of the day in camp is as follows: Reveille at 4 o'clock, roll call and breakfast call at 6, doctor's call at 6:30, guard mount and company inspection from 8 till 9, company drill 9 to 10, dinner call and roll call at 12 noon; in the afternoon, company drill from 2 to 3 o'clock, dress parade and supper call at 6, tattoo and roll call at 8, taps at 8:30, when all lights must be out and every man not on duty must be in his bunk. This is the way the days pass with a soldier in camp, in time of war.

(May, 1864)

Tuesday, 10th—We had an all day rain, and there was no drill or dress parade. The country around Clifton is very rough. There are but a few small farms, found only in the bottom land. Clifton is on the east bank of the Tennessee river about twenty-five miles below Savannah. The town has been burned and the people driven out, there being only four or five of the thirty log huts standing.

Wednesday, 11th—I was in a detail of a hundred men, with my corporal's squad, to go out on cattle guard. We had to herd about a thousand head of our beef cattle. At noon we were called in and our regiment, together with the Twentieth Illinois, was ordered to strap on our knapsacks, strike our tents and drive the cattle out about five miles farther on. We left our camp at 2 o'clock and at 3 reached Hardin's creek, in the direction of Huntsville, Alabama, where we found better range for the cattle, which was the object. There is more danger here of the rebel cavalry's making a raid and stampeding the herd, but it is thought our force is sufficiently large to guard the cattle.

Thursday, 12th—It is very foggy this morning and our camp is low and unhealthy. We had inspection this morning and then company drill for an hour. John White and I then took a walk, and going outside of the pickets, we climbed some very high bluffs and found some of the nicest springs that I have ever seen. The country is very rough and heavily timbered with chestnut and scrub oak. There are a few little clearings with log huts. Our teams went back to Clifton this morning for rations.

Friday, 13th—I went out as corporal of the picket this evening at 5 o'clock. There was in all a detail of one hundred and twelve sent out from the two regiments, besides the commissioned and non-commissioned officers. The guards are stationed from one to two miles from camp, where the cattle are corralled.

Saturday, 14th—The weather is quite warm and pleasant. A large fleet of transports arrived at Clifton this morning, loaded with troops and supplies, the wagons and teams of the Seventeenth Corps being on board. We also received a large mail.

News came that General Grant had defeated the rebels in a two days' battle before Richmond, though he lost about twenty thousand in killed and wounded. The news is almost too

(May, 1864)

good to believe. All is quiet here in the West. We are still herding cattle, but think we shall soon be relieved.

Sunday, 15th—We had regimental inspection this morning at 10 o'clock. Two regiments came out from Clifton as reinforcements for ours. We turned over all our tents, except one for every five men, and this evening received orders to be ready to march in the morning at 5 o'clock for Waynesburg, Tennessee. Jason Sparks arrived this evening from Iowa to join our company. He is well and happy.

Monday, 16th—Reveille sounded at 3 o'clock and at 5 we started on our way to Waynesburg. We reached the place at noon and went into camp for the rest of the day. The troops kept coming in from Clifton all the afternoon.[1] Our corps, the Seventeenth, is all together again, and now in command of General F. P. Blair. We have fine weather for marching, but the roads are very rough and stony, making it hard on our feet. The water is plentiful and very good, there being some healthful springs about here.

Tuesday, 17th—We marched fifteen miles today. Our brigade had the cattle in charge and at 10 o'clock we had to stop and let them rest, the heat and rough stony roads being too much for them. The other brigades of our corps passed us, going on ahead. We started again at 4 o'clock, but did not catch up with our corps and go into bivouac until late at night. In the country we passed through, only now and then are there small clearings with log huts. The people are poor and schoolhouses are very scarce through here.

Wednesday, 18th—The troops in advance of us started early this morning, but our brigade did not move until 11 o'clock. We had a hard day's march, having to cross a large swamp, wade four creeks, and cross one river twice; yet we covered fourteen miles with the cattle, and got into bivouac near Clarenceville[2] at 9 o'clock at night. Many of the men got sore feet, as a result of being in the water so much and then having to walk the rough, stony roads. The town of Clarenceville, they say, is almost deserted, only a few of the meaner sort of people remaining.

[1]They all left Clifton for Huntsville, Alabama.—A. G. D.

[2]This must have been Lawrenceburg, the county seat of Lawrence county, and on a direct line between Waynesburg and Pulaski.—Ed.

MOVING FORWARD TO JOIN SHERMAN

(May, 1864)

Thursday, 19th—We started our drove of cattle early this morning and the brigade broke camp at 8 o'clock and followed. We reached Pulaski at 2 o'clock, a distance of sixteen miles, and went into camp. Our road, rough and rocky, followed a winding creek which I think we had to wade twenty-four times during the day. I was corporal guard last night and having had no sleep, the hard day's march has almost worn me out.

Good news came from the Eastern army, also from the Cumberland army. The report is that General Grant has had a six days' fight at Richmond and that the rebels are whipped and on the retreat.

Friday, 20th—We are having nice weather. We lay here at Pulaski all day in order to draw rations and to rest. We spent the day in washing clothes and cooking navy beans and fresh beef. The troops of our corps were ordered to pack all extra clothing in their knapsacks and turn them over to the quartermaster, who would then send them by rail to Huntsville, where they are to be stored. We are to go in light marching order from now on, having but a blanket apiece. There is but little sickness in the corps and the men are in fine spirits. All are anxious to get through to the main army.

Saturday, 21st—Reveille sounded at 3 o'clock and at 5 we took up the line of march, our company being rear guard for the brigade. We marched seventeen miles and went into bivouac several miles beyond Elkhorn, which we reached at 1 o'clock. Here we waded the Elkhorn[1] river, which is from three to five feet deep and two hundred feet wide. The boys had a great deal of fun in wading across. The country is very rough and rocky, and the hard turnpike over which we marched most of the day made our feet very sore.

Sunday, 22d—We started at 5:30 this morning and marched till 2 o'clock, when we again went into bivouac. Our brigade today was just in front of the rear. We passed through some very fine country with well-improved farms. Today we bade old Tennessee farewell and entered Alabama.

What a cruel thing this war is! May God hasten the day when it will be brought to a close and our nation enjoy peace once more. Here in the army we have to march on Sunday as

[1] Now called Elk river. The town which our diarist calls Elkhorn was probably what is now Aspen Hill.—Ed.

(May, 1864)

other days. A soldier has to go through a great many hardships not thought of by others.

Monday, 23d—It has been very warm but pleasant for several days. Reveille roused us this morning at 3 o'clock and at 4 our brigade started, taking the advance. Our last night's bivouac is just twelve miles northwest of Huntsville and we had a fine road to travel on coming into town. There is some very fine country with splendid farms around Huntsville. We entered the town at 10 o'clock and went into camp, lying here the rest of the day. Here we got our knapsacks and a large mail. I received a letter and likeness from Miss G————. All of the non-veterans joined their regiments this afternoon. Our quartermaster received a consignment of clothing for the regiment.

Tuesday, 24th—We remained here at Huntsville all day resting. I went to the camp of the Fifty-ninth Indiana and found my cousin, Hamilton Shepherd, and the sons of some of our old friends from my old home at Bloomfield, Indiana. The order is that we are to start for Chattanooga[1] in the morning, and we again had to turn over our tents and baggage to the quartermaster, who will put them in storage.

Huntsville is a nice little town among the hills, and as in the case of most all of the villages here in the South, its citizens fled on the approach of the "mudsills," as they call us. There is a large spring here with a strong, steady flow of water, coming off a rocky cliff one hundred feet high, which supplies the town with water. The water runs into a large pool, from which it is pumped into an elevated tank by means of a water-wheel set near the cliff, and distributed over town through pipes.

Wednesday, 25th—We packed our knapsacks and sent them by rail to Rome, Georgia. The advance of our corps started early this morning for Decatur, Alabama, but our brigade taking up the rear did not leave Huntsville till in the afternoon. From Decatur we are to proceed to Rome, Georgia. We marched through fine farming country with good buildings, but as usual the people are gone and the farms are idle. Such is the effect of war, the citizens being afraid to remain while our armies are marching back and forth.

[1] Rome, Georgia. The order was later countermanded and the army, instead of going to Chattanooga, went to Rome via Decatur, Alabama. —A. G. D.

(May, 1864)

MOVING FORWARD TO JOIN SHERMAN

Thursday, 26th—We left our bivouac at 6 o'clock this morning and marched twelve miles. Within a few miles of Decatur we went into bivouac for the night. Advance brigades of our army were skirmishing with the rebels today and it is reported that the colonel of the Seventeenth New Jersey Regiment was killed. Our men captured a provision train and also took some prisoners. Our corps teams have been sent out for fodder.

Friday, 27th—We remained in bivouac until 2 o'clock waiting for rations. After getting our rations we crossed the Tennessee river by pontoon bridges and started on our way for Rome, Georgia. The railroad bridge of the Memphis & Ohio, here at Decatur, was destroyed by our gunboats soon after the battle of Shiloh. It took seventy-two pontoon boats to make our bridge. Our road today lay through a large swamp which it took some time for the artillery and provision trains to cross; besides we had some very rough country to cross, and did not get into bivouac until midnight.

Saturday, 28th—We started at 7 o'clock this morning and dragging along slowly with our heavy trains, went into bivouac when we reached Somerville at 3 o'clock. Most of our road was over very rough country and besides we had to wade one river, the bridges being gone. Somerville is a mere village with a courthouse, a few stores and about twenty dwellings.

Sunday, 29th—It was 9 o'clock before we got started this morning and though the country here between two mountains is very rough, we covered fourteen miles and went into camp in the mountains for the first time. Large foraging parties were sent out this morning to secure meat. Our advance lines had a skirmish with the rebels this afternoon. The health of the men is good, but many have sore feet from the hard marching.

Monday, 30th—The weather is getting quite warm and the roads are dusty. Our advance guard broke camp at daylight, while our brigade did not get under way until 10 o'clock. We crossed a ridge of mountains this afternoon and this evening went into camp in the valley close to Warrenton. The mountains are heavily timbered, mostly chestnut, and the soil is sandy and rocky. There are only a few small farms here and there. The men have gone to war, while the women and children remain with scarcely anything to live on.

(May, 1864)

Tuesday, 31st—We broke camp in the early morning and started on another day's march, our brigade leaving at 7 o'clock and taking up the rear. We climbed the mountains again and after marching sixteen miles went into camp on the very top. This has been a hard march; the men are suffering as never before from sore feet and some, giving out, had to be hauled in the ambulance. Then, too, we are on two-thirds rations because of the lack of transportation.

JUNE, 1864.

Wednesday, 1st—Our brigade started at 5 this morning, but covered only twelve miles. We marched down the Sandy mountains into the valley and went into bivouac along the banks of Sandy creek. The rear of the army did not get into camp until midnight. The wagon trains could move but slowly over the rough, rocky roads, and even then the teams are almost worn out. Many of the horses and mules lost their shoes and have broken hoofs and sore feet. Large foraging parties are sent out, but because of the poverty of the country they do not get much.

Thursday, 2d—A fine shower about noon cooled the air and laid the dust. The entire corps lay in camp all day, the men washing and mending their clothes, and the blacksmiths shoeing the horses and mules. We are in the valley between the Sandy and Lookout mountains, which are heavily timbered with pine and ash. The quartermaster's trains were sent out on forage today, but, although the farms in the valley are fairly good, there is little to be had, for the few farmers thought it useless to grow crops this summer.

Friday, 3d—It rained nearly all day and changed the dust into mud, which made the marching very heavy. We left camp at 8 o'clock and leaving the valley, traveled over a spur of Lookout mountain nine miles across. We marched eighteen miles today and bivouacked on the Chattanooga river. We passed a house of mourning today where lay the body of the head of the family, he having been killed just a few days before in a battle with Sherman's men. I never saw a sadder sight. The wife and daughters dressed in deep, rich mourning were most pitifully bewailing their loss. But some of our boys remarked that the people of the South had brought on this war themselves.

(June, 1864)

Saturday, 4th—We started at 8 o'clock and marched fifteen miles today. Have had rain for three days now, but late in the afternoon it cleared off. We had to wade a river, the water being only three or four feet deep, and the boys had great fun in trying to carry the powder on their heads to keep it dry. We were soaking wet from the rain so we did not mind wading the river. But the muddy roads make marching very hard, especially since we are kept on two-thirds rations when we might just as well have more. Large foraging parties were again sent out, but there isn't anything in the country to be had, although we traversed a level country between two mountains the whole day.

Sunday, 5th—Rain again this forenoon and clear this afternoon. We started early this morning, our regiment leading the advance division, and at 3 o'clock reached our destination, Rome, Georgia. The sixteen miles covered today was over very muddy roads, such as we have had for the last fifty miles, and all were greatly fatigued. Some of the men gave out completely and had to ride in the ambulance. News came that General Grant had surrounded Richmond, and that General Sherman was driving Johnston, but the report is too good to believe, yet I hope it is true.

Monday, 6th—It is quite warm. We started early this morning, and crossing the Coosa river on a pontoon bridge, passed through Rome for Kingston, about fourteen miles distant. We arrived at Kingston about 4 o'clock in the afternoon and went into camp. Kingston is on the railroad running from Chattanooga to Atlanta. Our forces routed the rebels from here about ten days ago. A large force of our men is stationed here. There is no news from the front. We are still in mountainous country, but there are some very nice farms in the valley with fine dwelling houses.

Tuesday, 7th—The weather continues warm. Our corps drew fifteen days' rations at Kingston this morning. We left the place at 10 o'clock, carrying five days' rations, the balance to be hauled by the supply trains. We marched twelve miles to Cartersville and went into camp. Our troops control the railroad, which is in running order to this place, but the rebels burned the bridge just before evacuating the town. Our men will soon have it rebuilt, using the old piers, which are intact. It is three hundred feet long and one hundred feet above the water. The rebels were very strongly fortified here at Cartersville, but they left the place without fighting because of our troops flanking them. Cartersville will be used as a base of supply for Sherman's army.

Wednesday, 8th—We moved forward early this morning, marching twelve miles to the little town of Ackworth, where we went into camp. We are now with Sherman's army, our corps being placed on the left in front of Atlanta. Our front is about twenty-five miles north of the city, while my division is back about ten miles farther. Sherman's forces now number about one hundred and fifty thousand men and it is thought that the rebels under Johnston have seventy-five thousand. Our army, in the main, is lying still today, though there is some skirmishing in the front. The rebels have fallen back about ten miles. The health of our men is excellent; they are in fine spirits and anxious for a fight.

Chapter XVIII.
The Battles Around Atlanta. In the Field Hospital.
June 9-July 11.

Thursday, 9th—The weather is fine—warm and pleasant. Our corps remained quiet and in its position all day. But orders have been given for the whole army to move forward in the morning. We commenced drawing full rations again today. I went out on picket this evening.

General Sherman is in command of all of our forces, with General Thomas in command of the right wing, General Hooker of the center, and General McPherson of the left. We have a large force of cavalry on each of the flanks. The country about Atlanta being so hilly and rough, it is exceedingly difficult to advance in front of the rebels, they having by far the better position.[1] They have a great deal better chance to kill our men than we have to kill them.

Friday, 10th—Our entire army moved forward early this morning. The teams were all left in the rear. We advanced our division about ten miles and went into bivouac at a place called Big Shanty. Our front drove in the pickets and did some brisk skirmishing and cannonading. The railroad station at Big Shanty and the houses have all been burned. Our army is prepared for a big fight. There is no news from Grant's army, but at last accounts things were working fine.

Saturday, 11th—Had a light shower yesterday, while today it rained nearly all day. We formed a line of battle this morning and moved forward. There was some sharp skirmishing, and our cannons were active, but the rebels did not reply. We advanced about a half mile and the rebels fell back inside of their rifle pits, a mile distant, at the foot of Kenesaw mountain. Each regiment then went to work throwing up its own rifle pits. There was some more sharp skirmishing, the rebels attempting to turn

---

[1] Sherman's plan was to get up as close as possible to the Confederates' works, build forts and rifle pits, and then move our right around their left, or our left around their right, thus flanking them and threatening their rear. By that means they would be compelled to evacuate their strong works without having the opportunity of fighting from behind them.—A. G. D.

our left, but we drove them back. The railroad is now in operation up to our army, and the first train came in to Big Shanty[1] today. News came that Lee had evacuated Richmond, but we could not believe the report.

Sunday, 12th—It rained steadily all day. Our forces did not advance any today, but they are still throwing up earthworks and planting batteries. There was some shelling at a few points today by our men and the skirmishing at times was quite lively on both sides. But because of so much rain the last two days, and since we have worked so hard building rifle pits, we are glad to remain quiet and get some rest. As we have no tents, the men have built "ranches" out of their rubber ponchos, for shelter and for resting places in which to get snatches of sleep. There are no tents except the hospital tents, and some of the officers have "fly tents" in order to keep their papers and books dry. Our wagon trains are kept in the rear for fear of our being suddenly shelled and compelled to fall back. The earthworks of both sides are in plain view of each other, all the timber between having been cut down, and the pickets are close enough together at night to engage in conversation.

Monday, 13th—It rained again nearly the whole day. We formed a line of battle early this morning, but soon returned to our "ranches" with orders to keep our accouterments on and be ready to form at a moment's notice. Skirmishing commenced early all along the line and there was cannonading from our side with no reply from the rebels. Things are progressing fine. There is no news from the army around Richmond. I wrote a letter today to Robinson Laport of the Twenty-fourth Iowa and received one from Miss Moore.[2]

Tuesday, 14th—No rain, but cloudy and quite cool. Skirmishing began again early this morning and our artillery threw shells into the rebels' works, but they would not reply. They are still fortifying their position. A rebel company consisting of thirty-five men came over to our lines today and gave themselves up. They informed us that there was a whole brigade that would surrender if given a chance, for they were tired

---

[1] This is the station where Andrews and his band captured an engine with tender one Sunday morning and started up North, but he and his men were all captured, and some of them were executed, while others were set at liberty.—A. G. D.

[2] Miss Moore, of Tipton, Iowa, wrote letters to encourage the soldiers.—A. G. D.

of retreating all the while. They also represented to our officers that Johnston's entire force numbered only sixty thousand men, and said that their artillerymen had orders not to fire when our artillery shelled, but to wait until our troops should make a charge, and then open up on us. There was one man of the Sixteenth Iowa killed today by a rebel sharpshooter.

Wednesday, 15th—The day has been clear and quite warm. This morning Company E was sent out as sharpshooters. During the night the Eleventh and Sixteenth Regiments had thrown up a new line of rifle pits, about a half mile in advance of the old one, and at noon today moved forward in line of battle into the new trenches. At the same time our skirmish line was ordered to advance on the rebel skirmish line, and it being our company's turn to go out on the line, we were deployed and advanced, driving in the rebel skirmish line for almost a half mile, pushing them back from their first and second lines of fence rails piled up for their protection. We approached so near to their rifle pits at the foot of Kenesaw mountain as to make it possible for their artillerymen to use grape and canister upon us, killing one man, William Alexander. The rebel skirmishers now received reinforcements, while our skirmishers on the left failing to come up with us, made a gap in our lines and left us in a very hot place for a little while, as it gave the rebels a cross fire on us, and we were compelled to fall back, thus losing some of the ground taken. But just then our colonel sent another company in double quick to relieve us, and our lost position was regained. We had become completely used up and lost one man killed, one mortally wounded, seven slightly wounded, and one man taken prisoner.[1] Our stretcher bearers, after the fight, raised the white flag and went to get the body of Alexander for burial.

Thursday, 16th—Skirmishing commenced again early this morning. The rebel batteries off on the left would fire a round or two and just as soon as our guns would open on them they would stop firing. General Leggett's Division on the left drove the rebels back about a mile, and there was some very heavy cannonading in the afternoon on the right, where it is reported that General Thomas made a charge on the rebels' left, around the rear and got possession of Pine Hills. It was reported

---

[1] As was supposed at the time. See note under June 16th.—Ed.

(June, 1864)

that at one point a rebel regiment, the Forty-third Mississippi, was ordered to make a charge on our lines and when they started their colonel ordered them to reverse arms, and they came marching right into our lines, surrendering themselves as prisoners of war. While our men were making demonstrations all along the line yesterday, about one thousand rebels were taken prisoners, some of them surrendering without firing a gun. They said that there was a great discontent in the ranks of their army around Atlanta; that they were tired of continually falling back, and that many had come to the conclusion that the war on their part could be nothing else than a failure. Company E is lying quiet today. The rough treatment we experienced yesterday was a hard blow to the company, for the loss of nine men from one company in a skirmish line, in less than four hours, does not often happen.[1]

Friday, 17th—Our brigade was moved out to the left of the Fourth Division during the night, and General Logan's Division occupied our former position. The Eleventh was at work nearly all night throwing up a new line of rifle pits, while the other regiments of our brigade occupied pits previously made by other troops. During the night Logan's Division was twice charged upon, but both times repulsed the attack. Skirmishing began early this morning and continued throughout the day. Our entire left wing was ordered to fall in all along the line and make a demonstration, by cheering and by opening our batteries. This was done to compel them to draw reinforcements from their left, while our right would then charge their weakened left.[2] During these demonstrations and skirmishing the captain of Company C was wounded by a sharpshooter, as was also a private in Company G.

[1] Our losses were as follows: William Alexander, killed; Lieutenant Alfred Carey, mortally wounded; John Zitler, a thumb shot off; Thomas R. McConnoll, a minie ball passed through thigh; John Ford, LeRoy Douglas, George G. Main and John Albin, slightly wounded. James Martin, it was thought at the time, had been taken prisoner, but on the fifth day after the skirmish his body was found by an Ohio regiment, lying with the bodies of two Confederate soldiers. They had made Martin a prisoner, it seems, but before they could get to the rear with him, a shell from one of our batteries exploded over them, killing all three. Then, as they were considerably back from our lines, the body was not found until the enemy had fallen back and our army had advanced; besides, our brigade in the meantime had moved two miles to the left.

Martin had both legs cut off by the shell. A captain from the Ohio regiment which had found his body, brought his silver watch, Bible, some letters and other articles found on his person, and turned them over to our captain, informing him how Martin, in all probability, lost his life.—A. G. D.

[2] This is strategy of war.—A. G. D.

THE BATTLES AROUND ATLANTA

(June, 1864)

Saturday, 18th—A light rain yesterday was followed by rain most of today, and all was quiet along the lines until late this evening, when there was heavy cannonading till late in the night. We were ordered to keep all accouterments on and our rifles at our sides during the night, for it is expected by our officers that the rebels will attack our left or evacuate. Deserters report that their men have orders to that effect. There has been some very hard fighting on our right this afternoon, and General Thomas has turned the rebels' left and pierced their center.[1] The news from Richmond is that General Grant is on the south of Richmond, that he has taken Fort Darling, and that he is going to change his base of operations.

Sunday, 19th—It rained hard all day. Cannonading commenced early this morning and was kept up all day, being very heavy in the center. We have outflanked the rebels' right and they have fallen back from their first line of rifle pits and have placed their heavy guns on high points of ground. It is supposed that they are on the retreat towards Atlanta, as it is reported that they have fallen back from two to four miles and are building strong earthworks. The First Brigade of our Fourth Division has now formed a line of battle beyond their former first line of rifle pits. The Thirteenth and the Fifteenth Iowa Regiments moved out in the front this afternoon.

The rain today has been a great benefit to those who are wounded. May God help them and stand by them, and may they return thanks unto Him! May they ever look unto Him for their support and help.

Monday, 20th—It has been quite warm today with rain this evening. Things were quiet all along the line until in the afternoon, when there was heavy fighting in the center, and all our artillery opened upon the rebels, without response from their guns. The heaviest cannonading that we have had yet was from our center, and it lasted for two hours. The rebels have fallen back, but still hold Kenesaw mountain and have their heavy batteries planted on the very top, while our men are along the north side of the mountain, slowly ascending it. Our regiment moved to the front again this evening and two companies, I and H, are out on picket.

[1] The final result of the demonstrations on the left the previous day —Ed.

(June, 1864)

Tuesday, 21st—Another all day rain and things were very still all along the lines until late in the afternoon when there was some brisk skirmishing. General Hooker made two charges on the rebel works yesterday; the first time he was repulsed, but the second time he carried them and took several hundred prisoners. General Osterhaus at the same time made a charge and took about two hundred prisoners. There is no news from Richmond.

Wednesday, 22d—It has cleared off and is quite warm today. The rebels commenced shelling us this morning, but did little damage, as their shells fell short of our lines, on account of their insufficient charges of powder, we suppose, and because their guns are too small to stand heavier charges. Our batteries opened up and exchanged shots with them for about two hours. Our men commenced throwing up heavy earthworks this evening. Company C went out on picket this evening. There have been no trains coming in to Big Shanty for the last two days on account of the rebels' destroying the railroad on this side of Chattanooga; but it will be repaired in a few days. Our army draws full rations with the exception of meat, of which we are allowed but three-fifths rations.

Thursday, 23d—We were up all night throwing up breastworks, finishing them about noon today. The rebels opened up their battery on Little Kenesaw mountain, but did no harm. General Leggett on the right made a demonstration before the rebel lines, but was not engaged and soon fell back again.[1] All is quiet on the right. The Sixteenth Corps was ordered out on an expedition with fifteen days' rations, but we do not know their destination. We received orders to be ready to march at a moment's warning, with two days' rations. William Cross of Company E returned from the hospital after an absence of ten months.

Friday, 24th—Our skirmish line was advanced late yesterday

---

[1] I remember quite distinctly seeing General Sherman with his staff officers riding along our lines taking in the lay of the country. They had just passed by where I was stationed, when they halted near one of our batteries and began using their field glasses, taking a view of the enemy's lines. At that same time a Confederate general with his staff rode out of the timber upon an open knoll to take a view of our lines with their glasses. This was too good a chance for our battery, so the gunners, taking good aim, fired five or six shots at the mark, and one of them hit and killed the Confederate general, who the signal corps reported was a General Pope. Our signal corps had learned the signs of the Confederate signal service and at once reported the facts. The Confederates claimed that General Sherman himself had aimed the shot which killed their general, but such is not the case.—A. G. D.

(June, 1864)

evening and the men worked all night building rifle pits to protect themselves today; I was on a detail that worked till 1 o'clock. The Fifteenth and Sixteenth furnished the skirmishers for the brigade, and the Fifteenth had two men killed. There was some skirmishing with heavy cannonading today. Our company with Companies F and G went out this evening after sundown to relieve the skirmishers, and we worked again most of the night throwing up rifle pits. Things are usually very quiet after night, though now and then skirmishing breaks out and arouses a little excitement.

Saturday, 25th—We remained out in the rifle pits till this evening, when we were relieved by the Fifteenth Iowa. John Esher was shot through the face this afternoon by a rebel sharpshooter. The shot was fired through one of the "portholes" under the head log of our defenses, where he was at the time loading his gun. The ball struck his jaw bone, knocking out some of his teeth, but it is thought that he will recover.[1] There is no news from Richmond.

Sunday, 26th—There was very little cannonading and skirmishing today. We drew two days' rations with orders to be ready to march at a moment's warning. Several brigades of the Fifteenth Army Corps are moving out to the rear, but we do not know their destination. The health of the troops is fine, although they are much fatigued. We have a great many wounded at the hospital, but it is reported that they are getting along fine.

May God hasten the day when this cruel war will be brought to a close, so that our nation may enjoy peace once more. May He hasten the day when the rebels will lay down their arms and return again to their homes. But we must remember that there may be many men yet who will fall for their country before it is free from this accursed secession. May God be with us and help us as we stand in need, for He is a God of battles.

Monday, 27th—There was a general line of battle formed this morning and orders given to make a charge all along the lines.

---

[1] Esher said to me, "I'm going to see what I'm shooting at," and walked up to peer through the porthole, when all of a sudden a ball crashed in, knocking him down, and as he fell back his heels kicked up. He was right by my side when he was struck and as he fell he cried out, "Oh, boys, I'm killed!" After he recovered, we laughed a great deal over it, at his expense, for he thought that now he was really killed. But although Esher recovered from the wound, yet he was deformed for life. His head was drawn down on the side of the wound, since the cords of the neck were shorter than on the other side.—A. G. D.

The center charged in full force, but as the flanks failed to charge, soon had to fall back. The Eleventh and Sixteenth Iowa furnished the skirmishers for our brigade and charged the rebels' skirmish line, but were driven back to their old line. Our side lost several in killed and wounded, and what little was gained did not pay for the loss of life. Company A of our regiment was in the charge and had one man killed; so close was he to the rebel works that our men had to raise the white flag in order to get his body. The Fifty-third Indiana made a charge on the rebel rifle pits and lost about forty men, taken as prisoners. When they made the charge, the rebels lay down in their pits, allowing them to come close up, when they rose up with their rifles drawn and said: "Come on, boys, we won't hurt you," and took them prisoners.

Tuesday, 28th—There was cannonading and skirmishing today on both sides, all along the lines, but our men did not attempt to advance the line of battle. We have orders to be ready to march at a moment's warning.

Wednesday, 29th—There was heavy cannonading on our side today, but the rebels did not reply. Our company was out on the skirmish line again, but I could not go with them on account of sickness. I have not been fit for duty since Saturday evening, the 25th, but on last Monday, the 27th, I was taken quite sick, having contracted the intermittent fever while digging the rifle pits along a branch infected with malaria. The weather was quite hot today, which is hard on the sick.

Thursday, 30th—The Seventeenth Army Corps have removed all their surplus baggage to the rear for the purpose of making a flanking movement on the rebels, who are reported to be falling back from their lines around Kenesaw mountain. Our artillery in the front is still in action, but the rebels make no reply.

JULY, 1864.

Friday, 1st—All is very quiet along the lines today. The rebels have built a strong line of works out along Nick-a-Jack creek, and it is reported that they are planning to retire from Kenesaw mountain and Marietta to their new line of works.

Saturday, 2d—All the sick have been removed to the field

hospital in the rear of the army. I was brought here to our division field hospital, near Big Shanty, with a few others. Our army supplies at Big Shanty have been removed by the general quartermaster, as the army has been ordered around to the right. The Fifteenth, Sixteenth and Seventeenth Corps are leaving the left flank altogether, and are hastening to the right wing. The rebels have now left Kenesaw mountain and Marietta and have moved around to their left so as to keep our right from flanking them.

Sunday, 3d—All is quiet. Our men are still marching around to the right. The Seventeenth Corps drove the rebels back about two miles, taking one line of their works. Wagon trains are going by the hospital day and night, and the roads are getting very dusty.

Monday, 4th—Our corps is still moving forward, and it is now along Nick-a-Jack creek. We learned here in the hospital that the corps lost several men killed and wounded in the skirmish fights yesterday. This has been a hard day for me, as I have to lie in the open without any shelter over me, the hospital tents being so crowded with the wounded. I have been taking some strong medicine the last two days, in the hope that it would break up the fever.

Tuesday, 5th—Our men are still advancing. The Eleventh Iowa made a charge on the rebels' left, on Nick-a-Jack creek, and took one line of rifle pits. We lost a few in killed and wounded. William Cross of Company E was killed by a piece of shell from the rebels' batteries; he had returned from the hospital to his company only about two weeks before. I am still in the hospital and no better. It is quite sultry today.

Wednesday, 6th—There is still skirmishing on the lines and some cannonading going on, but there is no general advance along the lines, except on the extreme left.

Thursday, 7th—It is quite warm. Still skirmishing and cannonading. The wounded in the hospital are getting along fine.

Friday, 8th—The weather is quite pleasant today. Wounded men are coming in from the front every day. Our men are strongly fortified in front of the rebel works, and within about a mile of the Chattahoochee river.

Saturday, 9th—The rebels left their rifle pits in the night and crossed the Chattahoochee river.[1]

Sunday, 10th—The sick and wounded were all moved today from the division hospital to Marietta. This could safely be done, now that the rebels have fallen back across the river. Marietta is not likely to be within the lines of a fierce battle, in case the rebels should come around on either flank of our army. It is very quiet all along the lines today.

Monday, 11th—A train load of the sick and wounded left today over the railroad for Rome, Georgia, where they are to go into the hospital. I stayed here at Marietta all day.[2] The general quartermaster has his headquarters here now since the railroad is in running order to this point. The supplies for the army are being taken from here by wagon trains and distributed along the lines as needed. A great many citizens are coming into Marietta for the purpose of going North to get away from the war region.

---

[1] General Sherman always moved his army by the right or left flank when he found the Confederate fortifications in front too strong to make a charge, and in that way the enemy had to fall back, leaving their strong position.—A. G. D.

[2] Mr. Downing thought that his fever was broken and that he might soon rejoin his company, yet he feared that he would have to go to Rome. There was some danger in going to Rome, because of a possible attack, and then he dreaded the thought of being confined in the general hospital.—Ed.

Chapter XIX.
In the Hospital at Rome, Georgia. Reports from the Front. July 12-September 23.

Tuesday, 12th—I was taken with the other sick and the wounded to Rome, to the field hospital of the Fifteenth, Sixteenth and Seventeenth Army Corps. We left Marietta at 10 a. m. and arrived at Rome at 6 p. m. No news.

Wednesday, 13th—There are a great many sick and wounded at this place. All of the vacant store buildings are filled with the sick, while the wounded are cared for in tents east of town. Nothing of any importance.

Thursday, 14th—I am with a large number of sick in a ward over a vacant store building. For the last four days I have had the camp diarrhea, and have become so weak that I have to lie on my cot all the time.[1] But we have a good doctor in this ward.

Friday, 15th—There is nothing new. We have very poor food here in the hospital, but we have good water. Rome was selected for our field hospital because of the good water and because it was on high, rolling ground, thus affording drainage. There are very few citizens living in Rome, they having gone before our army took possession of the town, some going to the North, others to the South. There was no burning of property here, our officers having placed guards about town to prevent it.

Saturday, 16th—The weather is pleasant. There is nothing of any importance.

Sunday, 17th—The same as ever. Am still in the hospital, but getting some better, and I am very thankful, for it is very disagreeable to lie sick in a field hospital. We have soldiers for nurses, and though they are convalescents, yet they are strong enough to care for the sick and wounded. They are glad to do everything possible for their comrades.

Monday, 18th—The weather is quite pleasant. There is nothing of any importance. All is quiet.

---

[1] Mr. Downing has an entry in his diary for every day, but wrote them at a later date, after he was convalescing.—Ed.

(July, 1864)

Tuesday, 19th—It is the same thing over and over. My fever is broken now and I am getting better. I just learned that there are three others of my company here in the hospital, all in different wards. They are Lieutenant Alfred Carey, Thomas R. McConnoll and John Zitler, all wounded on the skirmish line on June 15th at Noon-day creek at the foot of Kenesaw mountain.

Wednesday, 20th—Have had pleasant weather for a week now. Most of the citizens remaining here have been moved out of town, for the purpose of using their homes for hospitals. No news.[1]

Thursday, 21st—The same thing over and over, again and again.[2] All the available rooms in town have now been turned into hospital wards. We have single, iron cots with good mattresses, and the sheets and pillows are kept nice and clean.

Friday, 22d—The citizens remaining in town, after so long a time, have become quite reconciled. Nothing new from the front.[3]

Saturday, 23d—All is quiet. No news from the front. A great many sick and wounded are coming in from the front. Deaths occur here at the hospital every day.

Sunday, 24th—The weather is sultry. All is quiet, and no news from the front. I am gaining every day and can be up and around in the ward, but have not yet been out of doors.

Monday, 25th—It is hot and sultry. Lieutenant Carey died this morning here in the hospital, from his wounds, after suffering thirty-five days, he having been wounded on the skirmish line on the 15th of June. He was shot in the left thigh, the minie ball glancing from his hip and lodging near the spine. But the doctors were not able to locate it until after his death, when they removed it. I had not seen Lieutenant Carey from the time he was wounded until after he had died, being present when his body

---

[1] On this day David Hobaugh of my company was killed on the skirmish line. Our entire army moved forward making an advance on Atlanta.—A. G. D.

[2] On this day the Iowa Brigade made a charge on Bald Hill, in front of Atlanta.—A. G. D.

[3] In the battle of this day the Iowa Brigade was on the extreme left of the Seventeenth Corps, and all four regiments suffered in the number killed and wounded, besides losing many as prisoners of war. George Sweet of Company E was killed and Aaron Pierce was missing. The Sixteenth Iowa lost over two hundred and thirty, who were taken prisoners. This battle, known as the battle of Atlanta, proved to be the hardest fought battle for our brigade during the siege of Atlanta. Major General McPherson was killed in this battle, and the loss of our beloved McPherson was a great blow to the Army of the Tennessee. He was a noble man and kind to all under his command.—A. G. D.

was dressed for burial. John Zitler came over to my ward and we went down together. We saw his clothing and other articles packed by the chaplain, who has charge of all the effects of the deceased soldiers, and they will be forwarded to Mrs. Carey at their home in Cedar County, Iowa. Lieutenant Carey's body was buried in his uniform here at Rome, Georgia.

Tuesday, 26th—It is very warm. Still lying on my old cot. The hospital is one of the hardest places that I have found since I have been in the service; but when a soldier gets sick, he has to go there so that he can be taken care of. I have been in the United States service three years now, and this is the first time for me in the hospital. I hope that it may be the last time.

Wednesday, 27th—It is quite warm. Nothing of importance. One month ago today I was taken sick with the intermittent fever, at Kenesaw mountain.

Thursday, 28th—No news. All is quiet. I am still gaining strength slowly. We get very poor board here for a sick man to gain strength on, but we must make the best of it at present. The room we occupy, called a ward, is about one hundred feet long north and south, and fifty feet wide. There is a row of cots on each side. My cot is on the west side, and in the afternoons it is so hot that we can hardly stand it. There are windows in front and along the west side.

Friday, 29th—It is quite sultry today. Six deaths occurred today in the three wards of our building. One of the sick men, William Gibson of the Thirty-second Ohio Cavalry, died last night. He had been very sick, but was getting better, and just before he lay down for the night, told me that he felt better than for several days; but a few hours later he was dead, dying very suddenly. He left a small family. Life is indeed very uncertain. We should be prepared to meet death any moment, for we know not when the brittle thread of life will be broken, and we have to go to meet our Lord, prepared or unprepared.

Saturday, 30th—It is quite warm and sultry. We have a man in our ward who is very homesick; he sits on his cot and cries like a child. He has been promised a furlough, and I believe that if he could not get it he would die. All the wounded here able to take care of themselves on the way, are going home on thirty-day furloughs. Three from our company, Thomas R. McConnoll, John Zitler and John Hilton, are going. John Esher is not going until his wound gets better. A great many of the wounded men are dying, for the weather is so hot the wounds quickly mortify. No news from the front.

Sunday, 31st—Quite warm. It rained very hard this afternoon. There is no news of any importance. Everything appears so dull and the time passes so slowly. I am considered a convalescent now by the doctor and he has put me to work dealing out the medicine to the sick. Our chaplains here in the hospital hold preaching services in the churches of the town on Sundays. The convalescent soldiers make up the audience, as most of the citizens are gone, having given up their houses for hospital purposes.

AUGUST, 1864.

Monday, 1st—Quite warm and sultry. There isn't any news from the front. There is a force of about two thousand here under command of General Vandever, with an equal number of convalescents. The courthouse, located on the highest point of ground in Rome, is our citadel, strongly fortified with guns facing in all directions. The place is soon to be garrisoned with two regiments of negro troops, and the few remaining citizens are greatly agitated over the thought of being stopped on the streets by negro guards and required to show their passes.

Tuesday, 2d—We had a refreshing rain last night. Governor Stone of Iowa arrived at the hospital this morning, having come from the front, with an order from General Sherman granting a thirty-day furlough to the sick and wounded from the Iowa regiments here in the hospital. Those able for duty are to be sent to the front. News came from the front that the Iowa Brigade was badly cut to pieces in the battle of the 22d of July. Many of them were taken prisoners, including almost all of the Sixteenth Regiment. Among the killed are the major of the Thirteenth and the lieutenant colonel of the Fifteenth.[1] There is no news from General Grant's army.

[1] Later I learned that while the brigade's loss was great, yet Company E's loss was light. By a flank movement the brigade advanced a short distance upon Atlanta.—A. G. L.

IN THE HOSPITAL AT ROME, GEORGIA

(August, 1864)

Wednesday, 3d—Everything is quiet here in Rome, Georgia. There is no news from General Grant's army.

Thursday, 4th—It is warm and sultry. There is no news from the front. I am still serving the medicine to the sick.

Friday, 5th—It rained nearly all day. The troops here are receiving their pay today, some for one and others for two months. Since May 1st the Government has been paying the privates $16.00 per month, which is an increase of $3.00. But money here in Rome is of no particular benefit to a soldier, for there is nothing in town to buy, the only business men being the sutlers who are attached to the regiments in the front. All is quiet at this place.

Saturday, 6th—It is warm and pleasant again. This is general scrub-day for all the hospitals; the floors are scrubbed, clean sheets and pillow slips put on the cots, and clean underclothes are dealt out for the sick.

Sunday, 7th—A train came in this evening from the front loaded with the wounded from the Seventeenth Army Corps. They were wounded in the battles of July 21st, 22d and 28th around Atlanta. There is still no news from Grant's army.

Monday, 8th—This morning I was put in as head nurse of ward D, hospital number 4. My duty is to direct the nurses in dealing out medicine and attending to the needs of the sick.

Tuesday, 9th—A train loaded with wounded came in last night from Marietta, Georgia, and they were sent out to the field hospital east of town.

Wednesday, 10th—No news from the front. The sick in my ward are all getting along well, with the exception of two men who are suffering severely with inflammatory rheumatism. Some of the men are returning to the front, while others are going home on furloughs.

Thursday, 11th—A train loaded with sick and wounded came in this afternoon from the front. Some of our convalescents had to give up their cots to the sick, and go out to the field hospital, where they will occupy tents.

Friday, 12th—It rained nearly all day. I received a letter today from William Green, my bunk-mate out in the front. He reports that the loss of our company in the battles of July 21st

(August, 1864)

and 22d before Atlanta was four men: George Sweet and David Hobaugh killed, and H. Newans wounded, and Aaron Pearce is missing. I wrote a letter to Albert Downing this afternoon.

Saturday, 13th—This is general scrub-day, and we are cleaning up the wards of the hospital. We have good food for the sick served to them on their cots. The convalescents go out to the dining room for their meals. No news from General Grant's army.

Sunday, 14th—A hot, sultry day. There is no news of any importance. We are giving close attention to the very sick and the severely wounded, some of whom are dying every day.

A SET OF RESOLUTIONS.

Resolved, That I may from this day learn something new from the Scriptures every day, and that I may obey the laws of God as near as I can, in entreating my fellow men, and in doing good for the Master's sake.

Resolved, That I may once a day or more offer thanks to my Savior for his help; and, above all, that I may try to live a true Christian until death. May God help me so to live, is my prayer.

Monday, 15th—It is quite warm. All is quiet. There is nothing new from the front. A large number of men left the hospital this morning for the front. I would like to go, too, but the doctor tells me that I can do more good by staying here and caring for the sick. This is my birthday—twenty-two years old today.

Tuesday, 16th—There was a heavy rain this afternoon. All is quiet and there is no train in today from the front. I sold my American lever watch today for $33.50, which is $4.50 more than I paid for it in Davenport, Iowa.

Wednesday, 17th—No rain today—the first day without rain during this month. A train load of sick and wounded came in today from the front. The railroad is in running order again after the raid by General Wheeler, in which he tore up about two miles of track near Dalton, Georgia. It is reported that Wheeler has been captured with eight hundred of his men.

Thursday, 18th—It is the same old thing over and over. The first thing we do when sick and wounded soldiers come to the

(August, 1864)

hospital, is to pack all their clothing, blankets, knapsacks and the like, store their accouterments and guns in a dry place, and deal out to each a cotton shirt, drawers, socks and a pair of carpet slippers. When they get well, their clothes and equipment are returned to them, and in case of death their personal effects are turned over to the regimental officer, who sends them to their former homes.

Friday, 19th—A man by the name of Henry Neeley, a patient in our ward, died this afternoon of consumption. We were giving him cod liver oil, a tablespoonful six times a day. Nothing new from the front.

Saturday, 20th—This is general scrub day. We had a busy day in the hospital fitting out cots for the latest arrivals. Our ward is crowded to the limit, there being more sick and wounded here now than at any previous time. Our hospital number 4 contains only the sick. All is quiet. No news from General Grant.

Sunday, 21st—It is the same thing over again—lonesome, lonesome, lonesome. The first thing in the morning is to serve each man with food according to his condition and the doctor's orders, and then deal out the medicine. There is a death every day.

Monday, 22d—It is quite cool and pleasant this morning and things appear quite lively in town. I wrote a letter to Mr. G. G. Evans, Philadelphia, ordering a gold pen, for which I enclosed $5.00.[1]

Tuesday, 23d—Foggy this morning and sultry throughout the day. David Huff of our company died here today in the field hospital east of town, of the wound he received on the 12th of the month. He was a schoolmate of mine, and a good boy. He will be missed by all of the boys of the company.

Wednesday, 24th—William Snow died in our ward last night. This is a dreadfully hot day, and since our ward is so crowded, we make this a special scrub-day, to cool the atmosphere as well as to keep the place clean.

Thursday, 25th—There are now from five thousand to six thousand sick and wounded here, and still more are coming. Though some of the sick are gaining slowly, yet there are from

[1] Mr. Downing says that was the last of his $5.00, for he never heard from the order.—Ed.

five to six deaths daily; there have been as many as eight deaths in a day, and not less than three a day for the time the hospital has been established here. I am told that the dead are buried in the Rome cemetery. Most of the men are sent out to the front again just as soon as they can go. General Hospital, Ward D, Second Section, Second Division. Rome, Georgia.

Friday, 26th—A large number of the boys are going home on furloughs. Their papers came in from the front today, signed up, and the boys are to start home tomorrow. Thomas R. McConnoll and John Zitler of our company are among them. I am sending $25.00 home to father by John Zitler. That makes a total of $445.40 which I have sent home. A. G. Downing, Company E, Eleventh Iowa, Veteran Volunteers.

Saturday, 27th—All things are quiet. The furloughed men left on the train this morning for their homes. This has been another very busy day with us, being our regular clean-up day. No news from the front.

Sunday, 28th—No news. All things quiet. Rome, Georgia.

Monday, 29th—News came that General Grant had an engagement with the rebels on the Danville railroad near Petersburg, Virginia. The loss was heavy on both sides, but Grant succeeded in holding his place. The fight took place on the 21st of the month.

Tuesday, 30th—It is warm and sultry. There are not so many sick and wounded coming in as there were a few days ago. Quite a number, at their own request, are being sent out to the front. When the convalescents are able for duty, they can't stand it to remain here; the first thought is to get back into the lines. Taking care of the sick is no light work, if one does his duty. The worst is that there is so much sad, heart-rending work to do, ministering to the dying, taking down their farewells to be sent to their homes; then after death, we have to roll the bodies in their blankets and carry them to the "deadhouse," where other hands take charge and bury them without coffin or ceremony.

Wednesday, 31st—The same old thing over again. Nothing new from the front.[1] The sick and also the attendants here in

---

[1] Crocker's Iowa Brigade at this time was down at Jonesboro, below Atlanta, stationed on the Atlanta & Montgomery Railroad, which was one of the main roads running into Atlanta from the South. The losses in the brigade while there, were small.—A. G. D.

IN THE HOSPITAL AT ROME, GEORGIA 213
(August, 1864)

the hospital were mustered for pay today. This is muster day throughout the entire army.

SEPTEMBER, 1864.

Thursday, 1st—It is quite warm. Nothing of importance.[1] The number of men in the hospitals is decreasing rapidly, for so many are going home on furloughs and no more are coming in.[2]

Friday, 2d—Cloudy and warm—threatened rain. No news.[3] I wrote two letters today, one to Lewis Elseffer and one to Mrs. Mary Ham, Iowa City, Iowa.

Saturday, 3d—A report[4] came in today that General Sherman has his headquarters in Atlanta, and that the rebel army is in retreat with our army after them.[5] News came also of the surrender of Fort Morgan at Mobile, Alabama; also that General Grant is shelling Petersburg with fifteen-inch shells. All things are quiet here at Rome, Georgia.

Sunday, 4th—It is cool and quite pleasant. No news of any importance. The boys in my ward are all getting along fine, with the exception of two or three, and it is doubtful whether they will ever again be well.

Monday, 5th—Clear and quite pleasant. All things are quiet.[6]

[1] On September 1st Crocker's Iowa Brigade advanced from Jonesboro to Flint creek with the remainder of Sherman's army. The loss during the day was light.—A. G. D.

[2] This shows how completely in the dark our diarist-nurse was, as to what was going on around Atlanta.—Ed.

[3] On this day John Hilton of Company E was severely wounded in the right side at Lovejoy Station. This was the last day's fighting in the siege of Atlanta. Crocker's Iowa Brigade had been under fire eighty-one days out of the eighty-seven days of the siege—from June to September.—A. G. D.

[4] The information was gathered from a poster or news sheet about four inches wide and twenty-two inches long, printed on one side and sold among the soldiers at the hospital. Mr. Downing purchased one, which he has preserved, and thinks he paid ten cents for it.—Ed.

[5] General Sherman finally took Atlanta by a bit of strategy. He withdrew his army from the rifle-pits in front of Atlanta, and placing the Twentieth Army Corps across the Chattahoochee river to protect his base of supplies at Marietta, moved with the remainder of the army in a wide circuit by his right flank and got into the rear of Hood's army. It is said that when Sherman made this move, Hood, taking it for granted that Sherman had given up the siege, proclaimed the fact, and he and his army, together with the citizens of Atlanta, began celebrating the event with a great jollification. But when Hood, in the midst of their rejoicings, learned by courier the truth about Sherman's move, and that the Union army was in his rear in full force, he sent orders throughout his camp and the city, calling every man to arms. He immediately began the evacuation of Atlanta, destroying the ammunition and all army supplies.—A. G. D.

[6] Men were leaving every day for the front and but few were brought to our hospitals, since the Union army was in possession of Atlanta, where hospitals were being established, while those at Rome were to be closed just as soon as the sick there were able to go to the front.—A. G. D.

(September, 1864)

Tuesday, 6th—News came that General Sherman was still in pursuit of the rebels, and that he has captured a great many of them. This morning I was transferred from Ward D to Ward E as wardmaster, the master of Ward E having been sent to the front. I have charge of eleven sick men and they are getting along well. One poor fellow with a severe case of inflammatory rheumatism is entirely helpless.

Wednesday, 7th—The weather is still quite pleasant. There is nothing of any importance. All is quiet. Ward E is on the ground floor of the same building as Ward D, but at the rear of the building, and is a poor place to put sick men for any length of time, as it is poorly ventilated.

Thursday, 8th—Cool and cloudy with some rain today. All is quiet.[1]

Friday, 9th—It is clear and quite warm. The constant shifting of the sick and wounded men makes a great deal of work for the convalescents here. They are planning to close the hospitals here as soon as possible and the hospital equipment will be shipped either to Chattanooga or Nashville until needed. The field hospital at Atlanta is all that will be needed.

Saturday, 10th—A large number were sent to the front this morning. Jeremiah Argo of Company E, who had been among the wounded, was one of them. It is reported that the rebels are planning to raid this place, for we have but few soldiers here to defend it.

Sunday, 11th—This is a quiet day. I have only five boys in my ward now with one nurse. The ward is to be closed in a few days and some of the wounded out in the tents will occupy it.

Monday, 12th—No news. We have received no mail and no late papers for some time, because the main railroad to Atlanta has been torn up by the rebels for some distance between Nashville and Chattanooga.

Tuesday, 13th—All is quiet here at Rome. Another large squad of men was sent from the hospital to the front at Atlanta. Nearly every day there are some leaving for their homes on furloughs. I received a letter today from Lewis Elseffer; he is now a clerk at the headquarters of the Seventeenth Army Corps.

[1]Sherman's army went into permanent camp in the vicinity of Atlanta for a much needed rest. The camps were in the timber and the men had good water.—A. G. D.

IN THE HOSPITAL AT ROME, GEORGIA

(September, 1864)

Wednesday, 14th—The troops that went from here after General Wheeler into eastern Tennessee about a month ago, returned this morning, coming in on the train. They did not succeed in capturing Wheeler, but they had several skirmishes with him, in one of which it is reported that the notorious General Morgan was killed.[1] The expedition, made up of the Thirty-ninth Iowa and the Thirty-third Ilinois, experienced some hard marching. Dr. French, in charge of the hospital here and head physician of the sick wards, left today for Atlanta.

Thursday, 15th—The day has been pleasant. It is reported that the rebel cavalry is in strong force in this vicinity and it is a good thing that the expedition returned when it did.

Friday, 16th—There was quite an excitement early this morning when it was learned that the rebel cavalry was indeed here. All the convalescents in the hospital were armed and ordered out into the rifle pits. Wheeler's cavalry were in plain view across the river north of town. They did not come across, however, as they discovered that our garrison was in shape to give them a warm reception. All is quiet at present.

Saturday, 17th—The fight is all over and no one was hurt. The troops remained under arms all night to be in readiness for the rebels should they come across the river. Everything is quiet today.

Sunday, 18th—Have had a week of very pleasant weather. Our store of supplies here is small, as the army is to evacuate the place as soon as possible.[2]

Monday, 19th—The sick in the hospitals are getting along well. Part of the men here received two months' pay today, $32.00. The pay of soldiers has been raised to $16.00 per month since May 1, 1864.[3]

Tuesday, 20th—Rain most all day. More of the wounded from the field hospital out east of town started home today on thirty-day furloughs. The sick here are being transferred to

[1] This was another false report.—Ed.
[2] This proved to be my last Sunday at Rome, Georgia, for which I was very thankful. While there I saw more sick and wounded men than I ever wish to see again. While I was a convalescent working among the sick, giving out different kinds of medicine to forty or fifty men, I was under great responsibility, and it cost me many a night's sleep and rest.—A. G. D.
[3] The $32.00 I received was the first pay I got since leaving Davenport on Sunday, April 24, 1864.—A. G. D.

temporary hospitals down town, while the remainder of the wounded from the field hospital are taking the places vacated by them.

Wednesday, 21st—It rained all day. There is a rumor flying in the air here that the veterans of the Seventeenth Army Corps are to be mustered out of the service this fall, on account of not having been sworn in right. But we cannot yet believe such a report to be true; that would be too good a thing all at once. We hear that all is quiet in the East, on the Rappahannock.

Thursday, 22d—It is still raining, which makes the third day's rain. My ward was broken up today and the sick boys were transferred to Ward D in hospital number 4. We worked all afternoon making the ward ready for the wounded from the field hospital. I tried to get permission to return to my regiment today, but the doctor would not let me go. But all who are able, if not needed here, are to be sent to the front tomorrow.

Friday, 23d—I helped to move the field hospital into town this morning. Most of the wounded able to go, have been sent home on thirty-day furloughs, and some of the sick will also go soon. There is no news from Grant's army. I received a letter this morning from Miss G———. I received my knapsack and equipments and bidding good-by, left for Atlanta, Georgia. There was a squad of one hundred and seventy-five of us and we started at noon, going as far as Kingston, where we lay awaiting a train from the North. We left Kingston soon after dark.

(September, 1864)

Chapter XX.
Rejoining the Eleventh Iowa at Atlanta and the Pursuit of Hood. September 24-November 6.

Saturday, 24th—This morning found us lying at Acworth, Georgia, having arrived at about 11 o'clock in the night. There is an engine off the track about a mile east of town, and they are at work repairing the track and trying to get the engine back on. Eleven trains are waiting here, six going North and five South. We left Acworth at 2 p. m. and arrived at Big Shanty, where we again had to lie until night, waiting for the railroad to be repaired. The rebels tore up the tracks to the west of Kenesaw mountain, this afternoon. They had a small battery with them and threw some shells at the trains, but with the exception of hitting three or four cars, did no damage.

Sunday, 25th—We arrived in Atlanta about 9 o'clock last night. I stayed over night at the Soldiers' Home, in one of the vacant store buildings. I got my breakfast there and then with my knapsack on started for the headquarters of the Seventeenth Army Corps. From there I went to the headquarters of the Iowa Brigade and about noon joined my company. I was glad to see the boys. I received a large mail, one letter from father with $5.00 enclosed. Atlanta is quite a city, there being some fine buildings, one of the finest being the railroad station. But the town is low and in the timber.

Monday, 26th—The camp of the Seventeenth Army Corps is four miles south of town. We have a very nice camp here, the boys having built good bunks out of old lumber, in their wedge tents. Our tents had been stored at Huntsville, Alabama, and after the fall of Atlanta were sent forward. General Sherman's entire army is in camp here, and strongly fortified, just south of Atlanta. The army is to be paid off while in camp, the muster rolls having been sent in to the paymaster. All is quiet.

Tuesday, 27th—General Sherman issued an order removing all citizens from Atlanta, on account of the scarcity of food. There is only one line of railroad open from the North to Atlanta, and the rebels are destroying almost every day some portions of the track, thus delaying trains. All who take the oath of allegiance are sent north beyond the Ohio river, while those who refuse to take it are to go farther south; they can take their choice. General Sherman has notified Hood to come with wagons to a station south of Atlanta and take care of the citizens, as our teams will haul them to that station. A great many are taking the oath and going North, but some think themselves too good to take the oath. Some of the women are very strong secessionists, and spurn the idea of taking the oath, declaring that they would rather die.

Wednesday, 28th—Cloudy with some rain today. I went on picket this morning for the first time since coming back from the hospital. I was on a lookout post on the right of the picket lines of the brigade with four other men out of our brigade. All is quiet in front of the lines. I miss the four boys killed in battle while I was absent from the company—they were all good men, three of them being veterans.

Thursday, 29th—We were relieved from picket this morning at 8 o'clock. The men of the Eleventh Iowa have had no pay since leaving Davenport early in the spring, and some of the boys are pretty short of money; but they will get some soon, as the paymaster is expected to arrive any day. The rebels are becoming quite bold around Atlanta and along the railroads as far north as Nashville, Tennessee. It is reported that Hood is going to try to regain some lost ground. General Sherman has sent some of his troops north to reinforce the detachments guarding the railroads. There is no news from General Grant's army.

Friday, 30th—The weather is quite pleasant. Nothing of any importance. I have made loans to the boys of my company as follows: Samuel Bain, $5.00; John Ford, $5.00; Samuel Metcalf, $5.00; Burtis Rumsey, $3.00; William Green, $3.00, and Monroe Blazer, $1.00. I also loaned $5.00 to John Hemphill of Company I of the Sixteenth Iowa. All loans are to be paid back on next pay day. I paid a debt of $5.00 to Thomas Armstrong. I bought a gold pen from Jason Sparks for $5.00. All is quiet on the post.

OCTOBER, 1864.

Saturday, 1st—This afternoon the Third and Fourth Divisions of the Seventeenth Corps started on an expedition toward

(October, 1864)

Fairburn, Georgia, where, it is reported, there is a large force of the rebels. We marched about seven miles and went into bivouac for the night. I received a letter from David Cole of the Twenty-fourth Iowa. His regiment is now in the Shenandoah valley, Virginia.

Sunday, 2d—We started again early this morning, and after marching about six miles, came upon the rebels' rear guard. We did some skirmishing with them and chased them about two miles, when we let them go and started back to Atlanta. The rebels tore up a portion of the railroad track between Marietta and Acworth, and delayed our trains. Our expedition was sent out for the purpose of cutting off their retreat from Marietta, but we were too late. After marching six miles on our return, we went into bivouac for the night.

Monday, 3d—A heavy rain last night. We started early this morning and arrived in camp about 9 o'clock. This afternoon we received orders to prepare to march early tomorrow morning with fifteen days' rations. It is supposed that the expedition is going out towards Kenesaw mountain, as it is reported that Hood is moving north with the main part of his army, and that he is now in the vicinity of Kenesaw. The Fourteenth, Fifteenth and Seventeenth Corps are to move north, while the Twentieth and Twenty-third are to remain here at Atlanta. News came today that General Grant is within five miles of Richmond and that he has whipped the rebels at every point.

Tuesday, 4th—Rain early this morning. We stored away our tents in Atlanta and left in light marching order. The three corps started out on different roads, and the roads being muddy it made hard marching. We bivouacked for the night four miles west of Marietta, Georgia. The railroad bridge across the Tallahassee river here was partially destroyed by the rebels. They built a raft of logs and floated it down against the bridge, knocking out two piers. No news from the East.

Wednesday, 5th—The weather is pleasant. We were on the move early this morning, the Seventeenth and Fifteenth Corps marched out to the south of Kenesaw mountain, where we went into camp about noon. We lay here the rest of the day. The rebels, it is reported, are in force on Lost mountain. All is quiet.

(October, 1864)

Thursday, 6th—It rained nearly all day. We lay in bivouac all day, resting. We hear that Sherman with a part of his force is trying to surround the rebels in the vicinity of Lost mountain. The rebels left the railroad after tearing up about fifteen miles of track, burning the ties and twisting the rails. But the engineers will have it repaired in a few days, as there are thousands of trees along the way just the size for railroad ties. All is quiet along the line.

Friday, 7th—Weather clear and pleasant. Our division, now the Fourth of the Seventeenth Army Corps, started out to reconnoiter. We went in light marching order without teams or artillery and marching out about twenty miles to the southwest of Marietta came upon the rebels' pickets, at a place called Powder Springs. We drove them about four miles to the south, they not caring for a fight, and camped for the night. Our division was sent to find out whether or not the rebels are out in force along this road.

Saturday, 8th—We started back early this morning for Marietta and arrived in camp about noon. I was sent out on picket duty this afternoon. The entire Fifteenth Corps left on an expedition this afternoon, but their destination is not known. The rebels left Lost mountain, retreating to Dallas, Georgia. Our men captured some of their wagon trains. All is quiet again. No news from the North. Camp Eleventh Iowa, Marietta, Georgia.

Sunday, 9th—We were routed early this morning and left for Big Shanty, and arriving there in the afternoon went into bivouac. The Fifteenth and Seventeenth Army Corps were sent here to put the railroad track in repair. The rebels tore up about nine miles of track, burning the ties and twisting the rails. The engineers have to get out new ties and large details of our men are put to work cutting down trees and hewing the ties. It is reported that the rebels are going to the North.

Monday, 10th—A large detail from our regiment was put to work on the railroad. Three of us, Hiram Frank, John D. Moore and I, took French leave this afternoon and climbed to the top of Kenesaw mountain. It is a grand view from the mountain, but we had to pay for our sightseeing, for when we got back to camp we found that our command had left. They were ordered

(October, 1864)

to go on the double-quick to Altoona, Georgia, and we had to run about four miles before we caught up with them. Our bunkmates were carrying our knapsacks, haversacks, canteens and rifles, with all accouterments, and they were about as thankful as we were when we caught up with them.[1]

Tuesday, 11th—The weather has been cool and pleasant for several days. Our entire corps started early this morning at 2 o'clock, going as we suppose, to Kingston. We marched through to Cartersville, where we went into camp for the night.

We hear that there was a hard fight at Altoona yesterday with fearful loss of life on both sides, but Hood had to give up trying to capture the place. It is reported that Hood is now moving toward Rome, Georgia.

Wednesday, 12th—We started early this morning and marched to within five miles of Rome by midnight, when we went into bivouac for the rest of the night. We had to move very slowly on account of the teams giving out. Our horses and mules are getting very thin. This is because of the scarcity of forage, and then, too, the roads are very rough, which made it hard on them. Hood's force is thought to be about thirty thousand, while our army numbers fifty thousand men, of all arms, and the men are in fine shape. We received a large mail at Kingston, when passing through there this evening.

Thursday, 13th—We left our teams behind at Kingston and they did not catch up with us till this morning. We lay here in camp all day. About sundown we received marching orders and our division started for Adairsville, some fifteen miles distant from Rome. We left our teams and all artillery behind and marching through on a by-road, reached Adairsville by midnight.

Friday, 14th—At Adairsville we took a train composed of box cars and left for Resaca, where we arrived about 4 o'clock this morning. We at once left the cars and formed a line of battle. Here we lay all day. The remainder of our corps soon arrived, and later the Fourteenth Army Corps came up. The first division of our corps was sent out after the rebels. They found them on the railroad about six miles out between Resaca and Dalton, where

---

[1] General Corse had flagged Sherman for reinforcements, as Hood was trying to capture the place. Our army had about one million rations stored at Altoona. Sherman flagged: "Hold the fort; I am coming," and General Corse answered back that he'd hold the fort to the death if need be.—A. G. D.

they already had destroyed about fifteen miles of track. Our troops engaged in a skirmish there in which the Seventeenth Iowa were taken prisoners, but were at once paroled. It is reported that the commander of the post at Dalton surrendered the place without firing a gun. It is thought that the rebels are making for the mountains, and if they succeed in getting there before we do, it will be hard to trap them, as they are in their own country and among friends.

Saturday, 15th—We left Resaca early this morning, going out after the rebels whom we found at the south entrance of Snake Creek Gap. Here we formed a line of battle and skirmishing commenced. A small force of the rebels was behind some old works which our men had built last spring while advancing on Resaca. Finally two regiments of the Third Division made a charge upon them and routed them. Our loss was about fifty killed and wounded. The rebels then fell back through the pass, blockading it for about eight miles, by felling trees across the road. Our corps did not succeed in getting through the pass until about dark, and the Fifteenth Army Corps was still in our rear.

Sunday, 16th—We left bivouac early this morning and marched eight miles. We passed through Gooseneck Gap, about four miles long and quite narrow. The rebels did not take time to block this gap. The Fifteenth Corps being in the advance, came upon the rebels and engaged them in some skirmishing. The rebels are still falling back to the north. We are now in a mountainous country, and thinly settled, as it is so rough and rocky. The timber here is of chestnut and all varieties of oak.

Monday, 17th—We lay in bivouac all day, but at dark moved on about four miles and again went into bivouac. The weather has been very pleasant for some days. The muster rolls of the non-veterans of our regiment were made out today. They received their discharge papers, as their three years' service will be up tomorrow. There are twelve from our company: Albert Allee, John L. Ayers, John Ford, George Eicher, Padenarin McCarty, Ebenezer Rankin, George Mooney, Hugh C. McBirney, Joseph McKibben, Thomas R. McConnoll, Samuel Metcalf and Albert B. Stiles.

(October, 1864)

Tuesday, 18th—We started early this morning and reached Lafayette at 9 o'clock. We lay there for two hours when we took up our march for Summerville, Georgia, and went into bivouac within four miles of the town. The rebels are still moving to the north through the Blue mountains. We had two days' rations left in our haversacks this morning, when we received orders from the quartermaster that they would have to run us four days, as we could not draw any before that time. No news from the Eastern army.

Wednesday, 19th—We entered Summerville at 10 o'clock and remained there till noon, when we started for Galesville, Alabama. After marching fifteen miles, we went into bivouac on the banks of the Ogeechee river. All is quiet in front. The valleys through which we are marching are quite rich and there are some fine plantations which afford good forage. It is fortunate for us, as we have to get most of our living that way while on this expedition. Sweet potatoes are plentiful and then we also get some fresh pork.

Thursday, 20th—The same as ever. We marched twelve miles and went into camp near Galesville, Alabama. All of the forces of General Sherman which have been after Hood, came together at this place by different roads, and are now in bivouac. General Hardie of Hood's army is in front of us with his corps and still retreating. It is fine marching weather.

Friday, 21st—The Fourth, Fourteenth, Fifteenth, Seventeenth and Twenty-third Army Corps have concentrated here and are in bivouac. Foraging parties are sent out from the different corps, as there are some rich plantations in this section. Our corps moved camp today about four miles. All is quiet in the front. The report is that the rebels are retreating toward the Blue mountains.

Saturday, 22d—We lay in camp all day for the purpose of resting. But it appears to the rank and file of the men that Sherman must have given up trying to catch Hood, or else we would not remain so long at one place. The supply trains were all sent back to the main railroad line for provisions. I went out on picket this morning. The non-veterans of the Eleventh and Thirteenth Iowa Regiments were mustered out this morning, and left for Chattanooga, from which place they will start for home. All of the non-veteran officers from each regiment, except two or three, went out with the privates. It is fine weather for marching. No news from the Eastern army.

Sunday, 23d—The weather is getting pretty cool mornings, but we have plenty of wood to build fires in front of our shacks. All is quiet in the front. I was relieved from picket this morning. We had company inspection this evening.

Monday, 24th—Still lying in camp and all is quiet at the front. Large foraging parties are being sent out for food for the men and feed for the horses and mules. The valleys in this part of the country are thickly settled, but not more than half of the plantations have been cultivated this past season, as the negroes were taken south by their masters to keep them from falling into the hands of the "Yanks," and also to help build fortifications. The plantations that have been farmed were put mostly in wheat and corn. There are some large fields of corn which come in very handy for our army at this time.

Tuesday, 25th—Still lying in camp. The supply train of the Fifteenth Army Corps returned with rations late this evening, but the supply train of the Seventeenth Corps has not yet come in. It is reported that the army of the Tennessee is going on a march of four hundred miles. The route is supposed to be down through the States of Alabama and Mississippi and then up through to Memphis, Tennessee.[1] We are to take rations for thirty days and clothing for sixty days. The armies of the Ohio and of the Cumberland, it is said, are to garrison Atlanta[2] and also to hold the railroad between Atlanta and Nashville. The Twenty-third Army Corps moved out today to Cedar Bluffs.

Wednesday, 26th—The weather is quite pleasant. Nothing of importance. Still in camp. Our work, outside of regular picket duty, is very light here.

Thursday, 27th—Still lying in camp, and all is quiet.

Friday, 28th—Weather still pleasant. The Seventeenth Army Corps was reviewed by General Mower. We were out in full dress with knapsacks, haversacks and canteens on. There is to be only one battery to each division of the Fourteenth, Fifteenth,

[1] This was the first hint at "marching through Georgia," but the camp rumor had it Alabama and Mississippi.—Ed.
[2] We learned later that it was Chattanooga instead of Atlanta, and that the two armies were to be united under the command of General Thomas.—A. G. D.

(October, 1864)

Seventeenth and Twentieth Army Corps. The remainder of the artillery, with all defective wagons, horses and mules, is being sent back to Chattanooga. All things quiet in camp. We received orders to be ready to march in the morning at daylight.

Saturday, 29th—We were routed out at 2 o'clock this morning and at daybreak took up our march. We covered fifteen miles and went into bivouac near Spring creek. We reached Cedar Bluffs by 10 o'clock, where the Fifteenth Army Corps passed us, turning on a road to the right. About noon we crossed the Coosa river on a pontoon bridge and marched all the afternoon through a miserable swamp. The country is heavily timbered with white oak, and is thinly settled.

Sunday, 30th—We started early this morning and marched fifteen miles. We bivouacked for the night near Cave Springs. Large foraging parties were sent out which brought in great quantities of provisions and feed, this section not having been overrun by our armies. Cave Spring is a little village sixteen miles southwest of Rome, Georgia. The citizens all left their homes on the approach of our army. I was detailed on picket duty. All is quiet.

Monday, 31st—We lay in bivouac all day, this being a regular muster day, and the army was mustered. Foraging parties were again sent out. I was on picket continuously for twenty-four hours.

NOVEMBER, 1864.

Tuesday, 1st—We started early this morning and marched through to Cedartown and went into bivouac for the night. I was taken sick this morning and had to ride all day in the ambulance. This was my first experience in the ambulance.

Wednesday, 2d—We started early this morning and after marching fifteen miles went into bivouac near Van Wert, Georgia. It rained all day, and the roads became so slippery that it made hard marching. Some of the men gave out and had to be hauled.

Thursday, 3d—Still raining. Our march today covered sixteen miles and the troops are very much fatigued. We camped for the night in Dallas, Georgia, one division, the Fourth, going into vacant houses and buildings in the town. The citizens all left the place upon our approach. There had been a cotton mill here, but it was closed down last summer when the Yankees were besieging Atlanta.

Friday, 4th—Left Dallas this morning, marched ten miles, and went into camp near Lost mountain. I went out with a foraging party from our regiment. We brought in five head of cattle and seven hogs, and also some cane molasses and corn meal. We also searched for cabbage, but the negroes did not know what we meant; they said that they had never seen any such thing growing. We found very few citizens at home, mostly poor families at that; but the men were away in the rebel army.

Saturday, 5th—We left our fires early this morning and marching toward Marietta, went into bivouac for the remainder of the day and night within five miles of the town. Captain Anderson of Company A, Eleventh Iowa, arrived from Iowa this evening with one hundred and fifty conscripts for our regiment to serve one year. They are a fine lot of men to be conscripts; however, only half of them were drafted, the others being substitutes, each receiving from $150 to $800.

Sunday, 6th—Our division was moved in close to town today and went into camp. We received orders to remain here a few days, to draw clothing and receive our pay. This was glorious news. We pulled down vacant houses and proceeded to build bunks and "ranches" with the lumber, covering them with our rubber ponchos. The Sixteenth Iowa went out with the regimental teams for forage. Nine trains came in over the railroad from the north, loaded with provisions for the army stationed at the different points along the line, and at Atlanta. Things are quite lively in town today.

(November, 1864)

Chapter XXI.
Marching Through Georgia. Capture of Savannah. November 7, 1864-January 2, 1865.

Monday, 7th—It is cloudy and quite cool. The Eleventh Iowa received six months' pay this afternoon, besides another installment of the bounty. I got $148.00 in pay and $100.00 of bounty money. Our army is preparing to evacuate Atlanta. The general quartermaster is loading every train going north with the surplus commissariat and all extra army baggage. It is reported that our army is going to fall back as far as Chattanooga, and that we are to destroy the railroad as we go. There is a report that the army of the Tennessee is going on a long expedition further south.[1]

Tuesday, 8th—Still in camp. Some rain today. Ten train loads of army supplies left for the North. A great many refugees are being sent north, as it will be impossible for them to make a living down here during the coming winter. This is election day and everything is very quiet in camp, as political speeches are not allowed in the army. The election went off fine. Our regiment is strong for Old Abraham—three hundred and fourteen votes for Lincoln and forty-two for McClellan. I bought a watch of John Aubin for $18.50. Some of the boys are having lively times down town; they are going in on their nerves, to make up for lost time.

Wednesday, 9th—It is still raining. I went out on picket this morning. We received orders to be ready to move at a moment's notice, for the purpose of tearing up the railroad tracks. Citizens all around Atlanta, hearing that the Yankees are going to leave the place, are coming in larger numbers to go North. Women leave their homes and all they have, and with their children walk a distance of thirty miles, for the sake of getting to the North. Where both armies have been ravaging the country, the people are destitute—haven't anything to eat—and therefore they have to leave their homes. No news from the North.

[1] This was through Georgia, but as yet the men knew nothing definite.—Ed.

(November, 1864)

Thursday, 10th—All is quiet in camp. I borrowed $25.00 from William Barrett until next pay day. Several trains came in from the North this morning. We received a large mail. All men unable to stand the march on our Southern expedition are being sent North. Each regiment will be allowed but one wagon, and the number of headquarters wagons will be greatly reduced. Every man in the ranks will have to carry his shelter tent.

Friday, 11th—All is quiet in camp. We have company drill twice a day now for the purpose of drilling our conscripts. We received orders that the last mail would leave for the North tomorrow morning and that all who wanted to write farewell letters home would have to attend to it before that time. The rebel cavalry, about three thousand strong, made a raid on our forces at Atlanta, but were repulsed with heavy loss, for what little they gained.

Saturday, 12th—Our corps marched out on the railroad between Marietta and Big Shanty and tore it up, burning all the ties and bending the irons. The iron rails were thrown into the fires and then twisted up. The last train went North about noon, and no more mail will be sent out from this part of the army for forty days. The telegraph lines between Atlanta and the North were cut soon after the last train left. The railroad from Dalton south, wherever Sherman's army goes, is to be destroyed and all stations and public buildings burned.

Sunday, 13th—We started early this morning for Atlanta and after marching twenty miles went into camp for the night. A detachment of the Twentieth Army Corps is stationed at the railroad bridge crossing the Chattahoochee river. They will soon destroy the bridge, and also the track clear to Atlanta. All is quiet in the front. We burned everything in our camp yesterday that we did not need, and it seems that everything in sight is being burned. Every man seems to think he has a free hand to touch the match. The nice little town of Marietta which we left behind this morning will doubtless be burned before the last of Sherman's army leaves the place.

Monday, 14th—This morning was cool and pleasant. We started early and marched five miles, going into camp a mile south of Atlanta. We tore up the railroad tracks through Atlanta and

(November, 1864)

burned all the public buildings. There was a fine large station here, and a splendid engine house, but both were burned. Very few citizens are left in Atlanta. The Fourteenth, Fifteenth, Seventeenth and Twentieth Army Corps are in bivouac in the vicinity of Atlanta. They are concentrating here for the purpose of making a grand raid down South. We are to take forty days' rations with us, consisting of hardtack, coffee, sugar, salt and pepper, candles and soap, but we are to forage for meat as we march through the country. All is quiet.

Tuesday, 15th—Started early this morning for the Southern coast, somewhere, and we don't care, so long as Sherman is leading us. The Army of the Tennessee forms the right, while the Army of the Cumberland is moving off in the direction of Milledgeville, Georgia. There are about sixty thousand men of all arms, and they are in fine spirits and well clothed for the campaign. The roads are good and the weather fine for marching. We went into bivouac for the night about twelve miles from Atlanta. The country is very thinly settled and there is nothing to forage. All is quiet at the front—none of the rebels in sight.

Wednesday, 16th—Reveille sounded early this morning, and after marching twenty-five miles we went into bivouac tired and worn. Our division marched all day over a by-road on the inside of the right wing, and although the country was heavily timbered, yet we had a good road. We passed by some fine plantations, well improved with some good buildings. The Fourteenth and Twentieth Corps form the left wing and the Fifteenth and Seventeenth the right, both flanks being covered by the cavalry. There was some skirmishing off on our right in front of the Fifteenth Corps, but all is quiet in our front.

Thursday, 17th—We broke camp at 5 o'clock, marched eighteen miles, and went into bivouac for the night. Our regiment was train guard and the Sixteenth Iowa was rear guard of our brigade. We marched through some fine country today, and though heavily timbered, it is well improved. It is good country for foraging. We found plenty of fresh pork and all the sweet potatoes we could carry. The weather is delightful and there is no rebel in our front yet.

Friday, 18th—We were on the road by 8 o'clock and after marching ten miles, lay by until 10 p. m., when we were ordered

(November, 1864)

to fall in again. After an hour's march we came to the Ockmulgee river, which we crossed by pontoons at Ockmulgee Mills. The entire Seventeenth Corps came together again here and at 1 o'clock in the night we went into bivouac on the east side of the river. The Fifteenth Corps crossed the river by the same pontoon bridge. There is fine water power here and there are large mills. The country is very rough.

Saturday, 19th—There was some rain last night and the roads today are very slippery, which as the country is so hilly, makes difficult marching. We marched fifteen miles and went into bivouac. Our division was in the rear of the Seventeenth Corps, the infantry marching at one side of the road so that the artillery and wagon trains could move together and all go into bivouac earlier and at the same time. The country is thickly settled. The citizens on the approach of our army left their homes and fled to Macon. We passed through Hillsboro at 10 a. m., and the town being deserted, many of the vacant houses were burned by our men. We heard the sound of cannon off to our right in the direction of Macon.

Sunday, 20th—It is still raining and the roads have become so muddy that it is impossible for the artillery to keep up with the infantry. There are some well-improved plantations along the way which have had good crops this season and we find plenty of sweet potatoes and fresh pork. We are on short rations now and therefore have to forage a great deal. We also find enough forage for the horses and mules in the command.

Monday, 21st—We started on our march this morning in a rain which continued all day. We marched fifteen miles and went into camp. The artillery have the preference of the road and because of the muddy roads our division wagon train could not keep up. Our regiment was on train guard. We corralled the wagons four miles in the rear, where the First Division of the Seventeenth Corps went into bivouac, to safeguard the train, since the rebels' cavalry have appeared both in front and in the rear.

Tuesday, 22d—The weather has turned cold. We left our bivouac early this morning with the wagon train and at 10 o'clock caught up with our division at Gordon, where they were in camp last night. Gordon is fifteen miles from Milledgeville and is the junction of the railroad running from there to Savannah. General Sherman with the left wing of our army passed through here ahead of us, remaining in the town three or four days. We left Gordon about noon and marched ten miles on a by-road off to the right of our corps, going into bivouac near Irwinton, the county seat of Wilkinson county. This is a nice little town, but like all other places we passed through, is deserted, the citizens running away on the approach of our army, and leaving everything with the negroes. All is quiet at the front.

Wednesday, 23d—We started at 7 a. m. and marched twelve miles, when we bivouacked for the night. It is reported that a force of two thousand rebels is in our front beyond the Oconee river, and that there has been some skirmishing. We crossed the Savannah railroad here at Station No. 15. This station was burned last July by General Stoneman in his raid toward Macon, Georgia. The country is very heavily timbered, mostly pitch pine, but there are some very nice plantations. The negroes have all been run off to keep them from falling into the hands of our army. We are now on three-fifths rations and are foraging for meat.

Thursday, 24th—We lay in camp all day. The rebels are still in our front, and there is some cannonading off on our left where the Fourteenth and Twentieth Corps are on the move and destroying property. The Seventeenth Corps burned all the railroad property from Gordon down to the Oconee river. The first brigade of our division destroyed the railroad for some miles in this locality. The Iowa Brigade went out on the railroad this morning and worked for two hours. There was some skirmishing in our front and to our right. Our division supply train is lying at Station No. 15, the Fifteenth Iowa acting as train guard. We received orders to march in the morning at 5 o'clock.

Friday, 25th—Our brigade marched out early this morning and relieved the First Brigade at the railroad bridge across the Oconee river, the rebels being just beyond. We burned the bridge and after waiting there a short time, got orders to march back to Toomsboro, which place we reached by 7 p. m. From there we started for Hawkins Ford, some ten miles dis-

(November, 1864)

tant, and after marching six miles went into bivouac. The Fifteenth Corps came in on the same road in order to cross the river by our pontoon bridge, which the engineers commenced to build late in the evening, after our men had driven the rebels from the river—they had to leave or be taken prisoners.

Saturday, 26th—The weather is cool but quite pleasant. We lay in camp awaiting the completion of the pontoon bridge. At 10 o'clock we began our march and by 3 in the afternoon both corps had crossed the river. The Fifteenth Corps had an engagement with the rebels on the 22d inst. near Macon, and after the fight the rebels fell back and scattered, leaving their dead and wounded on the field. Their loss was about one thousand, while ours was only five hundred. Their force was mainly state militia and came out from town to attack our approaching army. It is reported that the rebels are concentrating some fifty miles ahead of us and are strongly fortifying themselves on the Ogeechee river. We are on two-thirds rations, but still we have plenty to eat.

Sunday, 27th—We started at 8 o'clock this morning, marched eight miles, and went into camp for the remainder of the day. On our march this forenoon our division, the Third, destroyed ten miles of the railroad east of the Oconee river. The Fifteenth Corps is off on our right about two miles, while the Fourteenth and the Twentieth with Kilpatrick's cavalry are off on the left, out toward Augusta, Georgia. All is quiet in front. This is a very fine country, thickly settled and with some very nice farms, though the soil is very sandy and there is considerable pine timber.

Monday, 28th—We started at 7 o'clock this morning, marched fifteen miles, and went into camp at 5 p. m. Our division took up the rear on our march today and we had good roads for marching, with the exception of a small swamp which lay in our path. This is a fine country and there is plenty of forage. All is quiet in front, the rebels retreating without putting up a fight.[1]

[1]Almost every day after leaving Atlanta large numbers of negroes, women, children and old men, came, some of them walking miles, to see the Yankees go by. The soldiers in the ranks would engage them in conversation and the odd remarks the negroes would make were often quite amusing. They were asked many questions, one as a joke, a favorite one with the boys, was asking the nice mulatto girls to marry them; the answer invariably would be in the affirmative. These incidents as well as others made a change, and broke the monotony of our long, weary marches.—A. G. D.

(November, 1864)

Tuesday, 29th—We left bivouac at 8 a. m. and marched twenty miles today, going into camp about dark. The Eleventh Iowa acted as rear guard. We had good roads, there being no hills. The country is very flat and heavily timbered and the soil is sandy, mixed with clay. We are on two-fifths rations now, but the country still affords additional rations, such as potatoes and pork. Our general direction is southeast on the west side of the Savannah and Macon railroad. All is quiet in front.

Wednesday, 30th—Weather pleasant. We broke camp at 8 o'clock and covered only ten miles by the close of the whole day's march, when we went into bivouac on the banks of the Ogeechee river. We had a bad road, it being almost one continuous swamp. Now and then there was a small farm with a log hut occupied by a poor woman and children, all the men and larger boys being off with the army.[1] All is quiet in the front, but the rebels keep close on our rear. It is reported that General Wheeler with his cavalry is in our rear. The boys all declare that it's the safest place for him to be, just so he doesn't get too close. This is the sixteenth day out from Atlanta and we have been on the march part of the time both day and night. We have had but little fighting, but we have destroyed one thousand miles of railroad and burned millions of dollars' worth of other property. Camp in the swamps of Georgia.

DECEMBER, 1864.

Thursday, 1st—A heavy fog this morning. Our division crossed the Ogeechee river early this morning, the other two divisions of the corps having crossed last night. We crossed near Benton Station on the Savannah railroad. Our brigade destroyed the railroad this forenoon all the way from Benton Station north to Sebastopol, on the road running to Augusta. Our entire corps destroyed about fifteen miles of railroad. We left Sebastopol about noon, and after marching eight miles through swamps, went into bivouac at dark. All is quiet.

Friday, 2d—We marched eleven miles today and went into bivouac after dark near the town of Millen. We passed through

---

[1] It has been truly said that Governor Brown of Georgia robbed the cradle and the grave, forcing all the boys and old men into the army at the time of their defense of Macon, where they were defeated and scattered by our Fifteenth Army Corps on November 22, 1864.—A. G. D.

some fine country with very large plantations. We crossed the east prong of the Ogeechee river about dusk, the infantry crossing over the railroad bridge and the artillery and teams by pontoon bridge. Millen is on the bank of this river and is a junction of the railroad running between Augusta and Savannah. We demolished the railroad all along the line.

Saturday, 3d—We started off on our railroad destroying this morning at 7 o'clock. Our corps destroyed about ten miles of road, from Millen down to Station No. 70, where we went into camp for the night. The Fourteenth and Twentieth Corps are off on our left, destroying the railroad from Millen toward Augusta. At Millen there was located one of those hell-holes, a rebel prison, where the rebels kept about thirteen hundred of our men as prisoners. They rushed them off on the train for Charleston, South Carolina, just before our army arrived. I never saw a feed-yard looking so filthy and forsaken as this pen.[1] We burned everything here that a match would ignite.

Sunday, 4th—Rain last night. The First and Third Divisions and the First Brigade of the Fourth Division destroyed the railroad this forenoon for a distance of ten miles. The Iowa Brigade acted as train guard. We covered fifteen miles today and went into bivouac near Cameron Station. For the last two or three days, we marched through fine country, though in some places it is very sandy and the land is heavily timbered with pine. The soil is very sandy, but the higher land is well improved and thickly settled. Good crops were raised the past season, the work having been done by old men and negro women. Most of the citizens have left their homes.

Monday, 5th—We started out at 6 o'clock this morning, and by 11 our corps had destroyed twelve miles of railroad. We then left the railroad and marching ten miles, over very fine roads, went into camp near Oliver Station. A force of eight thousand rebels left Oliver this morning for Savannah. They came into the town last night and throwing up earthworks made preparations for a fight, but this morning they concluded that they had better move on, or they would get hurt, and the infantry left without firing a gun. Our cavalry had a little skirmish with

[1] The treatment which our soldiers received in the Confederate prisons is the one dark, damnable stain that the South of that time will always have to carry. The North can forgive, but it cannot forget.—A. G. D.

(December, 1864)

them this morning. The Fifteenth Army Corps is on the west side of the Ogeechee river, but in advance of us, and perhaps the rebels were fearful of being cut off from Savannah.

Tuesday, 6th—We lay in camp all day. The day was spent in washing, cleaning and mending our clothes. The long march is beginning to tell on our clothing and shoes. My shoes are whole yet, but owing to so much sand, and wading through water, my feet are sore. My right foot is worn through on the bottom, and my toes are wet with blood every day. We are now within forty-five miles of Savannah, Georgia, and about ninety miles from Charleston, South Carolina. We can hear the large guns roaring from both places. The rebels are still retreating before us without much fighting. We are still in a rich country for foraging. Each regiment sends out its foraging party and we have plenty of sweet potatoes and fresh pork. We will have better roads now for marching as we approach Savannah. All is quiet in the rear of the army.

Wednesday, 7th—It rained all forenoon today, but because of the sand our road did not get muddy. We started at 7 this morning and after stepping off fifteen miles by 4 o'clock, we went into camp for the night. Our regiment led the advance of our corps. The rebels blocked our road by felling trees at the entrance to every swamp, thus delaying our march, since there were a good many swamps to cross. We had to build four or five small bridges, and also had to do some corduroy work. The First Michigan Engineers in advance of us had charge of the work.

Thursday, 8th—We left bivouac at 8 o'clock this morning, but owing to the roads, we moved very slowly, making only twelve miles before going into camp. Just before our regiment started into bivouac, we were ordered to stack arms and help our teams across a narrow swamp. We went about a half mile for rails, each man carrying from two to four, to corduroy the road so that the artillery and wagons could cross. Our cavalry had a skirmish with the rebels at noon today, when passing through Marlow Station, and captured a train of cars by cutting the railroad before the rebels could get the train past the station. We drew two days' rations today, with orders to make them last five days.

Friday, 9th—It is cloudy with a strong northeast wind. We

(December, 1864)

started early again this morning and after laying off ten miles went into bivouac. The Twenty-fifth New Jersey was on the skirmish line today, skirmishing commencing at 10 o'clock and continuing till dark. They lost four men killed and fifteen wounded. The First Division of our corps was in the front, and their quartermaster was killed by a ten-pound solid shot fired from a small cannon on a flat car which the rebels ran up and down the railroad. Our way today was through one continuous swamp, but we had a fine road, a high causeway which runs to Savannah. Our camp tonight lies within ten miles of Savannah.

Saturday, 10th—We broke camp at 6 o'clock this morning and moved forward five miles, driving the rebels all the way. Our division was in the advance in line of battle and drove the rebels back inside their main works. There was some heavy skirmishing and we had to throw up breastworks. Our loss during the day was fifteen in killed and wounded. We had four men wounded by the explosion of torpedoes which the rebels had buried in the road. General Sherman was riding with our column, and when informed of what had taken place, ordered that the prisoners of our division be placed in front to pass over the road first. The prisoners requested that one of their number be permitted to return to their headquarters to inform their commander of the peril in which they were placed. This was granted and there were no more torpedoes planted in the road after that. The prisoners dug up five torpedoes for us.

Sunday, 11th—The Twentieth Corps relieved our corps this morning and we moved to the right about five miles, taking the position occupied by the Fifteenth Corps, which moved still farther around to the right. We went into camp about 4 o'clock, and the Eleventh Iowa was sent out on the skirmish line, where we have good works built by the Fifteenth Corps. Skirmishing is not very brisk because of the wide swamp between us and the rebels. We are still on two-fifths rations and there is nothing to forage.

Monday, 12th—Our regiment was withdrawn from the rifle pits, the rebels having left during the night, and with our entire corps we moved about five miles to the right. Our division stacked arms until 3 p. m. when we fell in and marched two miles farther and again stacked arms. We now had to move over a

(December, 1864)

two-mile causeway from ten to thirty feet high, but the rebels having planted batteries within range of the road, we waited to move after dark. Our teams were all sent around about fifteen miles. We ran the blockade under cover of the night, the rebels opening their batteries on us, without doing any damage. We went into camp about 8 o'clock.

Tuesday, 13th—We lay in bivouac all day. Our rations ran out today and no more can be issued until we open up communications with the fleet. To do that we shall have to open a way to the coast. Our men have foraged everything to be found. The only thing that we can get now is rice, of which there is a great deal in stacks, besides thousands of bushels threshed out, but not hulled, and stored away in granaries. The Thirty-second Illinois went with a train from our brigade to forage. Fort McAllister was captured late this afternoon by a detachment of the Fifteenth Corps, General Hazen's Division. Our cracker line is open once more and there is great cheering in camp over the news.

Wednesday, 14th—The capture of Fort McAllister gives us our first communication with the North since the telegraph wires were cut at Marietta, Georgia, on the 12th of November. We have no rations yet, but will have crackers as soon as our men can remove the torpedoes from the Ogeechee river, which is thickly laid with them; then the transports can land provisions. There is great rejoicing in camp, as we have nothing left but unhulled rice. This we hull by placing a handful in our haversacks which we lay on logs and pound with our bayonets. Then we pour the contents from hand to hand, blowing the while to separate the chaff from the grains. All is quiet along the line, except occasional skirmishing. We had regimental inspection this afternoon. The foraging train of the Fifteenth Corps came in this afternoon with some forage. We are now in camp in a large rice plantation about ten miles south of Savannah.

Thursday, 15th—The weather is fine—days warm and pleasant and nights cool. The Thirty-second Illinois arrived in camp at 11 o'clock with sweet potatoes, fresh pork and corn for our brigade. We are still lying in camp without rations. We had company inspection and drill for the recruits. The First Division of the Fifteenth Corps advanced their skirmish line this morning toward the rebels' post south of Savannah. There was quite an artillery duel and some sharp skirmishing, but our men succeeded in gaining their position.

Friday, 16th—Left this morning at 8 o'clock for King's bridge over the Ogeechee river at a point fifteen miles from Savannah, where we again went into camp. All the torpedoes having been removed from the river, small boats can now come up to the bridge and land. Two boats came up with mail and some other articles. There were four tons of mail for the army. All is quiet along the line, but we have no rations yet. We still have plenty of rice with the hull on, but all the mortars upon the plantation have now been gathered together and the cavalry have put all the negroes of the plantation at work hulling rice.

Saturday, 17th—Large details of men from our division were sent out to cut and prepare timber for the engineers to build a wharf at the landing so that the boats can be unloaded more readily. Several hundred of us were at work, some cutting the trees—tall pines, others cutting them into proper lengths, and still others hewing and squaring the timbers. The teamsters then hauled them to the landing. Two more boats came up the river today, one loaded with hay for the mules, the other with our provisions. We received our mail today. All is quiet along the line and the weather is fine.

Sunday, 18th—This morning, as yesterday, there was a very heavy fog, continuing till about 9 o'clock. We drew one day's rations of hardtack, having been without bread of any kind for six days, during which time rice was almost our sole diet. Our company was partially reorganized today by promotions. Lieutenant Spencer was promoted to captain, J. A. White to second lieutenant, and I was made fifth sergeant. J. Tomlinson is to be made first lieutenant, but the promotion was not made today because his commission had not yet arrived.

Monday, 19th—Weather pleasant. Reveille sounded at 1 a. m. and at 2 o'clock our brigade started for the rifle pits in front of Savannah. The first brigade was left at the bridge to guard the landing and to unload the boats. A little before daylight, unnoticed by the rebels, we passed over the same causeway that we went down on, and after marching about nine miles we formed a line of battle and sent out skirmishers. We soon drove the

(December, 1864)

rebels across the swamp. They used grape and canister on us, but did little harm. At all the points where they have the roads blockaded, we have planted sixty-four-pounders, which keep their guns silent. There is some heavy cannonading and brisk skirmishing all along the lines.

Tuesday, 20th—Cloudy and windy this morning. Heavy cannonading with some skirmishing was kept up all day. Our batteries silenced the rebels' batteries at every point. Four companies from our regiment went out last night to reinforce the details on building fortifications. The walls of the forts are to be twenty feet thick. We have a miserable camping ground right on the edge of the swamp, but we cleaned up a camp and at 4 o'clock this afternoon had company inspection. We have very poor water to use, having to get it from the swamp. But we are now drawing full rations, for which we are very thankful. All is quiet in the rear.

Wednesday, 21st—The last artillery firing this morning was that of a thunderstorm. It seems that kind Providence wanted a hand in the capture of the city. We received orders about 10 o'clock to be ready to march at a moment's warning, and immediately we were ordered to march, as the rebels had evacuated the place. We started at once and before noon reached the edge of the city and went into camp, while a part of the army went in pursuit of the fleeing rebels. They left their outside works last night at 10 o'clock, and this morning left the city, crossing the Savannah river by pontoon bridges, under cover of their gunboats. Their rear guard is now five miles below, just across the river on the South Carolina side.

Thursday, 22d—It is quite cool. Our camp is just inside the city limits. We tore down several houses and fences with which to build "ranches," and then spent the rest of the day in cleaning accouterments and washing our clothes. The rebels, in their haste to get away, left about one hundred and fifty pieces of artillery and a large quantity of fixed ammunition. They also left hundreds of their sick and wounded soldiers here in the hospital.

Savannah is a very nice city, on high ground, affording a good view of the South Carolina coast. The town is well laid out, having wide streets and little parks at many of the intersections.

(December, 1864)

There are some fine churches here. A large number of business houses and office buildings are vacant. They had a printing press here for the making of paper money. I passed the building this morning where the press was located, and found on the sidewalk two bales of the currency, which some one had thrown out. The bundles were of about one hundred pounds each and the money consisted of tens and twenties. I helped myself to $50.00 and walked on. At the present time this money is below par. The boys are offering $1,000 to citizens for a loaf of bread, and some of the officers have offered from $4,000 to $5,000 for some one to curry their horses, but they can find no one who will accept their offers.

Friday, 23d—The citizens of Savannah have generally remained in their homes, only a few having left town. Four-fifths of the people are women and children, the rest being old men. They appear to be glad that our army has taken possession of the city, and most of them are willing to take the oath of allegiance. The people here are not so near starvation as they are in other places in this state. Two or three small boats came up the river from the coast, but they did not have any rations for the army, as there is danger from the torpedoes laid in the river. The torpedoes are being taken out as fast as the men can get to them.

Saturday, 24th—General Foster's command is still in pursuit of the fleeing rebels through South Carolina. They had an encounter yesterday with them, in which the rebels were completely routed. General Foster was wounded in the fight and was brought into town this morning. General Sherman[1] reviewed the Fifteenth Army Corps this morning. We had company drill this afternoon.

Sunday, 25th—This is a cloudy, cool day and a lonesome Christmas. We are on one-third rations now and poor prospects of getting more soon. We still have plenty of rice, although in

[1] While on our march through Georgia, all the men had a chance to see Sherman at close range, as he rode with the different corps, changing from one to another. As we approached Savannah, going in on the main road, which was rather narrow, he was with our corps, the Seventeenth, which had most of the fighting to do. I noticed that when he wished to get ahead to the front of the corps, he never would crowd the infantry aside, but instead rode alongside himself, leaving the good road for them. I have seen him ride this way, his horse on an ordinary walk, with his staff officers riding in single file behind him. Some of the boys would ask him questions, or make some joking remarks as to where we were going, and the general would seldom reply, but would always have a pleasant smile in recognition of the question asked. He won the respect of the boys, and they all had confidence in him.—A. G. D.

(December, 1864)

the hull, so we can get along. Large foraging parties were sent up the Savannah river to obtain rice straw for our beds and they brought in large quantities of rice still in the sheaf to feed the horses and mules. There are some very large rice plantations along the river and there is a great deal of rice not yet threshed. We had company inspection this evening. All is quiet.

Monday, 26th—Everything is quiet this morning, though for a while last night there was quite an excitement in town when a fire broke out. We are still lying in camp, with no particular duty to perform, though we are expecting orders every day to move down the river to Ft. Johnson, below Savannah. We are on half rations now, but today got large quantities of fresh oysters, all we can make use of. They were in the shell and were hauled into our camps by the wagon load, and sold to the boys by the peck or bushel. Governor Stone of Iowa arrived in camp today from Morehead City, North Carolina. He came to issue commissions to the officers of veteran regiments, and also to see that the sick and wounded Iowa soldiers in the field hospitals of the South were receiving good care.

Tuesday, 27th—All is quiet. There is no news of any importance.[1] The Fourteenth Army Corps was reviewed at 9 a. m. by General Sherman. The troops looked fine. The Fourteenth is a good corps. I sent in my subscriptions today for three papers: the Missouri Democrat at $2.00 per year, the Theological Journal, $2.00, and Harper's Weekly, $4.00. I think I shall have enough reading matter now for 1865, if I succeed in getting all my papers.

Wednesday, 28th—It was cloudy with some rain, though it cleared off in the afternoon and turned quite cool. Things are very quiet in camp, and our duty is light; we do not have even picket duty, as the cavalry are doing that on the outskirts. Near-

---

[1] The foragers or bummers, as they came to be called, presented at times some odd and amusing situations. Starting out early in advance of the command, they would do their pillaging, return to the main road to await the arrival of the command, and along in the afternoon we would find them, often loaded down with good things for their comrades to eat. They sometimes came upon rich plantations where the owners had about everything they wanted, including a well-filled larder. When there was no wagon at hand, they would look the premises over and, finding the family carriage and horse, they would load it down and start for the main line of march. I have often seen them with a fine family carriage filled with smoked meat, and on the outside were tied chickens, turkeys and geese, or ducks. Then, to cap the climax, one fellow would be seated in the carriage dressed in the planter's swallow-tail coat, white vest and plug hat, while another one would be astride a mule and dressed in similar fashion.—A. G. D.

(December, 1864)

ly all the citizens inside of our lines have taken the oath, swearing that they will not aid the Southern Confederacy. All of them express the view that the war will come to a close soon. We hope their view will prove true.

Thursday, 29th—The weather continues pleasant but cool. The glorious old Seventeenth Army Corps was reviewed at 9 a. m. by Major-General Sherman. The corps performed nicely and looked fine considering the campaign through which they have gone, and also considering the fact that they have not yet drawn new clothing. We formed our lines in the streets down in the city and the general rode along the lines to inspect them. We then marched along Front Street, where the general was stationed to review us. General Foster was also present as we passed in review. We got back into camp at 2 o'clock, having had a fine day for the review. Things are very quiet and there is no news of any importance. Small boats come up the river every day to bring rations and other army stores.

Friday, 30th—The Twentieth Army Corps was reviewed by General Sherman at 9 a. m. They came out with their flying colors and brass bands, making a big showing. But when there's a fight on hand they are not as forward as they might be; it suits them better to garrison a place after it has been taken. We have company drill once a day, and the substitutes have to drill twice a day when in camp. The Thirteenth and Sixteenth Iowa and the Thirty-second Illinois, moved their camps this afternoon to make room for the fortifications planned. Sherman has ordered Savannah to be strongly fortified. Heavy guns will be mounted so that no enemy can get close enough to do any harm with the ordinary field guns. The engineers went to work today laying out the places where the forts are to be built.

Saturday, 31st—Still in camp and on short rations at that, the quartermaster having cut us down to one-half rations. We cannot understand why this should be, though there must be a good reason for the order. The fire department of the city came out this morning for inspection by General Sherman, and made a fine appearance, considering that the city had been captured only ten days before.[1] Our men commenced today to fortify the city.

[1] It seems that there was the best of understanding between the people of Savannah and General Sherman. They tried to make it as pleasant for the Union army as they could, and Sherman treated them with great consideration.—A. G. D.

(December, 1864)

They are throwing up heavy earthworks ten feet through, protected by a ditch on the outside, ten feet deep by twenty feet wide at the top and ten feet at the bottom. The fortifications are built just inside the city. We have to tear down a great many houses in order to get lumber to support the earth thrown up, and with which to make platforms for the artillery.

And so this is the end of the year 1864. It has been a year of hard, active service for our brigade, as also for the entire corps. The Eleventh Iowa has done its part and suffered severely, Company E alone having lost seven men by bullet in the siege of Atlanta, besides a number having been severely wounded.

JANUARY, 1865.

Sunday, 1st—This is New Year's Day and my fourth in the army.[1] We did not have to work on the fortifications today, and as the weather was cloudy and cool we remained close to our "ranches." At 4 p. m. we had company inspection. We are still on two-thirds rations.

Monday, 2d—The weather is quite cool. I was detailed this morning to work on the fortifications. We are building the platforms, upon which will be mounted the large cannon, just outside of the forts and rifle pits. These are elevated from five to ten feet above the common level of the ground and then floored so that in wet weather the gunners will not have to be in the mud. A few nice residences have to be pulled down to make room for the works, but nothing like that we had to do at Vicksburg.

---

[1] The common belief among the men was that this would be the last New Year's Day spent in the army. Everything pointed to an early end of the war.—A. G. D.

Chapter XXII.
Raid Through South Carolina. January 3-March 7.

Tuesday, 3d—The First Division of the Seventeenth Army Corps embarked this afternoon on an unknown expedition.[1] They had to march down to the coast below the city in order to take ship. It is reported in camp that the rest of the corps, together with the Fifteenth Corps, is to follow in a few days, while the Fourteenth and Twentieth Corps, with Kilpatrick's cavalry, are to cross the Savannah river above the city and start on a grand raid through South Carolina. They are to move through North Carolina and Virginia, and finally land at Richmond.

Wednesday, 4th—A large detail from the Fourteenth Army Corps was at work today on the fortifications. The Third Division of the Seventeenth Corps marched down to the coast and this afternoon embarked upon the expedition. Our division, the Fourth, received orders to be ready to move in the morning. Our regimental quartermaster received a consignment of clothing for the men. I drew a rubber blanket, one shirt, one pair of drawers and a hat. I also purchased at one of the stores here a military cap for $6.00. Captain Spencer left for home today on a thirty-day furlough; I sent $200.00 home by him to father.

Thursday, 5th—The order for the Iowa Brigade to move was countermanded this morning, and we remained in camp all day. The weather has been pleasant and is quite warm today.

Friday, 6th—We left our camp this morning at 8 o'clock and marched down to the coast about four miles below Savannah. At 2 o'clock we embarked on the transports for Beaufort, South Carolina. Our regiment is on board a ship built in England as a blockade-runner for the Southern Confederacy, but which was finally captured by our navy at Savannah. It rained all forenoon, but by noon it had cleared off with a high wind blowing in from the ocean. Our ship, not having enough ballast, rocked frightfully in the gale, upsetting tables in the dining room and frightening many of the boys lest we should be turned over. The

---

[1] We learned later that the expedition sailed for Beaufort, South Carolina.—A. G. D.

(January, 1865)

sailors only smiled at our discomfiture. The rough sea made a great many of the boys sick, but our company being on the hurricane deck, did not become so sick. We reached Beaufort at 11 p. m., but cannot land, and so have to remain on the boats all night.

Saturday, 7th—This morning we found that during the night our ship was driven by the high wind upon a sand bar in the bay. Here we lay, a cold northwest wind blowing across our deck forty feet above the water. But we fared better than the boys below, for, on account of their being so sick, it was reported that their floor was difficult to stand on even after the ship had stopped. They ran a small side-wheel steamboat alongside of the ship and set a tall ladder on the wheelhouse, reaching up to our deck, and one by one we climbed down the ladder to the other boat, which hauled us to the shore. We were glad to leave that ship. Some of the boys declared that they would rather walk the entire distance than ride on any ship. We marched out about two miles from town and went into camp in a heavy pine timber. Here we have plenty of wood with which to build a good fire, as a cold rain commenced to fall this afternoon.

Sunday, 8th—It is quite cool. We lay in camp all day. We are once more drawing full rations, and it is well that we are, for there is absolutely nothing to forage here, not even rice in the hull. We have also received some of the Sanitary goods sent here for distribution. All is quiet at present and there is no news of any importance. Beaufort is a nice place, situated on an island, and has good shipping facilities. Goods of all kinds are sold here at reasonable prices, business being carried on much as in a Northern town. The Union army has been in possession of the place for some time. The entire Seventeenth Army Corps is here, but will move forward in a few days.

Monday, 9th—We remained in camp all day.[1] It rained most of the day. No news of any importance.

---

[1] I had been suffering with the toothache for some days when on this day it became so bad that I made up my mind to go to the doctor and have the tooth extracted. I arrived at the doctor's tent, he directed me to an ancient chair and asked me to show him the tooth. I pointed out the exact tooth, he hooked on, at the same time telling me to hold on to the chair, and pulled. He succeeded in bringing the tooth, but it was not the aching one. I however, concluded that one tooth at a time was enough, even if it was the wrong one, and returned to my rancho with the hope that it would soon quit aching. But the last state of that tooth was worse than the first.—A. G. D.

(January, 1865)

Tuesday, 10th—Our division moved out to the front about five miles and went into camp again. We had to move because we had burned up all the fallen timber around our camp, while at the new camp we will have plenty. It rained quite hard this afternoon and then turned colder at night. The country through which we passed is on a dead level, and the plantations lie idle. All of the buildings and fences were burned by our armies operating in this part of the state before our arrival.

Wednesday, 11th—It is clear and quite cool. We learn that a part of the Fifteenth Army Corps landed at Beaufort today and will come out this way and go into camp. We expect to be joined by the other two corps from Savannah as soon as they succeed in crossing the river, when we shall all move forward at the same time. We had company inspection today.

Thursday, 12th—All is quiet in camp. The weather is very pleasant and everything has the appearance of spring. The trees seem alive with birds, many different kinds, some of which are very sweet singers. Sometimes the sun is so bright that it reminds one of June days in the North. We received orders to be ready to march in the morning at daylight.

Friday, 13th—For some reason we did not break camp and get started until 4 p. m. and then moved only four miles and went into bivouac. We routed the rebels from the south bank of the Broad river and laid down the pontoons for the army to cross over. Two of our regiments crossed the river in skiffs at some point above or below after nightfall and routed the rebels from the river.

Saturday, 14th—Our army commenced to move at 7 this morning and by 10 o'clock the last detachment had crossed Broad river. We moved on about ten miles, driving the rebels and skirmishing with them all the way. The Iowa Brigade lost one man killed, a lieutenant of Company A, Fifteenth Iowa. The expedition consists of the Seventeenth Army Corps with General Foster's command on our left.

Sunday, 15th—The rebels fell back last night and our men pushed forward this morning. We moved six miles and again went into camp. One regiment and the Thirteenth Iowa was left at Pocotaligo for picket duty and to act as train guard for the

(January, 1865)

trains passing to and fro from Beaufort, hauling provisions out to the front for the army.

Monday, 16th—All is quiet in front. Company E moved back four or five miles to a large rebel fort on the main road to Beaufort, and on an inlet of the ocean. We are to remain here on picket duty until further orders. The main part of the regiment has fortified. Our company put up the "ranches" on a causeway.

Tuesday, 17th—Our brigade was inspected at 1 p. m. today by the brigade commander. There is very little sickness among the men in spite of the fact that we have been in this low, flat country for a fortnight. The land where we are stationed is barely above the sea level, and we easily see the effect of the tide on the water of the inlet.

Wednesday, 18th—The weather is very pleasant. We are still on duty guarding the main road to Beaufort. The trains have all gone in for supplies. All is quiet in front. This low country, before the war, was planted to cotton, the planters living in town while their plantations were managed by overseers and worked by slaves brought down from the border states. We can see rows of the vacant negro huts on these large plantations, set upon blocks so as to keep the floors dry. The negroes are all gone, being employed in the armies of both sections.[1]

Thursday, 19th—There is nothing new. We are still on picket on the main road to Beaufort.

Friday, 20th—It rained all day and the roads are becoming quite muddy.

Saturday, 21st—It is still raining. The teams are going back

[1] When I think of the vacant plantations I saw all through the South, when I recall the hardships of the negroes, and the different modes of punishment inflicted upon the slaves, all with the consent of the Southern people, then I can understand how they could be so cruel in their treatment of the Union prisoners of war. They put them in awful prison pens and starved them to death without a successful protest from the better class of the people of the South. The guards of these prisons had lived all their lives witnessing the cruel tortures of slaves; they had become hardened and thus had no mercy on an enemy when in their power. Many an Andersonville prisoner was shot down just for getting too close to an imaginary dead-line when suffering from thirst and trying to get a drink of water.

Not all Southerners were so cruel, for I lived in the same house with an ex-Confederate soldier from Georgia, when in southern Florida during the winter of 1911 and know that he had some feeling. He had been guard at Andersonville for a short time, and told me that he would have taken water to them by the bucketful, for he could not bear to hear the poor fellows calling for water; but that he did not dare to do it. This man's name was McCain, and at the time I met him his home was at College Park, Atlanta, Ga.—A. G. D.

(January, 1865)

and forth day and night, hauling provisions. The roads are so bad now at places that the teams get stuck in the mud.

Sunday, 22d—A detail from our regiment was sent out along the road today to help the loaded wagons across the deep mudholes, as they come through from Beaufort. It is reported that the Fourteenth and Twentieth Corps have crossed into South Carolina and are floundering in the mud bottoms of the Savannah river.

Monday, 23d—It is still raining, and our men have made a new landing within six miles of Pocotaligo. It is at one of the inlets which has a channel deep enough for small steamboats to come up. This will shorten the haul of our provisions about twenty miles—no small item in this land of sandy bottoms.

Tuesday, 24th—It is still raining, which makes the fifth day of steady rain, and at times it comes down in torrents. We are very fortunate in having shacks set up on the top of the old fort where we are located, for if we were camping down on the level ground, we could not possibly keep dry. Our duty is very light here, but we are getting awfully tired of the place, and hope that as we have a new landing for the provisions, we may be able to get away in a few days and move on to the front at Garden Corners, South Carolina.

Wednesday, 25th—It has cleared off now and is quite cool. It does not take long in this sandy region for the roads to dry off, and in three or four days they will be in good condition. We expect to leave here soon. The men are becoming very restless, being at one place so long. General Sherman and General Howard left for the front today.

Thursday, 26th—It is still clear and quite cool with the wind from the northwest. This is the coldest day we have had this winter here in the South, yet there is no ice even in a bucket of water.

Friday, 27th—We are still on duty at the old fort, and everything is going well. The trains have now quit going to Beaufort and we expect to receive orders to leave soon.

Saturday, 28th—Our company received orders to move on to the front tomorrow. The weather is quite pleasant. Some of the trains of the Fifteenth Corps came in from the landing this evening, but the corps has not yet arrived.

(January, 1865)

Sunday, 29th—Our company left camp in the old fort at 10 o'clock and reached the brigade headquarters at Garden Corners about noon. Our entire division then moved forward about ten miles and went into bivouac for the night. The roads were fine for marching, having had no rain for four days.

Monday, 30th—We marched about three miles this morning and then went into bivouac to await further orders. The report is that we are now ready to make the grand raid through South Carolina. The Seventeenth and Fifteenth Corps are to form the right wing, as in the campaign through Georgia, with General O. O. Howard in command. General Slocum is in command of the left wing, composed of the other two corps, the Fourteenth and Twentieth, while Kilpatrick's cavalry will take the flanks as rear guard. General Sherman is in chief command. General Foster, it is said, is either to remain here or move to Charleston.

Tuesday, 31st—We remained in bivouac all day and have heard no news. We drew some clothing today. Our camp is located about thirty miles northwest of Beaufort. The country is very level and heavily timbered, chiefly with pine. It is thinly settled and the farms are small with nothing of consequence raised on them. The people are poor, the women and children being left destitute, as the men have all gone off to the war.

FEBRUARY, 1865.

Wednesday, 1st—We left camp early this morning for the grand raid through South Carolina, under the command of General Sherman. But our march will not be an easy one, for the rebels will do their best to hold us in check. There are one hundred thousand men within a radius of twenty miles, and there's no telling how the campaign will end or who will be left dead or mortally wounded upon the field without a friend near. Cannon began booming in less than an hour, but we had no losses today. We moved foward about eight miles through Whiffy Swamp, driving the rebels all the way. On account of the bad road we had to travel, our division could not keep up with the rest of the corps, but went into camp about four miles in the rear. The Fifteenth Corps came up on our left to Hicky Hill, making a march of twenty miles.

(February, 1865)

Thursday, 2d—This is a beautiful morning and we started early on our march. We had better roads than yesterday, on higher ground, and covered thirteen miles. We drove the rebels forward all day, doing some lively skirmishing in the front. The rebels have all crossed the Salkehatchie river, but have possession of the two bridges about eight miles apart. We went into camp near the river. We lost some good officers and brave men in the skirmishing today. It makes one sorrowful to think that they have to be buried here in this God-forsaken swamp country.

Friday, 3d—It rained quietly nearly all day, and we remained in camp until 1 p. m., when we received marching orders. Our division under General Giles E. Smith then made ready to wade and swim the river midway between the two bridges. The river is one and one-fourth miles wide, having at least one hundred and thirty-three different channels or branches, from two to four feet deep. It took us an hour and a half to cross over, General Smith leading on foot, for no horse could go across. We were not allowed to talk or let our accouterments make any noise. We found the rebel pickets on the opposite side, but they fired only a single shot each and made for tall timber. We remained here on guard. The First and Third Divisions crossed the river above us and also drove in the rebel pickets.[1] Our teams and batteries were left in the rear.

Saturday, 4th—We remained in line of battle all night, not being allowed to build any fires. This morning we moved out about two miles nearer the upper bridge, the rebels having left the vicinity during the night. We remained here, fortifying the bridge. Our teams and batteries came across the bridge this morning. General Mower's division lost several men here at the bridge yesterday morning about the time that we were crossing below.[2]

Sunday, 5th—The atmosphere is clear and it is getting quite warm. We remained in our rifle pits all day, but had to put up our shelter tents, for we actually suffered from the heat. All is quiet in front. We had company inspection this morning and

[1] Our division, after successfully crossing the river, effected a lodgment on the main Charleston road just before the arrival of eight regiments which had been sent up to make good the enemy's position at this bridge.—A. G. D.
[2] There was a concerted move by the Union army all along the line.—Ed.

(February, 1865)

dress parade in the evening. We drew two days' rations to last ten days, but we have an abundance of forage. The boys brought in smoked bacon by the wagon load, also great quantities of corn meal, sweet potatoes, honey and other good things.

Monday, 6th—The weather changed again, and we had a rather cold, drizzling rain nearly all day. We left our trenches at 7 o'clock this morning and were all day in marching ten miles, the country being so very swampy. We had a great deal of corduroy to build, and the rebels blocked our way by burning a bridge over a deep channel in the swamp. There was some skirmishing in the front. We were ordered to leave all our surplus bacon in the company parade ground, and the quartermaster would send a wagon with the extra forage for us; but we were skeptical and carried all that our haversacks would hold.[1]

Tuesday, 7th—We had another all day, cold, drizzling rain. We left our bivouac at 7 o'clock and after marching fourteen miles stopped for the night. With every mile the road got better as we moved upon higher ground, and the forage also became more plentiful. Just after we had stacked arms to go into bivouac, our regiment was ordered to fall in again. We marched out on the Augusta and Charleston railroad to burn the bridge over the Edisto river, but the pickets, on hearing our approach, for it was too dark to see anything, all hastened across the bridge and set fire to it themselves. This saved us the trouble and we went back, reaching our bivouac about midnight, after marching in all about ten miles.

Wednesday, 8th—Our division started out on the railroad at 7 o'clock this morning and destroyed about ten miles of track. We then returned to camp for the rest of the day and night. All is quiet in front.

Thursday, 9th—We remained in camp until noon, when we moved forward again about ten miles and went into bivouac on the east bank of the Edisto river. The First Division waded the river to drive the rebels back so that the engineers with our corps could lay the pontoons for the corps to cross. The Fifteenth

---

[1] Our company alone left a load of the finest bacon, besides other articles. It was the last we saw of our store of surplus forage. We learned later that the officers took that way of having the forage left for the negroes and poor people of the vicinity, for we had cleaned the vicinity of everything.—A. G. D.

(February, 1865)

Corps crossed the river about a mile above. A great deal of property is being destroyed by our army on this raid. The familiar clouds of smoke are becoming more numerous every day, while out on the left we can count from ten to twenty of the red clouds in the heavens every night.

Friday, 10th—We lay in camp all day, but large foraging parties were sent out. They brought in great quantities of forage—pork and potatoes, also feed for the animals. The farming is all done here by the negro women and old men, the able-bodied men, white and black, being in the army. We received a large mail today, the first for a month. I got two letters and two packages.

Saturday, 11th—Very pleasant weather. We started at 8 o'clock this morning and moved forward twelve miles. There was some skirmishing in front, and our forces routed the enemy from some strong positions.[1]

Sunday, 12th—Our division relieved the Third Division on the skirmish line at the bridge this morning, while they went down the river about a mile, laid the pontoons and crossed over. The skirmishing was commenced at an early hour all along the line for a distance of fifteen miles. Our men threw shells across the river into Orangeburg, and the rebels left the bridge about 1 o'clock. Our division crossed the bridge two hours later and took possession of the town.[2]

Orangeburg is nicely situated on the north bank of the Edisto river, and on the railroad running from Charleston to Columbia. The town is almost deserted, but before the war it had a population of three thousand. We destroyed the railroad and went into camp for the night.

Monday, 13th—Our corps started out at 7 o'clock this morning and after destroying twenty-six miles of railroad, marched fifteen miles, on the State road from Charleston to Columbia, and went into camp. This is the finest road over which we have marched

[1] When the Confederates had good positions, they were unable to make a strong stand and retain them. For although they could delay our army for a time at the main crossings of rivers, there was always another part of our army reaching the same river by some byroad, which after crossing would flank them, or coming up in the rear would drive them out of their defenses.—A. G. D.

[2] The town was on fire when we arrived. The report was that the town was set on fire by a Jew, in revenge for the enemy's setting fire to his cotton, about fifty bales, when they evacuated the place. The high winds which prevailed rapidly spread the fire in spite of the efforts of the soldiers to extinguish it.

(February, 1865)

in all the South; it had mile posts and our division commander must have wanted to see how fast we could march, for we stepped off the fifteen miles in just three hours and fifteen minutes.

Tuesday, 14th—We started to move forward at 9 a. m. and after an easy march of twelve miles[1] went into camp for the night. The rebels are still retreating before us.

Wednesday, 15th—It rained all night, and this morning is quite cool. By 8 o'clock we were again on the move and covered ten miles in pushing the rebels back. The Fifteenth Corps on our right drove them back this afternoon behind their fortifications on the south bank of the Congaree river, then we had a regular artillery duel until after dark. We have been in the smoke of the burning pine woods and buildings almost continuously for the last few days. At times when marching on a road alongside the burning pine timber, we became so blackened from the smoke as to look like negroes, while the heat from the burning pitch was frightful.

Thursday, 16th—Early this morning cannonading was begun in front of the Fifteenth Corps, followed by some lively skirmishing, and the rebels were routed from their works and driven across the Congaree river. The Fifteenth Corps then marched up along the south bank of the river above the city of Columbia, to the forks, where the Saluda and Broad rivers form the Congaree, and crossed the Saluda on the pontoons. In the meantime our regiment was behind on train guard and did not come into action. We moved forward and with our corps went into camp for the night on the south bank of the Congaree, just opposite Columbia, the state capital.

Friday, 17th—The Seventeenth Army Corps remained all day on the south bank of the Congaree river, near the Saluda cotton mills, while the Fifteenth Corps early this morning crossed the

[1] It will be recalled that in the campaign through Georgia we went in extra light marching orders. Just before we began our raid through the Carolinas, at Pocotaligo, we received further orders which stripped us of all unnecessary articles. General Sherman himself had only a fly-tent at night.
Now I never could stand to carry a heavy knapsack, generally not carrying enough to make it keep its shape. Before we left Pocotaligo, therefore, in order to make it keep its shape and thus carry easier, I made a frame out of a cracker box, eighteen inches square by four inches in depth, and placed it in my knapsack, then rolling my fly-tent, four by seven feet, and around it my rubber poncho, making a roll about eighteen or twenty inches long, I strapped it on my knapsack and I was ready for the march. With this outfit, when I was well, I could easily march thirty to thirty-five miles a day. This I did without becoming fatigued, carrying besides, my rifle, cartridge-box, haversack with five days' rations, and my canteen filled with water.—A. G. D.

north fork, the Broad river, on pontoons, having laid them during the night, and moved down upon Columbia. But when they entered the place they found that the rebels had already left it. In the meantime the Thirteenth Iowa Regiment, being on our skirmish line in front of the city, crossed the river in skiffs and after a little skirmishing succeeded in placing their flag on the State House before any of the Fifteenth Corps even got into town.[1] So a part of the Seventeenth Corps was the first to enter Columbia.[2] Our corps crossed the forks late this afternoon and went into camp a short distance from town.

Saturday, 18th—Columbia was almost completely destroyed by fire last night. Only a few houses in the outskirts are left standing, and many people are without homes this morning. Columbia was a very nice town situated on the Congaree at the head of navigation. Three railroads run through the town. A new stone State House was being built, which it is said was to have been the capital of the Southern Confederacy. Last night I passed by the sheds where the fine marble columns for the build-

[1] This is precisely the substance of the original entry of Mr. Downing's diary. In the following footnote, after almost fifty years, he explains the flag episode more fully and also speaks incidentally of the burning of Columbia, though he makes no mention of it in his original; that he did not is, however, not to be wondered at, since such burnings were common. In his revision fifty years later he does not enter into the discussion of "Who Burned Columbia," but makes a single statement, which seems to hold the Confederates responsible.—Ed.

[2] It was a bright sunshiny day with a high wind blowing from the south. From where we were, on the south bank of the river just opposite the city, we could see men on foot and on horseback in the main street of Columbia, lighting the cotton bales which they before had piled up in the streets for defenses. In the forenoon a detachment of men from the Thirteenth Iowa Regiment crossed the river, and driving the enemy's skirmishers into the city, they placed their regimental flag on the State House, thus having the honor of being the first to place the Stars and Stripes on the capitol of the first state to secede from the Union.

The Thirteenth Iowa was in Crocker's Brigade, or the Third Brigade of the Fourth Division of the Seventeenth Army Corps. The boys of the Thirteenth Iowa made the mistake of not placing a guard about their flag, for about an hour after they had raised their flag, the Iowa Brigade in the Fifteenth Army Corps entered the city from the west, and the Thirtieth Iowa Regiment of that brigade, being on the skirmish line, naturally made for the State House. Upon approaching the capitol and seeing no Union soldiers around, they proceeded to investigate a little, and upon entering the building and finding no guard, they took down the flag of the Thirteenth Iowa, and put up their own instead. They then left a guard to defend it. The Thirteenth Iowa was without a flag for two or three days, when the Thirtieth Iowa finally returned to them their flag.

Our corps, the Seventeenth, moved up the river, and by dark had crossed the forks, the Saluda and Broad rivers, on the pontoons. As soon as we had stacked arms, I left for the city to replenish my haversack, which had become rather flat, and I did not get back to our bivouac until 2 o'clock in the morning, and then without anything to eat in my haversack. On entering town I passed by the abandoned Confederate commissary department, and seeing a great abundance of food stuffs, I thought that I would go down into town for a while, and then on my way back would fill up my haversack. But when I returned, I found the building in flames and food and all was in ashes before daylight.—A. G. D.

(February, 1865)

ing were carved and stored, and this morning they were all in ruins and the sheds in ashes. It is a sad sight to see the citizens standing in groups on the streets, holding little bundles of their most valued effects and not knowing what to do. It is said that some even came here from Charleston to escape Sherman's army. The people certainly have paid dearly for the privilege of seceding from the Union. The Seventeenth Corps passed through Columbia this morning and we were more than three hours in going through town. Our division marched out northwest along the railroad, destroying it all the way, and went into bivouac about six miles from town.

Sunday, 19th—We marched out on the railroad today and destroyed seven miles of track, then returned to camp, where we had left our knapsacks. We heard the sounds today of heavy explosions down in Columbia, and it is reported that our men have blown up the new State House.[1]

Monday, 20th—We continued our march northward today about ten miles, destroying six miles of railroad. All the railroads within twenty miles of Columbia have been destroyed, every tie is burned and every rail is twisted into a corkscrew. A sad accident happened yesterday afternoon in Columbia when a detail from the Fifteenth Army Corps was casting the fixed ammunition into the river. A man dropped a shell on the bank of the river, which exploding, caused other ammunition to explode and ignited a large quantity of powder, killing several soldiers and wounding twenty others. When Sherman heard of it, he is said to have remarked that one of his soldiers was worth more than all that ammunition or even the city of Columbia.

Tuesday, 21st—We left camp about noon and moved forward another ten miles. The First Brigade took the railroad, destroying it as they went.

Wednesday, 22d—We started at 6 o'clock this morning and marched about fifteen miles. Our brigade tore up two miles of

---

[1] The sound of the explosions in Columbia, which we heard on that day, was due to the destruction by our men of the fixed ammunition found there. General Sherman saved the beautiful new state capitol building, though it bore some of the ear marks of our shot and shell. The burning of Columbia resulted from the Confederates' setting fire to the bales of cotton in the streets; then at night some of the Union soldiers, getting too much poor whisky and burning with revenge, set fire to some of the vacant houses, and the high wind soon spread it over the whole town.—A. G. D.

railroad. We passed through Winnsboro at 10 a. m. The Twentieth Corps camped here last night and this morning moved north along the railroad. About half of the town is burned. We left the railroad at this place and marched eastward, going into camp within six miles of the Wateree river. There are large numbers of refugees at Winnsboro, well-to-do citizens having come from all parts of the South—from Vicksburg, Atlanta, and other places too numerous to mention. They came into this state, to this secluded town, thinking that the Yankees would never be able to set foot on the sacred soil of South Carolina. They declare now that they will go no farther, as it would be of no use, and we agree with them in this case.

Thursday, 23d—We broke camp at 7 o'clock this morning and marched ten miles, going into bivouac at Liberty Hill. At noon we crossed the Wateree river, at Perry's ferry, on a pontoon bridge which the Fifteenth Corps had laid and crossed on just ahead of us. Our division led the advance in the Seventeenth Corps, the other two divisions going into bivouac four miles in our rear.

Friday, 24th—We started on our march at 7 this morning, our division again taking the advance. We marched twenty miles, and all the way in a fearful northeast rain, accompanied by a high wind. The country is getting very rough. Some of our foragers have been horribly butchered by the rebels' cavalry during the last few days. Such atrocities as we have witnessed make the horrors of the battlefield seem like tender mercies. In one instance one of our couriers was found hanged on the roadside with a paper attached to his person bearing the words: "Death to all foragers." At another place we found three men shot dead with a similar notice on their bodies. Yesterday our cavalry in the direction of Chesterfield found twenty-one of our infantry lying dead in a ravine with their throats cut. There was no note giving a reason for the frightful murders.

Saturday, 25th—It rained all night, but today it is clear. We marched fifteen miles today through the mud. Our regiment is on train guard. We found Little Lynches creek flooded and we had to wade it, the water being waist deep. The Twentieth Corps crossed the creek above us, the day before, and we learned

(February, 1865)

that they raised the floodgates of a dam, letting the water in on us before we could get across. Our supply train had a hard time crossing. The water came up into the wagon boxes and a great deal of our hard bread got wet. We lost several beef cattle in the flood. The First Division did not come across this evening. The hills on this side of the creek are frightful and the mud is deep; when a wagon once settles in one of the holes, it takes a final rest, for no effort of man or beast can extricate it.

Sunday, 26th—We had another all-night rain, but it cleared off this morning. We started at 8 a. m. and marched ten miles, going into camp near the Big Lynches creek. Our division is still in the advance; the First Division did not yet come up with us. We have level country now, but for about twenty-five miles on each side of the Wateree river the land is very rough and covered with pine timber.

Monday, 27th—The day was clear and pleasant. About midnight last night our regiment was detailed to tear down an old mill to get material for the engineers with the pontoniers to build a bridge across the Big Lynches creek. We worked till 4 a. m., when we came in for a rest. This morning we took the advance again with the teams and worked all day in building corduroy to help the artillery and wagons across. When one layer of logs would go under in the mud, we had to put on another till all the teams had passed over. Our division got across late in the evening and went into camp about a mile beyond the creek.

Tuesday, 28th—We moved forward, in an all-day rain. The First Division took the advance, while the Third was in the center, and the Fourth in the rear. Our regiment was rear guard of the corps, and did not get into bivouac till 10 p. m. The corps upon going into bivouac late this afternoon threw up fortifications, for we are twenty miles in advance of the left wing, and have to lie here till they catch up. The Fifteenth Corps is away off to our right.

MARCH, 1865.

Wednesday, 1st—March came in with an all-day drizzling rain. We remained in bivouac all day. Large foraging parties were sent out, but did not succeed in getting anything, not even enough for the teams and the men that went out. The country is very thinly settled and the people here can hardly raise enough to live on. The soil is very sandy and the country is very heavily timbered, the trees being mostly pitch pine. There are some large turpentine camps about here.

Thursday, 2d—Still in camp. It was misty all day. One of our rebel prisoners was shot today at corps headquarters. He had to pay the penalty for the rebels' treatment of one of our men, from Company H, Thirty-fourth Illinois, whom they held as a prisoner and shot without provocation. When the prisoners at our headquarters were told that one of them had to pay the penalty, they drew lots, and it fell to a middle-aged man to die. The man was given time to write a letter to his family and then after bidding his comrades farewell, he was led out and shot.

Friday, 3d—It is still raining. We left our dismal camp at 7 a. m. and marched eleven miles, going into bivouac near Cheraw. The First Division of the Seventeenth Corps drove the rebels out of their works on Thompson creek and on through Cheraw and across the Great Pedee river. They captured seventeen cannon, three thousand stand of small arms and a number of prisoners. Cheraw is quite a business town and had been a manufacturing center for the rebel army. It is at the head of navigation on the Great Pedee river and has a railroad running to Charleston, South Carolina.

Saturday, 4th—We remained in bivouac all day. The Fifteenth Corps just came in on a road to our left and is to cross the Pedee ahead of the Seventeenth. The rebel skirmishers are just across the river and our skirmishers are keeping up a lively fusillade. Our engineers cannot lay the pontoons so long as the rebels are on the opposite bank of the river and the plan is to send a detachment above or below and cross the river after dark, and flank them. The foragers of the Seventeenth Corps were put in command of the colonel of the Ninth Illinois today and sent out on a raid to Society Hill, fifteen miles south of Cheraw on the railroad. They captured and destroyed two trains of cars loaded with ammunition and provisions, and then tore up the tracks for some miles and burned everything in town that would burn.

(March, 1865)

Sunday, 5th—The First Division of the Seventeenth Corps crossed the river last evening after dark and drove the rebels back. Our engineers then laid the pontoons and the troops began crossing at once. Our brigade passed through the town and crossed the river at noon and then continued our march for seven miles, when we went into bivouac for the night. Cheraw was nearly all burned to the ground before our men left it. The rebels burned the bridge across the river and upon evacuating the town set fire to it, and our men burned what remained. We are in a rich country again and forage is plentiful.

Monday, 6th—Pleasant weather. We started at 9 a. m., marched eight miles and went into bivouac near Bennettsville. We are marching through a fine country and have plenty of forage. There are no rebels in front of us at present. We are nearing the state line now between South Carolina and North Carolina, and our army has certainly made a wide path of desolation through the state.[1]

Tuesday, 7th—Weather is still pleasant. We started at 9 a. m. and marching eight miles, went into bivouac for the night. This is a fine country and we found plenty of forage again today. Negroes are putting in the crops, mostly corn. We saw some fine fields of winter wheat. There is very little cotton put in here.

---

[1] In our march through South Carolina every man seemed to think that he had a free hand to burn any kind of property he could put the torch to. South Carolina paid the dearest penalty of any state in the Confederacy, considering the short time the Union army was in the state, and it was well that she should; for, if South Carolina had not been so persistent in going to war, there would have been no war for years to come.—A. G. D.

(March, 1865)

Chapter XXIII.
March Through North Carolina. The Last Campaign. Johnston's Surrender to Sherman. March 8-April 26.

Wednesday, 8th—We started at 9 a. m. and marched seventeen miles, going into camp for the night at Floral College, North Carolina. It rained all day and the roads became very muddy. The First Brigade on guard with the supply trains is in camp about six miles in the rear. We entered the state of North Carolina about 10 a. m. and received orders that there should be no burning of property; that any soldier caught in the act of starting a fire should be shot on the spot.[1]

Thursday, 9th—It is still raining. The army started at 8 a. m. Companies C, D and E of the Eleventh Iowa were sent back to town on provost guard, to see that nothing was burned, until the First Division should come up. Our division is on the main road. The First and Third Divisions are on roads to our right, and the Fifteenth Corps is off on our left. We marched twelve miles today.

Friday, 10th—Started on our march again at 7 a. m. and made twelve miles today. It is still raining and the creeks and swamps are all overflowing. There was no show of keeping our clothing dry, for besides the rain, we had to wade some thirteen creeks and sloughs, some of them waist deep. This is a most God-forsaken stretch of country, and there is only now and then a small farm. I can't understand how anybody could live here; in fact, the citizens have all left their homes.

Saturday, 11th—It is clear again and quite pleasant. We were off at 7 a. m. and marched twelve miles. Went into bivouac within a mile of Fayetteville. Our division had the honor of driving the rebels out of town, but the Fourteenth Corps was placed on garrison duty. All of Sherman's forces, the four corps, are concentrating at this place to cross the Cape Fear river. Forage is very scarce, the country being so very poor, but we hope soon to strike rich country where we can fill our haversacks.

[1] This was a proper order, for the war was about over, and the order was generally respected.—A. G. D.

(March, 1865)

Sunday, 12th—We remained in our bivouac all day, the boys putting in the time in mending their shoes and clothing. The Fifteenth Corps came in today. The engineers laid the pontoons across the river. Fayetteville is just across on the east bank of the river, and is at the head of navigation, ninety miles from Wilmington on the coast. A boat came up this morning from Wilmington. Our men did not burn much property in town, only the public buildings were fired.

Monday, 13th—The Seventeenth Corps crossed the river this morning and marched out about a mile, where we halted till late in the afternoon, when we moved forward three miles and went into bivouac for the night. Three more boats came up from Wilmington today. They are to be loaded with the refugees and contrabands gathered up by Sherman's army.

Tuesday, 14th—I went out early this morning with the foraging party of our division, in search of feed for the horses and mules. We came to a rich plantation about four miles out, with corncribs well filled, and in a short time we had the wagons loaded. Some of us had been put to loading the wagons while others went to get the chickens and other things. After the boys had caught and loaded all the chickens and upset fully a hundred beehives, they called out, "The rebels are coming!" We had just finished loading the wagons, but that call was enough to frighten the teamsters, and they put the whip to the mules, starting off on a dead run. The road ran through a heavy timber, but it was wide and perfectly level, and they galloped the teams the whole way back to our bivouac. It was every fellow for himself, and I never ran faster in my life. A commissioner from Cornell College[1] was in camp today for the purpose of raising money to educate the orphan children of soldiers and sailors. Our company raised $229.00.

Wednesday, 15th—We were on the move at 7 a. m. and marched ten miles today. Went into bivouac near the Black river. The section of the country through which we passed today is almost one continuous swamp and heavily timbered. There is a small farm now and then. The corps took different roads and so we all got into bivouac earlier. Our division, the Fourth, had the center. When the road was wide enough the infantry

[1]College at Mt. Vernon, Iowa.

would march at one side, allowing the artillery and teams to occupy the roadway. This made it equal to a double column, and we could move faster and save time.

Thursday, 16th—We had a thunderstorm yesterday at 2 p. m. and today we had an all-day rain. We marched twelve miles in the mud, our division taking the lead. Our regiment crossed the South river after dark, on the stringers of the bridge, the rebels having burned a part of the bridge. The engineers have to lay the pontoons for the artillery and teams to cross. The country is very poor and forage is scarce.

Friday, 17th—Our division is still in the lead. We started at 7 a. m. and marched fifteen miles. Our regiment was train guard and we did not get into bivouac until midnight. The rebels are in our front and hard to drive; their main force, however, is on our left, in front of the Fourteenth and Twentieth Corps. It was clear today and quite pleasant.

Saturday, 18th—We started at 8 a. m. and marched twelve miles, the Third Division being in the advance. We had to cross a swamp four miles wide and the water in places was knee-deep. Our progress was slow because we had to lay a great deal of corduroy so that the artillery and trains could pass over the deep holes. A great many of the men are almost barefooted and their clothing is nearly worn out. The men on forage take everything in the clothing line that is fit to wear, regardless of the cut or color. Some have on white vests and straw hats, and occasionally one can be seen in the ranks wearing a swallow-tailed coat and white vest. This morning our men drew a few pairs of shoes, brought from Washington.

Sunday, 19th—We were off at 7 a. m. and marched ten miles through fine country. The roads were good and no swamps to cross. They had good crops here last year, and there was plenty of forage, so this evening we had our haversacks replenished. There was some heavy cannonading off on the left in front of the Twentieth Corps. The weather is fine.

Monday, 20th—Reveille sounded at 1 a. m. At 3 o'clock with the Fifteenth Corps in front, we took up the line of march and moved forward twenty-one miles, where we found the rebels fortified on the west side of the Neuse river near Bentonville.

(March, 1865)

We drove them back inside of their works, and forming a line of battle moved up as close to their works as we could, and then built a line of rifle pits. We left our wagon trains far in the rear under guard. The rebels' force is reported to be about thirty-five thousand men under the command of General Johnston. General Schofield has been moving up this way from the coast, and we just learned that he reached Goldsboro and took possession of the place this afternoon. We are informed that General Sherman will now open up communications from Goldsboro southeast to Newbern.

Tuesday, 21st—We advanced our line of battle a half mile, driving in the rebel skirmishers. Our loss was quite large in killed and wounded. All our artillery was brought into action and at times this afternoon the roar of cannon was fearful; but the rebels made no reply. Their loss in killed and wounded was large. There was some hard skirmishing on both sides. The Fifth and Twenty-fourth Corps under command of General Ord joined us this afternoon, thus reinforcing General Sherman's army. The army is in fine spirits for all that the men are poorly clothed and short of rations; but anything that General Sherman wants done now, they are willing to do. All know that when we gain this battle, we will have a short rest and a chance to draw some clothing, besides securing rations, for forage is scarce.

Wednesday, 22d—Companies E and F of the Eleventh Iowa were sent out at 6 o'clock this morning on the skirmish line, but there were no rebels to be seen in our front. They left during the night, crossing the Neuse river, and retreating towards Raleigh, the state capital. Kilpatrick's cavalry pursued them for several miles. The rebels fought in the pine woods, which were set on fire by the shells from our artillery. The fire compelled them to fall back, and they left their dead and wounded on the battlefield, to the mercy of the flames; the clothing was entirely burned off some of the bodies. The loss was very light on both sides. We remained all day in bivouac at the rifle pits, while the Fourteenth and Twentieth Corps moved back towards Goldsboro.

Thursday, 23d—An order from General Sherman was read this morning, stating that the campaign was over,[1] and that we

[1] This battle proved to be our last, and it is known as the battle of Bentonville. We took part later in the surrender of Johnston's army at Raleigh, N. C., but there was no battle then, or before the surrender, only a little skirmishing.—A. G. D.

should now prepare to take a short rest. We left the rifle pits at 7 o'clock, marched fifteen miles, and bivouacked within five miles of Goldsboro. Our army is concentrating there, and we are to get supplies, rest up, and prepare for another campaign.

Friday, 24th—We left bivouac at 7 a. m. and marched to the Neuse river, which we crossed near Goldsboro on a pontoon bridge. As we passed through town, we were reviewed by General Sherman, passing him by platoon form, and marching to martial music. The men looked pretty hard after such a long raid, ragged and almost barefooted; but we felt repaid, for we had accomplished the task which we had set out to do when we left Savannah. We went into camp north of town just outside of the town limits. Our corps, the Seventeenth, occupies the right center and the Twentieth Corps the left center, while the Fifteenth Corps occupies the right and the Fourteenth Corps the left. General Schofield's army, the Twenty-third, Twenty-fourth and Twenty-fifth Corps, is going into camp in the vicinity of Clinton.

Saturday, 25th—We remained in camp all day. Large foraging parties were sent out to get feed for the mules and horses. Our train loaded with supplies returned from Kingston, down on the river. A construction train came in from Kingston, repairing the railroad. The Twenty-third Corps from Schofield's army has been moved to Kingston. All the troops are in camp in and around Goldsboro, and it will be but a short time until all our supplies will be brought in from the coast by the railroad. The Thirteenth Iowa received three hundred recruits today.

Sunday, 26th—Pleasant weather. The Eleventh Iowa was sent out with a foraging train to get corn and fodder for the mules and horses of our brigade. They had to go a distance of thirteen miles to get the feed. I being on camp duty did not go. A train of cars came in from Newbern loaded with supplies for the army, and our quartermaster received some clothing for the regiment.

Monday, 27th—We cleaned up our camp today, and are building "ranches" with the expectation of staying here a while. We have a fine camp ground and plenty of water. Large foraging parties are sent out for corn and fodder. All is quiet in the front. No news of any importance.

Tuesday, 28th—We have had pleasant weather for several days, but today it is cloudy, with some rain. The men drew new clothing today just as fast as the quartermaster could receive the supply from the general quartermaster. Nearly every man in the regiment is drawing a full suit, out and out. Some of the men have to get new knapsacks, canteens and haversacks, while all are getting new shoes. I drew a pair of pants and a blouse, a pair of drawers and a pair of socks. Our regiment out on dress parade has the appearance of a new regiment.

Wednesday, 29th—It is quite rainy. We are now in spring quarters. Some of the boys in the regiment get teams from the quartermaster, go out to some vacant house or barn, and get what lumber they want to build "ranches." J. D. Moore and William Green went out this morning with a team and brought in a load of lumber, and then this afternoon we built a small house for our mess of four—Moore, Green, Jason Sparks and myself.

Thursday, 30th—It is quite stormy and rainy today. All is quiet in camp, and there is no news of importance.

Friday, 31st—Cloudy and windy today. We are ordered to have company drill four hours a day and dress parade at 5 o'clock in the evening. This is all the duty we have to perform; do not even have camp guard or provost duty. We have no picket duty to do, as the Twentieth Corps is out in front of us. We are drawing full rations now and have plenty of clothing. This is fine soldiering to what it was wading swamps in South Carolina. Nothing more for this month.

APRIL, 1865.

Saturday, 1st—The weather is pleasant. No news of any importance. The camp here is the best we have had since leaving Vicksburg. Our "ranch" is eight feet square, boarded up seven feet high, and has a gable roof of the proper pitch covered over with our rubber ponchos, nailed to the rafters; it will protect us from the worst rainstorm. Our bunks are raised two feet from the ground. We have a door to the "ranch," made of boards, and the latch-string hangs out.

Sunday, 2d—Regular camp routine is the order. We had company inspection this morning besides two hours' drill. A great many of us attended church in town this morning, also in the evening.

Monday, 3d—Fine weather continues, and camp routine the same. We are enjoying our fine camp ground, and to prevent our becoming stale, we have to keep up regular drill for our next campaign.

Tuesday, 4th—The quartermaster distributed new clothing today. I drew a hat, a pair of shoes and a pair of socks. We are enjoying full rations again, and also our new clothing. We no longer have to search our haversacks for a crumb of hardtack.

Wednesday, 5th—The regimental chaplains are occupying the pulpits of the different churches of Goldsboro and conducting nightly meetings. A large number of the boys are attending and a great many are coming forward and professing the name of the Lord. May the work continue until all have made the profession.

Thursday, 6th—News comes that General Grant has taken Richmond with five thousand prisoners and five hundred pieces of artillery. We also hear that Mobile has been taken with twenty thousand prisoners and a large number of guns. Glorious news!

Friday, 7th—Weather still pleasant. Company drill two hours a day. Our brigade came out in review and was inspected by General Smith. A statement was read to us by the assistant adjutant general of our brigade, stating our loss at Richmond, and also that of the enemy. Our loss was seven thousand killed and two thousand taken prisoners, while that of the enemy was forty thousand in killed, wounded and prisoners.

Saturday, 8th—All is quiet. Sherman's army received orders to march on the 10th. Our wagon trains are loaded with thirty-five days' rations, and we are to carry five days' rations in our haversacks. The news is so good that all are anxious to move at once. The boys are all happy, thinking that this will be our last campaign. Our brigade received orders to clean clothing and accouterments for regimental inspection.

Sunday, 9th—Very pleasant weather. Our division was inspected this forenoon by General Smith. Two regiments in the division did not pass inspection and were sent back to their "ranches" with the order to get themselves up in better style and

(April, 1865)

come back at 4 o'clock for inspection. The Eleventh Iowa was complimented for its neat appearance. We were ordered to come over to General Smith's headquarters at 5 o'clock in the evening to hold our dress parade. The officers of the two disgraced regiments were ordered to appear at his headquarters to see our regiment go through the manual of arms on our dress parade. We returned to our "ranches" much elated over the high compliments we had received from our division commander. We set to work at once preparing for our dress parade, not even taking time to cook our noon-day mess. A number of the boys were sent down town to buy all the white gloves and white collars they could find, besides shoe blacking and shoe brushes, and then we spent all the time till the parade in fixing ourselves up. We went over to the general's headquarters looking our best, and every move ordered by our colonel was nicely executed in the presence of the line officers of the other two regiments.[1]

Monday, 10th—Had an all-day rain. The entire army moved forward today, some starting at 8 a. m. We packed our knapsacks early this morning, but did not start until 10 o'clock. While we were waiting, some of the Twenty-fourth Iowa Regiment which had arrived at Goldsboro came over to our "ranches" for a visit. We boys had a visit from Homer Curtis of Company C, Twenty-fourth Iowa. We marched ten miles today. The Fifteenth and Seventeenth Corps form the right wing, the Twenty-third Corps, in command of General Schofield, the center, and the Fourteenth and Twentieth Corps form the left wing. Some heavy cannonading off on the left.

Tuesday, 11th—Weather quite pleasant. We started at 6 a. m. and marched twelve miles. Our march was very slow, the road being through one continuous swamp. We had to lay corduroy the whole way. Our division, the First, was in front of the corps, and there was some skirmishing in our front.

Wednesday, 12th—We started at 8 a. m. and marched five miles, all the way through one continuous swamp. News came to us this forenoon that General Lee had surrendered his entire army to General Grant. It was glorious news. We forgot all

[1] The next day when we started for Raleigh, one of those two regiments having marched out on the road ahead of our regiment, was ordered to halt while ours passed to the front. While we were marching by they could not find words strong enough to express their contempt for us.—A. G. D.

(April, 1865)

about our hard marching, and the whole brigade commenced singing songs—"John Brown's body lies a-mouldering in the grave, As we go marching on!"

Thursday, 13th—It rained nearly all day and I never saw it rain harder than it did this forenoon. We left our bivouac at 5 a. m. and marched eighteen miles. The roads are good now. The left wing of our army marched into Raleigh, the capital of North Carolina, the rebels having evacuated the place last night.

Friday, 14th—We started at 5 a. m. and marched twenty-one miles. We crossed the Neuse river at noon and passed through Raleigh about dusk, going into bivouac four miles west of town. Raleigh is a very nice place, and not a building was burned. Our division had the advance, the Eleventh and Thirteenth Iowa being on train guard.

Saturday, 15th—We started at 7 a. m., marched only four miles and went into camp again. News came from the front that Johnston had stopped fighting for the purpose of surrendering his army to General Sherman. It rained hard all day, but we don't mind that when hearing such glorious news as the surrender of Johnston. The Third and First Divisions remained in camp.

Sunday, 16th—The weather is warm and pleasant. We remained in bivouac all day. All is quiet in the front and both armies are resting under a flag of truce. Neither army is allowed to change its position while the agreement is in force.

Monday, 17th—News came that Abe Lincoln[1] had been assassinated at Washington, in a theater, also Secretary Seward and his son.[2] When the news came of the death of the president, the safety guards, placed at private houses to protect the families from violence, were relieved. General Sherman at once demanded an answer from Johnston by tomorrow, in regard to the surrender. Charles Correll of our company was put under arrest for saying that the president should have been shot three years ago. Correll has only been with the company since the 28th of last September, and then had been hired to enlist for a big sum of money. I went out on picket this morning.

[1] That a soldier should speak of Lincoln in such familiar terms was but natural. It was in no sense disrespectful. All through the war the President was spoken of as "Abe" Lincoln.—Ed.
[2] This shows again the unreliable character of the first reports.—Ed.

(April, 1865)

Tuesday, 18th—General Sherman went out to the front on the cars, and the two generals agreed upon the terms for the surrender of Johnston's army. Both armies are to go into camp and remain until the terms of surrender have been approved by the War Department at Washington. The Union army is to go into camp in the vicinity of Raleigh, and the rebel army in the vicinity of Chapel Hill. I came in from picket this morning, having been out on the picket line for twenty-four hours.

Wednesday, 19th—We struck our tents about noon and marched back about five miles, toward Raleigh, going into camp within three miles of town. We laid out our camp in regular order for the purpose of building small houses and covering them with our shelter tents.

Thursday, 20th—It rained some today. We spent the day in raising our tents. There is great rejoicing in camp. Many think that peace is made, and that in a few days we shall likely start for home.

Friday, 21st—Rain again today. All the men in the five different corps are at work fixing up their camp grounds. The army feels very sad and sorrowful over the death of the president.

Saturday, 22d—It is quite pleasant today. I went out with a team after a load of lumber for our company. We pulled down an old, vacant barn. No property is being burned and destroyed in this state, and only vacant buildings are torn down to get lumber with which to build "ranches." There is a large amount of land lying idle around here. The field where we have our camp has not been farmed for two or three years. But there are some fine wheat fields here and the wheat is just heading out. We have a fine camp; all of the tents are raised now, and our brigade has shade trees set in rows throughout our camp. There being no trees, we went to the timber and cut down small bushy pine trees for the purpose, setting them in the ground. Our camp looked so fine that the staff artist of Harper's Weekly took a picture of it for the paper.

Sunday, 23d—We had regimental inspection at 10 a. m. and this afternoon at 2 o'clock our division was reviewed by General Smith. The division came out in good style.

Monday, 24th—The Seventeenth Army Corps marched to Raleigh this afternoon and was reviewed by Lieutenant-General

Grant and Major-General Sherman. Their reviewing stand was in front of the governor's mansion. The army was glad to see their old commander once more. We received orders to move forward in the morning, since the terms of the surrender of Johnston's army were not approved by the War Department at Washington. This is not good news for us, but we are hoping that Johnston will surrender without more fighting.

Tuesday, 25th—We broke camp again and at 7 a. m. started to move forward, our division, the Fourth, taking up the rear. We marched six miles and went into camp for the night. All is quiet in the front. Deserters from Johnston's army are still coming in from the front. They declare that they do not want to do any more fighting, for they know that their cause is lost. They also expressed the belief that Johnston would surrender without fighting.

Wednesday, 26th—The weather is pleasant. We remained in camp all day. Lieutenant-General Grant and Major-General Sherman went to the front early this morning. The report came late this afternoon that Johnston had surrendered his entire army to Sherman. Great rejoicing in camp! Johnston is to retain one-seventh of his small arms until his men start for their homes.

FROM A PHOTOGRAPH OF SERGEANT DOWNING TAKEN AT LOUISVILLE, KENTUCKY, JUST BEFORE THE MUSTERING OUT, JULY, 1865.

Chapter XXIV.
Peaceful March Through Virginia and the Grand Review at Washington. April 27-May 27.

Thursday, 27th—We returned to our old camp just vacated and put our shelter tents over the old "ranches" again. By 1 p. m. the tents were all filled, we were at home once more and enjoying ourselves. The boys are now waiting for orders to start for their homes, but we are wondering which way we will go. Some think we will have to go back to the coast and take ship for New Orleans; but I guess we will leave that to General Sherman—he has never yet made a mistake in leading us.

Friday, 28th—The weather continues fine. We spent the day in washing and cleaning our clothing. We received orders to start for Washington at 8 o'clock in the morning, going by way of Richmond, Virginia. Great rejoicing in camp at the thought of going home—to come back no more. The report is that the four corps under Sherman, with Kilpatrick's cavalry, are going North, while the Twenty-third Corps under Schofield will remain at Raleigh until all of Johnston's men leave for their homes. He will take over the munitions of war surrendered by Johnston.

Saturday, 29th—Reveille sounded shortly after midnight and we had our knapsacks packed long before daylight. Some of the boys were so happy and excited that they did not sleep much during the night. At 7 o'clock we took up the march, stepping to music as we left our camp. We crossed the Neuse river about noon and after marching twelve miles for the day, went into bivouac. By order of General Howard we are to lay over here until Monday, when we will continue our journey. The Fifteenth Corps is taking a road to our right. General Sherman's headquarters wagons are going through with the Seventeenth Corps. The Thirty-second Illinois Regiment was taken from the Iowa Brigade and was brigaded with the First Brigade of the Second Division of the Seventeenth Corps. Our brigade is the First Brigade of the Fourth Division of the Seventeenth Corps.

Sunday, 30th—Remained in bivouac all day. We had a heavy rain last night, but it is clear and warm today. A man from the Fifteenth Iowa preached in our camp at early candlelight this evening.

MAY, 1865.

Monday, 1st—Our corps, the Seventeenth, took up the line of march at 6 a. m. and marched fifteen miles, going into bivouac at about 4 o'clock in the afternoon. No foraging parties are allowed on this march, and no railroad or any kind of property is to be destroyed. The army, by divisions, is to go into bivouac when convenient about 3 p. m. each day, and about three miles apart, so that the trains and artillery can get into their corrals before dark. We passed through Forestville and Wake Forest, towns a mile apart, at about noon today. We have good roads and fine weather for marching.

Tuesday, 2d—Weather pleasant. We started at 6:30 a. m. and marched seventeen miles today. We crossed the Tar river at 10 this morning, and passed through some very fine country this afternoon. There is nothing new.

Wednesday, 3d—We started at 5 a. m. and marched twenty miles today. Crops look fine. There are a great many rebel soldiers throughout the country here, who have just returned from the armies of Johnston and Lee. Our army, for the first time, is passing through the country without destroying property.

Thursday, 4th—We started at 8 a. m., marched four miles, and then lay over until 6 p. m., when we moved on four miles farther, passing the Third Division, and went into bivouac within a mile of the Roanoke river. The Fifteenth Corps is in advance of us and their rear crossed the river this evening. Our trains are all crossing the river tonight. Weather still pleasant.

Friday, 5th—It is quite warm. We left our bivouac at 3 a. m. and by 6 o'clock had crossed the Roanoke river. It is a fine stream. One of our drivers had an exciting experience in crossing the river last night, over the pontoon bridge. When he reached the middle of the bridge his leading mules became frightened at

(May, 1865)

the cracks between the boards and turned right around, upsetting the whole thing, and the six mules, wagon and all went overboard. When the driver saw what was going to happen, quick as a flash, he dropped down upon the bridge between the wheel mules and the wagon, thus saving himself. The mules and wagon were never seen again, as the Roanoke is very deep. We crossed the State line into old Virginia at 6:30 this morning. At 1 p. m. we crossed the Meherrin river and after marching twenty-six miles for the day went into bivouac. We have fine roads. News came that the two men who killed the president and stabbed Seward had been shot. All is quiet.

Saturday, 6th—We started at 5 a. m. and soon struck the Boydton plank road, which was quite good except at places, where it was a poor makeshift of a road. We marched twenty-five miles and went into bivouac for the night. I was sick all day and in order to keep up with the command I had to have the doctor order my knapsack and accouterments carried for me. Weather fine.

Sunday, 7th—Started at the usual time and marched eighteen miles today. We bivouacked in some old camps which our men had built during the siege of Petersburg, within two miles of town. I rode all the way today with the wagon train. A part of the Fifteenth Corps came in ahead of the Seventeenth Corps, but our corps beat the Fifteenth into Petersburg after all their running to beat us. The two generals in command of the Fifteenth and Seventeenth Army Corps started out, after crossing the Roanoke river, to see which corps could reach Petersburg first. So while one brigade of the Fifteenth Corps came into Petersburg first, the entire Seventeenth Corps arrived in town ahead of the Fifteenth.

Monday, 8th—We started at 7 a. m., and while passing through Petersburg by platoons, were reviewed by General Ord, in command at Petersburg. The Fifteenth Corps had to pass through the city in our rear. We crossed the Appomattox river at 9 a. m. and went into bivouac six miles out from Petersburg, making a march of only eight miles for the day. Petersburg is a lively place; business is going on regularly. The people are at work repairing the damages done by the war, and are even erecting new buildings. It is a fine city with beautiful country around, although badly cut up with fortifications. The town was strongly fortified.

Tuesday, 9th—We started at 3 o'clock this morning and marched fifteen miles, going into bivouac on the banks of the James river near Manchester. Sherman's entire army is arriving at this place and will lie here three or four days, after which we are to start for Washington City to be mustered out of the service.

Wednesday, 10th—Remained in camp all day. General Sherman's cavalry corps, under Kilpatrick, passed here on their way to Washington City. We are camped in plain view of the city of Richmond, once the capital of the so-called Southern Confederacy, but now desolate, its defenders having fled. It is partly burnt, the rebels having set it on fire before they left.[1] The weather is quite cool.

Thursday, 11th—The Fourteenth and Twentieth Army Corps started on their way for Washington City. Our corps remained in camp all day. The sick were all sent down to the wharf to go around by boat to Washington. The doctor had my name listed for that route, and I started to go, but got a release. I told the doctor that I should much prefer to march through with my company, if he would have my knapsack and accouterments carried for me in the wagons. He assured me that he would have them seen to and told me that I could rejoin my company, for which I am very thankful.

Friday, 12th—It rained very hard all night. We left our bivouac at 4 o'clock this morning and at 6 o'clock passed through Richmond.[2] The town looks fine and business seems to be good. We marched ten miles and went into bivouac on the Chickahominy river. The entire army is taking the same route and thus we cannot move fast.

Saturday, 13th—Started at 10 a. m. and marched twelve miles today. We went into bivouac for the night near Hanover Court House. It is quite swampy and the roads are very bad, on ac-

[1] The burning of Richmond by the Confederates seems so uncalled for. It was certainly very short-sighted, since they could not help knowing that their cause was lost.—A. G. D.

[2] The Union general in command at Richmond requested General Sherman to have his army pass in review through Richmond, but Sherman flatly refused, declaring that he would march his army around the city before he would do anything of the kind, and Sherman had his way as to how we should pass through.—A. G. D.

(May, 1865)

count of so much rain the last few days. The country through which we passed today is considerably cut up by fortifications and badly used up on account of the two armies passing back and forth so often over the same roads and fields. The citizens are back on their farms and are at work again. Details of our men are stationed all along the way, guarding their homes and property, to keep the army from destroying things. When the army gets past, the guards fall into line at the rear.

Sunday, 14th—It is quite warm. We remained in bivouac until 1 p. m., when we started and covered ten miles before night. We crossed the Pamunky river at 2 o'clock, after which the army divided, in order to get better roads. The Fourteenth and Seventeenth Corps took a road on the left, while the Fifteenth and the Twentieth marched on a road to the right. The roads through the lowlands are fearfully muddy.

Monday, 15th—We left bivouac at 5 o'clock this morning and marched eighteen miles. Went into bivouac for the night near the Fay river. The weather is quite warm and the roads are very bad.

Tuesday, 16th—Started at 4 a. m. and marched twenty miles today. We passed through Fredericksburg at 1 p. m., crossing the Rappahannock river at that place. On coming into Fredericksburg we marched along that stone wall by the bend of the river and looked down upon the lowland below where so many of our boys were marched to their death—at that terrible battle. It made me shudder to look down upon that horrible place. Fredericksburg seemed filled with Johnnies just returned from the war. At 5 o'clock we crossed the Poe river and went into bivouac.

Wednesday, 17th—We started at 4 o'clock this morning and marched thirty miles today. It was very hot and a great many of the boys gave out. Our division led the advance. We passed through some very fine country and the crops are looking fine.

Thursday, 18th—Some of the troops started quite early this morning, but our division left later, taking up the rear today. We marched fifteen miles and went into bivouac after crossing the Acon river, wading it just below the mouth of Bull Run creek, which empties into it. There are some fortifications here, it being near where the battles of Bull Run were fought.

Friday, 19th—Started at 10 a. m. and after marching fifteen miles, went into camp within four miles of Alexandria, Virginia. Sherman's entire army arrived today and all, including the artillery, which we kept with the infantry all the way, are in camp near Alexandria.

Saturday, 20th—There are three armies in camp here, the Army of the Potomac under General Meade, and the Armies of the Tennessee and of Georgia, both under General Sherman. We received orders that the Army of the Potomac would be reviewed by Lieutenant-General Grant on the 23d inst., and the armies under General Sherman on the 24th. The review is to take place in Washington City. It rained all day and it is very disagreeable in our camp on the commons of Alexandria. The firewood is so wet that it is almost impossible to get a fire to cook our food.

Sunday, 21st—It is still raining. We remained in our bivouac all day. Some of the troops are moving toward Washington for the grand review. News came that Jefferson Davis had been captured by General Wilson at a small place in Georgia, called Irwinville, in the county of Irwin.[1]

Monday, 22d—It is quite warm. Still in camp, and there's nothing of importance. We had company inspection at 2 o'clock this afternoon.

Tuesday, 23d—We started at 8 a. m. and by 10 o'clock had passed through Old Alexandria. We went into bivouac within three miles of Washington City. The Army of the Potomac was reviewed by the president of the United States and Lieutenant General Grant. Sherman's army is to be reviewed tomorrow.

Wednesday, 24th—This is a very pleasant day, for which we are all thankful. We left for Washington City at 8 o'clock, and crossing the Potomac river over Long Bridge, marched up to the south side of the capitol. Our column was formed on the east side of the capitol, and at 9 o'clock commenced to move forward past the reviewing stand. The Army of the Tennessee was in the advance, with the Army of Georgia following. General Sherman was riding at the head of his army and he passed down the avenue amidst loud cheering.

[1] The capture was effected on May 10th by Lieutenant-Colonel Pritchard, of the Fourth Michigan Cavalry, a detachment of General James H. Wilson's cavalry.—Ed.

(May, 1865)

The following officers were in command of the different departments: Maj. Gen. O. O. Howard was in command of the Army of the Tennessee, Maj. Gen. John A. Logan commanding the Fifteenth Corps, and Maj. Gen. Frank P. Blair commanding the Seventeenth Corps; the Army of Georgia was in command of Maj. Gen. Slocum, with Maj. Gen. J. C. Davis commanding the Fourteenth Corps, and Maj. Gen. Mower commanding the Twentieth Corps.

The reviewing stand was built on the south side of the avenue, and the army was reviewed by the president of the United States and Lieutenant-General Grant, together with members of the president's cabinet. There were about one hundred thousand spectators along the avenue, and there was great cheering while the army was passing. At times there was hearty laughter, when some of Sherman's "bummers" would fall in behind their regiments, displaying some of the articles, as trophies, which they had taken when marching through Georgia and the Carolinas.

We marched out across Rock creek about four miles northwest of the city and went into camp. Our knapsacks were brought around by the supply train.

Thursday, 25th—It rained nearly all day—at times very hard. We remained in camp all day and nothing of any importance occurred. Now that we are so near Washington, the boys are waiting their turns for passes to go to the city, for since there are so many provost guards there, it would not be safe to go without a pass.

Friday, 26th—It is raining again today, and the roads between our camp and the city are almost impassable. We are poorly fixed here for washing and cleaning our clothing. The long march from Goldsboro, North Carolina, has been pretty hard on our clothes. We have not received any pay since November, 1864, and some of the boys are getting pretty short of change.

Saturday, 27th—It is cloudy and still raining some. I received a pass and with six other boys of our company went to the city to spend the day. We went through some of the public buildings, the capitol, patent office and the treasury building; they are fine buildings, all being built of marble. We viewed the

White House from the street, and went through the Smithsonian Park, which is very beautiful indeed.

The city is full of soldiers viewing the sights. But there is one thing which seems to cast a gloom over the city, and that is, that our beloved President Lincoln is not in the White House, that he was not here to greet us when we passed down Pennsylvania avenue, and that he had to be taken off by the hand of an assassin just when the war was over.

Chapter XXV.

The Mustering Out. Return to the Harvest Field. May 28-July 31.

Sunday, 28th—It is clear and pleasant today. We cleaned up our camping ground and put up our "ranches" in regular order. News came that the rebel general, Kirby Smith, commanding south and west of the Mississippi, had surrendered his army and the navy.

Monday, 29th—It is reported in camp that the western men in General Sherman's army will be transferred to Louisville, Kentucky, by rail and by transports on the Ohio, there to be mustered out of the service. The veterans are anxious to get their discharge, for since the war is over we have no desire to remain in the army.

Tuesday, 30th—The weather is pleasant and seems to be settled. There is nothing new.

Wednesday, 31st—I got a pass and went to the city again. I spent most of the day in the patent office and in the Smithsonian Institution. I also got my watch repaired, which cost me $3.00. The city seems to be astir; new buildings are growing up all over and some of the Government buildings are being improved. Except for the presence of so many soldiers in the city, no one would think that a four years' war had just ended. The city needs most of all paved streets, for in wet weather they get very muddy and the city looks no better than a country town. The Washington monument is not yet finished and from a distance it looks like a large smokestack with the top lacking. A part of the Fifteenth Corps left for Louisville today, but all men whose time is out by October 1st were left here to be mustered out at once. All of the eastern men in Sherman's four corps are to remain in Washington for the present. We had a temperance talk here this evening by William White Williams. I bought a medal of honor from him. Everything is going along fine.

JUNE, 1865.

Thursday, 1st—The weather is quite sultry. There is nothing of importance. Our camp duty is very light here. The ground is rough, and it would be impossible to find a place for a drill ground or even a parade ground.

Friday, 2d—For the first time we saw mustered-out soldiers leaving for their homes today.

Saturday, 3d—The weather continues quite hot. All men in our brigade whose time is out by the 1st of October were mustered out today and they turned over their guns and accouterments. Twelve boys from our company received their discharge and will be sent home.

Sunday, 4th—We had company inspection this morning. The weather is very hot and we all remained close to our "ranches" today. We could not go to the city anyway, for without a pass it is difficult to get by the provost guard.

Monday, 5th—This forenoon we had a temperance speech by Wm. Roach of Iowa at the headquarters bivouac of the Eleventh Iowa. Blank pledges of the Washington Temperance Society were distributed and a good many of the boys signed the blanks after they were filled out.[1] The men mustered out from our division, the Fourth, started for their homes this afternoon. The Government furnishes them transportation to their home states.

Tuesday, 6th—We received orders to leave for Louisville, and drawing four days' rations turned over to the general quartermaster our regimental teams and wagons. We expect to start in the morning. The Third Division of our corps started this morning, while the First Division left yesterday morning. The troops are leaving Washington as fast as the railroads can furnish cars; they even bring in all the open cars not in use and crowd the soldiers onto them until there is no standing room. Large numbers of soldiers have already left for their homes, while others are going to different cities to remain in camp for a while.

Wednesday, 7th—The First Brigade of our division left at 5 o'clock this morning for Louisville. Our brigade left camp at 3 o'clock this afternoon and marched to the Baltimore & Ohio station, where we boarded the cars. We were put on open coal cars,

[1] Mr. Downing was among the number.—Ed.

and there were so many to the car that we could not lie down and straighten out.[1]

Thursday, 8th—We left Washington City at 1 a. m. and arrived at the junction of the Baltimore & Ohio railroad about 8 o'clock, where we changed to the line running through Harper's Ferry, which place we passed through. Our brigade is in the rear, the Eleventh Iowa being on the rear train, as we were the last regiment to leave Washington, D. C. The day was very hot and many of us being crowded on the open cars suffered terribly under the hot sun. We arrived at Cumberland about midnight, where we were served with hot coffee by the Sanitary Commission Society.

Friday, 9th—Our train ran all night, except for two or three times when we were standing on some sidetrack. Arriving at the foot of the Cumberland mountains our train was divided and another engine put on to pull one-half the train up the mountains. The train moved up very slowly, which gave us a chance to get off and cut some sassafras bushes, which we nailed on the sides of the cars for shade, for the sun was terribly hot, and the weather was very sultry. By noon we reached the top of the mountains. At 4 p. m. we arrived at Grafton, Virginia, where we received hot coffee from the Sanitary Commission. Here we left the Baltimore & Ohio road for Parkersburg, Virginia, over the Ohio & Virginia Railroad. We passed through a great many tunnels between Grafton and Parkersburg, one being four thousand one hundred and thirty-eight feet long. The citizens along our route today seemed to be very loyal, cheering us all along the way. It reminded us of our home folks.

Saturday, 10th—We had a heavy thunderstorm and rain early this morning, which made it very disagreeable for us on our open coal cars. We arrived at Parkersburg on the Ohio at daylight and left the cars. We cooked and ate our breakfast and then at about 8 o'clock went aboard the transports, and at 4 o'clock in the afternoon we left for Louisville, Kentucky. The Eleventh Iowa and the Thirty-second Illinois Regiments are on board the transport "Empress." We have a fleet of five boats, which besides the "Empress" are the "Nord," "America," "Revenue" and "Edinburgh," the headquarters boat. All the boats are heavily

---

[1] It was nothing short of disgraceful for the Government to treat the soldiers that way after the war. The War Department should have taken more time to move the soldiers from the city.—A. G. D.

loaded and we are crowded, but it is much more pleasant than in the open coal cars, and while the sun is hot, it is not so oppressive as on the railroad.

Sunday, 11th—Our boats ran all night. This is a bright sunshiny Sunday. All went well and everything was quiet until about 4 p. m. when our boat struck a snag. We were nearing Manchester, Ohio, when we ran upon an old sunken stone barge, the bottom of our boat was torn off and it sank in less than three minutes. The captain, quick to see the danger of our going down in midstream, ordered the boat turned toward the Kentucky side of the river, and we were within twenty feet of the bank when it sank stern first, going down at an angle of about forty-five degrees. In the excitement several men jumped overboard, but were rescued by men in canoes from Manchester. Tears were shed by the ladies of Manchester, thinking that, of course, a great many would be lost, but all were saved in one way or another. Regardless of the danger some of the boys on the sinking boat broke into the steward's pantry and filled their haversacks with the good things in store. Our regiment was now divided, and put on the other already crowded boats. Company E, with H, G and B, went upon the "Nord"—and as usual, Company E got the hurricane deck.

Monday, 12th—The boats ran all night, and we passed Cincinnati about 1 a. m. At daylight we landed at Ornod, Indiana, remaining there about two hours, till the fog lifted. We arrived at Louisville about 4 p. m., and disembarking, marched out about eight miles below town where we went into bivouac. This is a miserable place for the troops to camp, being very low, the next thing to a swamp, and heavily timbered; we cannot remain here long without its resulting in a great deal of sickness.

Tuesday, 13th—We had a thunder shower early this morning. The Eleventh Iowa signed the muster rolls this morning and we expect to get our pay in a few days. The Army of the Tennessee is in camp in and around Louisville. The veterans are becoming very much dissatisfied, as they were expecting to be discharged as soon as the war was over, but there is no sign of their being discharged very soon; besides that, we are kept in ignorance of it all, not knowing what they are going to do with us. Some of the boys think that we shall be sent down to Texas on duty, while others believe that we shall receive our discharge within a month or six weeks.

Wednesday, 14th—The weather is sultry. We occupied the day in cleaning our clothing and accouterments. The long journey of eight hundred miles on coal cars and transports was pretty hard on our clothes as well as trying on the men, for we had no protection from the hot sun nor shelter from the rain. The farmers around here are harvesting, and the grain looks fine.

Thursday, 15th—The men found so much fault with our camp on the low ground and made so much complaint about it at headquarters that our division was ordered to move to higher ground. We moved today to a large piece of sparsely-timbered land, high and rolling, where we will have a fine camp. It is about two miles south of Louisville. The Fourteenth Army Corps and one division of the Twentieth Corps, with the exception of the eastern men in these two corps, have arrived at Louisville.

Friday, 16th—Pleasant weather. We cleaned up our camping ground today and built "ranches" covering them with our rubber ponchos. General Hinkenlooper, a West Pointer, is in command of our brigade and has given orders to put on camp guard.

Saturday, 17th—Still pleasant. We have not yet received our pay. A part of the Fifteenth Corps has been paid, and the paymaster is paying the men of the First Brigade.

Sunday, 18th—We had regimental inspection at 10 a. m. by Captain Foster. The weather is very hot and this afternoon we had a heavy thunderstorm. I was sergeant of the regimental guard and during the night, on account of the rain, I had the guard relieved.

Monday, 19th—It is very pleasant, having cleared off during the night. We had regimental inspection again this morning. Our camps are filled with all kinds of agents from the city, trying to sell their nostrums to the boys; even the "dents" come out to pull teeth or to clean them for the boys.

Tuesday, 20th—Very pleasant weather. I sold my watch to Samuel Bair for $25.00, receiving $20.00 in cash, the balance remaining unpaid. They have fine macadamized roads out from the city, and there are men working on them all the time, but they would be killing on soldiers marching over them.

(June, 1865)

Wednesday, 21st—The Second Brigade of the Fourth Division of the Seventeenth Army Corps received their pay and embarked this morning for St. Louis.

Thursday, 22d—The Eleventh Iowa received eight months' pay, besides $100.00 of bounty money. I received $243.45, $34.00 of it being clothing money.[1] I expressed $105.00 home, John D. Moore sending some with mine. The boys of Company E settled for their year's clothing. The furloughed men started for their homes this evening.

Friday, 23d—The Thirteenth Iowa received their pay today. A great many of the boys expressed their money home.

Saturday, 24th—Weather pleasant. The Fifteenth Iowa received their pay today. I received a pass, and in charge of four boys of the company spent the day in Louisville. The city is patrolled by large numbers of provost guards and I had to carry my pass in hand all the time. I bought some clothes and several articles to take home. My bill came to $26.40, as I spent $8.50 for a pair of pants, $9.00 for a jacket, and $3.75 for an album, besides other articles.

Sunday, 25th—Rain this afternoon. We had company inspection this morning and dress parade at 5 o'clock this afternoon. The paymaster finished paying the Fifteenth Iowa and then paid part of the Sixteenth Iowa.

Monday, 26th—Quite sultry today. They finished paying the Sixteenth Iowa. Money is quite plentiful, as the veterans received more than $200.00 each. General W. W. Belknap went home on leave of absence and Brig. Gen. B. F. Pitts is in command of our division.

Tuesday, 27th—Quite sultry today. Nothing of any importance.

Wednesday, 28th—We still have brigade guard. There is a great deal of dissatisfaction in the veteran ranks on account of their not having been discharged yet. The Indiana troops are finding the most fault, as they can almost see their homes just across the Ohio river, but dare not cross over. They have been making an effort through the Louisville papers to get General Sherman to

---

[1] When a soldier did not draw all the clothing the Government allowed him, he was allowed the money instead. Sergeants were allowed more than privates, receiving $20 per month.—A. G. D.

tell them why they are not being discharged. Sherman answered them also through the press, assuring them that the Government will discharge them just as soon as it can get to them.

Thursday, 29th—I am on brigade guard again, being sergeant of the guard. Each day we have on guard from our brigade two commissioned officers, three sergeants, six corporals, and one hundred and thirty-eight privates. One of the commissioned officers, a captain, is officer of the day for the brigade, while the other, a lieutenant, is officer of the day for the regiment. We have to wear our white gloves on guard.

Friday, 30th—The weather is sultry. Nothing of importance today.

JULY, 1865.

Saturday, 1st—The weather is quite hot and sultry. We are looking forward to going home soon, and expect to receive such an order any time, though we have not yet heard of one having been issued.

Sunday, 2d—Things are working fine. Company inspection this afternoon. On account of the heat, the men remained in their "ranches" until time for dress parade at 5 o'clock in the evening. We cannot go to the city to attend church without a pass, since there is a brigade guard around the brigade.

Monday, 3d—Reveille sounded at 1 a. m. for the Iowa Brigade, and at 2 o'clock we started for the city, marching down to the wharf for the purpose of escorting General Sherman from the landing to the residence of Mr. Osborne, the editor of the Louisville Journal. The general looks fine; he never looked better to us boys.

Tuesday, 4th—General Sherman reviewed the Army of the Tennessee today for the last time, our division passing in review at 9 a. m. He made a short speech—a farewell address—to all the troops. He told us that we had been good soldiers, and now that the war is over and the country united once more, we should go home, and as we had been true soldiers, we should become good citizens. This is a rather dull Fourth. I stayed in camp the rest of the day after the review, but in the evening I went down town to a theater—Wood's theater—for the first time in my life.

For a while today there was a lively time in camp when a lot of the boys tried to break through the guard line. When they failed at that, they next made a raid on the sutlers, who have been doing a big business since our arrival at Louisville. Before the officer of the day could get guards to the sutlers' tents, the boys had secured a considerable amount of booty.

Wednesday, 5th—An order from the War Department came today, ordering the mustering out of all the soldiers of the Army of the Tennessee. All is quiet.

Thursday, 6th—It is hot and sultry, but as our duty is light we can stay in our "ranches" and keep out of the hot sun. All are happy at the thought of going home soon.

Friday, 7th—Our officers have commenced to make out the discharge papers and the muster rolls. The blanks came this morning and the officers of each company have expert penmen at work filling them out.

Saturday, 8th—Captain Spencer returned to our company today. He is in ill health and it is supposed that he has consumption. He is a fine officer, tall, and as straight as an arrow. He is kind to his men at all times, on or off duty. We still have dress parade every evening.

Sunday, 9th—It rained all day and all of us not on guard remained in our "ranches." Our camp is on rolling ground and so the water runs off quickly. In this camp we have no bunks built up from the ground, for there was no tearing down of houses to get timbers, but we have straw on which to lay our ponchos. For a roof we have a pole resting on two forks, with four rubber ponchos stretched over the pole and the ends fastened to the ground.

Monday, 10th—The men of the Fifteenth and Seventeenth Army Corps are raising a subscription for the purpose of erecting a monument in memory of the lamented Gen. James B. McPherson,[1] the old commander of the two corps, who was killed in the battle of Atlanta on the 22d day of July, 1864. I gave $5.00 myself, the whole company raising $75.00.

[1] Major-General McPherson was a noble man, a Christian gentleman, kind to the officers and men in his command, and the men of his two corps placed him equal to any of the generals in the army, East or West.—A. G. D.

(July, 1865)

Tuesday, 11th—Troops are leaving daily for their homes. The boys are all active in getting everything squared up with one another before leaving for their homes. We get passes to the city as often as we can, to buy things we want before leaving the army for good. The boys are getting small photo gems taken to exchange with one another; I have already received over sixty in exchange.

Wednesday, 12th—Very pleasant weather. Our regimental muster-out rolls are almost ready.

Thursday, 13th—I was on camp guard this morning, detailed as sergeant of the brigade guard. This thing of camp guard is about played out, and I suppose it is my last.[1] The guard house or tent has become so dirty that the men on that relief do not want to stay there while not on their beats. I took their names this morning and allowed them to go back to their own tents.

Friday, 14th—I had a time getting the men out this morning when starting around the brigade to relieve the second relief, some refusing to come out of their tents. I finally started with what guards I had, and when I came to a guard for whom I had no man as relief, I told him to fall in behind and go to the guard tent, thus leaving his beat vacant. After I had made the round, I went to the tents of the absentees and ordered them out, each to his own beat number, adding that if they refused I would have them arrested and put in the guardhouse. I went to one chap's tent the third and last time, and I tell you he did some lively stepping to reach his beat. He was a member of the Sixteenth Iowa. Our muster rolls and discharge papers were all finished to-day and the accounts with the regimental quartermaster were all squared up; everything has now been inspected and reported ready for mustering out. All the property belonging to the quartermaster will be turned over to him tomorrow morning. Some of the boys in the regiment have bought their Springfield rifles of the Government, paying $7.00 for them. I bought my rifle, as did more than half of the boys of Company E. These are the rifles we received at Cairo, Illinois, in May, 1864. We are entitled to our knapsacks, haversacks and canteens, and of course are taking them with us.

[1] This proved to be the last time that we were on duty of any kind.—A. G. D.

(July, 1865)

Saturday, 15th—Our regiment, the Eleventh Iowa Veteran Volunteers, was mustered out this morning at 9 o'clock. We were relieved from all duty and turned over to the general quartermaster the regimental teams and everything that does not belong to the individual officers or men. The papers for the rest of the brigade have not yet been made out.

Sunday, 16th—It rained all day, and having no duty of any kind, we remained in our "ranches." We had no services of any kind today, but as we had our last dress parade, and as this is our last Sunday in camp, we should have had some minister come out from the city for our last religious services in camp.

Monday, 17th—We had our last reveille early this morning. We took down our rubber ponchos, packed our knapsacks, and at 5 o'clock started for the boat landing, where we took the ferry for New Albany, Indiana, crossing the river below Louisville. On our way up the river we passed the headquarters of Generals Logan and Belknap, and each delivered a short speech to us. At New Albany we took the train for Michigan City, leaving at 10 o'clock. We had fairly good passenger cars, but the train was a slow one, as it often had to switch onto sidings to let other trains pass.

Tuesday, 18th—We are still pushing on towards home and everything is all right. Our train ran all night, except when standing on some sidetrack. We arrived at Michigan City a little after dark and changed cars for Chicago.

Wednesday, 19th—Our night along the lake shore was quite cool. We arrived in Chicago this morning at 2 o'clock, and then marched to the Rock Island station, where at 8 o'clock we took train for Davenport, Iowa. We arrived at Davenport at 5 p. m. A large crowd of citizens was at the station to receive us, among them our old colonel, William Hall, who gave us an address of welcome.[1] Although he was suffering from sickness, he came to welcome us, and as he could not stand on a platform, he remained in his carriage to address us. We then marched up to old Camp McClellan, where we shall remain till we get our discharge and

[1] "I cannot stand long enough to make a speech, I can only say to the citizens of Davenport, in response to the warm and generous welcome that they have extended to my comrades of the Eleventh Iowa, and myself, that the record we have made as good soldiers from the State of Iowa, while fighting in defense of our common country, will be duplicated by the record we shall make as good citizens, when we shall have returned to homes and loved ones."—Roster Iowa Soldiers II, p. 282.

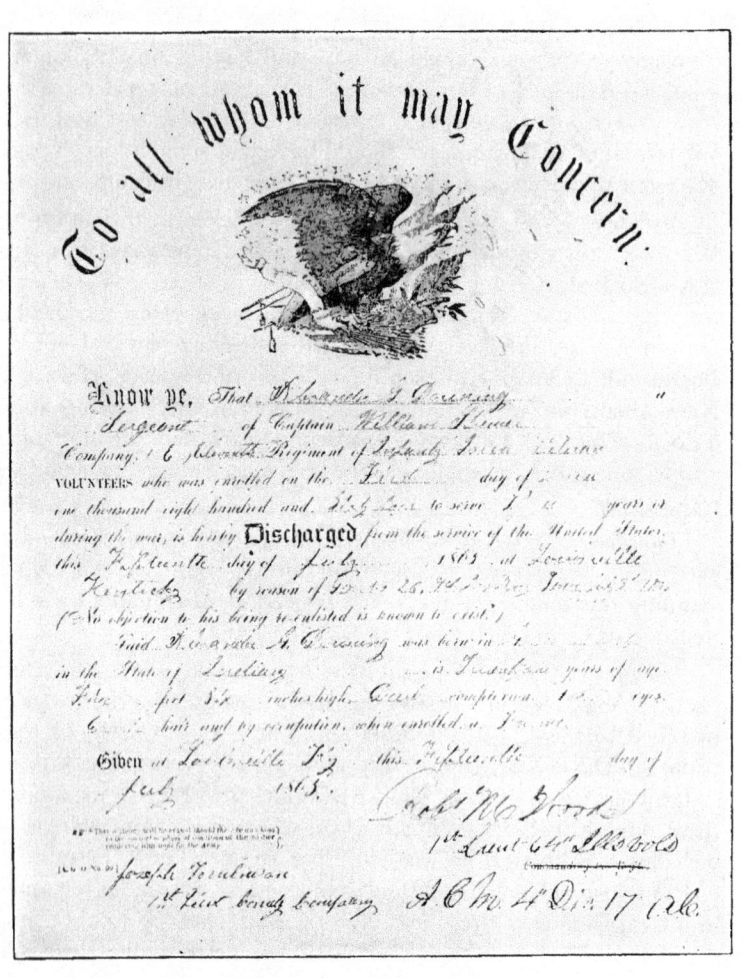

FACSIMILE OF SERGEANT DOWNING'S DISCHARGE CERTIFICATE.
ISSUED AT LOUISVILLE, KENTUCKY, JULY 15, 1865.

pay, which we expect in two or three days. The Second and Seventh Iowa have just received their pay and are striking out for home.

Thursday, 20th—We remained in camp all day. No pay yet.

Friday, 21st—It rained all day. No pay yet. Most of the boys are staying down in town. There is nothing of importance.

Saturday, 22d—Weather quite pleasant today. Our regiment was paid off this afternoon, and we received our discharge. This makes us free men again and we at once left Camp McClellan for town. I went to the Davis House and stopped for the night. Mr. Hatch came to Davenport for a load of us.

I bought some clothing this afternoon, the first citizen's suit which I was permitted to wear in four long years. I also bought a good watch for $50.00, which with my clothing, $41.50, amounted to $91.50.

The Sixteenth Iowa arrived this morning from Louisville, Kentucky. The men of our brigade, on being discharged, seem to be scattering to the four ends of the earth; even the boys of Company E, after bidding one another farewell, are going in all directions.

Sunday, 23d—I started for home, thirty miles distant, with Abner Hatch, who had come down from our neighborhood with a team for the purpose of taking a load of the boys home. We left Davenport at 7:30 o'clock this morning and I reached home at 5 p. m. I found my folks all well. I am at home this time never to go to war again. It was a fine day for a ride in Iowa; it had rained yesterday, and though it was somewhat cloudy, the prairies never looked so nice and green as they did today.

Monday, 24th—It rained all day. I remained at home and brought my diary up to date.

Tuesday, 25th—I went into the harvest field and worked all day at binding wheat.

Wednesday, 26th—Working in the harvest field is making me quite sore, as it is the first of the kind I have done in the last four years.

Thursday, 27th—It is the same thing and nothing of importance.

Friday, 28th—I went out to Tipton today, and in the evening had a fine visit with Miss ————.

Saturday, 29th—Home again from my visits. I have worked three full days now in the harvest field.

Sunday, 30th—I went to church this morning and in the evening went to visit friends, old and new.

Monday, 31st—Today I again went out into the harvest field.

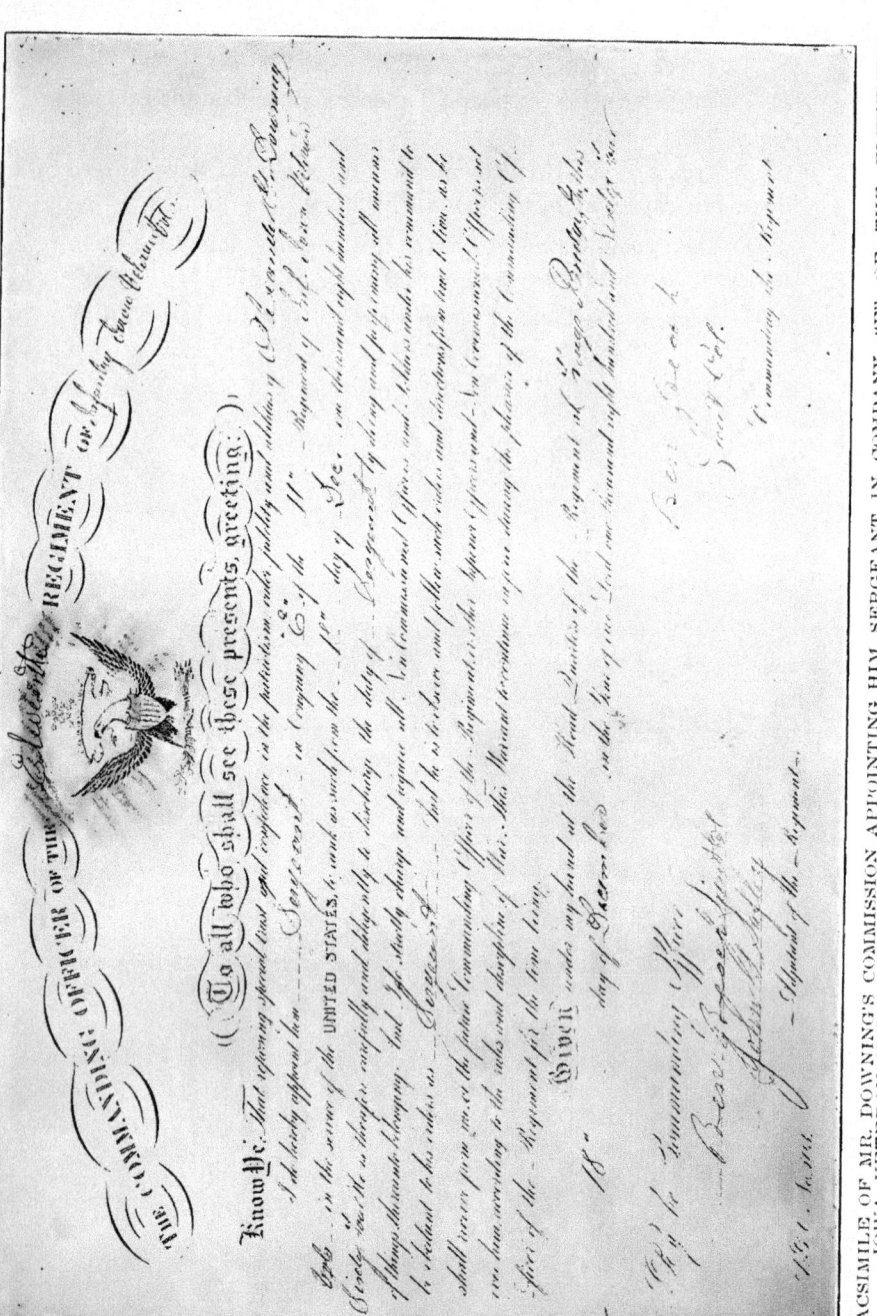

FACSIMILE OF MR. DOWNING'S COMMISSION APPOINTING HIM SERGEANT IN COMPANY "E" OF THE ELEVENTH IOWA VETERAN VOLUNTEERS. THE APPOINTMENT WAS MADE DURING THE SIEGE OF SAVANNAH, AND IS DATED DECEMBER 18, 1864, AT KING'S BRIDGE, GEORGIA.

APPENDIX

AUTOBIOGRAPHY OF ALEXANDER G. DOWNING.

I first saw daylight early on Monday morning, the 15th day of August, 1842, in a log house of one room, on the northeast corner of block 14, in the town of Bloomfield, Green county, Indiana. My father at that time had a small tanyard on said block of land, but had to give up the tanning business finally, on account of quicksand in the well from which he drew the water to fill his tanning vats. My father and his twin brother came from West Virginia[1] in their boyhood days and located at Salem, Indiana. While living there they learned the tanner's trade. Their father, my grandfather, came from Ireland when a young lad and later served his adopted country in the Revolutionary War. After the war he settled in Virginia. My mother was from North Carolina and was of English ancestry. She died when I was almost two years old, and my only sister died six months later. In 1846 my father married again and moved upon an eighty-acre farm two miles east of Bloomfield, which became the first family homestead. There my five half-brothers were born. Our combined ages are, on this 14th day of June, 1914, 396 years, while our combined time in Iowa is three hundred and sixty years.

I attended school two summers, during the last two years we lived in Indiana. It was in a log schoolhouse, located in heavy timber. It had no floor, nor even a window, though there was a small hole in one side of the building to give light when the door was shut. The door was made of split staves, and hung by wooden hinges; the accustomed latch-string was on the outside. There was not a nail in the entire building. I attended my first Sunday School at this schoolhouse, my cousin being the superintendent. He gave me a Sunday School book, the reading of which at that time of my boyhood days has guided me to this day in living the better life.

In May, 1854, father pulled up stakes and left for Iowa. We had one team of horses and three yoke of oxen, with two wagons loaded with the family bedding, clothes and utensils, besides

[1] Then western Virginia.—Ed.

enough dried fruit to last two years. We also took along a small herd of young cows and heifers.

It was my lot to drive those cattle. I was in my twelfth year and with the one hired man walked the whole way, driving the herd. I had just received from my uncle a new pair of boots for the journey; but those boots almost proved my undoing. My uncle had bought our eighty-acre farm, upon which was a ten-acre field of fall wheat, having been sown in the standing corn. He told me that if I would cut the stalks he would buy me a new pair of boots for our journey. That spring I went at the job with father's old iron hoe, which had a dogwood handle, and whacked down that ten acres of cornstalks, earning my boots. On our way to Iowa we encountered so much rain and water that the boots became so shrunken and stiff I could scarcely get them on and off; I had to leave them on for days at a time. The result was that my feet became very sore and calloused, and to this day I have a callous place on the bottom of one foot caused by the pegs in those boots.

We crossed the Mississippi river at Davenport, Iowa, on Sunday morning, June 11, 1854. It was a hot, foggy morning, but soon clouded over and by the next day we had to travel in a cold, all day, northeastern rainstorm. In all we were on the road twenty-two days, and we had rain at some time during the day for eighteen of those days.

Father had come to Iowa in the fall of 1852 and had entered two hundred and forty acres of land eight miles east of Tipton, the county seat of Cedar county. After he had the land surveyed he bought forty acres more, of timber land, four miles distant. Here he cut forks and poles for the frame and then went to Davenport for the lumber with which to build our shanty to live in during the summer. Davenport was thirty miles distant, and it took him three days with an ox team to make the trip.

In the latter part of the summer I had to drive the three yoke of oxen hitched to a breaking plow while the hired man held the plow handles, to break twenty acres of prairie. The grass and blue stem were so high and always so wet that I never thought of being dry until in the afternoon. There were so many rattle-snakes that I had to wear those "store" boots all that summer, to protect my feet. While the hired man and I were breaking prairie, father was building our house, a one and one-fourth story building, into which we moved some time in November. He also built a sod stable, covering it with slough grass. Besides this, he with the help of two hired men cut and stacked about sixty tons of the blue stem for hay. We built a rail fence around the stacks and then during the winter, we threw the hay over the fence to feed the cattle.

The two hired men we had were both from Indiana and late in the fall they went back, as they were afraid of freezing to death in Iowa. Our first winter, though, was not bad; in fact, it was one of the finest winters I have ever seen in Iowa, and I have now (1914) seen sixty of them in the State. The nearest schoolhouse was four miles away and overcrowded at that, so I received no schooling that winter. Father would go to the timber every day with Ben and Head, a faithful yoke of oxen, to make rails and posts, bringing home a load at night. He would reach the timber usually by daylight and very often would not get home till long after dark. I thus, with some help from my younger brothers, had to do the chores, cut the stove wood, and carry it into the house. The fine, dry winter was a great blessing to father, as he had to work every day in getting out the material with which to fence the farm the next spring.

That spring, 1855, we put in a crop on the twenty acres which we broke the summer before, sowing twelve acres to wheat and planting eight acres to corn. It was my task to harrow and smooth down that tough sod. Father had made a forty-tooth, "A-harrow," and with Ben and Head hitched to it, I harrowed that twenty-acre field over and over. It seemed as if I walked several thousand miles in getting the twelve acres of wheat covered. Father had told me to lap the harrow about one-half each time, and in my anxiety to do so I kept calling whoa-haw to the oxen almost continuously. One day father said to me, "Bud" (for that was my nickname then), "if I had a dollar for every time you said whoa-haw, I could retire for life a rich man."

After putting in the wheat I helped father fence in sixty acres of land with a two-rail fence, building in all one mile and sixty rods of fence. I dug the post holes and father set the posts, and then nailed on the rails while I held them in place.

The old stage road from Davenport to Cedar Rapids ran across our farm right where we had fenced it in, but the stage route had not yet been changed. One day the stage from Davenport, heavily loaded with passengers, came through and the driver, following the old road, drove right up to the new fence to find his way blocked; and in place of following the new road about twenty rods up around the corner, he with the help of some of his passengers was going to tear down the fence. Father was at work a short distance away and seeing the move they were making, simply called out to them to be careful what they were doing. That settled the matter; the driver uttered a few "damns" and then went up the new road around the corner. The first railroad engine had just entered Iowa, having been brought across the Mississippi river on the ice by the piece and then put together at Davenport. Soon thereafter the old stage route was abandoned altogether.

At that time there were few houses to be seen on all that vast prairie. From our home we could count but four or five small homes, and we could see for miles in all directions without anything to break the view. It was a mile to our nearest neighbor.

That summer father cut our first crop of wheat in Iowa with a cradle. I raked the swathes into bundles with a hand rake, while the hired man bound them into sheaves. In the fall before father had broken up a large hazel patch for a garden, and I planted a part of it in watermelons. They did well, and late in the season I sold in all $6.00 worth of melons to the "movers" going west on the old territorial road which was now turned to run close by our house. I counted that $6.00 over a great many times, and each dollar then looked as big as a base drum head does today. But alas! The six silver dollars went to a local shoemaker for making six pairs of cowhide shoes for us six boys, and that was the last I saw of the $6.00.

Our second winter in Iowa was spent in the same way as the first. There was no schoolhouse near, and for the second time I got no winter's schooling. Instead, I remained at home to do chores and "smash up" the stove wood. Father again went to the timber every day with the same yoke of oxen to make a load of rails, or posts, or to cut a load of firewood, as occasion required.

During the summer of 1856 we farmed on a larger scale than the year before, and we bought a reaper to cut our grain. Then came the cold winter of '56 and '57, with six to eight feet of snow on the level. This "winter of the deep snow" was followed by the "wet summer of '57." Our wheat crop was so badly blighted that we took none of it to mill. We had to use old wheat for food as well as for seed the following spring. The years of 1858 and 1859 were uneventful years. The times were hard, money was very scarce, and what little there was to be had was wild-cat money in the bargain.

The year of 1860 was another rather dull year, though in the late summer the political excitement ran high, the main topic being the South and slavery. I united with the church in November, 1860, becoming a member of the Disciples' Church.

In 1861 there was no improvement over the past three years, and the finest wheat ever grown would not bring over thirty cents a bushel, while corn was only ten cents a bushel. That spring the Civil War broke out, and after I helped father through with the harvest, I enlisted in the army and was away from home in the war for four long years. While in the army I participated in thirty-eight battles and skirmishes, and was mustered out in July, 1865.

When I came home from the war, I helped finish the harvest and then in the fall worked with a threshing outfit. I went through the winter without any occupation and then in the spring of 1866 I decided to put in a crop. I farmed eighty acres and cleared above all expenses $600.00 in six months.

In the fall of 1866 I thought that my occupation for life should be that of a merchant and decided to go into business. I went to London, Iowa, and bought an interest in a general store. After six months of experience I found out that merchandising was not my calling and sold out, losing in the whole transaction $1,200.00, or $200.00 per month. I decided then to make farming my calling and in the spring of 1867 broke up one hundred and twenty acres of prairie. I bought the best team of horses I could find, paying $400.00 cash for them, and went to breaking prairie.

On the 9th of May, 1867, I was married to Miss Mary E. Stanton, daughter of J. W. Stanton, a prosperous farmer of my home neighborhood. In 1868 we built a house on York Prairie, two miles north of Bennett, Iowa. Here for a period of seventeen years, I was engaged in general farming and stock raising. My father died in 1877 and I settled up his estate, which was worth about $50,000.00. He owned over five hundred acres of land, all well improved, besides a large amount of personal property. In 1881 I built one of the largest barns in Cedar county at that time, requiring over one hundred thousand feet of lumber. It would stable one hundred head of cattle, had bins to hold five thousand bushels of grain, and the hayloft would hold one hundred tons of hay. In the fall of 1885 I sold my farm of two hundred acres and bought a badly run down farm of one hundred and sixty acres. My old farm was all in grass, and at my sale in September of that year I sold over one hundred head of cattle, high-grade Durhams. I rented out the new farm I had bought for a term of ten years and quit farming for good.

Being somewhat broken in health, we moved to Colfax, Iowa, that same year for the benefit of my health. We remained there until the 1st of March, 1887, when we moved to Des Moines, Iowa, where we have made our home ever since. Having no living children we decided to endow a medical chair in Drake University and gave for that purpose $25,000.00. Later we gave $5,000.00 to the Medical Library of the University, and since have given $2,000.00 to establish the Downing Prizes in Drake University.

> Signed this 11th day of June, 1914, by Alexander G. Downing, in his seventy-second year and his sixtieth year in the State of Iowa.

SOME OBSERVATIONS.
By A. G. D.

BROTHERS IN COMPANY E.

Twelve families are represented in Company E by two brothers each, and one by three brothers. John W. and Samuel Albin—John W. slightly wounded June 15, 1864, on the skirmish line on Noon-day creek, Kenesaw Mountain in Georgia. Robert and William Alexander—William killed on the skirmish line June 15, 1864, on Noon-day creek at the foot of a spur of Kenesaw Mountain. John M. and Sylvester Daniels—John M. received a wound on one hand at Shiloh April 6, 1862, and was discharged for disability on October 13, 1862. John W. and William Dwiggans—William died of typhoid fever December 28, 1861, and John W. died from wounds received at Shiloh May 7, 1862. John W. and William Esher—John W. was severely wounded June 25, 1864, at Kenesaw Mountain and discharged for disability March 20, 1865. Allen and Carlton Frink—Carlton killed at Shiloh April 6, 1862. Dean and John Ford—John had his right thumb shot off at Vicksburg and then slightly wounded on the skirmish line June 15, 1864, on Noon-day creek, Kenesaw Mountain. Ezra and Samuel McLoney—Ezra killed at Shiloh April 6, 1862. Francis and Reuben Niese—Reuben died March 2, 1865, in McDougal's Hospital near New York City. Ebenezer and James Rankin. Burtis H. and James K. Rumsey—James K. died at Chattanooga, Tennessee, February 2, 1865. George W. and Wilson Simmons—George W. wounded at Shiloh April 6, 1862, and died of his wounds May 12, 1862; Wilson died of lung fever April 15, 1862. Daniel, George and Henry Sweet—George killed in battle July 22, 1864, near Atlanta, Georgia; Henry L. died of fever in the Division Hospital in Tennessee, May 4, 1862.

CASUALTIES IN COMPANY E.

Killed in action, 11. Died of wounds, 4. Died of disease, 14. Discharged for disability, 15. Taken prisoners, 6. Deserters, 4.

Absent on account of sickness for short periods, 32. Absent on account of slight wounds, 31. Total casualties, 117, or a fraction over 82 per cent of the 142 men in the company during the four years' service. There were those who were sick and marked not fit for duty, yet who did not leave the company, and there were others slightly wounded who likewise did not leave the company. Then, there were those, who for the same causes, had to go to the hospitals and be absent from the company for weeks at a time. The regimental surgeon would examine all cases, and it was left to his decision as to what a man had to do.

CROCKER'S IOWA BRIGADE.

Crocker's Iowa Brigade was composed of the Eleventh, Thirteenth, Fifteenth and Sixteenth Infantry Regiments. The regiments enlisted in the months of September and October, 1861, and were organized into a brigade April 27, 1862. There were in all 6289 enlisted men in the brigade.

The regiments had the following numbers, rank and file:

    Eleventh,   1297   Fifteenth, 1767
    Thirteenth, 1788   Sixteenth, 1441

The record of re-enlistments in the different regiments at Vicksburg, Mississippi, January, 1864, is as follows:

    Eleventh,   420   Fifteenth, 440
    Thirteenth, 450   Sixteenth, 415

The casualties numbered 4773, or seventy-six per cent of the strength of the brigade. The record of the officers and men who died during the war is as follows:

	Killed in battle	Wounded	Died of wounds and disease	Total dead
Eleventh	90	234	148	238
Thirteenth	117	313	176	293
Fifteenth	140	416	231	371
Sixteenth	101	311	217	318
	448	1274	772	1220

The miles traveled in marching during the war are, by years:

	By land	By boat and railroad
1862	495	581
1863	470	651
1864	1979	1660
1865 (to July 24)	1622	440

This makes a total of 4566 miles traveled by land and 3332 miles by boat and railroad, with a grand total of 7898 miles.

BATTLES ENGAGED IN BY CROCKER'S BRIGADE.

1862.

Shiloh, Tenn., April 6th.
Advance on Corinth, Miss., April 28th to May 30th.
Iuka, Miss., September 19th, 20th.
Corinth, Miss., October 3d, 4th.
Waterford, Miss., November 29th.

1863.

Lafayette, Tenn., January 2d.
Richmond, La., January 30th.
Siege of Vicksburg, May 20th to July 4th.
Oakridgetown, La., August 27th.
Monroe, La., August 29th.

1864.

Meridian, Miss., February 24th.
Big Shanty, Ga., June 10th.
Noon-Day Creek, Ga., June 15th.
Brushy Mountain, Ga., June 19th.
Kenesaw Mountain, Ga., June 27th to July 1st.
Second Advance on Nick-a-Jack Creek, Ga., July 3d, 4th, 5th.
Advance on Atlanta, Ga., July 20th.
Charge on Bald Hill, Ga., July 21st.
Battle of Atlanta, Ga., July 22d.
Ezra Church, Ga., July 28th.
Advance on Atlanta, Ga., August 3d.
Before Atlanta, Ga., August 3d to August 16th.
Atlanta & Montgomery R. R., Ga., August 28th.
Jonesboro, Ga., August 31st to September 1st.

Flynt Creek, Ga., September 1st.
Lovejoy Station, Ga., September 2d.
Fairburn, Ga., October 2d.
Snake Creek Gap, Ga., October 15th.
Savannah, Ga., December 10th to 21st.

The battles from June to September are known as the Siege of Atlanta. During this period of eighty-seven days Crocker's Brigade was under fire eighty-one days.

1865.

Garden Corners, S. C., January 14th.
River Bridge, Salkahatchie Swamp, S. C., February 2d.
Big Salkahatchie Swamp, S. C., February 3d.
North Edisto River, S C., February 9th.
Columbia, S. C., March 3d.
Fayetteville, N. C., March 11th.
Bentonville, N. C., March 20th, 21st.
Raleigh, N. C., April 13th.

INTEMPERANCE IN THE ARMY.

Intemperance in the army during the war was the cause of much disturbance, and, to the men using intoxicating liquors, it was a curse. Men who were good men when sober, became, when intoxicated, regular demons. There were more men ordered bucked and gagged by officers for drunkenness than any other cause, and that just for the reason that a drunk man will talk or fight.

The only trouble I had with any of the boys in my company was at Louisville, Kentucky, just before we were mustered out. One of the boys came back to camp from the city so drunk that he could hardly walk. I was out in front of my "ranch," cleaning my rifle and accouterments, and, as I was the first man he happened to see upon his return, he was ready for a fight at once. I, of course, kept out of his way and soon a number of other boys came out, captured him, took him to his "ranch" and tied him to a post. There he remained till he "cooled off."

HARDSHIPS OF WAR.

Some people think that being in a battle is all there is to war. While experience in battle is a dreadful thing, it is by no means the only hardship in war. Here are some of the hardships and dangers aside from being under fire: in a field hospital; suffering from wounds or from any of the many diseases to which a soldier is subject; on long marches, sometimes for days and even nights at a time, or on picket line for a day and a night without sleep; in rain or snow, and that without protection, or perhaps in digging trenches all night for protection the next day, or in remaining in the rifle pits for days and nights at a time, and in addition, drinking stagnant water, thus causing fevers; then for days and weeks at work, building heavy fortifications, and besides all at times on short rations, when an ear of corn would be a Godsend—these are some of the many hardships. But above all things, starving to death in a Southern prison required more courage than going into any battle fought during the Civil war.

MY PAY FROM THE GOVERNMENT.

While in the army, I received as my pay, $700.00, as bounty money, $500.00, and for clothing, $40.00, making a total of $1,240.00. Besides this I received from the State of Iowa, $24.00.

Privates received $13.00 per month to May 1, 1864, after which time they received $16.00. Sergeants received $22.00 per month.

ROLL OF CO. E.

JOHN W. ALBIN—Age, 18; residence, Newport; nativity, Iowa; enlisted, March 7, 1864; mustered, March 7, 1864; private; wounded, June 15, 1864; mustered out, July 15, 1865.

SAMUEL ALBIN—Age, 18; residence Linn county; nativity, Iowa; enlisted, April 9, 1864; mustered, April 11, 1864; private; mustered out, July 15, 1865.

ROBERT ALEXANDER—Age, 22; residence, Tipton; nativity, Ireland; enlisted, September 2, 1862; mustered, September 12, 1862; private; mustered out, June 2, 1865.

WILLIAM ALEXANDER—Age 22; residence, Tipton; nativity, Ireland; enlisted, September 21, 1861; mustered, October 5, 1861; veteran; reenlisted, January 25, 1864; private; killed in battle, June 15, 1864.

ALBERT ALLEE—Age, 18; residence, Tipton; nativity, Indiana; enlisted, September 21, 1861; mustered, October 5, 1861; private; wounded, June 21, 1864; mustered out expiration of term, October 17, 1864.

JEREMIAH A. ARGO—Age, 18; residence, Springfield; nativity, Ohio; enlisted, April 20, 1864; mustered, April 20, 1864; private; mustered out, July 15, 1865.

THOMAS ARMSTRONG—Age, 18; residence, Tipton; nativity, Pennsylvania; enlisted, September 23, 1861; mustered, October 5, 1861; veteran; reenlisted January 1, 1864; private; mustered out, July 15, 1865.

JOHN L. AYERS—Age, 21; residence, Mechanicsville; nativity, Ohio; enlisted, October 10, 1861; mustered, October 5, 1861; private; mustered out expiration of term, October 17, 1864.

SAMUEL BAIN—Age, 21; residence, Cedar Bluff; nativity, Ohio; enlisted, September 28, 1861; mustered, October 5, 1861; veteran; reenlisted, January 1, 1864; private; mustered out, July 15, 1865.

EGBERT BANKS—Age, 25; residence, Davenport; nativity, New York; enlisted, October 6, 1864; mustered, October 6, 1864; private; mustered out, July 15, 1865.

CORYDON BARKER—Age, 28; residence, Grinnell; nativity, Kentucky; enlisted, September 23, 1864; mustered, September 23, 1864; private; discharged for disabilities, May 10, 1865.

WILLIAM BARRETT—Age, 20; residence, Cambridge; nativity, Maine; enlisted, September 13, 1861; mustered, October 5, 1861; veteran; reenlisted, January 1, 1864; private; 4th Corporal January 1, 1865; mustered out, July 15, 1865.

FRED BARTIMER—Age, 19; residence, Davenport; nativity, Germany; enlisted, October 3, 1864; mustered, October 4, 1864; private; mustered out, July 15, 1865.

JOHN R. or W. BATDERF—Age, 30; residence, Tipton; nativity, Pennsylvania; enlisted, September 14, 1861; mustered, October 5, 1861; private; 4th Corporal December 12, 1861; discharged for disabilities, July 25, 1862.

GEORGE BERRIMAN—Age, 21; residence, Tipton; nativity, Ohio; enlisted, September 9, 1861; mustered, October 5, 1861; veteran; reenlisted, January 1, 1864; private; mustered out, July 15, 1865.

MONROE S. BLAZER—Age, 21; residence, Springfield; nativity, Virginia; enlisted, March 2, 1864; mustered, March 2, 1864; private; mustered out, July 15, 1865.

JOHN W. BOLTON—Age, 18; residence, Tipton; nativity, Iowa; enlisted, September 21, 1861; mustered, October 5, 1861; private; promoted, 4th Corporal September 10, 1862; discharged for disabilities, March 9, 1863.

BENJAMIN BOSSERT—Age, 18; residence, Tipton; nativity, Pennsylvania; enlisted, October 1, 1861; mustered, October 5, 1861; veteran; reenlisted, January 1, 1864; private; mustered out, July 15, 1865.

PETER R. BRADSHAW—Age, 19; residence, Tipton, nativity, Iowa; enlisted, September 28, 1861; mustered, October 5, 1861; reenlisted, January 1, 1864; private; mustered out, July 15, 1865.

ANDREW BRIDGER—Age, 24; residence, Tipton; nativity, West Virginia; enlisted, March 3, 1864; mustered, March 3, 1864; private; discharged for disabilities, May 26, 1865.

ABRAHAM BROWN—Age, 34; residence, Tipton; nativity, Pennsylvania; enlisted, October 1, 1861; mustered October 5, 1861; private; promoted, wagoner; died of disease, January 2, 1864.

ASA S. BRUNSON—Age, 33; residence, Tipton; nativity, Ohio; enlisted, September 30, 1861; mustered, October 5, 1861; veteran; reenlisted, January 1, 1864; private; wounded, September 5, 1864; mustered out, July 15, 1865.

WILLIAM H. BUCK—Age, 25; residence, Davenport; nativity, Ohio; enlisted, October 7, 1864; mustered, October 7, 1864; private; mustered out, July 15, 1865.

JOHN R. BUCKMAN—Age, 18; residence, Le Claire; nativity, Illinois; enlisted, August 26, 1861; mustered, October 15, 1861; private; killed in battle, April 6, 1862.

HENRY L. CANFIELD—Age, 22; residence, Davenport; nativity, Indiana; enlisted, September 28, 1864; mustered, September 28, 1864; private; mustered out, June 2, 1865.

ALFRED CAREY—Age, 25; residence, Tipton; nativity, New York; enlisted, August 20, 1861; mustered, October 5, 1861; office, 3d Sergeant; 2d Lieutenant April 7, 1862; 1st Lieutenant October 1, 1862; wounded, June 15, 1864; died of wounds, July 25, 1864.

WASHINGTON CARL—Age, 23; residence, Tipton; nativity, Iowa; enlisted September 28, 1861; mustered, October 5, 1861; veteran; reenlisted, January 1, 1864; private; mustered out, July 15, 1865.

NATHAN CHASE—Age, 18; residence, Tipton; nativity, Illinois; enlisted, September 16, 1861; mustered, October 5, 1861; veteran; reenlisted, January 1, 1864; private; mustered out, July 15, 1865.

WILLIAM CHOWIN—Age, 39; residence, Davenport; nativity, England; enlisted, October 7, 1864; mustered, October 7, 1864; private; mustered out, July 15, 1865.

ELMORE CHRISMAN—Age, 25; residence, Tipton; nativity, Ohio; enlisted, September 28, 1861; mustered, October 5, 1861; private; wounded, April 6, 1862; discharged for disabilities, December 2, 1862.

MAJOR CHRISTMAS—Age, 38; residence, Tipton; nativity, England; enlisted, September 20, 1861; mustered, October 5, 1861; veteran; reenlisted, January 1, 1864; private; mustered out, July 15, 1865.

JOEL H. CLARK—Age, 24; residence, Ireland; nativity, New York; enlisted, August 20, 1861; mustered, October 5, 1861; 1st Sergeant; transferred, Inv. Corps March 15, 1864; no record.

JOHN F. COMPTON—Age, 36; residence, Ireland; nativity, England; enlisted, October 5, 1861; mustered, October 5, 1861; 1st Lieutenant October 5, 1861; killed in battle, April 6, 1862.

DWIGHT D. COMSTOCK—Age, 36; residence, Davenport; nativity, New York; enlisted, September 21, 1864; mustered, September 21, 1864; private; mustered out, June 2, 1865.

CHARLES CORRELL—Age, 20; residence, Davenport; nativity, Ohio; enlisted, September 28, 1864; mustered, September 28, 1864; private; mustered out, June 2, 1865.

GEORGE CROAK—Age, 20; residence, Le Claire; nativity, Pennsylvania; enlisted, August 26, 1861; mustered, October 5, 1861; private; killed in battle, April 6, 1862.

WILLIAM CROSS—Age, 25; residence, Tipton; nativity, New York; enlisted, September 20, 1861; mustered, October 5, 1861; private; killed in battle, July 5, 1864.

ORRIN CULVER—Age, 26; residence, Grinnell; nativity, Ohio; enlisted, September 23, 1864; mustered, September 23, 1864; private; mustered out, June 2, 1865.

GEORGE CUSH—Age, 25; residence, Cedar Rapids; nativity, Germany; enlisted, August 20, 1861; mustered, October 5, 1861; veteran; reenlisted, January 1, 1864; private; mustered out, July 15, 1865.

JOHN M. DANIELS—Age, 26; residence, Tipton; nativity, New York; enlisted, September 24, 1861; mustered, October 5, 1861; 1st Corporal; discharged for disabilities, October 13, 1862.

SYLVESTER DANIELS—Age, 33; residence, Inland; nativity, New York; enlisted, August 20, 1861; mustered, October 5, 1861; veteran; reenlisted, January 1, 1864; drummer; mustered out, July 15, 1865.

FERDINAND DAVIS—Age, 22; residence, Davenport; nativity, Indiana; enlisted, September 22, 1864; mustered, September 22, 1864; private; mustered out, June 2, 1865.

PATRICKS DEMPSEY—Age, 20; residence, Davenport; nativity, Canada; enlisted, September 23, 1864; mustered, September 23, 1864; private; deserted, November 13, 1864.

ROLL OF CO. E.   305

JOHN A. DICKSON—Age, 19; residence, Davenport; nativity, Maine; enlisted, October 4, 1864; mustered, October 4, 1864; private; mustered out, July 15, 1865.

LEROY DOUGLAS—Age, 20; residence, Cedar County; nativity, Pennsylvania; enlisted, September 30, 1861; mustered, October 5, 1861; veteran; reenlisted, January 23, 1864; private; wounded, June 15, 1864; mustered out, July 15, 1865.

THEODORE DOUGLAS—Age, 18; residence, Tipton; nativity, Pennsylvania; enlisted, September 24, 1861; mustered, October 5, 1861; private; no record.

ALEXANDER G. DOWNING—Age, 18; residence, Inland; nativity, Indiana; enlisted, August 20, 1861; mustered, October 5, 1861; veteran; reenlisted, January 1, 1864; private; 6th Corporal March 1, 1864; 5th Corporal; 4th Sergeant January 1, 1865; mustered out, July 15, 1865.

DAVID DRAUCKER—Age, 23; residence, Tipton; nativity, Pennsylvania; enlisted, August 20, 1861; mustered, October 5, 1861; veteran; reenlisted, January 1, 1864; private; fifer; mustered out, July 15, 1865.

LORENZO D. DURBIN—Age, 35; residence, Tipton; nativity, Ohio; mustered, October 5, 1861; 2d Lieutenant September 22, 1861; 1st Lieutenant April 7, 1862; resigned, September 28, 1862.

JOHN W. DWIGGANS—Age, 19; residence, Tipton; nativity, Ohio; enlisted, September 23, 1861; mustered, October 5, 1861; private; wounded, April 6, 1862; died of wounds, May 7, 1862.

WILLIAM DWIGGANS—Age, 19; residence, Tipton; nativity, Iowa; enlisted, September 23, 1861; mustered, October 5, 1861; private; died of disease, December 28, 1861.

CHARLES EDDY—Age, 25; residence, Davenport; nativity, Canada; enlisted, October 3, 1864; mustered, October 3, 1864; private; mustered out, July 15, 1865.

GEORGE W. EICHER—Age, 22; residence, Woodbridge; nativity, Ohio; enlisted, September 23, 1861; mustered, October 5, 1861; private; mustered out expiration of term, October 17, 1864.

LEWIS ELSEFFER—Age, 18; residence, Woodbridge; nativity, New York; enlisted, September 12, 1861; mustered, October 5, 1861; veteran; reenlisted, January 1, 1864; private; 6th Corporal; 4th Corporal January 1, 1864; 3d Corporal May 1, 1864; 1st Corporal January 1, 1865; mustered out, July 26, 1865.

JOHN W. ESHER—Age, 25; residence, Woodbridge; nativity, Pennsylvania; enlisted, September 23, 1861; mustered, October 5, 1861; veteran; reenlisted, January 23, 1864; wounded, June 25, 1864; discharged for disabilities, March 20, 1865.

WILLIAM ESHER—Age, 23; residence, Inland; nativity, Pennsylvania; enlisted, September 20, 1861; mustered, October 5, 1861; mustered out, July 15, 1865.

WILLIAM C. FALLS—Age, 33; residence, Tipton; nativity, Virginia; enlisted, August 30, 1862; mustered, August 30, 1862; mustered out, June 2, 1865.

JOHN FERREN—Age, 24; residence, Davenport; nativity, Ireland; enlisted, October 11, 1864; mustered, October 11, 1864; mustered out, July 15, 1865.

FRANK FISHER—Enlisted, October 5, 1861; rejected by mustering officer.

DEAN FORD—Age, 23; residence, Tipton; nativity, Indiana; enlisted, September 21, 1861; mustered, October 5, 1861; veteran; reenlisted, January 1, 1864; private; mustered out, July 15, 1865.

JOHN FORD—Age, 23; residence, Tipton; nativity, Indiana; enlisted, September 14, 1861; mustered, October 5, 1861; private; wounded, June 15, 1864; mustered out expiration of term, October 17, 1864.

JAMES FOSSETT—Age, 21; residence, Inland; nativity, Ohio; enlisted, September 26, 1861; mustered, October 5, 1861; 6th Corporal; discharged for disabilities, October 17, 1862.

HIRAM FRANK—Age, 42; residence, Tipton; nativity, New York; enlisted, September 24, 1861; mustered, October 5, 1861; veteran; reenlisted, January 1, 1864; 3d Corporal; 6th Sergeant October 16, 1862; 4th Sergeant May 1, 1864; 2d Sergeant November 1, 1864; mustered out, July 15, 1865.

GOTTHES JOHN FREDERICK—Age, 18; residence, Davenport; nativity, Germany; enlisted October 7, 1864; mustered, October 7, 1864; private; mustered out, July 15, 1865.

ALLEN FRINK—Age, 22; residence, Tipton; nativity, New York; enlisted, September 26, 1861; mustered, October 5, 1861; private; wounded, April 6, 1862; no further record.

CARLTON FRINK—Age, 18; residence, Tipton, nativity, New York; enlisted, September 26, 1861; mustered, October 5, 1861; private; killed in battle, April 6, 1862.

WILLIAM H. GREEN—Age, 21; residence, Tipton; nativity, Ohio; enlisted, August 20, 1861; mustered, October 5, 1861; veteran; reenlisted, January 1, 1864; private; 5th Corporal January 1, 1865; mustered out, July 15, 1865.

THOMAS M. HAINES—Age, 24; residence, Tipton; nativity, New York; enlisted, September 21, 1861; mustered, October 5, 1861; private; killed in battle, April 6, 1862.

JOHN W. HARDIN—Age, 20; residence, Jefferson City; nativity, Missouri; enlisted, December 19, 1861; mustered, December 19, 1861; private; hospital June 30, no record.

HARRISON HARRICE—Age, 25; residence, Tipton; nativity, Maryland; enlisted, September 24, 1861; mustered, October 5, 1861; private; discharged for disabilities, July 14, 1862.

PITT B. HARRINGTON—Age, 21; residence, Tipton; nativity, Michigan; enlisted, September 17, 1861; mustered, October 5, 1861; veteran; reenlisted, January 1, 1864; private; mustered out, July 15, 1865.

ABNER H. HATCH—Age, 25; residence, Tipton; nativity, New York; enlisted, September 14, 1861; mustered, October 5, 1861; private; discharged for disabilities, August 13, 1862.

LEWIS P. HAZEN—Age, 30; residence, Davenport; nativity, Ohio; enlisted, September 28, 1864; mustered, September 28, 1864; private; mustered out, June 16, 1865.

NICODEMUS D. HENRY—Age, 19; residence, Cedar County; nativity, Ohio; enlisted, April 19, 1864; mustered, April 19, 1864; private; mustered out, July 15, 1865.

AUGUSTUS F. HERRICK—Age, 19; residence, Davenport; nativity, New York; enlisted, October 8, 1864; mustered, October 8, 1864; private; mustered out, July 15, 1865.

JOHN HILTON—Age, 18; residence, Davenport; nativity, Missouri; enlisted, April 25, 1864; mustered, April 27, 1864; private; wounded, July 5, 1864, and September 2, 1864; mustered out, July 15, 1865.

ROBERT L. HILTON—Rejected by mustering officer October 5, 1861.

DAVID HOBAUGH—Age, 21; residence, Toronto; nativity, Indiana; enlisted, September 17, 1861; mustered, October 5, 1861; veteran; prisoner, October 4, 1862; reenlisted, January 1, 1864; private; killed in battle, July 20, 1864.

DAVID HUFF—Age, 21; residence, Inland; nativity, Indiana; enlisted, August 20, 1861; mustered, October 5, 1861; veteran; reenlisted, January 1, 1864; private; 2d Corporal; 1st Corporal May 1, 1864; wounded, August 12, 1864; died of wounds, August 23, 1864.

CHARLES J. JOHNSON—Age, 22; residence, Mechanicsville; nativity, Ohio; enlisted, October 5, 1861; mustered, October 5, 1861; private; died of disease, November 25, 1863.

FRANK JOHNSON—Age, 19; residence, Tipton; enlisted, October 5, 1861; mustered, October 5, 1861; reenlisted, January 1, 1864; private; mustered out, July 15, 1865.

JOHN C. JOHNSON—Age 18; residence, Marshall County; nativity, Ohio; enlisted, March 23, 1864; mustered, March 23, 1864; private; mustered out, July 15, 1865.

JOHN KINNAN—Age, 22; residence, Tipton; nativity, Pennsylvania; enlisted, September 16, 1861; mustered, October 5, 1861; veteran; reenlisted, January 1, 1864; private; mustered out, July 15, 1865.

CRAVEN LANE—Age, 19; residence, Tipton; nativity, Indiana; enlisted, September 21, 1861; mustered, October 5, 1861; private; died of disease, January 3, 1862.

JOHN LETT—Age 19; residence, Tipton; nativity, Ohio; enlisted, September 21, 1861; mustered, October 5, 1861; veteran; reenlisted, January 1, 1864; private; 3d Corporal January 1, 1865; mustered out, July 15, 1865.

AUGUSTUS LOBSHEIR—Age, 22; residence, Woodbridge; nativity, Germany; enlisted, September 25, 1861; mustered, October 5, 1861; veteran; reenlisted, January 1, 1864; 5th Sergeant; 2d Sergeant October 1, 1862; Sergeant-Major November 1, 1864; discharged for disabilities, July 17, 1865.

JOEL LONG—Age, 22; residence, Cedar Bluff; nativity, Iowa; enlisted, September 30, 1861; mustered, October 5, 1861; wagoner; mustered out, July 15, 1865.

ROLL OF CO. E.

PETER LONG—Age, 18; residence, Davenport; nativity, Ohio; enlisted, October 11, 1864; mustered, October 11, 1864; private; deserted, November 11, 1864.

HUGH C. McBIRNEY—Age, 21; residence, Mechanicsville; nativity, Canada; enlisted, September 26, 1861; mustered, October 5, 1861; private; 3d Corporal; mustered out expiration of term, October 17, 1864.

PADENARIN McCARTNEY—Age 39; residence, Tipton; nativity, Pennsylvania; enlisted, September 23, 1861; mustered, October 5, 1861; private, discharged—?[1]

THOMAS McCONNOLL—Age, 24; residence, Tipton; nativity, Pennsylvania; enlisted, August 26, 1861; mustered, October 5, 1861; private; wounded, June 15, 1864; mustered out, expiration of term, October 31, 1864.

EBENEZER McCULLOUGH—Age, 23; residence, Davenport; nativity, Ohio; enlisted, October 1, 1861; mustered, October 5, 1861; private; died of disease, August 3, 1862.

JOSEPH McKIBBEN—Age, 26; residence, Tipton; nativity, Ireland; enlisted, September 23, 1861; mustered, October 5, 1861; private; mustered out, expiration of term, April 1, 1865.

EZRA McLONEY—Age, 25; residence, Tipton; nativity, Ohio; enlisted, September 28, 1861; mustered, October 5, 1861; 4th Sergeant; killed in battle, April 6, 1862.

SAMUEL S. McLONEY—Age, 33; residence, Inland; nativity, Ohio; mustered, October 5, 1861; appointed Captain October 5, 1861; mustered out, expiration of term, October 26, 1864.

ROBERT McWILLIAM—Age, 36; residence, Grinnell; nativity, Scotland; enlisted, September 23, 1864; mustered, September 23, 1864; private; mustered out, July 2, 1865.

GEORGE G. MAIN—Age, 32; residence, Lowden; nativity, New York; enlisted, September 19, 1861; mustered, October 5, 1861; 4th Corporal; wounded, January 15, 1864; mustered out, July 8, 1865.

JAMES MARTIN—Age, 19; residence, LeClaire; nativity, Ohio; enlisted, August 26, 1861; mustered, October 5, 1861; veteran; prisoner, October 4, 1862; reenlisted, January 1, 1864; private; killed in battle, June 15, 1864.

SAMUEL METCALF—Age, 25; residence, Tipton; nativity, Vermont; enlisted, August 20, 1861; mustered, October 5, 1861; private; mustered out, expiration of term, October 17, 1864.

GEORGE MOONEY—Age, 22; residence, Tipton; nativity, Ohio; enlisted, September 9, 1861; mustered, October 5, 1861; private; mustered out, October 18, 1864.

JOHN D. MOORE—Age, 20; residence, Inland; nativity, Indiana; enlisted, March 23, 1864; mustered, March 23, 1864; mustered out, July 15, 1865.

DANIEL MOWERY—Age, 24; residence, Tipton; nativity, Pennsylvania; enlisted, September 20, 1861; mustered, October 5, 1861; discharged for disabilities, March 27, 1863.

MARION Z. MUSCHOTZY—Residence, Lookout Station, Mo.; enlisted, January 17, 1862; private; deserted, June, 1862.

FRANCIS NEESE—Age, 21; residence, Fort Dodge; nativity, Indiana; enlisted, September 28, 1864; mustered, September 28, 1864; private; mustered out, June 2, 1865.

REUBEN NEESE—Age, 26; residence, Fort Dodge; nativity, Indiana; enlisted, September 28, 1864; mustered, September 28, 1864; private; died of disease, March 2, 1865.

HENRY NEWANS—Age, 18; residence, Tipton; nativity, Canada; enlisted, September 23, 1861; mustered, October 5, 1861; veteran; reenlisted, January 1, 1864; private; wounded, July 22, 1864; mustered out, July 15, 1865.

JAMES NEWCOM—Age, 26; residence, Tipton; nativity, Pennsylvania; enlisted, October 17, 1861; mustered, October 17, 1861; veteran; reenlisted, January 1, 1864; private; 5th Corporal; 3d Corporal. January 1, 1863; 2d Corporal May 1, 1864; 3d Sergeant October 27, 1864; 1st Sergeant January 1, 1865; 2d Lieutenant July 29, 1865; mustered out, July 15, 1865.

FOREST NOWLIN—Age, 18; residence, Davenport; nativity, Pennsylvania; enlisted, October 10, 1864; mustered, October 10, 1864; private; mustered out, July 15, 1865.

CULVER ORRIN—See Orrin Culver.

[1]See Downing's Civil War Diary, p. 222.

WILLIAM PATTEN—Age, 19; residence, Tipton; nativity, Indiana; enlisted, September 26, 1861; mustered, October 5, 1861; veteran; reenlisted, January 1, 1864; private; mustered out, July 15, 1865.

AARON PEARCE—Age, 21; residence, Tipton; nativity, Ohio; enlisted, September 22, 1861; mustered, October 5, 1861; veteran; reenlisted, January 1, 1864; private; prisoner, missing in action July 22, 1864; mustered out, July 15, 1865.

ABRAHAM PENCE—Rejected October 5, 1861.

ALEXANDER RAGAN—Age, 18; residence, Tipton; nativity, Pennsylvania; enlisted, April 20, 1861; mustered, October 5, 1861; private; died of disease, September 9, 1863.

EBENEZER RANKIN—Age, 22; residence, Mechanicsville; nativity, Ireland; enlisted, September 26, 1861; mustered, October 5, 1861; private; 4th Corporal; mustered out expiration of term, October 17, 1864.

JAMES RANKIN—Age, 21; residence, Mechanicsville; nativity, Ireland; enlisted, September 26, 1861; mustered, October 5, 1861; veteran; reenlisted, January 1, 1864; private; mustered out, July 15, 1865.

EDWIN D. REAVES—Age, 21; residence, Tipton; nativity Ohio; enlisted, September 21, 1861; mustered, October 5, 1861; private; discharged for disabilities, April 15, 1863.

CHRISTIAN REIGART—Age, 18; residence, Tipton; nativity, Pennsylvania; enlisted, September 28, 1861; mustered October 5, 1861; private; discharged for disabilities, November 2, 1861.

JOHN T. RICE—Age, 22; residence, Lowden; nativity, Virginia; enlisted, September 17, 1861; mustered, October 5, 1861; private; died of disease, April 19, 1862.

ROSCOE R. ROYSTER—Age, 29; residence Fort Dodge; nativity, Iowa; enlisted, September 28, 1864; mustered, September 28, 1864; private; mustered out, June 2, 1865.

BURTIS H. RUMSEY—Age, 18; residence, Tipton; nativity, Ohio; enlisted, October 1, 1861; mustered, October 5, 1861; veteran; reenlisted, January 1, 1864; private; mustered out, July 15, 1865.

JAMES K. RUMSEY—Age 23; residence, Davenport; nativity, Ohio; enlisted, April 6, 1864; mustered April 6, 1864; private; died of disease, February 2, 1865.

JAMES RYON—Age, 27; residence, Davenport; nativity, Canada; enlisted, October 12, 1864; mustered, October 12, 1864; private; deserted, November 13, 1864.

ALBERT B. SILES—Age, 23; residence, Wyoming; nativity, New York; enlisted, September 28, 1861; mustered, October 5, 1861; 7th Corporal; 2d Corporal; mustered out expiration of term, October 17, 1864.

GEORGE W. SIMMONS—Age, 22; residence, Tipton; nativity, Ohio; enlisted, September 21, 1861; mustered, October 5, 1861; private; wounded, April 6, 1862; died of wounds, May 12, 1862.

WILSON SIMMONS—Age, 21; residence, Tipton; nativity, Ohio; enlisted, September 23, 1861; mustered, October 5, 1861; private; died of disease, April 15, 1862.

ADAM C. SMITH—Age, 29; residence, Tipton; nativity, New York; enlisted, August 20, 1861; mustered, October 5, 1861; private; died of disease, 1863.

JASON C. SPARKS—Age, 21; residence, Le Grand; nativity, Indiana; enlisted, March 31, 1864; mustered, March 31, 1864; private; mustered out, July 15, 1865.

WILLIAM SPENCER—Age, 26; residence, Davenport; nativity, Pennsylvania; enlisted, August 20, 1861; mustered, October 5, 1861; 2d Sergeant; 2d Lieutenant October 1, 1862; Captain October 27, 1864; mustered out, July 15, 1865.

ORLANDO STOUT—Age, 18; residence, Tipton; nativity, Iowa; enlisted, September 21, 1861; mustered, October 5, 1861; veteran; reenlisted, January 1, 1864; private; mustered out, July 15, 1865.

DANIEL E. SWEET—Age, 23; residence, Tipton; nativity, Pennsylvania; enlisted, August 20, 1861; October 5, 1861; veteran; reenlisted, January 1, 1864; 2d Corporal; 1st Corporal; 5th Sergeant May 1, 1864; 3d Sergeant January 1, 1865; mustered out, July 15, 1865.

GEORGE SWEET—Age, 18; residence, Tipton; nativity, Wisconsin; enlisted, January 1, 1864; mustered, January 6, 1864; private; killed in battle, July 22, 1864.

HENRY L. SWEET—Age, 20; residence, Tipton; nativity, Pennsylvania; enlisted, August 20, 1861; mustered, October 5, 1861; 8th Corporal; died of disease, May 4, 1862.

ROLL OF CO. E.

HENRY M. SWIFT—Age, 18; residence, Boone county; nativity, Missouri; mustered, December 19, 1861; private; died of disease, June 23, 1862.

MILTON SWIFT—Supposed to be Henry M. Swift.

ODELL THORNE—Age, 20; residence, Louden; nativity, Ohio; enlisted, September 17, 1861; mustered, October 5, 1861; veteran; reenlisted, January 1, 1864; private; mustered out, July 15, 1865.

GEORGE M. TITUS—Age, 22; residence, Louden; nativity, Pennsylvania; enlisted, September 18, 1861; mustered, October 5, 1861; veteran; re-enlisted, January 1, 1864; fifer; 5th Sergeant January 1, 1865; mustered out, July 15, 1865.

JOSEPH TOMLINSON—Age, 24; residence, Tipton; nativity, New York; enlisted, September 14, 1861; mustered, October 5, 1861; veteran; re-enlisted, January 1, 1864; private; 3d Sergeant; 1st Sergeant May 1, 1864; 1st Lieutenant December 17, 1864; Captain July 29, 1865; mustered out, July 15, 1865.

GEORGE W. TOYNE—Age, 27; residence, Tipton; nativity, England; enlisted, August 20, 1862; mustered, August 30, 1862; private; mustered out, June 2, 1865.

GEORGE W. TUTHILL—Age, 30; residence, Davenport; nativity, New York; enlisted, March 25, 1864; mustered, March 25, 1864; private; mustered out, July 11, 1865.

PETER VINRICHE—Age, 32; residence, Louden; nativity, France; enlisted, September 18, 1861; mustered, October 5, 1861; veteran; re-enlisted, January 1, 1864; private; mustered out, July 15, 1865.

SALEM WADE—Age, 21; residence, Davenport; nativity, New York; enlisted, September 23, 1864; mustered, September 23, 1864; private; mustered out, June 2, 1865.

LEROY WALDO—Age, 22; residence, Davenport; nativity, Ohio; enlisted, September 28, 1864; mustered, September 28, 1864; private; mustered out, June 2, 1865.

DARIUS WATERHOUSE—Age, 25; residence, Davenport; nativity, New York; enlisted, January 27, 1864; February 11, 1864; private; mustered out, July 15, 1865.

JOHN A. WHITE—Age, 22; residence, Wyoming; nativity, Michigan; enlisted, September 20, 1861; mustered, October 5, 1861; veteran; re-enlisted, January 1, 1864; 5th Corporal; 4th Sergeant October 16, 1862; 3d Sergeant May 1, 1864; 2d Lieutenant October 27, 1864; 1st Lieutenant, July 29, 1865; mustered out, July 15, 1865.

MILTON G. WAGGINS—Age, 18; residence, Tipton; nativity, Ohio; enlisted, September 9, 1861; mustered, October 5, 1861; veteran; re-enlisted, January 1, 1864; private; 8th Corporal April 25, 1862; 7th Corporal; 5th Corporal January 1, 1864; 4th Corporal; 2d Corporal January 1, 1865; mustered out, July 15, 1865.

GEORGE T. WILLCOTT—Age, 20; residence, Inland; nativity, Ohio; enlisted, August 20, 1861; mustered, October 5, 1861; died of disease, May 12, 1862.

JOHN ZITLER—Age, 19; residence, Tipton; nativity, Pennsylvania; enlisted, September 24, 1861; mustered, October 5, 1861; veteran; re-enlisted, January 1, 1864; wounded, June 15, 1864; mustered out, July 15, 1865.

INDEX

Abbeville, taken, 85, 86; army left, 88;
Abercrombie, Major, drilled Eleventh Iowa after Shiloh, 44; in command of regiment, 49; drill by, 83;
Ackworth, Ga., train through, 217, 219,
Adairsville, Ga., marched through, 221.
Albin, John, wounded, 198,
Alexandria, Va., army at, 276,
Alexander, William, killed, 197,
Allee, Albert, mustered out, 222,
Allotment rolls, inaugurated, 84; discontinued, 133
Anderson, Lieutenant, return of, 48; captain, arrived with conscripts, 226
Armstrong, Thomas, loan from, 183; loan, 218,
Army of Cumberland, on march through Georgia, 229,
Army of the Tennessee, on march through Georgia, 229,
Argo, Jeremiah, 180; to the front, 214
Atlanta, Georgia, movement upon, 199; battles around, 209; field hospital, 214; provisions for army, 226; to be evacuated, 227; citizens leaving for north, 227; raid on, 228; evacuated, 229;
Ayers, John I. mustered out, 222,

Baker, Nathaniel B., Adjutant General of Iowa, in charge of Camp McClellan, 5; reviewed Eleventh Iowa, 17; at the front, speech, 120,
Bain, Samuel, loan, 218,
Baltimore and Ohio railroad, station of, 280; long tunnel, 281,
Banks, General, at Port Hudson, 121, 132
Barrett, William, loan from, 228,
Batderf, John, company cook, 12
Bayou Lee, crossed, 137.
Bayou Mason, army through, 137, camp near, 139,
Bayou Said, camp near, 138
Beauregard, General, evacuating Corinth, 50
Belknap, General W. W., home on leave, 284; speech by, 288
Beaufort, S. C., army landed, 245; description of, 245,
Benton Barracks, at St. Louis, 19; parade ground at, 20; accident at, 20, 21
Benton Station, on Savannah railroad, 233,
Bentonville, N. C., rebels fortified at, 262, 263, battle of, 263,
Bible, presented by John Moore, 11; reading, 40; discussion about, 57; reading of, 106, 107, 108
Big Black river, bridge across, 116; camp at, 125, 129; on guard at, 126; post at, 155; camping grounds, 165; return to, 171,
Big Shanty, bivouac at, 195, 196; supplies removed from, 283; train through, 217; railroad at, 220; destruction of railroad, 228,
Blair, General, division of, 113, 115; command of, 118; command of Seventeenth Corps, 188; in grand review, 277,
Blazer, Monroe, loan, 218
Bolivar, Tennessee, 60; on guard, 62; "corporal the guard," 63; on picket at, 64; night watch, 66; Fort Hall, 67; leave, 68
Boonesboro, Missouri, raid on, 24
Boonville, Missouri, 24; in pest-house, 25
Bounty, veterans', 156, 157; expiration of, 161; money, 173
Bragg, General, at Corinth, 77; defeated at Dalton, 156; retreating, 157
Brandon, Miss., burned, 167

Brown, Abraham, died in hospital, 161
Buckman, John R., killed at Shiloh, 42
Buell, General, arrived at Shiloh, 42; to central Tennessee, 52
Burnside, General, expedition, 121; at Chattanooga, 143

Cadle, Richard, quartermaster of Eleventh Iowa, 15
Cairo, Illinois, 36, 37; concentration camp, 174, 175, 183; description of, 184; transports back to, 185
California, Missouri, 25; flagpole raising, 26; company to, 33; hospital at, 34; leaving, 35
Camp, routine, at Camp McClellan, 14; life in, 20; newspapers in, 21; at Savannah, Tennessee, 37; in Jones' field, 38; unhealthy, change of, 46, 47, 48, 49, 52; clean up for inspection, 55; near Corinth, 72; beautiful camping ground, 76; in fine shape, 79; on Scott creek, 81; flooded, moved, 73; near Abbeville, 86; receive mail, 91; smallpox in, 92, 93; at Memphis, 94; camp on Mississippi, 96, 97; moved to higher ground, 98; muddy, smallpox in, 101; moved, 106; excellent, 110; Vicksburg, 111; sickness in, 131, 141; poor ground, 132; protecting from sun, 133; good, 134; dangerous, 138; bunks, 142; reading, and writing letters, 146; at home again, 148; flooded, built new, 150, 151; wash day in, 157; inspection of, 158; duties light, 162; guarded by convalescents, 166; cleaning up, preaching in, 172; at Cairo, 183; robbery in, 184; at Clifton, routine, 186; lying in, making repairs, 192; at Atlanta, 223, 224; leave, at Galesville, 225; at Atlanta, 228; in Georgia swamps, 233; in rice plantation, 237; in Savannah, 239; quiet, in, 241; in pine timber, 245; fuel for, 246; lie in camp, 252; before Columbia, 253; in bivouac at Cheraw, 258; at Goldsboro, 264; building "ranches," 265; routine, 265, 266; near Raleigh, 269; return to, 271; preaching in, 272; at Alexandria, 276; at Washington, D. C., 277; temperance address in, 279; light duties, 280; at Louisville, 282; moved, 283; waiting in, 285; description of, 286; get passes to city, 287; last Sunday in, 288; at camp McClellan, 289
Camp McClellan, at Davenport, 5; return to, 6; troops from Tipton arrive at, 11; concentration at, 181, 182; return to, 288; receive discharge at, 289
Canton, Miss., camp at, 170, 171
Cape Fear river, 260
Cape Girardeau, Missouri, 36
Carey, Lieutenant Alfred, to solicit recruits, 152; wounded, note, 198; in hospital, death of, 206; burial of, 207
Carterville, Georgia, evacuated, 193; base of supply, 194; marched through, 221
Carthage, La., train through, 112; loading boats at, 114.
Cave Springs, village of, 225
Cedartown, Ga., in bivouac, 225
Centralia, Ill., passed through, 175; stopped at, 183
Chambers, Captain Alexander, of regular army, 12; battery of six guns, 38; Colonel, command Iowa Brigade, 120; released from command, 127; again command of Iowa Brigade, 128; command of post, 131; General, review by, 164
Champion Hills, battle of, 116.
Chapel Hill, N. C., Johnson's army at, 269
Chaplain, preaching in camp, 13; regular preaching by, 15, 17; no preaching, 28; new chaplain, 62; without, 86; preached to regiment, 98; without, 105; sermon, first in six months, 123; at hospital, Rome, 208

312 DOWNING'S CIVIL WAR DIARY

Charleston, S. C., news from, 131; besieged, 143; army at, 162; prisoners sent to, 234
Chase, Nathan, in fight, 78; a veteran, 159; got into trouble, 185
Chattahoochee river, army along, 203, 204
Chattanooga, Tennessee, taken, 143; lost to South, 156; bivouac on river, 192; railroad from, 193; railroad destroyed, 200; hospital equipment, 214; surplus supplies, 225; army to, 227
Cheraw, S. C., manufacturing center, 258; burned, 259
Chickamauga river, battle on, 143
Chrisman, Elmore, wounded at Shiloh, 42
Christmas, first in army, 26; gloomy, 89; officers' episode, 159; lonesome, 254
Christmas, Major, on furlough, 133
Citizens, in Vicksburg, 154; gold and silver of, 158; for military duty, 159; without passes, 162; fled, 167; not molested, 170; levy on, 171; leaving, 190; destitute, 191; sorrow in home, 192; vacating war zone, 204; leaving Rome, Ga., 205; at Rome, 206; agitation of, 208; removal of, 217, 218; flee, 226; gather at Atlantic, 227; flee, 230, 231, 234; oath of allegiance at Savannah, 240, 242; left destitute, 249; back on farms, 274; cheering soldiers, 281
Clarenceville, Tennessee, town of, note, 188
Clark, Henry, veteran of Company E, 180, 182
Clark, Joel H., elected orderly, 10; "scouting" expedition, 30
Clifton, Tennessee, army to, 184; journey to, 185; in camp at, 186; town of, 187
Clinton, Miss., pass through, 130; taken, 166
Clothing, orders concerning, 16; settlement for, 51; for regiment, 58; consignment of, 83; need of, 89; bill of, 90; from storage, 95; overcoats and blankets for regiment, 103, 119; discarded, 113; allowance for, 127; for regiment, 133; washing, 141; new uniforms, 185; for regiment, 190; in hospital, 211; waiting for, 226; wearing out, 235; consignment of, 244; mending, 261; shoes, 262; distributed, 265; washing and cleaning, 277; cleaning, 283; money allowed for, 284
Cold Water, Miss., marched through, 90
Cole, David, letter from, 219
Columbia, S. C., State road to, 252; capture of, 253, 254; burning of, 254; explosions at, 255
Columbus, Miss., Johnson's army at, command of, 131
Company E, Eleventh Iowa Infantry, completed, election of officers, 10, 12; nativity of men in, 13; uniforms for, inspection, 19; proud of drillmaster, 20; after "secesh," 24; in winter quarters, 26, 27; vaccination of men, 29, 31; religious services, 30; celebration of fall of Forts Henry and Donelson, 33; return to California, 33; company cook, 33; prayer meeting, 32, 33, 34; mending clothes, 35; on boat, 36; last drill by Compton, 40; in battle of Shiloh, 41, 42; rifles from battlefield, 44; at Bolivar, Tennessee, 64; on Patrick's plantation, 65, 66; on forage, 71; washing squads, 78; corporal reduced, 81; danger from sharpshooters, 86; inspection of, 110; skirmish line, 117; in cotton sheds, 119; in the canebreakes, 121; reserve and police duty, 121, 122, 123; joins regiment on Big Black River, 125; furloughs, note, 133; picket service, 142, 143; in form again, 145; enlistments in, 158; veterans of, 159, 160; veteran company, 161; election of officers, 164; veterans greeted, 176, 177; dinner for, 178; reported for duty, 182; on skirmish line, 197; lying quiet, losses, 198; throwing up rifle pits, 201; on skirmish line, 202; non-veterans mustered out, 222; reorganized, 238; losses in, 243; on picket duty, 247; impatient to move, 248; moved forward, 249; on provost

INDEX 313

guard, 260; subscription for Cornell College, 261; on skirmish line, 263; settled for clothing, 284; men purchase rifles, 287; bidding farewell, 289;
Compton, John F., Englishman, drill-master, 9, 10; chosen first lieutenant, 10; in manual of arms, 15; praise for, 20; New Year's chicken dinner to company, 27; after "secesh" assassin, 29, 33; drills company for last time, 40; killed at Shiloh, 42
Congaree river, struggle for, 253
Corinth, advance on, 46, 47; evacuation of, 50, 51; Union army in, 51, 52; fortifications at, 53, 54; deserted, 56; orchards around, 58; army return to, 68; movements about, 69; important point, 71; battle of, 73; battlefield of, 76; Government wells at, 77; fortifications of, 78; knapsacks in storage, sick in hospital, 80
Cornell College, commissioner from, 261
Conscripts, (see Recruits)
Coosa river, pontoon bridge across, 193, 225,
Copperheads, to hunt down, 103; denounced, 178; activity of, 179
Correll, Charles, arrest of, 268
Croak, George, killed at Shiloh, 42
Crocker's Brigade, (See Iowa Brigade)
Crocker, Colonel of Thirteenth Iowa, 15; General in command of brigade, 82; note, 102; headquarters of, 105; brigadier general, command of Iowa brigade, 111; takes command of Seventh Division, 112; division at Natchez, 152; in Meridian expedition, 166; capture of Enterprise, Miss., 168
Cross, William, in fight, 78; returns from hospital, 200; killed, 203
Curtis, Homer, at home, 177; visit of, 267
Cush, George, frightened, 64; a veteran, 159

Dallas, Ga., enemy to, 220; marched thru, 225, 226
Dalton, Ga., railroad near, 210; capture of 221, 222; railroad from, destroyed, 228
Daniels, Sylvester, returns home, 9; on furlough, 133
Davenport, Iowa, camp at, 5; return to, 6; troops arrive at, 11, 175
Davis, General J. C., in grand review, 277
Davis, Jefferson, plantation of, 114; news of capture, 276
Decatur, Miss., camp at, burned, 168; in bivouac, 169; march to, 190; army thru, 191
Decatur, Alabama, army thru, 191
Deserters, to be brought back, 102, 154; confederate, 199
"Dog" tents, 82
Dodge, General, re-enforcements for, 132
Douglas, Leroy, on picket, 72; a veteran, 160; wounded, note, 198
Downing, Albert, half brother of Alexander G., 3; letter to, 109, 210
Downing, Alexander G., in the harvest field, 3, 4; birthday, enlisted, 4; to Camp McClellan, his father's advice, note, 5; home on pass, back to camp, 6; drill and rations, 7; perplexity of, 8; returns home, enrolled in State service, 9; visits home before leaving for camp, 10; to Tipton, to Camp McClellan with Eleventh Iowa, 11; sworn into United States service, cook for company, 12; camp routine, 14; received State pay, 17; on the "Father of Waters," 18, 19; sent money home, 19; on guard at Benton Barracks, 20; first experience in tent, 22; first pay from United States Government, 23; first march after enemy, 23, 24; experiences of, 25; Christmas dinner, 26; marked "not fit for duty," 27; vaccinated, 29, 30; sent money home, 30; cook for mess No. 1, 31; boat to Cairo, 36; in battle of Shiloh, 40, 43; burying dead, 44; opinions of Shiloh, note, 44, 45; enters Corinth, 52; sends money home, on guard at General Todd's headquarters, 53; first

314 DOWNING'S CIVIL WAR DIARY

time on fatigue, 54; picks blackberries, 55; sees doctor, sells apple pies, 61; experience, 62; birthday, 63; hard march, 68; buys poncho, 69; on picket, 72; at the battle of Corinth, 73; description of chase, note, opinion of, 74; first offence and punishment, 81; signed allotment role, 84; note, 89; account of supplies, 90; on guard, 93; loan to Lieutenant Spencer, 94; with thirteenth Iowa, work on levee, 97; letter to John D. Moore, "likeness" taken, 99; letter to brother John, 100; note, 101; diary, 103; guard at headquarters, sent money home, 105; draw clothing, 107; reading Bible, 106, 107, 108; cooked for officers' mess, 107; letter to Jason Sparks, 108; money sent home, 109, 133; bread for officers' mess, slept in bed, 111; pay as cook, 112; digging trenches, 121; writes letter for comrade, 122; strict orders on picket, 123, 124; filling canteens, 128; hard experience, 129; gold pen, 131; views Vicksburg, on patrol, 134, 135; experience, 136, 137, 138; opinions of, 140, 141; ague, 142; return to duty, 143; on fatigue and provost duty, 144; to church, 145; on soldiers' voting, 147; sends money home, 150; paying soldiers, 153; provost guard, 154; on patrol guard, 156; Christmas dinner, 159; New Year's day prayer, 160; re-enlisted, 161; strict orders on patrol, 162; at church services, elected fifth sergeant, 164; corps headquarters' guard, 166; headquarters' guard, 171; on guard at round house, 173; promotion of, started on furlough, 174; at Cairo, made purchases, reached home, 175; greetings, 176; dinners at Mrs. Curtis', 177; lamentations, 178, visits, 180; expiration of furlough, 181; swapped watches, left for front, 182; at Cairo, 183; certificate of discharge, 184; first detail as corporal, 185; Corporal's squad, 186, 187; outside of pickets, 187; expressed feeling, 189; visits cousin, 190; description of battle, 197; feelings expressed, 199; prayer, 201; taken sick, 202; to division hospital, 203; condition, note, 204; to field hospital, Rome, Ga., 205; convalescent, 206; describes burial of Carey, 207; head nurse, 209; resolutions of, birthday of, 210; money sent home, 212; ward master, 214; increase of pay, 215; left hospital, 216; return to regiment, 217; loans to comrades, 218; with comrades climbed Kenesaw Mountain, 220; on picket, ride in ambulance, 225, bounty, 227, feet sore from marching, 235; promoted to fifth sergeant, 238; obtains Confederate money, 240; subscribes for papers, 241; sent money home, 244; observations, note, 247; carrying heavy load, 253; notes on Columbia, S. C., 254; building corduroy, 257; note on S. C., 259; opinion of country, 260; last battle, note, 263; with mess at Goldsboro, 265; describes camp at Raleigh, 269; rejoicing in camp over Johnston's surrender, 270, 271; account of crossing Roanoke river, 272, 273; ill, decides to march, 274; describes homeward march, 275; description of grand review, 276, 277; medal of honor, 279; description of journey, 281; account of sinking of transport, 282; command of guard, 283; sent money home, visits Louisville, 284; attends theater, 285; on Fourth of July, 285, 286; estimate of General McPherson, note, 286; sergeant of brigade guard, 287; trip home, 288, 289; returns to harvest field, 289, 290;

Downing, Andrew, half-brother of Alexander G., 3
Downing, George, half-brother of Alexander G., 3
Downing, John, half-brother of Alexander G., letter to, 100; referred to, 179
Downing, Paul, half-brother of Alexander G., 3
Dressers Battery, 38; location of, 40
Drilling, at Tipton, 9, 10; at Camp McClellan, 13, note, 16, 17; at Ben-

INDEX 315

ton Barracks, 20, 21; on Jones' Field, 39, 40; after Shiloh, 44; for punishment, 48; dispensed with, 54, 58; on rough ground, 84; brigade and company, 105; division, 107; regimental, 111; on march, 112; at Grand Gulf, 113; battalion, 114; renewed, 134; by regiments, 148; in marksmanship, 153; regular, 163, 164; new recruits, 185; order for, 186; conscripts, 228, 240; regular, 265, 266; dress parade, 286; last dress parade, 288

Durbin, Lorenzo D., chosen second lieutenant, 10; arrived in camp, 12; after horse thief, 29; scouting, 30

Dwiggans, John W., wounded at Shiloh, 42; died, note, 48

Edisto river, army crosses, 251, 252

Eicher, George, on guard, 93; mustered out, 222

Eighth Iowa Infantry, forming, 4, 5, 6; four men drummed out, 7

Election, soldiers' vote, 147; presidential, 227

Eleventh Iowa Infantry, chaplain of, 7; building barracks, 12; completed, 14; guns and equipment, uniforms received by quartermaster, 15; first review in new uniforms, orders to leave for South, 17; en route for St. Louis, march through Muscatine, 18; at Benton Barracks, 19; marching orders, 21; to Jefferson City, 22; up Missouri River, 23; ordered to California, Missouri, 25; in winter quarters, note, 27; regiment reunited, 34; up the Tennessee, 37; at Pittsburg Landing, camp of, 38; called under arms, 40, battle of Shiloh, 40; directed by Grant, 42; in battle of Shiloh, 41-42, second day, 42-43; inspected for pay, 47; on picket, 52, 53, 54, 55; guarding orchard, 56; loss from disease, 59; guarding railroad, 62; routine, 66; leave Iuka, 72; in battle of Corinth, 73; on fortifications, 78; note, 80; without chaplain, 86; pay, 94; start to Vicksburg, 95; to Lake Providence, 99; smallpox in, 101; to Greenville, 102; wedge tents for, officers' resolutions, 103; pay, 104; Sibly tents for, 105; received Enfield rifles, 106; toward Vicksburg, 106; pay, 108; health of, 109; strength of, 112; through Louisiana plantations, 114; expedition of, 116; movements of, 117; sappers of, 120; to rear, 121; expedition of, 123; pay of, 127; escort for wagons, 128; Major Foster in command, 133; on expedition, 136; rear guard, 137; to Vicksburg, 140; no chanplain, 142; picket service, 146, 147, 148, 149; pay, 153; on picket, 157; re-enlistments, 158; veterans sworn in, 159; roll call for re-enlistments, 160; a veteran regiment, 161; sworn in, 163; election of officers, 164; on furlough, 174; at Camp McClellan, 181; mustered, on board transports, 184; new uniforms, 185; rifle pits of, 197; building rifle pits, 198; to front, 199; on skirmish, 202; charge of, 203; no pay, 218; camp of, 220; non-veterans mustered out, 223; six months' pay, 227; strong for Lincoln, 227; on train guard, 229; rear guard, 233; on fortifications, 239; part in campaign, 243; at Pocotaligo, 246, 247; at Edisto river, 251; cross South river, 262; foraging train, 264; new clothes for, 265; complimented on dress parade, 267; temperance pledge, 280; entrains, 281, on board transports, 281; muster-rolls signed, 282; received pay, 284; muster-out rolls, 287; mustered out, 288

Elkhorn, Tenn., march through, note, 189

Elseffer, Lewis, elected first sergeant, 164; clerk, 176; letter to, 213; letter from, 214

Esher, John, on guard, 93; wounded, note, 201; in hospital, 208

Esher, William, on picket, 72

Fairburn, Ga., march to, 219

Farmington, Tenn., campaign, 47, 48

Fayetteville, N. C., army at, 260, 261
Fifteenth Army Corps, to move north, 219; on expedition, 220; at Galesville, 223; on return, 225, 229; in engagement, 232; in advance, 235; foraging train, 237; reviewed, 240; leave Savannah, 244; landed at Beaufort, 246; supply trains, 248; at Hicky Hill, 249; engagement before Columbia, 253; entering Columbia, 254; detail from, 255; camp of, 264; on right wing, 267; race with Seventeenth Corp, 273; paid off, 283; subscription for monument, 286
Fifteenth Iowa Infantry, in Iowa Brigade, 30; battle of Corinth, 73; at Lafayette, 91; guard wagon train, 130; on furlough, 174; on transports, 184; to front, 199; on skirmish, 201; in battle, 208; on move, 219, 220, 221; on march, 222, 229; train guard, 231; landed at Beaufort, 234; received pay, 284.
Floral College, N. C., near state line, 260
Foraging, at Lookout Station, 28, 29, 30, 32; government's policy, 57; on "secesh" plantation, 60; guards taken off, 62; for corn, 71; poor, 77; orders against, 81; cotton, 86, corn and cotton, 87, corn, 89; scalding water for foragers, 104; oats, 131; green corn, 134; on expedition, 137; party caught, 138; sweet potatoes, 139; for meat, 167; plenty forage, 168, 170; parties, 169; for meat, 191; poor country, 192; parties, 193, 223, 224, 225; plenty forage, 226; for meat, 229; on march through Georgia, 230; for meat, 231; plenty forage, 232; sweet potatoes and pork, 235; rice in sheaf, 241; description of foragers, 241; surplus bacon, 251; destruction of property, 252; treatment of foragers, 256; country poor, 257, 258; capture of cars, 258; plenty forage, 259; forage scarce, 260; exciting episode, 261; clothes taken, 262; parties, 264; forbidden, 272
Force, Brigadier General, F. M., command at Clifton, 186
Ford, John, wounded, 122, note, 198; loan, 218; mustered out, 222
Fort Donelson, taken with prisoners, 33
Fort Henry, taken, 33; dilapidated, 37
Fort McAllister, capture of, 237
Fort Robinet, at Corinth, 73
Fort Johnson, below Savannah, 241
Fossett, James M., bunk-mate, 12; on boat, 18; sent to hospital, note, 22, 26; at home, 177
Fossett, Thomas, did not re-enlist, 12; of Twenty-fourth Iowa, 177
Foster, Major Charles, with Le Claire boys, 5; word from, 8; relief for Company E, 125; speech on re-enlisting, 161; speech by, 178
Fourteenth Army Corps, to move north, 219; campaign, 221; at Galesville, 223; on march through Georgia, 229; destroying railroad, 231; reviewed by Sherman, 241; to start on raid, 244; floundering in mud, 248; on garrison, 260; camp of, 264; on left wing, 267; arrived at Louisville, 283
Fourth of July, celebration, 56; fall of Vicksburg, 126; at Louisville, Ky., 285, 286
Frank, Hiram, elected third sergeant, 164; climbing Kenesaw Mountain, 220
Fredericksburg, Va., site of battle, 275
Frink, Carlton, scouting, 29; killed at Shiloh, 42

Galesville, Ala., concentration at, 223
Gambling, "chuck luck," 109, 153, 154, 158
Garden Corners, S. C., headquarters of army, 247, 248
Glascow, Missouri, captured powder at, 24
Goldsboro, N. C., 263; in camp at, 264
Goodrich's Landing, camp at, 136; returned to, 139

INDEX 317

Gordon, Ga., camp at, 230; railroad junction, 231
Grand Gulf, fighting at, prisoners taken, 112, news from, 112; army at, 113; boats for, 114; camp at, 115; quiet at, 116
Grand Junction, marches through, 80; Sixth Division at, 81; provisions to, 82; camp at, 83; fast at, 86
Grant, General Ulysses S., Fort Henry and Fort Donelson, 33; reviews army at Pittsburg Landing, 39; at Shiloh, 42; confidence in, 78; inspection by, 79; command of, 85; inspection by, 88; at Vicksburg, 98; failure of, 112; successes, 115; at Jackson, 116; surrounding Vicksburg, 117; confident, 122; siege of Vicksburg, 123; surrender of Vicksburg, 126; review of Iowa Brigade, 146; orders from, 152; at Chattanooga, 155; at Dalton, Ga., 156; praise for, 157; head of armies, 173; before Richmond, 187, 189; news from, 193; no news from. 195, 199, 208, 209, 210, 211; engagement, 212; at Petersburg, 213; no news from, 218; near Richmond, 219; at Richmond, 266; receives surrender of Lee, 267; joins Sherman, 270; review of armies, 267, 277
Great Pedee river, army crosses, 258
Green, William, on furlough, 150; to camp McClellan, 180; letter from, 209; loan, 218; hauling lumber, 265

Haines' Bluff, army post, 109; attack on, 112; Eleventh Iowa at, 116; taken, 117; army at, 119
Haines, Thomas, experience and death at Shiloh, 41, 42
Hall, Lieutenant Colonel William, in command at California, Missouri, 26; at home, 49; returns with Mrs. Hall, from home, 55; return from home, 108; wife of, 110; takes command of Iowa Brigade, 112, 127; again in command of Brigade, 132; in command of regiment, 145; welcome to comrades, 288
Halleck, General, command of, 51
Ham, Mrs. Mary, letter to, 213
Hardie, General, of Hood's army, 223
Hare, Colonel Abraham M., of the Eleventh Iowa, arrived in camp, 14; in charge of regiment, for drill, 16; in battalion drill, 20; in command of First Brigade, 38; inspection of regiment, 39; at home, 49; returns to camp, 55; drill, 58; inspection of regiment, 59; resignation of, 77
Harper's Ferry, passes through, 281
Hatch, Mr., party for veterans, 177
Hatchie river, camp near, 60
Hazen, General, forces of, 237
Hemmenway, Mrs., gives a dance, 28
Hemphill, John, loan, 218
Hillsboro, Ga., marched through, 230
Hillsborough, Miss., burned, 167; bivouac, 169
Hilton, John, furlough for, 208; wounded, note, 213
Hinkenlooper, General, command of Iowa Brigade, 283
Hobaugh, David, killed, note, 206, 210.
Holly Springs, Miss., rations, 81; moved upon, 85; base of supplies, 87; recaptured, 88; devastation of, 89; recapture of, note, 90
Holmes' plantation, camp on, 111; planted to cotton, 114
Hood, General, notice from Sherman, 218; moving north, 219; force of, 221; retreating, 223
Hooker, General, at Port Hudson, 124; command of, 195; charges of, 200
Hospital, in siege of Vicksburg, 117; confederate, 138; filled, 141; sick improving, 143; boys leaving, 144; near Big Shanty, 203; at Marietta, 204, at Rome, Ga., 204, 205; description of, 206, 207; preaching services, 208; scrub day, 209; crowded, routine, 211,

212; men leaving, note, 213; changes in, 214; services slackening, 215
Howard, General O. O., with Sherman, 248; command of right wing, 249; orders from, 271; in grand review, 277
Huff, David, returns home, 9; on picket, 72; elected second sergeant, 164; died in hospital, 211
Hunter, General, reviewed Iowa Brigade, 161
Huntsville, Ala., transports for, 183; destination, 184; driving cattle toward, 186; knapsacks sent to, 189; army at, description of, 190; tents stored at, 217
Hurlbut, General, after Price, 74; division, 166; tax on citizens, 171

Illinois Central, railroad, 175; over the, 182
Inland, Ia., peace meeting at, 4; enlisted men at, 5; boys from, 9, 176; loyal people of, 177; meeting at, 178
Iowa Brigade, announcement of, 30; formation of, 46; movement on Corinth, 48; camp of, 61; garrisoning Iuka, 70, 71; at battle of Corinth, 73; praise of, 102; resolutions by officers, 104; embarked for Vicksburg, 110; quarters of, 111; loses Croker, Colonel Hall in command of, 112; expedition of, 118, 119; on Big Black River, 124; health of men, 128; return to Big Black river, 131; to Vicksburg, 132; rumored expedition, 134; on expedition, 136; lead in march, 140; building camp, 144; recovering health, 144; relief expedition, 147; target shooting, 153; becomes veteran brigade, 161; in expedition, 165; preparing to leave on furlough, 173; non-veteran battalion, 174; in charge of cattle, 186; note, 206; news from, 208; at Atlanta, note, 213; destroying railroad, 231; train guard, 234; embarked for Beaufort, 244; in engagement, 246; inspected, 247; review of, 266; Thirty-Second Illinois, taken from, 271; leaving Washington, 281; escort for General Sherman, 285
Irwinton, Ga., bivouac near, 231
Iuka, Mississippi, battle of, 69, 70; evacuation of, 72

Jackson, Miss., Johnson at, 127, 128; taken, 130; recaptured, 148, 166
Jefferson City, Missouri, 22; in camp, 24; headquarters, leave, 25; return to, 36
Johnson, Frank, a veteran, 160
Johnston, General Joseph E., in siege of Vicksburg, 118; on Big Black river, 122, 123; cut off, 125; at Jackson, 128; retreating, 130; at Columbus, 131; forces of, 197, 263; estimated force, 194; surrendering to Sherman, 268; agrees to terms of surrender, 269; surrenders to Sherman, 270; men and munitions of, 271; soldiers of, 272
Jones' Field, camp of Eleventh Iowa, 38, 39; parade ground, 39, 40; after battle of Shiloh, 42, 43

Kansas, First Infantry, 96; infantry in skirmish, 100
Kenesaw Mountain, 195; battle of, 197; held by confederates, 199; lines around, 202; rebels left, 203; expedition towards, 219
Keokuk, Ia., "secesh" fight at, 6; false report, 7; Eleventh Iowa at, 18
Kilpatrick, General, cavalry of, 232; to start on raid, 244; as rear guard, 249; pursuit of enemy, 263; to leave for north, 271; cavalry of, 274
Kingston, Ga., passed through, 193; train through, 216; marched through, 221
Kingston, N. C. (Kinston), supplies from, 264
Kirkwood, Governor Samuel J., visits troops on train, 11

La Grange, Tenn., provisions from, 83; knapsacks in storage, 84, 85, 89, 92

INDEX 319

Lafayette, Tenn., on guard at, 90, 91
Lake Providence, La., levee at, 99; cemetery, 100; fire in, 102; flooded, 105, 106; desolation of, 107; levee at, 108; waters from lake, 131
Laport, Robinson, letter to, 196
La Salle, Ill., passed through, 175, 182
Lauman, General, division of, 116; arrival of, 118
Le Claire, Ia., boys from, 5; to raise company, 8; boys from, at Tipton, 9
Lee, General Robert E., news from, 115; news of battle of Gettysburg, 128; report from, 196; surrender of, 267
Lett, John, cook for officers' mess, 122
Liberty Hill, S. C., bivouac at, 256
Lichtenwalter, Solomon, sent money by, 183
Liggett, General, division of, 166; in battle, 197; demonstration of, 200
Lincoln, President, call for troops, 3; proclamation for fasting and prayer, 10; solider vote for, 227; assassination of, 268; sorrow for, 278
Logan, General, command of, 89; division of, 101, 106, 124; at Monroe, 138; returned to Vicksburg, 140, 148; in command of, 147; division of, 151; charged upon, 198; in grand review, 277; speech by, 288
Long Bridge, army crosses, 276
Lookout Station, Missouri, winter quarters at, 26, 27; country around, 30; leave, 33
Lost Mountain, rebels on, 219
Louisville, Ky., detachments leaving for, 279, 280, 281; in camp at, 282; country around, 283; army left, 288

McArthur, General, inspection of Sixth Division, 79; command of, 82; division drill by, 83; headquarters, 98; speech, 108; review by, 110; inspection by, 145
McBirney, Hugh C., corporal, 93; mustered out, 222
McCarty, Padenarin, mustered out, 222
McClellan, General, retreat from Richmond, 56; small vote for, 227
McClernand, General John A., command of, 38; reviews division, 39; general review by, 40; in battle of Shiloh, 41
McConnoll, Thomas R., loan, 154; at Cairo, 180, 181; wounded, note, 198; in hospital, 206; furlough for, 208; on furlough, 212; mustered out, 222
McCullough, Ebenezer, died, 62; reference to, 144
McKibben, Joseph, mustered out, 222
McLoney, Captain Samuel S., provisional, company disbanded, 8; company for the state service, 9; chosen captain, 10; on scout, 32; returns from furlough, 55; pay to Downing, 112; musters company, relief of company, 125; on furlough, 141; re-elected captain, 164
McLoney, Ezra, Sergeant, killed at Shiloh, 42
McPherson, General, Seventeenth Army Corps, 82; camp of, 99; inspection by, 103; headquarters of, 117, 120; inspection by, 145; speech on re-enlisting, 161; headquarters of, 167, 168, 169; at Canton, 170, 171; corps, 184; command of, 195; killed, note, 206; monument for, 286

Macon, Ga., engagement near, 230, 232
Mail, at Lookout Station, 32; at Memphis, 91; at Lake Providence, 100; none received, 127; in hospital, 214, 216; at Atlanta, 217; at Kingston, 221; last before march thru Georgia, 228
Main, George G., wounded, note, 198
"Marching through Georgia," first hint of, 224, 227; preparation for,

228; start on, 229; number of men, 229; destruction of property, 233
Marietta, Ga., evacuation of, 202, 203; sick and wounded to, 204; the wounded from, 209; railroad at, 219; possible destruction of, 228
Marlow Station, Ga., skirmish with rebels, 235
Martin, James, a veteran, 160; killed, note, 198
Memphis, concentration at, 91; provisions from, 92; camp at, 94; leaving, 95; hospital at, 114; stop at, 175
Memphis and Charleston Railroad, guarding, 90; country along, 92
Meridian, Miss., expedition to, 162, 165; captured, 168; destruction of railroads about 169; orders on expedition, 171; results of expedition to, 171, 172
Metcalf, Samuel, loan, 218; mustered out, 222
Michigan City, passed through, 288
Milledgeville, Ga., marched through, 229
Millen, Ga., army through, 233; rebel prison at, 234
Milliken's Bend, camp at, 110
Mills, William, of Sanitary Commission, 109
Mobile, Ala., riots in, 144; surrender of Fort Morgan, 213
Money, Confederate, plenty and cheap, 240.
Mooney, George, mustered out, 222
Monroe, La., railroad to, 111; expedition to, 136; description of, 138; expedition to, note, 141
Moore, John, Mexican war veterans, 12, 181
Moore, John D., presents Bible to Alexander G. Downing, 11, 12; letter to, 85, 99; enlisted, 176; to camp McClellan, 180; climbed Kenesaw Mountain, 220; hauling lumber, 265; money sent home, 284
Moore, Miss, letters to soldiers, 196
Morton, Miss., burned, 167
Moscow, Tenn., march through, 90
Mower, General, 224; losses, 250; in grand review, 277
Muscatine, Iowa, Eleventh Iowa at, 18

Nashville, Tenn., hospital equipment, 214
Negroes, servants adopted, 57; built breastworks, 60; on plantation, 65; at Holly Springs, 85; at work, 97; work on canal, 100; picking cotton, 101; entering army, 104; work by, 105; regiments of, 108; regiments at Duck's Point, 120; refugees, 131, 136, 148; regiments of, 143; washing clothes, 157; military duty, 159; refugees from Meridian, 169, 170; troops for Rome, Ga., 208; carried off, 231; on line of march, 232; put to work, 238; huts on plantations, 247; women farming, 252; putting in crops, 259; refugees and contrabands, 261
Neuse river, 262; rebels crossed, 264; army crosses, 271
Newans, H., a veteran, 160; wounded, 210
Newbern, N. C., supplies from, 264
Newcom, James, a veteran, 160
Nick-a-Jack, Creek, works along, 202; army along, 203

Oak Ridge, camp on, 137, 138, 139
Ockmulgee Mills, Ga., on river, 230
Oconee, river, army crosses, 231
Ogeechee river, bivouac on, 223; rebels fortifying at, 232; bivouac on, 233; crossed, 234; King's bridge over, removing torpedoes from, 238
Ohio river, rising, 183
Oliver Station, army at, 234
Orangeburg, S. C., town of 252

INDEX 321

Ord, General, army of, 127; in pursuit of enemy, 128; in battle of Bentonville, 263; in command of Petersburg, 273
Osterhaus, General, charge of, before Atlantic, 200
Oxford, Miss., army at, 87, 88; college at, 88

Paducah, Ky., stopped at, 37
Pamunky river, army crossed, 275
Parkersburg, Ohio, train through, 281
Patrick, plantation of, 65, 66
Pay, of soldiers, increased, 209, 215; soldiers send money home, 108
Pearl river, crossed, 129, 130, 166, 170
Pemberton, General, siege of Vicksburg, 123; note, 121, 125; surrender, 126
Perkins' Landing, below Vicksburg, 114, plantation, 114
Petersburg, Va., Grant near, 212, 213; Sherman's army through, 273
Pierce, Aaron, missing, 210
Pitts, B. F. Brigadier General, in command, 284
Pittsburg Landing, Tenn., mobilization at, 37, 38; troops returning to, 52; teams to, 53; reminder of, 186
Pocotaligo, S. C., on guard at, 246, 248; new landing near, 248
Pomutz, Major, command of non-veterans, 174
Pope, General, command of, 47, 48, 50, 51
Port Hudson, report from, 97, 104; siege of, 115, 121, 122; reports from, 124
Posten's Grove, church at, 4
Potomac river, 124; army of, 134, 276
Preaching, (see Chaplain).
Price, General, retreat from Corinth, 74
Price, Hiram, provisioning troops, note, 7
Prisoners, taken north, 95; taken, 112, 113; at Jackson, Miss., 128; paroled at Vicksburg, 129; to Vicksburg, 130; leaving Vicksburg, 132; at Atlanta, 202; at Union, at Millen, 234; placed in advance, 236; retaliation in treatment of, 248; treatment of, retaliation, 258
Providence, Missouri, 23
Provisions, expensive, 98; hauling, 113, 114; trains of, 128, 129; trains unmolested, 130; high price, 132, 150; hauling, 144; market house for, 154, 155; trains, 169; transports and wagons for, 180; wagon trains, 192; distribution of, 204; supply trains, 224; nine trains of, 226; supply train, 231; by boat, 238; hauling, 247, 248; difficulties of hauling, 257
Pulaski, Tenn., army at, 189
Purdy, Tenn., 47

Quimby, General, division of, 102; division of, 105, 109, 110.

Ragan, Alexander, death of, 144
Raleigh, N. C., occupied, 268; army at, 269
"Ranches," built of ponchos, 196; built from vacant houses, 226; built at Savannah, 239; at Goldsboro, 264; description of, 265; at Washington, 279; shelter of, 280, 286
Rankin, Ebenezer, mustered out, 222
Rankin, James, becomes veteran, 160
Rations, at Camp McClellan, 7, 11; served on long tables, 17; first taste of hard-tack, 19; preparation of, 23; at Lookout Station, 28, 29; prepared by company cook, 33; cooking on boat, 36; wild fruit, 54, 55; apples and peaches, 58; bacon and fruit, etc., 58, 59, 62; cooking, 63; foraging for, 71; out of, 75; "gruel," 81, 82; short, arrived, 82; hauling, 83; portions, 84; full, 86; burned,

322   DOWNING'S CIVIL WAR DIARY

88; half, 89; hot coffee, 90; short of, 91; arrived, 92; draw full, 93; high cost, 98; desiccated potatoes, 101; cost of potatoes, on march, 109; variety, 112; waiting for, 118; wild fruit, 122, 124, 125; issued to Confederates, 126; green corn, 130; high cost of, 132; fresh bread, 133, 134; to negroes, 136; high at Vicksburg, 150; twenty days', 165; short, received, 169; beef cattle, 186; cooking, 189; short of, 192; at Kingston, 193; full, 195, 200; foraging for, 223; forty days, 229; sweet potatoes and fresh pork, 230; three-fifths, 231; two-thirds, 232; two-fifths, 233, 236; rice in hull, 237; drew hard-tack, 238; on full rations, 239; one-third, 240; half, fresh oysters, 241; half, 242; two-thirds, 243; variety of, foraged, 251; full, 265; loaded, 266

Recruits, arrived from Iowa, 82; in manual of arms, 185; drilling at Clifton, 186; conscripts from Iowa, 226; drilling conscripts, 228

Redstone, expedition to, 159

Remington, Chauncy; chaplain for Eleventh Iowa, 62

Reseca, Ga., marched through, 221

Rice, John T., wounded at Shiloh, 42; died, 42; burial of, 45

Richmond, La., army through, 111

Richmond, Va., news from, 57, 115, 196; no news from, 200; objective, 244; capture of, 266; go by way of, 271; condition of, 274

Rifles, Belgian, distributed, 39, 41; from battlefield, 44; Springfield rifles, 183; Enfield exchanged for, 184; men purchase their, 287

Roanoke river, army crossing, episode, 272, 273

Rome, Ga., en route for, 190, 191; passed through, 193; sick and wounded to, 204; hospital at, 205; conditions at, 209; quiet at, 212, 213, 214; threatened, 215

Rosecrans, General, at Iuka, 69, 70; division of, 89; report from, 104; at Chattanooga, 143; defeat of, 146; command of, 159

Rumsey, Burtis, sickness of, 54; becomes veteran, 180; loan, 218

Salkehatchie river, struggle for possession of, 250

Saluda river, cotton mills on, 253

Sanitary Commission, goods from, 108, 109; goods distributed, 245; service of, 281;

Savannah, Ga., march toward, 234; approach to, 235; camp near, 236; advance upon, 238; evacuated by rebels, 239; description of, 239, 240; citizens take oath of allegiance, 241, 242; to be fortified, 242; fortifications at, 243;

Savannah, Tenn., landing at, men in camp, 37

Schofield, General, department of, 159; possession of Goldsboro, 263; army of, 264; command of left wing, 267; at Raleigh, 271; in grand review, 277

Scott County Fair, 8

Sebastopol, Ga., destroying railroad to, 233

Second Illinois Cavalry, 23

Second Iowa Cavalry, in camp at the Fair Grounds, 6; in Camp Halt, 8; made up of Allen's Grove boys, 13; new troops for, 14; at Corinth, 51; back to Corinth, 74

Seventeenth Army Corps, question of arming negroes, 108; hospital of, 117; re-enlistments in, 161; raid, 165, 167; provision train of, 168; on veteran's furlough, 173; supply train, 175; at Cairo, 183; reorganized, 184; arrived at Clifton, 187, 188; begins action at Atlanta, 195; flank movement, 202; movement of, 203; hospital of, 205; the wounded from, 209; veterans of, 216; camp of, 217; on move, 219, 220; at Galesville, 223; reviewed, 224; on return, 225; destroying property, 228; on march through Georgia, 229; burned railroad property, 231; reviewed by Sherman, 242; leaving Savannah, 244; landed at Beaufort, 245; on expedition, 246;

INDEX 323

march on State road, 252; on bank of Congeree, 253; entering Columbia, 254; marched through Columbia, 255; threw up fortifications, 257; foragers of, 258; crosses Cape Fear river, 261; camp of, 264; on right wing, 267; in review at Raleigh, 269, 270; started on march homeward, 272; arrived at Petersburg, 273; in camp near Richmond, 274; receiving pay, 284; subscription for monument, 286

Seward, Secretary, report concerning, 268

Shepherd, Hamilton, of Bloomfield, Indiana, 190

Sherman, General, rear of Vicksburg, 85; report from, 91; at Haines' Bluffs, 112, 116, 117; against, Johnston, 123; pursuing enemy, 127, 128; at Jackson, Miss., 128; re-enforcement for, 129; capture Jackson, Miss., 130; to Chattanooga, 146; attacked, 153; at Knoxville, Tenn., 155; expedition of, 162, 165; driving Johnston, 193; forces of, 194, 195; episode, note, 200; strategy of, note, 204; order from, 208; capture of Atlanta, 213; pursuit of enemy, 214; order removing citizens, 217, 218; forces of, 220, 223; through Georgia, 231; orders, 236; at close range, note, 240; reviewed troops, 241; inspects fire department, 242; left for the front, 248; starts on grand raid, 249; at Columbia, note, 255; forces concentrating, 260; to open communications, 263; orders from, 263, 264; orders for army, 266; negotiations with Johnston, 268; terms of surrender of Johntson, 269; reviews army, terms of surrender of Johnston, 270; army to start for Washington, 271; at Richmond, 274; in grand review, 276, 277; army to be mustered out, 279; answers critics, 284, 285

Shiloh, battle of, preliminaries, Union camp, 38, 40; first day, 40-42; second day, 42, 43; losses, 42, 43, 48; Mr. Downing's reflections on, footnotes, 43, 44, 45; arrival of troops after, 43, 44; celebration of at Tipton, 178

Sibley tents, 78, 82; at Memphis, 94; exchanged for wedge tents, 105

Simmons, George W., wounded at Shiloh, 42; died, 48

Simmons, Wilson, death of, 45

Sixteenth Army Corps, on Meridian expedition, 165, 167, 168, 170; at Vicksburg, 171; Red river expedition, 173; supply train of, 175; orders to, 200; on skirmish, 202; movement of, 203, hospital of, 205

Sixteenth Iowa Infantry, in Iowa brigade, 30; at Iuka, 70; joke on, 92; with wagon train, 130; rifle pits of, 197; on skirmish, 201, 202; in battle, 208; on forage, 226 rear guard, 229; moved camp, 242; received pay, 284; arrived at Davenport, 289

Sixth Division, at Holly Springs, 85; cotton stores, 86, 87; grist mill for, 86; at Memphis, 94; question of arming negroes, 108; review of, 110; in winter quarters, 153

Slocum, General, command of left wing, 249; in grand review, 277

Smith, Giles E., General, division of, 250; brigade inspection by, 266, 267; review by, 269

Smith, General Kerby, surrender of, 279

Smithsonian Institution, visit to, 278, 279

Solider vote, (see Election)

Sparks, Jason, letter from, 100, 108; to enlist, 178; measles, 180; gold pen from, 218; with mess, 265

Sparks, Mr., at home of, 6, 178, 180

Sparrow's plantation, camp on, 99, 100, 105, 107

Spencer, Sergeant William, on scouting expedition, 30; loan; 94; elected first lieutenant, 169; promoted to captain, 238; on furlough, 244; returns to camp, in ill health, 286

Society Hill, S. C., 258

Somerville, Alabama, village, army through, 191

South Carolina, army on raid through, 244, 248, 249; seek refuge in, 256; feeling, note, 259
Southern Confederacy, ship built for, 244; new capital for, 254; 274
St. Louis, mobilization at, 19; soldiers to, 30; ordered to, 35; army leaves, 36
Stanton, J. W., supper for veterans, 176
Stearns, Captain, of Eighth Iowa, securing enlistments, 9
Steele, General, division of, 112
Stephenson, General, command of expedition, 136; orders of, 138; expedition of, 139
Stiles, Albert B., mustered out, 222
Stone, Governor William, speech to Iowa Brigade, 120; candidate for governor, 147; at hospital Rome, 208; arrived in camp at Savannah, 241
Stout, Orlando, taken prisoner, 60; becomes a veteran, 160
Strong, General William E., estimate of Iowa Brigade, 102
Summerville, Ga., village of, 191; marched through, 223
Supplies (see provisions)
Sweet, Daniel, 30; on furlough, 133; return of, 154
Sweet, George, killed, 210
Sweet, Henry L., death of, 48

Tallahatchie river, 85; bridge over, 87
Tennessee river, transports up, 37, 185; crossed by pontoons, 191
Tensas river, channel of, 108
Thirteenth Iowa Infantry, new barracks, 13; new companies for, 14; sworn in, Marcellas M. Crocker, colonel of, 15; new uniforms for, 17; arrived at Jefferson City, 25; at Pittsburg Landing, 38, 53; on expedition, 97; to Lake Providence, 99; Captain Elrod of, 101; to Greenville, 102; with Eleventh, 116; on provost guard, 142; picket service, 146, 147, 148, 149; at Messenger's Ford, 148; sworn in as veterans, 163; started on furlough, 173; on board transports, 184; moved to front, 199; in battle, 208; non-veterans mustered out, 223; moved camp, 242; Pocotaligo, 246, 247; flag on State house, 254; receiving pay, 284
Thomas, General George H., command of, 195; charge of, 197; in battle, 199
Tipton, county seat, 3; news, 4; new company formed, 9; drilling at, 10; troops leave, 11; visitors from, 14; celebration at, 178; boys of, 179
Titus, Mark, on furlough, 135
Toly, Tom, farm hand, 3, 4
Tomlinson, Joseph, company cook, promoted to first lieutenant, 238; elected second lieutenant, 184
Townsend, General, speech on arming negroes, 108
Toyne, George, loan to, 134
Tuttle, General, in command at Bolivar, Tenn., 60; brigade of, 127; expedition to Jackson, candidate for governor, 147; division left, 157; division of, 165
Twenty-third Army Corps, at Atlanta, 219; at Galesville, 223; on return, 224; camp of, 264
Twentieth Army Corps, at Atlanta, 219; destroy bridge, 228; on march through Georgia, 229; destroying railroads, 231; reviewed by Sherman, opinion of, 242; to start on raid, 244; floundering in mud, 248; driving enemy, 262; camp of, 264; on left wing, 267

Uniforms, for Eleventh Iowa received, 15; cost, "dog-collars," 16; new, 185, 265

INDEX

Valentine's Day, 32
Vandever, General William, in command at Rome, Ga., 208
Van Dorn, cavalry of, 92
Van Wert, Ga., in bivouac, 225
Veterans, order concerning, enlistments, 156; urging enlistments, 157; sworn in, 159; re-enlisting slow, 160; excitement in camp, bounty discontinued, 161; restless in camp, 162; regiments of, 163; on furlough, 173, 174; reception for, 176, 177, 178; gathering at Davenport, 181, 182; gathering at Cairo, 183; new equipments for, 184; rumored discharged, 216; commissions to officers, 241; dissatisfaction among, 284;
Vicksburg, Sherman before, 91; start toward, 95; batteries at, 98; ran blockade at, 101; report from, 102; troops to, 103; cannonading at, 104; movement upon, 106, 110; troops toward, 107; sickness in siege of, 111, 112; run blockade to, 113; siege of, 115, 116, 119; fall threatened, 120; bombardment, 123; Forts blown up, 124; surrender of, 126; rejoicing over fall of, 127; provisions from, 129; troops returning to, 131, 132; expedition back to, 139; returned to, 140; sickness in camp, 141, 142; provost duty, 144; fortifying, 145, 149; guarding, 146; provisions at, moving camp, 150; winter quarters, fortifications, 151, 152; spies on fortifications, 154; quiet at, use of coin, 158; woman banished from, 160; icefloe, 162; damage to, 164; refugees, 170; return to, 171; opinion concerning, 173, 174

Wallace, General, 47
Warrenton, Ga., country around, 191
Washington, D. C., army to start for, 271; starting for, 274; grand review at, 276, 277; description of, 278, 279
Washita river, La., 136
Wateree river, army crosses, 256; rough country, 257
Waterford, battle at, 85, 86
Waynesburg, Tenn., camp at, 188
Wheeler, General Joe, cavalry, 170; report concerning, 210; raid of, 215; cavalry of, 233
Whiffy Swamp, S. C., marched through, 249
White, John A., scouting, 29, 30; bed to sleep in, 111; elected fourth Sergeant, 164; with Downing outside of lines, 187; promoted Second Lieutenant 238;
White river, expedition, 96
White House, visit to, 278
Whittlesey, John S., chaplain of Eleventh Iowa, 14; died, 54
Willey, Mr., visit with, 4; family of, 179, 180
Wilmington, North Carolina, boat from, 261
Wilson, James F., at the front, 120
Wilson's Creek, battle of, 3, 4
Winnsboro, S. C., refugees at, 256

Yazoo river, floods, 109; country around, 119; expedition up, 121; crops along, 134

Zitler, John, wounded, note, 198; in hospital, 206, 207; furlough for, 208; on furlough, 212

Made in the USA
Monee, IL
08 July 2020